# Federal Tax Policy and Charitable Giving

A National Bureau
of Economic Research
Monograph

# Federal Tax Policy and Charitable Giving

Charles T. Clotfelter

The University of Chicago Press
*Chicago and London*

CHARLES T. CLOTFELTER is professor of public policy studies and economics and vice-provost for academic policy and planning at Duke University.

The University of Chicago Press, Chicago 60637
The University of Chicago Press, Ltd., London
© 1985 by The University of Chicago
All rights reserved. Published 1985
Printed in the United States of America
95  94  93  92  91  90  89  88  87  86  85      5  4  3  2  1

**Library of Congress Cataloging in Publication Data**

Clotfelter, Charles T.
  Federal tax policy and charitable giving.

  (National Bureau of Economic Research monograph)
  Bibliography: p.
  Includes index.
    1. Income tax—United States—Deductions—Charitable
contributions—Mathematical models.   2. Corporations—
United States—Charitable contributions—Mathematical
models.   3. Voluntarism—United States—Mathematical
models.   4. Charitable bequests—United States—
Mathematical models.   I. Title.   II. Series.
HJ4653.D4C56   1985                336.2'06            84-16336

ISBN 0-226-11048-6

### Relation of the Directors to the
### Work and Publications of the
### National Bureau of Economic Research

1. The object of the National Bureau of Economic Research is to ascertain and to present to the public important economic facts and their interpretation in a scientific and impartial manner. The board of Directors is charged with the responsibility of ensuring that the work of the National Bureau is carried on in strict conformity with this object.

2. The President of the National Bureau shall submit to the Board of Directors, or to its Executive Committee, for their formal adoption all specific proposals for research to be instituted.

3. No research report shall be published by the National Bureau until the President has sent each member of the Board a notice that a manuscript is recommended for publication and that in the President's opinion it is suitable for publication in accordance with the principles of the National Bureau. Such notification will include an abstract or summary of the manuscript's content and a response form for use by those Directors who desire a copy of the manuscript for review. Each manuscript shall contain a summary drawing attention to the nature and treatment of the problem studied, the character of the data and their utilization in the report, and the main conclusions reached.

4. For each manuscript so submitted, a special committee of the Directors (including Directors Emeriti) shall be appointed by majority agreement of the President and Vice Presidents (or by the Executive Committee in case of inability to decide on the part of the President and Vice Presidents), consisting of three Directors selected as nearly as may be one from each general division of the Board. The names of the special manuscript committee shall be stated to each Director when notice of the proposed publication is submitted to him. It shall be the duty of each member of the special manuscript committee to read the manuscript. If each member of the manuscript committee signifies his approval within thirty days of the transmittal of the manuscript, the report may be published. If at the end of that period any member of the manuscript committee withholds his approval, the President shall then notify each member of the Board, requesting approval or disapproval of publication, and thirty days additional shall be granted for this purpose. The manuscript shall then not be published unless at least a majority of the entire Board who shall have voted on the proposal within the time fixed for the receipt of votes shall have approved.

5. No manuscript may be published, though approved by each member of the special manuscript committee, until forty-five days have elapsed from the transmittal of the report in manuscript form. The interval is allowed for the receipt of any memorandum of dissent or reservation, together with a brief statement of his reasons, that any member may wish to express; and such memorandum of dissent or reservation shall be published with the manuscript if he so desires. Publication does not, however, imply that each member of the Board has read the manuscript, or that either members of the Board in general or the special committee have passed on its validity in every detail.

6. Publications of the National Bureau issued for informational purposes concerning the work of the Bureau and its staff, or issued to inform the public of activities of Bureau staff, and volumes issued as a result of various conferences involving the National Bureau shall contain a specific disclaimer noting that such publication has not passed through the normal review procedures required in this resolution. The Executive Committee of the Board is charged with review of all such publications from time to time to ensure that they do not take on the character of formal research reports of the National Bureau, requiring formal Board approval.

7. Unless otherwise determined by the Board or exempted by the terms of paragraph 6, a copy of this resolution shall be printed in each National Bureau publication.

*(Resolution adopted October 25, 1926, as revised through September 30, 1974)*

To my parents
James and Caroline Clotfelter

# Contents

# Preface

In answer to a question about the possible effects of eliminating the charitable deduction in the nation's income tax, Ronald Reagan replied that Americans "are the most generous people on earth" and that they would remain so without a deduction (*Wall Street Journal*, 7 July 1982, p. 4). The question was prompted by one of several major proposals for reforming the U.S. tax system, a low-rate comprehensive income tax. Indeed, concern over economic incentives, the effects of inflation, tax compliance, and distributional equity appears to have reached a new level in the United States. From 1976 to 1983 an average of one major tax bill was enacted every two years, and there is mounting discussion of comprehensive tax reform. As the question to the president suggests, one source of concern amid these actual and potential tax changes is the effect they will have on charitable giving. This question is a particularly important topic now, following recent cuts in federal social-welfare expenditures. In fact, the philanthropic sector has long shown a keen interest in tax provisions affecting their support and operation.

This book concerns the relation between federal taxes and charitable giving. Its objective is to present and discuss econometric evidence on this relationship in order to assist in the evaluation of tax policy. The aim of the book is not to make policy recommendations, however, but rather to provide evidence and a framework for analysis of policy. I attempt to review the body of applied econometric analysis in the area and to extend that analysis in several areas using four basic sets of data. One of these data sets has been used previously to study charitable giving. Two others have has been adopted for the present study to include the most recent data on contributions. A fourth has not previously been analyzed for this purpose. In addition to this statistical estimation, I present results based on computer simulations of charitable giving, one of which is a revised version of a model used in a previously published paper. Because of the technical nature of many of the issues dealt with, some parts of the text cannot be made fully accessible to all readers. Where such technical topics are unavoidable, I have attempted to include more generally comprehensible discussion in hopes that the book can be of use to those not trained in economics and statistical methods.

The National Bureau of Economic Research provided the major support for this book. I am also grateful for the support I received from Drake University, where I am employed, and from the University of North Carolina, where I spent a sabbatical semester. Throughout the project, I have benefited from the able and industrious research assistance of Susan Cowan and from the skillful manuscript preparation of Dante Noto and Patsy Terrell. In addition, I received assistance from Richard Bostic, Mark Gallo, William Long, Mayre Loomis, Stan Paskoff, and Allyson Tucker. Karl-Heinz Paqué, Thomas Petska, Thomas Rosen, and Roy Wyscarver provided me with useful unpublished data. For helpful comments and discussions, I am grateful to Elizabeth Boris, Arthur Clarke, Daniel Feenberg, Daniel Frisch, Pamela Gann, H. Gregg Lewis, Ralph McCaughan, Richard Schmalbeck, John Siegfried, B. J. Stiles, Emil Sunley, and members of the tax group at the National Bureau. In addition, I have benefited from many discussions I have had over the past decade with my coauthors on papers dealing with individual charitable giving: Martin Feldstein, Lester Salamon, and Eugene Steuerle. Finally, I am grateful to Lucile, James, and John Clotfelter for their indulgence over the period I have worked on this project.

# 1 Tax Policy and Support for the Nonprofit Sector: An Overview

The nonprofit sector—as distinct from government and the for-profit sector—plays a more important role in the United States than in any other industrialized economy. Encompassing such institutions as colleges and universities, not-for-profit hospitals and research institutions, churches and other religious organizations, museums and cultural institutions, and charitable organizations of many varieties, this sector historically has performed many functions that in other countries are the primary responsibility of government. It employs over 10 percent of the labor force and over twice the number of federal-government employees (Weisbrod 1980, p. 26). At the same time, the United States is distinctive in the degree to which it subsidizes the nonprofit sector through its tax system. Its provisions for the deductibility of charitable gifts in addition to the tax exemptions accorded to nonprofit institutions are unparalleled in scope. Although the interrelationships that have evolved between government, nonprofit institutions, and the legal structure are the result of hundreds of years of complex social development, it seems by no means accidental that this special reliance on nonprofit institutions and these favorable tax provisions have developed side by side.

In recent years, however, there has been evidence of increasing concern about the vitality of the nonprofit sector and the adequacy of federal tax provisions affecting charitable giving. One source of concern has been the standard deduction, introduced as a simplification into the income tax system over forty years ago, but blamed for reducing incentive to make contributions. Public commissions in the 1960s and 1970s investigated the role of tax policy in philanthropic giving and made their recommendations to Congress. One of those—the Commission on Private Philanthropy and Public Needs, known as the Filer Commission—began its report by recommending several basic changes in the tax treatment of contribu-

1

tions (Commission on Private Philanthropy and Public Needs 1977, pp. 3–21). For its part, Congress has responded with changes in tax provisions affecting charity, most recently passing a law that would extend the charitable deduction to nonitemizers by 1986. Even so, there is widespread concern about the adequacy of support for the nonprofit sector. Proposals to eliminate the corporation income tax or to replace the income tax with a "flat-rate" comprehensive tax would have implications for charitable giving. In addition, cuts in federal spending for social programs under President Reagan reduced an important revenue source for nonprofit organizations at the same time it increased the demand for many of their services. Rising labor costs and other developments within the nonprofit sector combined with slow growth in private support have caused one commentator to conclude that the sector as a whole "is in serious and growing difficulty" (Nielson 1979, p. 3). Needless to say, such concerns have heightened interest in the role of the tax system in influencing the level and distribution of private support for charitable and other nonprofit organizations.

The purpose of the present study is to examine one important aspect of the relationship between the tax structure and the nonprofit sector: how federal taxes affect charitable giving. Specifically, it examines the effect of tax provisions on contributions by individuals, corporations, and estates, on grants by foundations, and on volunteer work. The focus is on the connection between policy variables and behavior as observed in econometric anaylsis and other empirical study. To give the reader perspective for this investigation, it is useful to begin by providing, first, an overview of the nonprofit sector and the role of charitable giving in it and, second, a brief description of the major federal tax provisions affecting charity. The chapter concludes with an outline of the remaining chapters.

## 1.1 Charitable Giving and the Nonprofit Sector

Before focusing on charitable organizations and contributions made to them, it is useful to have a general sense of the size and function of the nonprofit sector as a whole. Table 1.1 presents data for major categories within the nonprofit sector based on returns for tax-exempt organizations in 1975. The organizations are divided according to whether contributions made to them are generally deductible in calculating federal income taxes. Of the 220,000 nonprofit organizations filing returns in 1975, the largest single group was in fact charitable organizations. Often referred to by the Internal Revenue Code section applying to them, such "501(c)3 organizations" include religious, educational, cultural, scientific, and social-welfare organizations. This category represented over a third of all nonprofit organizations, based on number of returns, and over a half of total receipts of the sector, although these figures are probably underestimates since some religious groups do not submit returns. Charitable organizations represented an even larger share of contributions received—some 83 percent based only on 1975 returns and almost 90 percent counting all organizations.[1] The most important other category, based on receipts, was civic clubs such as Lions and Rotary. Other significant categories included voluntary employee beneficiary associations, labor and agricultural groups, business groups, and life insurance associations. As numerous as these other nonprofit organizations were, however, table 1.1 makes clear that charitable organizations account for a sizable portion of the entire nonprofit sector.

Measured in terms of dollars contributed, charitable giving in 1982 amounted to about $60 billion. Table 1.2 provides estimates of giving from four sources for selected years between 1955 and 1982. The estimates are published in the annual volume *Giving U.S.A.*, a widely cited source of data on charitable contributions. Worth noting, however, is that the estimation procedures underlying these figures are not described in print and should be taken as rough approximations only. For 1982, contributions by living individuals accounted for about four-fifths of the total, some $49 billion. The remaining one-fifth was shared by bequests from estates (about $5 billion), corporations ($3 billion), and foundations ($3 billion). These numbers involve some double counting since foundations act as intermediaries, as is discussed below, but these figures serve to give a general idea of relative magnitudes. Over the period 1955 to 1982, the real level of total giving has almost tripled, from $11 to $29 billion in 1972 dollars. This growth has also tended to exceed that of national income; total giving rose from 2.0 percent of national income in 1955 to 2.5 percent in 1982. Over this period, individual donations have averaged about 80 percent of the total. Contributions by corporations have declined slightly in importance, and foundation grants have dropped significantly. Bequests have fluctuated over time, being particularly sensitive to large gifts.

Two forms of charitable giving are not shown in table 1.2. The most important is volunteer work. In 1980 as many as 80 million Americans did some volunteer work, spending the equivalent of about 8 billion hours in such activity. The market value of this time has been estimated to be on the order of $60 billion, suggesting that estimates of giving such as those shown in table 1.2 measure about half of the economic resources contributed to charitable organizations (Weitzman 1983, p. 270). In addition, the dollar amounts in table 1.2 do not directly reflect contributions made on fiduciary income tax returns for trusts and estates. Representing for the most part gifts not otherwise reflected on personal income or estate tax re-

---

1. Total receipts by charitable organizations were some $28 billion in 1975 (see table 1.2, netting out foundation grants). Adding the $11 billion yields 89 percent for contributions to 501(c)3 organizations.

**Table 1.1**     **Tax-Exempt Organizations, 1975**

| Type of Organization | Number of Returns | Receipts in Millions of Dollars | | Applicable Code Section |
| --- | --- | --- | --- | --- |
| | | Total | Contributions, Gifts, and Grants | |
| *Tax-Deductible Contributions Generally Allowed* | | | | |
| Corporations organized under act of Congress | 665 | 527 | 11 | 501(c)1 |
| Charitable, religious, educational, and scientific organizations | 82,048 | 65,544 | 17,110 | 501(c)3 |
| Cemetery companies | 1,518 | 255 | 5 | 501(c)13 |
| War-veterans organizations | 1,921 | 130 | 7 | 501(c)19 |
| *Tax-Deductible Contributions Generally Not Allowed* | | | | |
| Title-holding companies for exempt organizations | 3,263 | 490 | 23 | 501(c)2 |
| Civic leagues, social-welfare organizations, and local associations of employees | 28,064 | 19,558 | 681 | 501(c)4 |
| Labor, agricultural, and horticultural organizations | 28,258 | 5,028 | 120 | 501(c)5 |
| Business leagues, chambers of commerce, and real estate boards | 17,530 | 3,890 | 230 | 501(c)6 |

| | | | | |
|---|---|---|---|---|
| Social and recreational clubs | 18,228 | 2,535 | 32 | 501(c)7 |
| Fraternal beneficiary societies | 12,066 | 2,134 | 46 | 501(c)8 |
| Voluntary employees' beneficiary associations | 4,285 | 6,806 | 1,926 | 501(c)9 |
| Domestic fraternal societies | 4,674 | 507 | 21 | 501(c)10 |
| Teachers' retirement-fund associations | 49 | 100 | 6[a] | 501(c)11 |
| Local benevolent life insurance associations | 4,975 | 3,725 | 17 | 501(c)12 |
| State-chartered credit unions | 1,610 | 2,259 | 1[a] | 501(c)14 |
| Mutual insurance companies or associations | 864 | 59 | 0[a] | 501(c)15 |
| Farmers cooperatives organized to finance crop operations | 36 | 54 | 18[a] | 501(c)16 |
| Supplemental unemployment-benefit trusts | 496 | 959 | 244 | 501(c)17 |
| Employee-funded pension trusts | 42[a] | 13[a] | 7[a] | 501(c)18 |
| Other organizations[b] | 9,605 | 309 | 62 | — |
| TOTAL | 220,197 | 114,890 | 20,565 | |

*Source*: Sullivan and Coleman 1981, pp. 7–8, figure 1; p. 10, table 1.

[a]Estimates based on small samples.

[b]Organizations not specified included trusts for prepaid group legal services (covered in section 501(c)20), black lung trusts (501(c)21), religious and apostolic associations (501(d)), farmers' cooperative associations (521(a)), cooperative hospital service organizations (501(e)), and cooperative service organizations of operating educational organizations (501(f)). Contributions to the last two types of organizations are generally tax deductible.

**Table 1.2    Estimated Charitable Giving by Source, Selected Years**

| Year | Individuals | Corporations | Bequests | Foundations | Total | Total in 1972 Dollars | Total as Percentage of National Income |
|---|---|---|---|---|---|---|---|
| | *Amounts in Billions* | | | | | | |
| 1955 | $ 5.71 | $0.42 | $ 0.24 | $ 0.30 | $ 6.67 | $10.96 | 2.0 |
| 1960 | 7.63 | 0.48 | 0.57 | 0.71 | 9.39 | 13.67 | 2.3 |
| 1965 | 10.36 | 0.79 | 1.02 | 1.13 | 13.30 | 17.89 | 2.3 |
| 1970 | 15.92 | 0.80 | 2.13 | 1.90 | 20.75 | 22.69 | 2.6 |
| 1975 | 24.24 | 1.20 | 2.23 | 1.65 | 29.32 | 23.31 | 2.4 |
| 1980 | 39.88 | 2.60 | 2.86 | 2.81 | 48.15 | 26.95 | 2.3 |
| 1982 | 48.69 | 3.10 | 5.45 | 3.15 | 60.39 | 29.14 | 2.5 |
| | *Percentage of Total Giving* | | | | | | |
| 1955 | 85.6 | 6.3 | 3.6 | 10.6 | 100.0 | — | — |
| 1960 | 81.3 | 5.1 | 6.1 | 7.6 | 100.0 | — | — |
| 1965 | 77.9 | 5.9 | 7.7 | 8.5 | 100.0 | — | — |
| 1970 | 76.7 | 3.9 | 10.3 | 9.2 | 100.0 | — | — |
| 1975 | 82.7 | 4.1 | 7.6 | 5.6 | 100.0 | — | — |
| 1980 | 82.8 | 5.4 | 5.9 | 5.8 | 100.0 | — | — |
| 1982 | 80.6 | 4.5 | 9.0 | 5.2 | 100.0 | — | — |

Sources: *Giving U.S.A.* 1983, p. 36; U.S. Council of Economic Advisers 1983, p. 186.

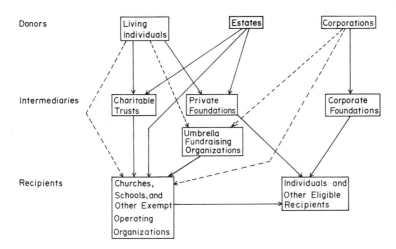

**Fig. 1.1**    Principal flows of charitable contributions and transfers. Solid lines signify flows of cash or other assets. Dotted lines denote flows of voluntary services as well as monetary flows.

turns, contributions by fiduciaries were some $600 million in 1974, or about 2 percent of total giving.[2] Because of their small size these contributions by fiduciaries are not covered in the present study.

In order to show the relationship among these categories of giving as well as the connection between them and support of nonprofit organizations, figure 1.1 traces the major flows of money and volunteer services from donors to recipients in the nonprofit sector. There are three classes of original donors: living individuals, the estates of decedents, and corporations. Individuals and corporations may contribute money or volunteer services. The gifts of money may go directly to tax-exempt organizations or may pass through some tax-exempt intermediary institution. These intermediaries include charitable trusts, private foundations, and corporation foundations.[3] Because the intermediaries essentially are conduits for previous gifts, it is strictly incorrect to add, for example, foundation grants to other donations. However, the timing of such grants may be so far removed from the original gifts that it can be useful to show them along with contributions from original donors. Umbrella fund-raising organizations such as community foundations or the United Way act as a central collection point for contributions, which are then distributed to operating nonprofit agencies according to an established formula. Such

2. See U.S. Internal Revenue Service, *Statistics of Income—1974, Fiduciary income tax returns* 1977 for the most recent published data on charitable deductions by fiduciaries. Whether fiduciary contributions are reflected in the *Giving U.S.A.* estimates is unclear.

3. Recipient organizations such as religious organizations may also act as conduits by making grants to other charitable groups.

organizations receive money and volunteer services primarily from individuals and corporations, though they might well receive support from, say, foundations as well. The ultimate recipients of charitable giving are the hospitals, museums, churches, and colleges that make up the service-providing "retailers" of the nonprofit sector. Most of the organizations in this category are eligible to and do receive tax-deductible contributions directly from individuals and corporations. Some ultimate recipients are nonexempt organizations or individuals, gifts to whom are typically not deductible for individuals or coporations but which may nevertheless receive grants from foundations.

Although charitable giving is an important source of support for operating nonprofit organizations, it is by no means the only source. Table 1.3 presents a summary of aggregate receipts and expenditures in 1980 for the entire "philanthropic sector"—those nonprofit organizations eligible for tax-deductible contributions. Total expenditures for this sector were $129 billion.[4] To cover this amount, organizations raised $60 billion through sales of goods and services and $69 billion from subsidies, of which private donations constituted the most important component—about $45 billion. For this group of nonprofit organizations, therefore, charitable contributions represented about 35 percent of total support.

A more detailed breakdown of sources of support is given in table 1.4. Based on a survey of nonprofit organizations in Philadelphia, the percentage distribution reflects an unweighted average of distributions of indi-

**Table 1.3**      **Receipts and Expenditures of Philanthropic Organizations, 1980 ($ billions)**

| Receipts | | | Expenditures | |
|---|---|---|---|---|
| Sales | | $60 | Purchases of goods and | |
|   To businesses | $ 4 | |   services | $ 43 |
|   To households | 30 | | | |
|   To government | 26 | | Salaries | 75 |
| Subsidies | | 69 | Capital costs (including | |
|   Private donations | 45 | |   rental property) | 11 |
|   Government grants | 8 | | | |
|   Investment income | 7 | | | |
|   Rental value of property | 9 | | | |
| TOTAL | $129 | | TOTAL | $129 |

*Sources:* Estimates of Gabriel Rudney, "Toward a Quantitative Profile of the Nonprofit Sector," in Program on Non-profit Organizations 1981, p. 3.

4. To avoid double counting, these figures omit foundation grants to other organizations (Program on Non-profit Organizations 1981, p. 3).

Table 1.4    **Sources of Support for Nonprofit Institutions in Philadelphia, 1973 and 1978**

| Source | Percentage of Total Support | |
|---|---|---|
| | 1973 | 1978 |
| Private sources | | |
| Foundation grants | 4.9 | 6.3 |
| Individual gifts—direct | 7.8 | 7.9 |
| Federated funds (including United Way) | 10.1 | 7.8 |
| Special benefit events | 1.5 | 1.1 |
| Trusts and bequests | 7.4 | 7.3 |
| Subtotal | 31.6 | 30.3 |
| Government | | |
| Federal | 14.7 | 14.8 |
| State and local | 16.4 | 19.1 |
| Subtotal | 31.1 | 33.9 |
| Self-generated income | | |
| Fees (including tuition) | 22.6 | 21.8 |
| Sales of merchandise | 2.7 | 2.7 |
| Membership dues | 2.8 | 2.6 |
| Income from endowment | 3.9 | 3.9 |
| Income from other assets | 5.3 | 4.8 |
| Subtotal | 37.3 | 35.8 |
| TOTAL | 100.0 | 100.0 |

*Source:* Reiner and Wolpert 1981, p. 26, table 1.

vidual organizations.[5] These figures imply that nonprofit groups on average received support from three sources in approximately equal amounts: private sources, government, and sales of other self-generated income. The two most important sources of private support were direct gifts from individuals and transfers from umbrella fund-raising organizations, each with 8 percent of total support in 1978. Bequests and transfers from trusts and foundations were also an important source, together accounting for about 14 percent of support. Not only is charitable giving an important

5. Thus the relative size of institutions plays no part in these calculations as is the case in table 1.2.

source of support for nonprofit organizations, therefore, but many organizations receive this support by means of intermediaries, such as trusts, foundations, and umbrella fund-raising bodies.

### 1.1.1   Support by Recipient Group

In considering the implications of tax policy for charitable giving, it is often important to go beyond aggregate measures to observe the relative importance of giving for the major recipient groups within the nonprofit sector. Probably the best summary of the importance of giving for these groups is a simple tabulation of total contributions by major groups, as is given in table 1.5 for the years 1960 and 1982. The most striking aspect of the distribution for either year is the large share of contributions that go to religious organizations. For 1982, giving to religious organizations accounted for 47 percent of the total. Educational and health institutions were next in importance, each accounting for 14 percent of total giving. Social service organizations claimed 11 percent, and arts and humanities another 8 percent of total giving. Between 1960 and 1982, the largest relative increase was recorded by arts and humanities organizations: their share increased from 2 to 8 percent. Increases in shares also occurred in the civic and public and the health and hospital groups. Groups whose shares fell during the period were social services, religion, and education.

The relative importance of charitable gifts as a source of support also varies by subsector. Table 1.6 presents a distribution of funding sources by major recipient group in 1974. This tabulation shows that, for the nonprofit sector as a whole, private contributions and government funds each provided about 30 percent of total support, with the remaining 40 percent coming from dues, sales, and endowment income, corresponding roughly to the distribution given in table 1.4. Among the major recipient groups, religious organizations were most dependent on charitable gifts for sup-

Table 1.5        **Charitable Giving by Recipient Group, 1960 and 1982**

| Recipient Group | Giving (in billions) | | Percentage of Total | |
|---|---|---|---|---|
| | 1960 | 1982 | 1960 | 1982 |
| Religion | 4.79 | 28.06 | 51.0 | 46.5 |
| Education | 1.50 | 8.59 | 16.0 | 14.2 |
| Social services | 1.41 | 6.33 | 15.0 | 10.5 |
| Health and hospitals | 1.13 | 8.41 | 12.0 | 13.9 |
| Arts and humanities | 0.19 | 4.96 | 2.0 | 8.2 |
| Civic and public | 0.09 | 1.67 | 1.0 | 2.8 |
| Other | 0.28 | 2.37 | 3.0 | 3.9 |
| TOTAL | 9.39 | 60.39 | 100.0 | 100.0 |

*Source: Giving U.S.A.* 1983, p. 38.

Table 1.6    **Distribution of Support for Nonprofit Organizations, by Recipient Group, 1974**

| Recipient Group | Philanthropy | Service Charges and Endowment Income | Government Funds | Total |
|---|---|---|---|---|
| Religion | 94 | 6 | — | 100 |
| Health | 11 | 47 | 42 | 100 |
| Education | 32 | 56 | 12 | 100 |
| Other | 31 | 35 | 34 | 100 |
| TOTAL | 31 | 40 | 29 | 100 |

*Source:* Report of the Commission on Private Philanthropy and Public Needs, cited in Sumariwalla 1983, p. 195.

port, receiving some 94 percent of all revenues from contributions. Given the lack of fees or government funding for religious activities, this dependence is not surprising. Health organizations, in contrast, showed the least dependence on contributions, with almost 90 percent of their revenues being derived from service charges, government support, or endowment income. Education and other nonprofit groups received about 30 percent of their revenues from contributions. In summary, churches and other religious organizations are distinctive in their dependence on charitable giving and the large share of all giving that they receive. Educational institutions and hospitals each account for the second largest share of contributions, but the former depends on these contributions to a greater extent. Religious institutions aside, nonprofit organizations receive a sizable part of their funding from self-generated revenues and government support.

## 1.2    Philanthropy and Tax Policy

Two cornerstones underlie U.S. tax policy toward charitable activity: the deductions for contributions allowed in major federal taxes (the personal income tax, the corporate tax, and the estate tax) and the tax-exempt status generally accorded nonprofit institutions. The tax exemption is of general importance to the nonprofit sector and is discussed below. As for the tax deductions, the size of individual giving suggests that the charitable deduction in the personal income tax is of preeminent importance. Adopted in 1917, four years after the enactment of the individual tax itself, the provision allows the deduction of individual contributions of cash or other assets made to eligible organizations up to certain limits. Since 1917 the deduction has been modified in two principal ways. First, the introduction of the standard deduction in the 1940s as a major simplification measure effectively eliminated the charitable deduction for a majority of taxpayers. Second, a provision of the 1981 Economic Recovery Tax Act calls for a phasing in of a new charitable deduction for nonitemizers. If implemented as planned, this provision would give all taxpayers an opportunity to deduct contributions. As will become clear in later chapters, the effect of provisions such as these cannot be evaluated without reference to the overall structure of the income tax and its tax rates. In addition, state income taxes usually allow a deduction for gifts similar to the federal deduction and thus are another influence on contributions.

The debate over these provisions has pitted those who think the deduction is an effective and appropriate incentive for charitable giving against those who believe that simplification or equity would be better served with less favorable provisions for contributions. These issues are as relevant in recent discussions of low-rate comprehensive income taxes as they were in the debate over the standard deduction in 1941. The majority of such "flat-rate" tax schemes, would, for example, eliminate the charitable deduction altogether.[6] Levels of giving may also be influenced by the structure of taxes and tax rates. The debate over provisions affecting charitable deductions is therefore framed by normative questions of their equity, the importance of tax simplification, and the comparative value of public and nonprofit provison of services as well as by the factual question of how taxes affect contributions.

Besides the charitable deduction in the individual tax, two other deductions and a separate set of related provisions affect charitable giving directly. First, charitable bequests made as part of the disposition of estates are deductible without limit in calculating the federal estate tax. Individuals wealthy enough to be subject to the estate tax may choose between making deductible contributions during life or deductible charitable bequests at death. Second, contributions made by corporations are deductible up to a limit in calculating the corporate income tax. In addition to these provisions, the tax law allows individuals to set up foundations or charitable trusts and deduct the value of gifts made through them. As with the income tax, state taxes are generally similar to their federal counterparts in how charitable gifts are treated.

In addition to these four sets of provisions directly affecting charitable contributions, the tax-exempt status accorded to eligible nonprofit organizations has significant indirect impact. Except for unrelated business earnings, nonprofit organizations are not subject to income taxation. In addition, they are generally exempt from property taxation at state and local levels. Although these provisions certainly influence the growth,

6. For further discussion of these issues, see Teitell 1977, p. 486, and U.S. Congress, Senate 1980.

cost, and vitality of nonprofit functions, their effect on the level of charitable contributions is indirect. In much the same way, the structure and
performance of the nonprofit sector are influenced by the whole panoply
of relevant laws and regulations, and this structure and performance in
turn may affect the level of private charitable contributions.

## 1.3 Scope of the Present Study

The remainder of the book focuses on the effect of federal tax provisions on the level and distribution of charitable contributions in the United States. The laws and specific tax provisions related to the operation of
nonprofit organizations are for the most part not dealt with. Nor is there
any examination of the behavior of nonprofit organizations themselves—
with the exception of foundations. Instead, the study focuses on the behavior of donors and foundations and the effect of taxes on that behavior.
In addressing these positive questions, the study makes extensive use of
and reference to econometric analyses. Without the application of multivariate models of analysis, the task of identifying the independent effects
of tax provisions on giving in the presence of other influences would be
hopeless rather than merely difficult. At the same time, an effort is made
throughout the exposition to provide comprehensible summaries of abstract models and econometric estimates where they are presented.

In order to investigate the positive question of how taxes affect contributions, it is necessary to begin with a model of giving itself. The models
adopted in this study are based on the basic economic theories of individual and firm behavior, although some important variants are discussed.
Using these basic models, it is possible to make predictions concerning the
effects of changes in the tax structure, including changes in the deductibility of contributions. How these effects vary by income and age are of
great importance in evaluating tax policies toward the nonprofit sector.
Other questions, though, are also of considerable practical interest. For
example, it is useful to ask whether and how the giving behavior of different individuals is related. Or, what is the relationship among the volunteering, lifetime donations, and bequests undertaken by an individual?
And, is individual giving influenced by the level of government spending
or is it affected only by the taxation side of public budgets?

For the most part the present study leaves aside the normative questions
involved in determining what constitutes proper treatment of charitable
contributions within the tax system. Chapters 2 through 7 are restricted to
an evaluation of positive questions of effect or likely effect. The positive
questions are necessary for a full assessment of these issues of tax policy,
but they are of course not sufficient. In order to provide a framework for
a more complete analysis, the last chapter discusses normative as well as
positive issues.

Chapters 2 and 3 examine the effect of the personal income tax on individual charitable contributions. Chapter 2 focuses on the determination of the behavioral relationship itself, describing the most important tax provisions relevant to individual giving, theoretical predictions about tax effects, and econometric analyses of the question. Particular attention is devoted to the data, models, and estimation procedures used in this empirical work. The studies are reviewed for their implications for various hypotheses regarding individual giving. The final section of the chapter reviews econometric analyses using data for other countries. Chapter 3 traces the implications of the estimates of econometric models by simulating the likely effects of actual or possible tax provisions. These include such options as a charitable deduction for nonitemizers, a tax credit for contributions, or the complete elimination of the deduction. In addition, the implications of general tax changes such as the institution of a flat-rate comprehensive tax and changes in the standard deduction are considered. Simulation models focusing on changes in giving over time are also presented. These models focus on the effects of inflation, tax rate changes, and, in particular, the provisions of the 1981 tax act. The chapter devotes attention to the methods of simulation as well as to the results.

Chapter 4 examines the implications of tax policy for volunteering. Following a description of the tax treatment of volunteer work, income tax effects within the theory of the household's allocation of time are discussed. Given the possibilities for work, volunteering, other household work, and leisure, and for interactions in time use between spouses, the theoretical problem is quite complex indeed. Previous econometric work on volunteering with implications for tax effects is then reviewed, followed by a new analysis of volunteering by women.

Chapter 5 examines corporate contributions and the effect of the charitable deduction in the corporate income tax. The tax treatment is described, and implications of economic models of the firm are developed. Previous econometric analyses of corporate giving—their data, methods, and results—are then described. Finally, an econometric analysis of aggregate data on corporate contributions over the period 1936 to 1980 is presented. Special attention is devoted to the variation in corporate income and in the price of gifts over time and across asset classes.

The next two chapters deal with charitable bequests and philanthropic foundations. Chapter 6 describes the estate tax and the importance of bequests for various nonprofit activities. First it reviews the results of three econometric analyses of charitable bequests and then presents an analysis of a sample of 1976 estate tax returns. Finally, the resulting estimates are used in considering the effect of recent tax changes on bequest giving. In chapter 7 the role of private foundations within the larger charitable sector is described along with the tax legislation affecting them. Particular attention is paid to the Tax Reform Act of 1969, which contained a comprehensive set of taxes and requirements related to private foundations.

The final chapter—chapter 8—summarizes the study and suggests a framework for considering the behavioral findings described here. Although it makes no policy recommendations, the chapter discusses normative principles relevant to a more complete assessment of tax policy toward charitable giving. Like the rest of the study, this discussion is limited to a consideration of contributions by donors and foundations and does not extend to a consideration of such issues as governance, management efficiency, or responsiveness in the operation of nonprofit agencies themselves.

# 2 Contributions by Individuals: Estimates of the Effects of Taxes

Gifts by living individuals account for the lion's share of charitable contributions in the United States. Accordingly, the present examination of the effect of taxes on contributions begins by considering just such contributions. Section 2.1 provides some statistical background by tracing the growth of individual contributions over time and describing its distribution by various characteristics. Section 2.2 provides a brief description of the provisions of the tax law affecting charitable contributions. The next section discusses the theoretical analysis of the effect of income tax provisions on contributions within a standard economic model of individual behavior. The implications of alternative behavioral assumptions are also considered. Section 2.4 describes the data, estimation methods, and basic results of econometric studies of giving by individuals. In discussing both the theoretical and empirical models, the effects of the tax-defined price of giving and net income are afforded special attention. And section 2.5 continues this discussion by focusing on particular issues of behavior and estimation technique arising from this work. The final section discusses econometric work on the effect of tax policy on charitable giving for other countries. Discussion of the implications for tax policy of observed giving behavior is deferred to chapter 3.

## 2.1 The Size and Distribution of Individual Contributions

As in all other areas of empirical study, our knowledge about the magnitude of charitable contributions is limited by the availability and quality of data on the subject. If one accepts the definition of contributions in the tax law—gifts to certain nonprofit organizations, but not direct gifts to other individuals—contributions may readily be measured for taxpayers who itemize their deductions. For households who do not itemize their deductions, however, information on giving is rarely available. In order to give a general idea of the magnitude of contributions over time in the United States, table 2.1 presents estimates from three sources. Although the series shows that these appear to be roughly comparable to each other, there is considerable variation in the methodologies that have been used to

**Table 2.1**    **Estimates of Contributions by Individuals, 1929–81 (current dollars, in billions)**

| Year | Andrews Estimate (1) | Giving U.S.A. Estimate (2) | Personal Income (3) | Estimated Contributions (2 or 3) as Percentage of Personal Income (4) | Nelson Estimate (5) |
|---|---|---|---|---|---|
| 1929 | 1.067 |      | 85.8  | 1.24 |      |
| 1930 | .981  |      | 76.9  | 1.28 |      |
| 1931 | .843  |      | 65.7  | 1.28 |      |
| 1932 | .702  |      | 50.1  | 1.40 |      |
| 1933 | .637  |      | 47.2  | 1.35 |      |
| 1934 | .662  |      | 53.6  | 1.24 |      |
| 1935 | .727  |      | 60.2  | 1.21 |      |
| 1936 | .830  |      | 68.5  | 1.21 |      |
| 1937 | .943  |      | 73.9  | 1.28 |      |
| 1938 | .884  |      | 68.6  | 1.29 |      |
| 1939 | .967  |      | 72.4  | 1.34 |      |
| 1940 | 1.064 |      | 77.9  | 1.37 |      |
| 1941 | 1.556 |      | 95.4  | 1.63 |      |
| 1942 | 2.108 |      | 122.6 | 1.72 |      |
| 1943 | 2.535 |      | 150.8 | 1.68 |      |
| 1944 | 2.691 |      | 164.5 | 1.64 |      |
| 1945 | 2.772 |      | 170.0 | 1.63 |      |
| 1946 | 2.929 |      | 177.6 | 1.65 |      |
| 1947 | 3.240 |      | 190.1 | 1.70 |      |
| 1948 | 3.319 |      | 209.0 | 1.59 |      |
| 1949 | 3.447 |      | 206.4 | 1.67 |      |
| 1950 | 3.688 |      | 227.2 | 1.62 |      |
| 1951 | 4.286 |      | 254.9 | 1.68 |      |
| 1952 | 4.545 |      | 271.8 | 1.67 |      |
| 1953 | 4.779 |      | 287.7 | 1.66 |      |
| 1954 | 4.789 |      | 289.6 | 1.65 |      |
| 1955 |       | 5.71 | 310.3 | 1.84 |      |
| 1956 |       | 6.08 | 332.6 | 1.83 |      |
| 1957 |       | 6.52 | 351.0 | 1.86 |      |
| 1958 |       | 6.79 | 361.1 | 1.88 |      |
| 1959 |       | 7.26 | 384.4 | 1.89 |      |
| 1960 |       | 7.63 | 402.3 | 1.90 | 7.89 |
| 1961 |       | 7.96 | 417.8 | 1.91 | 8.13 |
| 1962 |       | 8.50 | 443.6 | 1.92 | 8.58 |

(*cont.*)

Table 2.1 (*continued*)

| Year | Andrews Estimate (1) | Giving U.S.A. Estimate (2) | Personal Income (3) | Estimated Contributions (2 or 3) as Percentage of Personal Income (4) | Nelson Estimate (5) |
|------|------|------|------|------|------|
| 1963 | | 9.03 | 466.2 | 1.94 | 8.93 |
| 1964 | | 9.55 | 499.2 | 1.91 | 9.55 |
| 1965 | | 10.36 | 540.7 | 1.92 | 9.98 |
| 1966 | | 11.33 | 588.2 | 1.93 | 10.61 |
| 1967 | | 12.15 | 630.0 | 1.93 | 11.33 |
| 1968 | | 13.36 | 690.6 | 1.93 | 12.50 |
| 1969 | | 14.71 | 754.7 | 1.95 | 13.27 |
| 1970 | | 15.92 | 811.1 | 1.96 | 14.0 |
| 1971 | | 17.02 | 868.4 | 1.96 | 14.6 |
| 1972 | | 18.19 | 951.4 | 1.91 | 15.80 |
| 1973 | | 20.43 | 1065.2 | 1.92 | |
| 1974 | | 22.33 | 1168.6 | 1.91 | |
| 1975 | | 24.24 | 1265.0 | 1.92 | |
| 1976 | | 26.57 | 1391.2 | 1.91 | |
| 1977 | | 29.22 | 1540.4 | 1.90 | |
| 1978 | | 32.79 | 1732.7 | 1.89 | |
| 1979 | | 36.39 | 1951.2 | 1.87 | |
| 1980 | | 39.78 | 2160.4 | 1.84 | |
| 1981 | | 44.51 | 2415.8 | 1.84 | |

*Sources:* Col. (1), estimates by F. Emerson Andrews, given in Kahn 1960, p. 63, table 16; col. (2), *Giving U.S.A.* 1982, p. 34; col. (3), 1929–38: U.S. Bureau of the Census 1960, p. 139; 1939–81: U.S. Council of Economic Advisers 1983, p. 185; col. (5), Nelson 1977b, p. 131.

estimate total giving.[1] Thus care should be taken in interpreting these figures. The two basic sets of estimates from Andrews (Kahn 1960) and the American Association of Fund-Raising Counsel's *Giving U.S.A.,* suggest that contributions have risen in relation to personal income between 1929 and 1981. As a percentage of personal income, contributions have increased from about 1.3 to 1.8 percent over the period. Despite this overall increase in the average contribution rate, the trend since 1970 has been negative, with the ratio falling from a peak of 1.96 in 1970 and 1971 to 1.84 in 1980 and 1981.[2]

At any one time, contribution levels obviously vary among individuals. Not surprisingly, they vary markedly by income level. Table 2.2 gives re-

1. For discussions of methodologies used in estimating contributions by individuals, see Kahn (1960, chap. 4), Dickinson (1970), and Nelson (1977a).

2. The shorter series on contributions produced by Nelson implies that the ratio of contributions to personal income fell throughout the 1960–72 period, from 1.96 to 1.66.

Table 2.2          Average Contributions by Household Income, 1973

| Income | Average Income | Average Contributions | Average Contributions as Percentage of Average Income |
|---|---|---|---|
| Under $4,000 | $ 1,942 | $ 75 | 3.9 |
| $4,000-7,999 | 5,906 | 122 | 2.1 |
| $8,000-9,999 | 8,974 | 208 | 2.3 |
| $10,000-14,999 | 12,365 | 327 | 2.6 |
| $15,000-19,999 | 17,191 | 523 | 3.0 |
| $20,000-29,999 | 23,685 | 720 | 3.0 |
| $30,000-49,999 | 36,174 | 1,455 | 4.0 |
| $50,000-99,999 | 66,004 | 5,552 | 8.4 |
| $100,000-199,999 | 130,363 | 16,988 | 13.0 |
| $200,000-499,999 | 280,255 | 38,950 | 13.9 |
| $500,000 or more | 1,008,653 | 70,501 | 7.0 |
| All | $ 10,251 | $ 459 | 4.5 |

*Sources:* Average income: U.S. Internal Revenue Service, *Statistics of Income—1973, Individual Income Tax Returns* 1976, p. 7; average contributions: Morgan, Dye, and Hybels 1977, p. 161, table 1.

sults taken from the National Study of Philanthropy, a survey taken in 1974 covering contributions in 1973. The table shows that average contributions rose monotonically with income, from $75 for households in the lowest income group to over $70,000 for households with incomes over $500,000. The percentage of income contributed also rose with income between $4000 and $500,000. The ratio falls with income at the lowest income levels, which agrees with similar tabulations using other data.[3] Figure 2.1 uses data for itemized deductions to plot the relationship between income and the proportion of income contributed. In each case, a U-shaped curve is evident over some range.[4]

It may be tempting to make conclusions, using information on the correlation between contributions and income, about the income elasticity of individual contributions. For example, one might conclude from the rise in the contributions-to-income ratio since 1929 that contributions have an elasticity greater than one. This reasoning may yield incorrect conclusions, however. Unlike the determination of the income elasticity for a consumer good where the price of the good is constant, the tax-defined net price of giving created by the charitable deduction typically varies over time and among income classes. In addition, taxes affect the amount of disposable income available after taxes. Indeed, one of the principal ob-

3. See, for example, Clotfelter and Steuerle (1981, p. 406).
4. For further discussion of this U-shaped relationship, see Clotfelter and Steuerle (1981, pp. 405-7). Among the possible factors in explaining the U-shape, the high proportion of older individuals, whose wealth is high relative to their incomes, may be important.

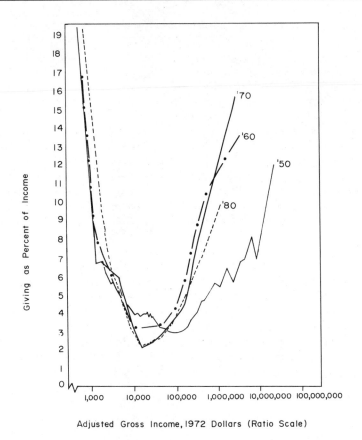

Adjusted  Gross  Income, 1972  Dollars  (Ratio  Scale)

**Fig. 2.1**                Giving as a percentage of income by income, selected years.

jectives of the econometric analysis of charitable contributions has been
to determine the independent effect of taxes.

The examination of average contributions masks significant variability
in contributions among households of a given income level. Tables 2.3
and 2.4, which show the distribution of giving in relation to income, indicate substantial inequality in personal propensities to make contributions.
Grouping households according to the proportion of their gross income
contributed makes it clear that households earning a relatively small portion of total income account for a disproportionate share of contributions. Table 2.3, based on survey data for 1973 covering itemizers and
nonitemizers alike, shows that households contributing more than 20 percent of their income accounted for about 11 percent of income but over 60
percent of all contributions. At the other end, households accounting for
55 percent of income gave only 8 percent of all gifts. Table 2.4 presents
similar data based on tax returns for itemizers only. It shows that there is

considerably more equality in propensities to contribute among itemizing taxpayers only than among all households. Itemizing taxpayers with 2 percent of the total income made about 21 percent of all contributions for this group. At the lower end, taxpayers with 62 percent of income gave only about 17 percent of all gifts. There is, then, considerable variation

**Table 2.3    Distribution of Contributions and Income, 1973**

| | | Weighted Cumulative Distribution | |
| --- | --- | --- | --- |
| Contributions as Percentage of AGI[a] | Unweighted Number of Households | Income | Contributions |
| 0 | 154 | 1.3 | 0 |
| 0–2 | 1,043 | 39.7 | 3.7 |
| 2–4 | 455 | 55.3 | 8.2 |
| 4–6 | 235 | 65.1 | 12.9 |
| 6–8 | 106 | 73.4 | 19.1 |
| 8–10 | 119 | 79.2 | 24.4 |
| 10–15 | 120 | 86.8 | 34.6 |
| 15–20 | 52 | 89.3 | 39.2 |
| 20–30 | 36 | 93.1 | 49.0 |
| 30–50 | 24 | 94.9 | 55.9 |
| Greater than 50 | 49 | 100.0 | 100.0 |
| TOTAL | 2,393 | | |

*Source:* Tabulations from the National Study of Philanthropy. See Morgan, Dye, and Hybels 1977 for a description of this data set.
*Note:* Intervals include the upper limit.

**Table 2.4    Distribution of Contributions and Income, Itemizers Only, 1983**

| | Cumulative Distribution | | |
| --- | --- | --- | --- |
| Contributions as Percentage of AGI | Returns | Adjusted Gross Income | Contributions |
| 0 | 12.5 | 6.2 | 0.0 |
| 0–2 | 62.6 | 61.9 | 16.7 |
| 2–4 | 80.8 | 81.0 | 34.1 |
| 4–6 | 87.2 | 87.7 | 44.9 |
| 6–8 | 91.2 | 91.6 | 53.7 |
| 8–10 | 93.7 | 93.9 | 60.5 |
| 10–15 | 97.0 | 96.9 | 72.4 |
| 15–20 | 98.1 | 98.0 | 78.7 |
| 20–30 | 99.1 | 99.0 | 86.1 |
| 30–50 | 99.8 | 99.8 | 96.0 |
| Greater than 50 | 100.0 | 100.0 | 100.0 |

*Source:* Unpublished tabulations, based on 1983 tax model, Office of Tax Analysis, 10 December 1984.
*Note:* Intervals include the lower limit.

among households in propensities to contribute, and this is much more so among all households than among those who itemize their deductions.

### 2.1.1   Contributions by Type of Recipient

The organizations to which individuals contribute include churches and other religious groups, schools and colleges, hospitals and health organizations, community-welfare organizations, combined appeals, and other causes and organizations. Table 2.5 presents information regarding the distribution of individual gifts based on three different sources of data—a tabulation of itemized tax returns in 1962 and household surveys covering 1973 and 1978. The most apparent fact is that contributions to religious organizations account for the largest share of individual giving, over 60 percent in each case. The distribution of nonreligious gifts, however, either is more variable or information on it is less certain, or both. Giving to seemingly well-defined groups as education and hospitals appears to vary markedly, suggesting either some change in giving patterns or noncomparabilities between data sources. Giving to education exceeds 9 percent of the total in the 1973 and 1978 surveys but is only 3.6 percent among itemizers in 1962. By the same token, gifts to hospitals appear to have had a relative increase between 1962 and 1978. To what extent these

**Table 2.5**          **Percentage of Total Contributions by Type of Organization: Comparison of Three Data Sources**

| Type of Organization | Itemized Tax Returns 1962 (1) | National Study of Philanthropy 1973 (2) | Gallup Survey 1978 (3) |
|---|---|---|---|
| Religious | 60.9 | 62.2 | 66.8 |
| Education | 3.6 | 9.5 | 9.8 |
| Higher | — [a] | 6.8 | — |
| Other | — | 2.7 | — |
| Medical and health | | 6.8 | 15.1 |
| Hospitals | 1.5 | — | 4.5 |
| Other health | — | — | 10.6 |
| Other charitable | 14.2 | | — |
| Culture | — | 2.7 | — |
| Combined appeals | — | 8.1 | — |
| Other | 19.8 | 10.8 | 7.0 |
| Total | 100.0 | 100.1 | 98.7[b] |

*Sources:* Col. (1), U.S. Internal Revenue Service, *Statistics of Income—1962, Individual Income Tax Returns* 1964, p. 6, table E; Morgan, Dye, and Hybels 1977, p. 208, table 38 (percentages exclude unidentified gifts); Gallup Omnibus 1979, p. 8.

[a]No data given for category.

[b]Total does not equal sum of classes; possibly due to rounding.

differences are due to differences in methods of classifying gifts is unclear. Furthermore, comparisons are inhibited by differences in the categories used.[5]

The surveys do agree on the finding that the distribution of giving varies markedly by income level. Table 2.6 presents the distribution by income level based on households' four largest gifts in 1973. The proportion of gifts made to religious organizations is largest in the lower-income classes. For example, identified religious gifts accounted for 59 percent of all contributions and 88 percent of identified gifts, for those with incomes below $10,000. This pattern is similar to that of the 1962 gifts.[6] In contrast, giving to higher education grows in importance with income, accounting for 24 percent of all gifts or almost a third of identified gifts. Similarly, the importance of gifts to cultural institutions and combined appeals increases with income.

A number of writers have suggested that, in analyzing charitable contributions, it is useful to distinguish religious gifts from other contributions. Schwartz (1970a, p. 1269) refers to the inclusion of religious gifts in charitable contribution figures a "distracting element, since religious giving is not clearly philanthropic."[7] The reasoning would appear to be that a large portion of the expenditures of religious groups pays for salaries, buildings, and operating expenses for local congregations, leaving a relatively small portion for transfer outside the congregation. Needless to say, it is impossible to measure the "philanthropic" components in such diverse groups as churches, universities, or local service organizations. Some kinds of personal benefits may be derived from gifts to each, but even these benefits tend to be somewhat public and subject to "free rider" behavior.

One concrete way of describing the nature of religious giving is by examining the pattern of expenditures made by religious groups. By and large, expenditures for worship, religious education, and operation account for the bulk of religious expenditures. An estimate of "nonsacramental" expenditures—those for social welfare, health functions, and

5. Because the 1962 distribution implies contributions for education and health much smaller than those in *Giving U.S.A.*, the 1973 distribution is used in chapter 3 for simulations.

6. The proportion of gifts made to religious organizations fell from 71 percent for itemizers with incomes below $2000 in 1962 to 3 percent for those with incomes over a million dollars (U.S. Internal Revenue Service 1964, *Statistics of Income—1962, Individual Income Tax Returns*, p. 6, table E).

It is also interesting to note that a similar distributional pattern can be observed in contributions data for West Germany. Unpublished data provided by Karl-Heinz Paqué for 1974 shows that deducted contributions (other than the church tax) rose from about 0.1 percent of gross income at the lowest income levels to 0.6 percent in the highest bracket. Since these contributions probably include little if any religious giving, these figures suggest a strong income effect for nonreligious giving similar to that found in U.S. data.

7. See also Taussig 1967 and Vickrey 1962.

**Table 2.6    Contributions by Type of Organization and Income, 1973 (percentage)**

| Income | Religion | Education | | Combined Appeals | Medical and Health | Culture | Other Major | Not Iden- tified[a] | Total |
|---|---|---|---|---|---|---|---|---|---|
| | | Higher | Other | | | | | | |
| $0–9,999 | 59 | 1 | 0 | 2 | 3 | 0 | 2 | 33 | 100 |
| $10,000–19,999 | 67 | 1 | 0 | 3 | 3 | 0 | 4 | 22 | 100 |
| $20,000–29,999 | 59 | 2 | 1 | 5 | 4 | 0 | 10 | 19 | 100 |
| $30,000–49,999 | 42 | 5 | 7 | 6 | 3 | 3 | 6 | 28 | 100 |
| $50,000–99,999 | 16 | 9 | 1 | 10 | 11 | 4 | 19 | 30 | 100 |
| $100,000–199,999 | 10 | 14 | 5 | 9 | 10 | 5 | 6 | 41 | 100 |
| $200,000–499,999 | 8 | 27 | 6 | 10 | 11 | 6 | 8 | 24 | 100 |
| $500,000 or more | 9 | 24 | 3 | 6 | 6 | 9 | 16 | 27 | 100 |
| TOTAL | 46 | 5 | 2 | 6 | 5 | 2 | 8 | 26 | 100 |

Source: Morgan, Dye, and Hybels 1977, p. 208, table 38.
[a]Information regarding donees was obtained only for the four major gifts of each donor; therefore additional giving could not be allocated to donee categories.

nonreligious education—amounted to about 18 percent of total revenues for major religious groups in 1972. A survey of 178 local churches in 1972 showed that 79 percent of total expenditures covered operating costs and another 10 percent paid for buildings and capital improvements. Only 11 percent of total expenditures went to cover special-purpose or restricted uses (Interfaith Research Committee 1977, p. 402). However, these figures may understate the amount of redistributional giving to the extent that they omit special offerings. Despite this possible bias as well as the lack of more specific categories, the available data do suggest that sacramental functions account for a preponderance of church expenditures and that a relatively small part of religious spending is redistributional in nature.[8]

## 2.2   The Tax Treatment of Individual Contributions

The distinctive feature of U.S. tax treatment of charitable contributions is the deduction allowed for taxpayers who itemize their deductions. Besides the general tax-exempt status of nonprofit organizations itself, the income tax deduction is probably the most important single tax policy affecting the vitality of the nonprofit sector in the United States. By reducing taxable income and thus tax liability, the deduction has the effect of lowering the net cost of making donations. It was adopted in 1917, four years after the enactment of the first personal income tax, and was available to all of the relatively limited number of Americans who paid income taxes through the 1920s and early 1930s.

### 2.2.1   The Standard Deduction

As the income tax expanded its coverage and raised its rates, however, a standard deduction was introduced in 1944 along with payroll deductions in an effort to achieve high compliance with a minimum of administration. Many low- and middle-income taxpayers elected this standard deduction, leaving only a portion of the taxpaying public eligible to deduct their contributions. Table 2.7 traces the proportion of taxpayers who itemized their deductions for selected years between 1945 and 1980. The table also gives the maximum standard deduction allowed a married couple. As one would expect, the proportion of taxpayers who find it advantageous to itemize deductions has risen as the real value of the standard deduction has fallen. Because of its effect on the number of taxpayers who can itemize their contributions, the standard deduction has been

8. Even a socially active church like the Riverside Church in New York devoted only about 19 percent of its budget to benevolences in 1949 (Andrews 1950, p. 174), though these budget figures probably omit some special offerings earmarked for redistributional purposes. For a discussion of the redistributional character of religious expenditures, see Schaefer 1968, pp. 29–30.

Table 2.7    Itemization and the Standard Deduction in Selection Years, 1945–80

| Year | Proportion of Tax Returns with Itemized Deductions | Maximum Standard Deduction[a] for a Joint Return | |
|------|---------------------------------------------------|---------------|--------------|
| | | Current Dollars | 1972 Dollars |
| 1945 | 17.0 | $ 500 | $1319 |
| 1948 | 16.4 | 1000 | 1888 |
| 1950 | 18.8 | 1000 | 1867 |
| 1952 | 22.1 | 1000 | 1726 |
| 1954 | 27.1 | 1000 | 1679 |
| 1956 | 31.4 | 1000 | 1593 |
| 1958 | 35.5 | 1000 | 1514 |
| 1960 | 39.7 | 1000 | 1455 |
| 1962 | 42.5 | 1000 | 1416 |
| 1964 | 41.4 | 1000 | 1374 |
| 1966 | 40.9 | 1000 | 1303 |
| 1968 | 43.7 | 1000 | 1212 |
| 1970 | 47.9 | 1000 | 1093 |
| 1972 | 35.0 | 2000 | 2000 |
| 1974 | 35.7 | 2000 | 1738 |
| 1976 | 30.8 | 2800 | 2115 |
| 1978 | 28.7 | 3400 | 2260 |
| 1980 | 31.0 | 3400 | 1897 |

*Source:* U.S. Internal Revenue Service, *Statistics of Income, Individual Income Tax Returns,* various years.
[a]Beginning in 1977, the standard deduction was made a fixed amount and renamed the "zero bracket amount."

viewed as "a threat to the continued existence of private non-profit activity" (Kahn 1960, p. 46). In response to this concern, Congress included in the Economic Recovery Act of 1981 a provision that would gradually phase in an "above-the-line" charitable deduction applicable to nonitemizers as well as itemizers.[9] If it is continued beyond its present expiration date of 1986, this extension of the charitable deduction would represent a substantial change in tax policy towards the nonprofit sector to the extent that itemization is an important influence on the level of contributions.

### 2.2.2   Other Limitations on Deductibility of Contributions

Congress has imposed two basic kinds of limitations, besides the standard deduction, on the deductibility of contributions: limits on the amount that can be deducted and restrictions on what kinds of organiza-

9. In 1982 and 1983, 25 percent of the first $100 of contributions was to be deductible for nonitemizers. The amount was to increase to 25 percent of the first $300 in 1984, 50 percent without limit in 1985, and all contributions in 1986.

tions are qualified to receive tax-deductible gifts. Presently, individuals may deduct contributions up to 50 percent of their adjusted gross income, although gifts to certain organizations must not exceed 20 percent. The limit was originally 15 percent of taxable income for gifts to all charitable organizations, then was expanded for virtually all taxpayers to 15 percent of adjusted gross income in 1944, to 20 percent in 1952, and to 30 percent for certain charities in 1954 (Liles and Blum 1975, pp. 25, 30–31).[10] The present maximum of 50 percent was adopted in 1969.[11] Charities for which the 50 percent limitation applies include all churches, public charities, educational institutions, government agencies, and certain private foundations.[12] The 20 percent limit applies to all other charitable organizations, including most private foundations. Contributions to the first group of charities that exceed the 50 percent limit may be carried forward as deductions for five years, but no carry-over is allowed for contributions over the 20 percent limit applying to other charities.

Table 2.8 presents information on the charitable deduction by income class for 1980. Both marginal tax rate and giving rise with income. Over 90 percent of itemizers make some charitable contribution, with the proportion rising above 95 percent among taxpayers with incomes over $30,000. Only 0.2 percent of itemizers reached the limit on deductibility, and the value of gifts exceeding the limit was 6 percent of deductible contributions. The limit on contributions was most often exceeded in the highest income classes, with more than 4 percent of taxpayers with incomes over $500,000 reaching the limit. These nondeductible gifts exceeded 20 percent of giving in each of the three highest income categories. The table also suggests, however, that the usage of the carry-over allowed for such deductions over the limit roughly corresponds to the incidence of nondeductible contributions. This suggests that virtually all qualified contributions are deductible either in the year made or in the years immediately following.

Integrated with the questions of which gifts are deductible and what limit applies is the tax code's specification of the kinds of organizations eligible to receive deductible gifts. To begin with, gifts to individuals, no matter how sincere the altruistic motive, are not deductible. Only donations to certain nonprofit organizations are eligible to be deducted. Ever since the deduction was originally enacted, the list of qualifying organiza-

10. A special provision enacted in 1924 for the benefit of an heiress-nun allowed an unlimited deduction for taxpayers who had contributed over 90 percent of their incomes in each of the previous 10 years. This provision was relaxed somewhat in 1954 to require such giving in 8 of the last 10 years and was phased out in 1974 by the Tax Reform Act of 1969 (Liles and Blum 1975, pp. 26, 32; Goode 1976, p. 161n.).

11. Tax Reform Act of 1969 (*Internal Revenue Acts* 1971, pp. 301–2).

12. These foundations include "operating" foundations and foundations designed primarily as a temporary conduit for contributions. See Arthur Andersen and Company 1982, p. 3.

**Table 2.8    Income, Tax Rates, and Contributions by Itemizers, 1980**

| Income | Average Income | Marginal Tax Rate[a] | With Charitable Deductions | Exceeding Contributions Limit | With Carry-overs | Average Contributions | In Cash | Not Deductible |
|---|---|---|---|---|---|---|---|---|
| | | | Percentage of Itemized Returns | | | | Percentage of Contributions | |
| Under $5,000 | 3,030 | 0 | 43.5 | 1.7 | 0.5 | 173 | 94.3 | 21.6 |
| $5,000–10,000 | 7,820 | 0 | 78.1 | 0.9 | 0.8 | 436 | 93.5 | 4.4 |
| $10,000–15,000 | 12,663 | 0.16 | 88.1 | 0.2 | 0.2 | 513 | 92.7 | 7.6 |
| $15,000–20,000 | 17,636 | 0.21 | 89.6 | 0.0[b] | 0.0[b] | 523 | 94.6 | 0.3 |
| $20,000–25,000 | 22,563 | 0.24 | 91.9 | 0.1 | 0.8 | 565 | 92.4 | 3.0 |
| $25,000–30,000 | 27,491 | 0.28 | 93.7 | 0.0[b] | 0.0[b] | 624 | 93.1 | 0.9 |
| $30,000–50,000 | 37,461 | 0.32 | 95.8 | 0.1 | 0.1 | 858 | 90.6 | 0.9 |
| $50,000–100,000 | 64,770 | 0.49 | 96.8 | 0.1 | 0.1 | 1,725 | 84.3 | 2.5 |
| $100,000–200,000 | 132,294 | 0.59 | 97.1 | 1.0 | 1.0 | 4,531 | 69.5 | 19.6 |
| $200,000–500,000 | 282,571 | 0.70 | 97.4 | 2.0 | 2.0 | 13,449 | 50.5 | 27.5 |
| $500,000–1,000,000 | 667,516 | 0.70 | 97.8 | 4.2 | 5.7 | 46,402 | 43.7 | 38.4 |
| $1,000,000 + | 2,085,475 | 0.70 | 97.8 | 5.5 | 5.5 | 202,547 | 40.0 | 21.0 |
| TOTAL | | | 91.9 | 0.2 | 0.3 | | 83.8 | 6.1 |

*Source:* U.S. Internal Revenue Service, *Statistics of Income—1980, Individual Income Tax Returns* 1982, pp. 56–57, table 2.1.

*Note:* Ranges include the lower limit.

[a]Marginal tax rate computed using class averages for married taxpayers filing jointly.

[b]Less than 0.05.

tions has included religious, charitable, educational, literary, and scientific organizations. In addition, this list has been expanded periodically, to include such organizations as medical research groups, state university endowment funds, governmental units, and "publicly supported" nonprofit organizations (Liles and Blum 1975, pp. 34–35). Amendments in 1918 and 1934 have stipulated that they must be domestic organizations and not be engaged in lobbying (pp. 25–26).[13] The limit of 50 percent of income applies to such organizations as universities, hospitals, community chests, charitable groups, and churches. Examples of organizations for whom gifts are subject only to the 20 percent limit are veterans' organizations and private foundations.[14]

Gifts of property are generally deductible at cost or at full market value, depending on the type of asset. Donated property may include such items as used clothes and household items, art objects, real estate, or financial assets. For most gifts of property with long-term capital gains made to charities qualifying for the 50 percent limit, no tax is levied on the capital gains. Combined with the full deduction of the market value, this provision creates an added incentive to contribute assets with large, accrued capital gains. Consider a taxpayer in the 50 percent tax bracket with a $10,000 stock holding that he originally purchased for $5000. Assuming a 40 percent inclusion rate for long-term capital gains, two options among those open to this taxpayer are (1) to increase his disposable income by $9000 ($10,000 − (0.5)(0.4)$5000) by selling the stock and (2) to contribute the stock, receiving a $5000 tax reduction from the deduction. When compared to the option of selling the stock and consuming the proceeds, the amount of consumption foregone due to contributing the stock is $9000 less the tax reduction of $5000, or $4000. In contrast a $10,000 gift of cash would reduce consumption opportunities by $5000.

There are several limitations to the general treatment described here as well as a host of possible forms in which various assets may be given. First, gifts to organizations qualifying for the 50 percent limit cannot exceed 30 percent of income in the form of property.[15] Second, deductions for donations of property subject to capital gains taxation made to private foundations or other "20 percent-type organizations" or donations of "tangible personal property" unrelated to the recipient organizations' tax-exempt functions are reduced by 40 percent of the amount that would have been taxed as long-term capital gain had the asset been sold. In addition, gifts of inventory, assets subject to short-term capital gains, and items produced by oneself are not generally deductible at their full fair

13. See also Goode 1976, pp. 160–61.
14. See Goode 1976, p. 165, and *Internal Revenue Code* 1982, sec. 170(b). See chap. 7 for a discussion of the legal definition of a private foundation.
15. The 50 percent limitation applies only if the deduction is reduced by 40 percent of appreciation. See *Internal Revenue Code* 1982, sec. 170(b)(1)(c) and 170(e)(1)(B).

market value (Goode 1976, p. 167, 167n; *Internal Revenue Code* 1982, sec. 170(e)(3)). Before 1969 donors in high tax brackets could usually contribute an appreciated asset at even lower net cost—and sometimes make a profit—by selling the asset at cost and taking a deduction for the appreciated portion. The treatment of such "bargain sales" was tightened in 1969, however, by requiring the taxpayer to include a portion of the gain in taxable income.[16]

Finally, gifts may be made through trusts or trustlike arrangements. A trust establishes an endowment, a specified combination of income and remainder payments from that endowment, and a trustee to administer the fund. Similar arrangements can be set up with universities or other charitable organizations in which the organization administers the fund. The tax consequences are the same. One form of trust is a charitable trust, which distributes both income and remainder interests to charity. A deduction is allowed for the present value of payments at the time the trust is established. In contrast, a split-interest trust has both charitable and noncharitable beneficiaries. It may be a charitable income (or lead) trust, which pays a fixed amount or proportion to a charitable organization, or a charitable remainder trust, which assigns income to noncharitable beneficiaries for a period, designating the remainder for a charitable organization. A charitable deduction is allowed for either type as long as the various interests are paid according to a predetermined nondiscretionary formula. For example, charitable remainder trusts qualify for a deduction if the income beneficiaries receive a fixed periodic payment (an annuity trust) or a fixed percentage of assets (a unitrust). A pooled-income arrangement, in which the noncharitable beneficiary receives income from funds invested and managed by a university or other charity, similarly qualifies.[17] Among its attractive features, a split-interest trust offers a means of providing a beneficiary with the income from an asset during his or her life while at the same time obtaining a charitable deduction and reducing the eventual estate tax base. At one time, giving through charitable income trusts also offered a way to make contributions beyond the percentage limitation for deductible gifts, but changes in the law in 1969 have severely limited this possibility for trusts of less than a ten-year dura-

16. For example, consider a taxpayer in the 60 percent bracket holding $10,000 worth of stock with a basis of $6000. Selling the stock would net $8800 after taxes. Contributing the stock to a charity would reduce taxes by $6000 (.6 x 10,000), for a net cost of $2800 compared to realization. With a bargain sale, the taxpayer sells the stock to a charity for $6000 and, under the pre-1969 rules, obtains a $4000 deduction with $2400 in tax reduction, for a total return of $8400 and a net cost of only $400. See Penick (1960, p. 117) for similar illustrations and *1980 U.S. Master Tax Guide* (1979, p. 941) for an explanation of the post-1969 law.

17. For discussions of the tax treatment in this area, see Penick 1960, pp. 118–28; Taggart 1970; Griswold and Graetz 1976, pp. 923–30; *1980 U.S. Master Tax Guide* 1979, p. 167; Sorlien and Olsen 1970, pp. 221–24; or Petska 1983, pp. 1–5.

tion.[18] Despite their variety and attractive features, trusts are used by relatively few taxpayers for making charitable gifts. In 1979 there were about 2000 charitable trusts, accounting for $56 million in contributions, and almost 14,000 split-interest trusts, corresponding to another $61 million (Petska 1983, p. 5). Together, these payments were less than one-half of 1 percent of all individual giving.

### 2.2.3   Tax Policy and the Deduction's Incentive Effect

In the debate over tax policy since the introduction of the income tax, the role of the charitable deduction in encouraging donations has been directly addressed on several occasions. Because of the emphasis in the present study on the impact of taxation on contributions, it is useful to note both the importance that such incentives have played in the policy debate as well as to review the prevailing opinion among tax scholars as to the deduction's incentive effect.

*The Charitable Deduction, 1917*

In the debate that accompanied congressional action to add the charitable deduction in 1917, proponents of the change justified the deduction in large part because of its presumed incentive effect. Senator Hollis, the sponsor of the amendment, argued that rising income tax rates would hurt contributions by reducing the "surplus" out of which gifts are made: "we impose these very heavy taxes on incomes, [and] that will be the first place where these very wealthy men will be tempted to economize, namely, in donations to charity" (*Congressional Record,* 7 September 1917, p. 6728).[19] That the tax effect would primarily be felt at higher incomes follows from the limited coverage of the early income tax. The bill passed in 1917, for example, levied no tax on net incomes below $37,700 in 1982 dollars and applied tax rates as high as 15 percent only for net incomes above $300,000, in 1982 dollars.[20] Once the deduction was adopted, its significance apparently was not lost on nonprofit organizations. Cornell University, for example, cited the law in its endowment drive in 1919, pointing out that wealthy individuals would bear only a fraction of the cost of gifts they made (*New York Times,* 1 December 1919, p. 14).

---

18. See Penick (1960, p. 128) for an explanation of how the income limits could be stretched through trusts with lives as short as two years. This was possible because the present value of the charitable interest was deductible while the charitable income interest was not taxable to the taxpayer. Current law requires the taxation of such income, thus offsetting the original deduction if the marginal tax rate is constant.

19. See also Kahn (1960, p. 46) and Liles and Blum (1975, p 25) for discussions of the incentive issue in connection with the adoption of the deduction.

20. The consumer price index relative to 1972 ( = 100) was: 38.4 in 1917 and 289.1 in 1982 (U.S. Bureau of the Census 1960, p. 126; U.S. Council of Economic Advisers 1983, p. 221). The 15 percent bracket in the 1917 bill began at $40,000 (*Congressional Record* 7 September 1917, p. 6727).

*The Standard Deduction, 1944*

The growing coverage of the income tax during World War II motivated a proposal in 1944 to introduce a standard deduction as an alternative to itemized deductions. Combined with a withholding system for wages, the standard deduction greatly simplified tax compliance for most taxpayers. The proposal brought on a storm of opposition on the basis that the incentive effect of the charitable deduction would be lost. Representative Carl Curtis stated, "This bill, when carried into effect, means that the individual who gives a portion of his hard-earned money in contributions will have the same amount of taxes withheld from his wages as if he had given nothing" (*Congressional Record,* House, 3 May 1944, p. 4029). Church and other nonprofit organizations opposed the standard-deduction proposal as written, some advocating a payroll deduction linked to employees' anticipated donations.[21] In opposition, Senator Vandenburg expressed "doubt whether many contributors in [the] lower brackets are motivated in their philanthropy by tax-reduction aims" (*Congressional Record,* Senate, 19 May 1944, p. 4706). In the end, the Congressional debate came down to weighing the costs of reduced incentives against the simplification the standard deduction would bring about.[22]

*The Charitable Deduction for Nonitemizers, 1981*

A third issue that raised the question of the incentive effect of the charitable deduction was the proposal to allow nonitemizers to deduct their gifts in addition to those who already itemized their deductions. Proposed in 1979 as a means of counteracting the presumed effect of declines in itemization on giving, this bill was opposed by the Treasury due to the projected revenue losses involved. An important issue in the hearings was whether the increases in contributions would be more or less than those revenue losses. The Senate hearings on the bill focused on such seemingly technical questions as the size of the incentive effect at lower incomes and the lag in taxpayers' response to changes in the tax law. (U.S. Congress, Senate 1980, esp. pp. 51–69 and 217–35).

*Scholarly Opinion on the Incentive Effect*

Despite the arguments made for the charitable deduction and against the standard deduction, many commentators have expressed skepticism concerning the deduction's annual incentive effect. Reviewing trends in contributions in the 1920s, Syndnor Walker concluded that "the ratio between income and contributions is so consistent throughout the period as to suggest that giving is more definitely regulated by habit or tradition

21. See *New York Times,* 5 December 1943, p. 1; 4 March 1944, p. 11; 5 May 1944, p. 8; 25 May 1944, p. 19; 20 July 1944, p. 31; 16 September 1944, p. 16; and 1 December 1945.

22. For editorial support of simplification, see "To Simplify Taxes," *New York Times,* 5 May 1944, p. 18.

than by changes in income, tax rate, or any external circumstance (Kahn 1960, p. 47). Similarly, Kahn (pp. 71–72) concluded that the incentive effect of the deduction was weak because the introduction and extension of the standard deduction in 1941 and 1950 had no discernible effect on the proportion of income being contributed.

This view remained the prevalent one into the 1970s. Noting the scarcity of reliable research on the effect of the deduction up to that point, Aaron (1972, p. 211) concluded that "the numbers of charitable contributions suggest that it is inconceivable that the effect could be very large in the aggregate." Aaron was particularly dubious regarding the existence of a large incentive effect for taxpayers with incomes below $15,000 (p. 211). Likewise, Vickrey (1975, p. 157) argued that the price elasticity of contributions was below one in absolute value, stating: "there is grave doubt whether the deduction actually achieves to any detectable extent the intended function of stimulating gifts by individuals, as distinct from merely supplementing such gifts with a government contribution derived from what would otherwise have been tax revenue" (p. 153). Hood, Martin, and Osberg (1977) agreed, commenting that an elasticity greater than one in absolute value "strains credulity" (p. 661). In a 1973 survey, fewer than half of households interviewed said they thought the deduction stimulated giving. However, this proportion rose markedly with income, with over 70 percent of those with incomes over $50,000 believing that the tax deduction is a spur to giving (Morgan, Dye, and Hybels 1977, table 19).

Despite the doubt that exists about the existence and size of the income tax's effect on individual contributions, it is clear that taxpayers who itemize their deductions do contribute more than nonitemizers. As table 2.9 shows, itemizers contribute as much as twice or more what non-

Table 2.9    **Average Giving by Income and Itemization Status, 1973**

| Income | Itemizers | Nonitemizers |
|---|---|---|
| Less than $4,000 | $   119[a] | $   69 |
| $4,000–7,999 | 215 | 89 |
| $8,000–9,999 | 314 | 117 |
| $10,000–14,999 | 407 | 201 |
| $15,000–19,999 | 600 | 329 |
| $20,000–29,999 | 800 | 354 |
| $30,000–49,999 | 1,564 | 171[a] |
| $50,000–99,999 | 5,679 | 3,190[a] |
| $100,000–199,999 | 17,106 | 816[a] |
| $200,000–499,999 | 39,763 | 8,892[a] |
| $500,000 or more | 71,316 | 5,000[a] |
| Overall average | $   775 | $   140 |

*Source:* Morgan, Dye, and Hybels 1977, p. 193.
[a]Based on fewer than 25 observations.

itemizers at the same income level give. Itemizers in the $10,000 to $14,999 income class, for example, gave an average of $407, compared to $201 for nonitemizers. To what extent this difference is due to a price effect, some itemization effect, or other tax considerations is a central question in empirical work on charitable contributions.

## 2.3   Taxation and the Theory of Charitable Behavior

Students of social behavior, economists included, have devoted considerable attention to the study of altruism and helping behavior. In apparent violation of the simple economic model of egoistic utility maximization, helping behavior is observed in charitable contributions, volunteering, disaster relief, rescues at sea, public policies of redistribution, much neighborhood crime prevention, donations of blood, and intrafamily gifts and sacrifices.[23] Obviously, the nature of this giving and helping varies from case to case. In assessing the effect of income taxation on individual charitable behavior, it is useful to begin by summarizing the major theories that have been offered to explain helping behavior in general. These theories are discussed in the context of utility maximization. The effects of tax deductibility and other tax policies on the individual's opportunity set are then discussed. Finally, the possibility that government spending may "crowd out" private giving is considered.

### 2.3.1   Theories of Helping and Giving

Although the lines cannot be drawn precisely, it is possible to distinguish several possible motivations for helping and giving. As shown by the survey responses summarized in table 2.10, the reasons offered for making contributions suggest various dimensions of unselfish as well as self-interested motives. For example, 44 percent of respondents mentioned "belonging" as their first or second reason for making religious gifts, while the same percentage mentioned receiving benefits from giving to higher education. In contrast, pressure was cited most often as a reason for giving to combined appeals. In trying to explain giving in theory, one useful classification (Obler 1981) distinguishes three basic motivations: altruism, reciprocity, and direct benefit.

*Altruism*

Altruism, behavior that has little or no observable selfishness, may be founded on sympathetic feelings for others, social norms, or individual feelings of commitment. Economists, with characteristic homeliness, de-

---

23. For analyses of various manifestations of helping behavior, see Bolnick 1975, 1978; Clotfelter 1980a; Douty 1972; Hochman and Rodgers 1969; Hammond 1975; Landes and Posner 1978a, 1978b; Macauley and Berkowitz 1970; and Titmuss 1971. For a thorough review of the social science literature, see Gonzalez and Tetlock, n.d.

**Table 2.10    Reasons for Giving, by Donee Organization, 1973[a]**

| Type of Organization | Approve, They Need Money, Feel Obligated | Get Some Benefit | "Belongs" | Pressure, Quota | Other, DK, NA | Number of Gifts |
|---|---|---|---|---|---|---|
| Religious | 69% | 8% | 44% | 2% | 6% | 1,649 |
| Combined | 66 | 4 | 2 | 25 | 15 | 750 |
| Community, other | 77 | 21 | 8 | 3 | 14 | 480 |
| Health | 53 | 27 | 2 | 6 | 24 | 686 |
| Higher education | 66 | 44 | 3 | 2 | 19 | 441 |
| Other education | 74 | 29 | 2 | 0 | 17 | 133 |
| Social welfare | 77 | 13 | 2 | 1 | 16 | 293 |
| Cultural | 75 | 21 | 8 | 0 | 12 | 107 |
| Overall averages and total | 67% | 13% | 23% | 5% | 13% | 4,539 |

*Source:* Morgan, Dye, and Hybels 1977, p. 204, table 34.

[a]Numbers are sums of percents of first and second mentions for each reason among those who gave $100 or more in 1973. Percentages are based on gifts to various donee organizations, not dollars of giving. The question posed was: Why did you give to this organization?

scribe the sympathy and compassion that individuals commonly feel for their fellows as a manifestation of the interdependence of individual utility functions. Thus individual A may value his own consumption $X_a$ as well as that of his neighbor B: $U_a = (X_a, X_b)$. If the marginal utility of $X_b$ is positive, then A's contributions to B take on the usual characteristics of the consumption of ordinary economic goods.[24] One implication of preferences of this kind is that donations will depend on the relative, not absolute, well-being of potential recipients.

Behavior in this case can be illustrated by an individual's choice between personal consumption and charitable contributions, as shown in figure 2.2. Other kinds of helping behavior are ignored. In the absence of tax deductibility, the individual's after-tax income $0_b$ ($= 0_a$) is divided between personal consumption and contributions as shown by the budget line $ab$. The indifference curves $U_I$ and $U_I*$ illustrate two different preference sets. In both, contributions to person B is a good and the indifference curves are negatively sloped over the range shown.[25] The equilibrium for indifference curve $U_I$ includes both personal consumption and charitable contributions and, as drawn, satisfies the usual conditions for a utility maximum. In the absence of a tax deduction, the optimum point $E_I$ is the point at which the marginal rate of substitution between contributions and own consumption is equal to one. In contrast, the marginal rate of substitution of $U_I*$ is less than one, resulting in a corner solution of no contributions, despite the fact that contributions have positive marginal utility. The fact that about 16 percent of all households contributed nei-

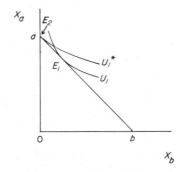

**Fig. 2.2**     Alternative preference sets for own consumption ($X_a$) and consumption of another ($X_b$).

24. A may value B's utility, income, or particular consumption components. For an analysis of the implications of interdependent utilities, see Hochman and Rodgers 1969. For an application to charitable contributions, see Schwartz 1970a.

25. The marginal utility of contributions may fall to zero as B becomes better off. See Hochman and Rodgers 1969 or Throsby and Withers 1979, p. 249.

ther cash nor volunteer time in 1981 indicates that this corner solution is not uncommon (Gallup Organization 1981, p. 24).

Social norms constitute another source of altruistic behavior. Often reinforced by social pressure, norms produce behavior that is indistinguishable from that arising from interdependent utility functions. Whether such social mechanisms arise to prevent "free rider" behavior or for other reasons, it is argued that they are an important determinant of giving and other charitable behavior.[26] In the presence of norms, the act of making contributions is assumed to increase utility. Thus preferences may be described by the same kind of indifference curves as those used to illustrate charity based on interdependent variables, as shown in figure 2.2.

Sen (1977) has argued, however, that not all altruistic behavior must necessarily increase utility. Instead of explaining all giving in terms of the standard model of utility maximization, Sen distinguishes a sense of duty or commitment that may lead individuals to do things plainly not in their own best interest. Obviously, this criticism goes to the heart of economic theory itself. As such, it is a theory that can be neither analyzed in terms of the assumption of utility maximization nor utilized in assessing the likely effects of tax policy on individual giving.

*Reciprocity*

In contrast to altruism, reciprocal helping involves the consideration that help may be returned. Obler (1981) argues that mutual-aid associations and churches, both characterized by aid or assistance among members, have high components of reciprocal giving. The argument has been carried to the level of the social community by viewing much helping behavior as a kind of social insurance. According to this view, philanthropy and everyday helping behavior are part of an informal mutual insurance pact whereby society's fortunate compensate the less fortunate.[27] To the extent to which this is important, then, people act charitably for the same reason they buy insurance. Since this kind of giving brings the benefit of

26. An explanation of how group pressures may inspire philanthropic behavior is given by Bolnick (1975, p. 220): "assuming the existence of an organization to direct and administer a charity drive, we can expect this group to generate communications to the community at large. Depending on the status of this organizational core and the amount of norm-sending generated, there will be a tendency for members of the community to contribute. These individuals in turn will generate chains of primary group pressures, tending to induce more contributions. In addition, the members of the organizing group will each generate a chain of primary group pressures, the strength of these pressures varying with the prestige of the initiators. Through these channels of influence, much of the community will be exposed to direct and/or indirect social pressures to contribute to the charity, and will base their decisions upon the strength of thse pressures, the utility derived from giving to the particular project, and the cost of choosing to contribute." As to the effectiveness of peer pressure, Morgan, Dye, and Hybels (1977, p. 274) report that 45 percent of their sample believed that people would give more if the amount given were made public.

27. See, for example, Douty 1972; Becker 1974, p. 1084; Landes and Posner 1978b; and Hirshleifer 1978.

potential return aid, the standard economic model shown in figure 2.2 would again apply. How much giving of this sort would be forthcoming depends, of course, on the shape of the indifference curves, which in turn is a function of the importance and effectiveness of that potential aid.

### Direct Benefit

Finally, helping may arise out of some more immediate or tangible benefit. Individuals may volunteer for organizations in order for their families or themselves to consume services. Thus Sunday-school teachers and soccer coaches often supervise their own children. As Olson (1971, p. 34) explains this kind of participation, "in a very small group, where each member gets a substantial portion of the total gain simply because there are few members in the group, a collective good can often be provided by the voluntary, self-interested action of the members of the group." Donors may derive more ethereal personal benefit from making contributions as well. Weisbrod (1978b, p. 34) describes the character of such benefits:

> The extent to which narrow self-interest lies behind the donations of money and time to non-profit organizations is little understood, but there can be no doubt that donors often do benefit through the making of business contacts and the receipt of favorable publicity for good deeds. Having a library, park, or college classroom building named after a donor can be viewed as reflecting philanthropy but it can also be viewed as the reward for a donation—and, hence, as a form of purchase. Even small donors frequently receive tangible and direct returns in such forms as receipts of a "free" magazine, access to organized meetings with like-minded people, or other information, goods, or services, in return for their tax-deductible "gifts," "donations," "voluntary contributions," or membership dues. The motivation of those who make these contributions are doubtless complicated.

To the extent that contributions "buy" such tangible or intangible consumer goods, contributions again fall naturally into the standard utility-maximization framework, as shown in figure 2.2. An extension of this model is called for, however, in the case that contributions actually increase own consumption over some range. For example, a proprietor's contribution to local charities may increase profits through favorable publicity. Or, individuals may gain valuable job skills from volunteer work, particularly women who may have been out of the labor market for some time.[28] In such cases it is unnecessary to postulate that donors receive any direct utility from helping others since helping is literally its own reward. Thus individuals who are indifferent about the well-being of

28. Mueller 1975 emphasizes this reason for volunteer activity. See chap. 4.

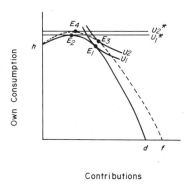

**Fig. 2.3**          Contributions with gains from giving.

beneficiaries will contribute or help. Figure 2.3 illustrates the choice for an individual who can gain income over some range by making contributions. The solid curve *hd* is the budget line after taxes but with no tax deductibility. Optimal contributions are positive whether the donor values making the gift itself ($U_1$) or is indifferent ($U_1^*$). If contributions are deductible at a constant rate, the budget set swivels in a counterclockwise direction to *hf*, causing contributions to increase under both preference assumptions. Although such a positively sloped budget set is conceivable, the remainder of this section is confined to the analysis of the usual negatively sloped budget sets.

To sum up, helping behavior in the form of donations or charitable actions may be divided, roughly, into altruism, reciprocal helping, or strictly self-interested activity. Except for Sen's notion of commitment, this behavior can be analyzed in terms of a general utility-maximization model. Where no monetary gain is expected, helping based on interdependent utilities, norms, or personal consumption all look the same, though the underlying motivations obviously differ greatly. For the purpose of predicting individual behavior, there is little practical difference between helping others because sympathy inspires it, society expects it, or tastes demand it. In analyzing the effects of income tax treatment, therefore, individuals are simply assumed to value contributions and their own consumption as two goods and to maximize utility subject to a tax-defined budget constraint.

### 2.3.2    The Effect of Income Taxation

If an individual's giving behavior can be explained in a way consistent with utility maximization, the effect of income taxation on giving can be analyzed using conventional microeconomic models. The individual is seen as deriving satisfaction from contributions ($G$) and his own consumption of other goods ($X$): $U = U(X, G)$. Where gross income is $Y$ and taxes are a function of income and contributions ($T(Y,G)$), the maximization problem is

(1)                    maximize $U(X,G)$,

(2)                    subject to $Y - T(Y,G) = X + G$.

Using primes to denote partial derivatives, the resulting equilibrium condition is

(3)                    $$\frac{U'(G)}{U'(X)} = 1 + T'(G).$$

Since $T'(G)$ is the rate at which taxes are reduced per dollar of contribution, equation (3) states that the marginal rate of substitution between contributions and own consumption is equal to the net-of-tax "price" of making contributions. Where contributions are a deduction in calculating taxable income, the marginal effect of contributions is the negative of the marginal tax rate, $T'(G) = -T'(Y)$, and (3) reduces to

(3')                    $$\frac{U'(G)}{U'(X)} = 1 - T'(Y).$$

In order to analyze the likely effect of the tax treatment of charitable contributions, it is useful to examine in detail several existing or possible tax provisions.

*Deductibility*

The most important tax provision affecting charitable contributions in the United States is, of course, the deduction allowed for such gifts. Figure 2.4 shows the individual's budget lines under a progressive income tax with and without a deduction for contributions. The line $ab$ is the budget set when there is no deduction, and its slope is $-1$, reflecting the fact that a dollar of contributions costs a full dollar in this case. The height of the budget line $0a$ is after-tax income. The line $acdef$ is the budget set in the presence of a charitable deduction. The segmented nature of the budget line reflects the progressivity of the rate structure. The tax rate at which contributions are deducted will usually decline at some point as increasing contributions place the taxpayer in a lower marginal rate bracket. The slope of segment $ac$ is $-(1 - m_l)$, where $m_l$ is the marginal tax rate applying to the first dollar of contributions. The slopes of succeeding segments become steeper as the applicable marginal rate falls. If there is a ceiling on the deduction of contributions—here assumed to be point $e$—the slope becomes $-1$ thereafter. The optimal point shown in the figure for a taxpayer receiving a deduction is $E_2$, in segment $de$, corresponding to the tax rate $m_3$, where $m_3 < m_1$. At $E_2$ the marginal rate of substitution between contributions and own consumption is $(1 - m_3)$.

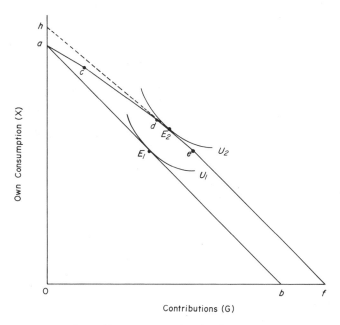

**Fig. 2.4**          Effect of income tax deduction for contributions.


In general, then, the deductibility of contributions has an income effect and a substitution effect. If giving is a normal good, both effects will tend to encourage contributions. If the individual chooses a point on the initial segment of the budget line (*ac*), the deduction is equivalent to a reduction in the price of contributions, and the budget line turns counterclockwise on point *a*. If another budget line is chosen, however, the progressivity of rates implies a result different from this standard effect. For example, moving from budget line *ab* to segment *de* amounts to combining two changes: (a) a price reduction from 1 to $(1 - m_2)$ and (b) an exogenous increase of *ah* in disposable income. The amount *ah* has been referred to as the "tax schedule premium," which arises from the higher rate(s) at which some inframarginal contributions were deducted from income. In estimating and predicting tax effects on giving, this additional income effect ideally should be taken into account.

In order to make the connection between the hypothetical rate schedule implied in figure 2.4 and actual income taxes, table 2.11 presents the budget set for a taxpaying household with average income in 1980. Mean values of exemptions and deductions were chosen for the income class corresponding to mean adjusted gross income (AGI) in 1980 ($37,461). Since budget lines will generally be different for each household, the case presented can only be illustrative. Maximum own consumption for this

**Table 2.11    Budget Line Segments for Average Itemizing Household, 1980 (adjusted gross income = $37,461)**

| Contribution Range | Tax Liability at Lower Contribution Level[a] | Net Income Less Contributions at Lower Contribution Level | Price of Giving in Range[b] | Tax Schedule Premium[c] | |
|---|---|---|---|---|---|
| | | | | Total | As Percentage of 31,055[d] |
| $    0–554 | $6406 | $31,055 | 0.63[e] | $    0 | 1 |
| 555–5,854 | 6201 | 30,705 | 0.68 | 28 | 0.1 |
| 5,855–10,254 | 4505 | 27,101 | 0.72 | 527 | 1.7 |
| 10,255–14,454 | 3273 | 23,933 | 0.76 | 1333 | 4.3 |
| 14,455–18,554 | 2265 | 20,741 | 0.79 | 2313 | 7.4 |
| 18,555–18,730 | 1404 | 17,502 | 0.82 | 3526 | 11.4 |
| 18,731[f]–36,094 | 1367 | 17,363 | 1.00 | 6930 | 22.3 |

*Note:* Calculations based on joint return in 1980 with AGI of $37,461. Average figures for the $30,000–50,000 AGI class were also used: excess itemized deductions—$4564; contributions—$858; exemptions—$3300.

[a]Taxable income is AGI − (exemptions) − (lower contribution level) − (other excess itemized deductions).

[b]One minus marginal tax rate in range.

[c]The tax schedule premium is the difference between first-dollar net income and the hypothetical net income implied by extrapolating the appropriate budget segment. Where $P_1$ is .63, $P_i$ = price applying to a given segment, and $G_i$ is the minimum contribution level for a segment, the premium is $G_i(P_i - P_1)$.

[d]First-dollar net income.

[e]First-dollar price of giving.

[f]Fifty percent limitation on deduction as percent of AGI is assumed to apply.

household (corresponding to $0a$ in figure 2.4) is $31,055, and the price of initial gifts (the "first-dollar" price) is 0.63. Since no contributions over half of AGI are deductible,[29] the price of giving becomes 1.0 beyond gifts of $18,731. If this hypothetical household gave the average amount for the $30,000–50,000 class, $858, the table shows that the second budget segment, corresponding to a price of 0.68, would be chosen. In this case, the extra-income effect due to the tax schedule premium is $28, or 0.1 percent of beginning net income. For this premium to amount to as much as 4 percent of net income, contributions would have had to be about 12 times the actual average for the class. On the other hand, if other deductions had been about $500 more, or $300 less, the average gift of $858 would have been located on the initial budget segment. Despite the theoretical nonlinearity of tax-defined budget sets, therefore, the figures in this table suggest that the average household in practice faces a nearly linear budget set and that the effect of tax deductibility is quite close to that of a simple price decrease.

Within the general utility-maximization framework used here, it is possible to identify particular preferences that yield special cases of the effect of tax deductibility on giving. One interesting special case is that of the "target giver." If the target is stated in terms of gross contributions, the individual's giving will not be affected by income or price changes. Alternatively, the target may be stated in terms of contributions net of subsidy, or "sacrifice." As Feldstein and Lindsey (1981, pp. 21–22) note, a target level of sacrifice implies that decreases in price will lead to equi-proportional increases in gross contributions, resulting in the same behavior as would be observed for an individual with a unitary price elasticity.

### Changes in Tax Rates

Although not explicitly a policy directed toward charitable giving, changes in the tax rate schedule will generally have an effect on the individual's choice between giving and own consumption. Such tax rate changes may arise from tax legislation or from inflationary "bracket creep." To illustrate the effect of a tax rate change, consider a proportional increase in all tax brackets. The result of this tax increase would be to shift the budget set toward the origin and to make it steeper. In other words, there would be an income effect discouraging contributions (if giving is a normal good) and a substitution effect encouraging contributions. The net effect of a given tax increase would depend on the size of the income and price elasticities and on the nature of the tax cut itself.[30]

---

29. The 50 percent limit is assumed.
30. For further discussion of these effects, see Schwartz 1970a, p. 1272.

*Tax Credit*

One logical alternative to a charitable deduction is a tax credit—a reduction in taxes by some proportion of charitable contributions. While the price of giving under a deduction depends on the taxpayer's marginal tax rate, under a credit all taxpayers would face the same price of giving. With a tax credit of $100n$ percent for contributions, taxes would be $T = f(Y) - nG$ where $f(Y)$ is the tax function, and the price of giving in equation (3) would be $1 - n$. Figure 2.5 illustrates the effect of a tax credit by showing a credit of 25 percent ($n = 0.25$). Such a credit has the same effect as a price subsidy, with both the income and substitution effects leading to more contributions when giving is a normal good. As can be seen by comparing figures 2.4 and 2.5, a tax credit at rate $n$ will have precisely the same effect on giving (cash gifts) as a deduction for a taxpayer whose marginal tax rate is $n$ if the equilibrium occurs in the budget set's first segment. Otherwise, the deduction will have a larger income effect by virtue of the rate "progression premium," although this difference may be quite small. If a tax credit were substituted for the present deduction, however, the prices faced by most taxpayers would change since there would likely be a single tax-credit rate $n$ for all taxpayers. The price of giving for taxpayers with marginal tax rates above that rate would increase, and the price for taxpayers with low tax rates would fall. Since both the size of gifts and the intended beneficiaries tend to vary by the income of donors, a tax credit is likely to result in markedly different size and distribution of total contributions, a possibility considered in more detail in chapter 3.

*Multiple Deduction*

Another alternative to a simple charitable deduction is a deduction for some multiple of contributions. While this multiple could in principle be

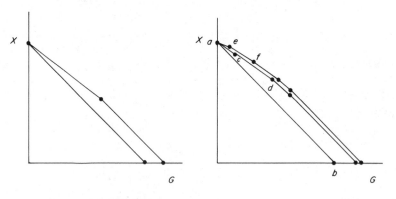

Tax Credit of 25 Percent          Deduction for 150 Percent of Contributions

**Figs. 2.5 and 2.6**   Effect of tax credit and multiplied deduction in contributions.

less than 100 percent, proposals to alter this proportion, such as that made by the Commission on Private Philanthropy and Public Needs, have focused on increasing the deduction percentage beyond 100.[31] Figure 2.6 illustrates the effect of a multiple deduction by showing how a deduction of 150 percent affects the budget set. This provision pushes the budget set out from $acd$ to $aef$. The initial price of giving falls from $(1 - m_l)$ to $(1 - rm_l)$, where $r$ is the deduction rate (in this case, 1.5) and $m_l$ is the taxpayer's marginal tax rate applicable to the first dollar of contributions. For any given deduction rate $r$, the higher the taxpayer's marginal tax rate, the greater the percentage point decrease in the price of giving.

One special case of the multiple deduction arises in connection with gifts of appreciated property. As Schwartz (1970a) first pointed out, the fact that capital gains on donated assets are generally not taxable reduces the price on such gifts from $(1 - m)$ to $(1 - m - m_c g)$, where $m_c$ is the marginal tax rate on capital gains and $g$ is the gain-to-value ratio. If $u$ is the portion of long-term gains included in taxable income, the price is $(1 - m(1 + ug))$. This tax treatment is equivalent to a multiple deduction of cash proceeds of $100(1 - ug)$ percent.

*Deduction Floor*

A special case of the charitable deduction is a deduction allowed only for contributions over some minimum amount or floor.[32] This floor might be an absolute dollar amount or might be calculated as some percentage of gross income. Proposals for deduction floors have been supported as ways to maintain incentives to give while reducing the revenue cost of the deduction. The existence of a standard deduction may also act as a deduction floor for some taxpayers. Whether the standard deduction is a constant amount or is calculated as a percentage of income, it is advantageous to taxpayers to choose the standard deduction as long as itemized deductions are less. A taxpayer whose potential itemized deductions other than contributions are $100 less than the standard deduction effectively receives no deduction for his first $100 of contributions. There is an effective floor of $100: only when contributions exceed that amount will tax liability be reduced. For taxpayers facing either type of deduction floor, the price of giving is 1 initially; then it falls when the floor is exceeded.

The budget set for an individual confronting a deduction floor is shown as $abd$ in figure 2.7. The budget set without the deduction is $abc$, and the floor is $e$ dollars of giving. Along the segment $ab$ the price of giving is 1, but it falls to $(1 - m_l)$ in the first segment to the right of $b$, where $m_l$ is the applicable marginal tax rate. Unlike the budget set applying to the unlim-

---

31. See Commission on Private Philanthropy and Public Needs 1977, p. 4. For discussions of the multiple deduction, see Hood, Martin, and Osberg 1977 or Throsby and Withers 1979.
32. A floor has an analogous effect for a tax credit.

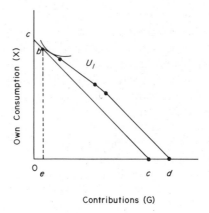

Contributions (G)

**Fig. 2.7**          Effect of tax deduction with floor on contributions.


ited deduction, the budget set in this case is no longer convex from above. As suggested by the hypothetical indifference curve $U_I$, discontinuous jumps in desired contributions could occur with very small changes in the tax rate, net income, or the floor amount.

The analysis of giving with a deduction floor raises two important issues—one econometric and one behavioral. First, the effective floor created by the standard deduction creates a class of taxpayers who become itemizers only by virtue of their charitable gifts. For such "borderline" itemizers, the price of giving the first dollar of contributions is one, and it is incorrect to assume that itemization status is independent of the choice about how much to give. This point is considered in section 2.4 of this chapter.

The behavioral issue raised by the case of a deduction floor is the possibility that taxpayers under such a plan might tend to "bunch" their gifts, say in alternate years, in order to obtain maximum benefit from the deduction. Clearly, this possibility points up one limitation of using a one-period model to examine contribution behavior. One way to see the implications of a floor for the pattern of giving over time is in a simple two-period model of contributions. Suppose an individual is prepared to contribute, in present value terms, $S$ dollars net of taxes over two years and that gifts above a floor of $M°$ dollars are deductible at rates $k_1$ and $k_2$ in the two years. Figures 2.8 and 2.9 show the two-period opportunity set for various floor levels.[33] Because only gifts over the floor receive the deduction, the maximum net gift of $S$ in year 1 yields a gross gift of $M° + (S–M°)/(1-k_1)$. When the floor is relatively large, as in figure 2.8 ($M_1$) the opportunity set can be markedly nonconvex from above. Fur-

33. For constructing figures 2.8 and 2.9, $k_1 = k_2 = .33$ and the rate of interest is .10.

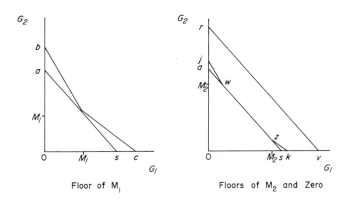

**Fig. 2.8 and 2.9**   Contributions with a deduction floor in a two-period model.

thermore, if there is a high degree of substitutability between gifts in either year, indifference curves will tend to be flat and bunching of gifts in one year or the other is likely to occur. In contrast, when the floor is either very high or very low, it is less likely that bunching will occur. In figure 2.9, a high floor of $M_2$ yields a nearly straight budget set of $jwzk$. When no floor exists, the budget set is the straight line $rv$. Whether bunching will occur thus depends on the relative size of the floor, the deduction rate, and the degree to which gifts in one year substitute for gifts in another. Although there appear to be some forces favoring relatively constant periodic gifts, at least to the extent that contributions follow involvement in organizations, it is quite conceivable that a floor could encourage alternate-year timing of gifts.[34]

### 2.3.3   Relative Income, Government Expenditures, and "Crowding Out"

A final question of considerable theoretical interest is how the well-being of potential recipients affects donations. If giving is motivated by interdependence in utility functions, one might predict that donations would increase as potential recipients become more needy. Two empirically testable implications follow from this reasoning. First, donors motivated by interdependence in utility functions will tend to give more as the income of recipients, relative to theirs, falls. As Becker (1974, p. 1084) states, "an increase in the incomes of both recipients and givers should not increase giving by as much as an increase in the incomes of givers alone." Accordingly, some of the empirical studies discussed in the following sections include relative income as an explanatory variable for giving.

---

34. For a further discussion of contributions in the presence of deduction floors, see Feldstein and Lindsey 1981 and the discussion of simulation methods in chap. 3.

A second implication of utility interdependence, one that is directly applicable to public finance, is that government expenditures will tend to crowd out private giving to the extent that government programs make recipients better off or provide similar services to those provided through charitable organizations. How complete this effect is depends upon how closely substitutable government services are with private gifts and what exactly enters the utility functions of donors. If donors care only about recipients' income levels, a public-income maintenance program may well completely supplant private charity. If, however, donors value attributes that cannot be provided by government, or if donors value the act of giving itself, private giving is less likely to be crowded out. Rose-Ackerman (1981) suggests that government programs could even encourage private giving, depending on the difference in public and private services, the scale economies of charities, regulations imposed on charities, and the effects of increased government and on information about charities. Obler's (1981, pp. 33, 36) observations about charities in an English village are interesting in this regard. He found that only one new social-welfare charity had arisen since the rapid rise in government health and welfare programs. Over the same period, in contrast, the number of recreational and self-help groups had mushroomed, suggesting that the primary crowding out that resulted from the growth of the welfare state occurred in areas where government programs were most closely substitutable with charitable activities.

### 2.3.4  Conclusion

This section has reviewed alternative explanations for giving, noting that most are consistent with the standard economic model of utility maximization subject to a budget constraint. By focusing on the effects of various tax provisions on possible combinations of consumption and contributions, it is possible to show the effect of tax provisions on an individual with given income and preferences. In general, tax inducements have income and substitution effects, both of which encourage giving if giving is a normal good. It is useful, however, to summarize several assumptions implicit in this basic model. First, both labor supply and gross income are assumed to be constant. By and large, therefore, the models neither allow for the possibility that giving will increase income, nor do they make allowance for tax effects on volunteer time. Second, the model rests on the assumption that making contributions increases an individual's utility. As for contributions motivated by Sen's notion of commitment, there seems to be no direct way to adapt models based on utility maximization for the purpose of predicting the effects of income taxation on contributions. The conclusion of this section is conditioned, therefore, on the assumption that contributions, at least over some range, increase utility. Third, the basic model deals with optimization in a single period and does not consider multi-period effects of tax policies.

## 2.4  Econometric Studies of Contributions by Individuals: An Overview

Since 1967 there have appeared over a dozen econometric studies of charitable giving by individuals. Using different kinds of data and various model specifications, they have examined the effect on contributions of income, the income tax, and a host of other factors. This section reviews this empirical literature, focusing on the models and variables used to specify the individual's decision to contribute. Results contained in the studies are then described.

### 2.4.1  Model and Variables

Analogous to the specification of demand functions in consumer theory, an individual's "demand" for contributions usually takes the form

(4)  $$G = f(Y, P, Z),$$

where $G$ measures contributions, $Y$ is disposable income, $P$ is the "price" of giving, and $Z$ is a vector of other explanatory variables. Although the connection between utility and demand functions is seldom made explicit, it is possible to derive specific utility functions consistent with particular demand functions by utilizing the condition for utility maximization that the price of giving is equal to the marginal rate of substitution between giving and other goods.[35] In most empirical studies the demand function takes the log-linear form:

(5)  $$G = AY^a P^b e^{hZ},$$

where $A$, $a$, and $b$ are constants and $h$ is a vector of constants. For estimation purposes, (5) can be transformed by taking logarithms:

(6)  $$\ln G = \ln A + a \ln Y + b \ln P + hZ,$$

leaving a form that is linear in its parameters. A principal assumption implicit in the adoption of the log-linear model is, of course, that the income and price elasticities are constants. Several of the most important issues of specification in this literature come down to a question of whether this constant elasticity assumption is valid.

### Contributions

The measure of contributions $G$ is invariably based on the dollar value of gifts made. This is not surprising, since contributions are reported in dollars on tax returns and counted in dollars by recipient organizations; however, the dollar value of contributions is not necessarily an ideal mea-

---

35. For example, the function $U(G, Y, Z) = (1/(a+1))G^{a+1}Z^c + (1/(b+1))Y^{b+1}Z^d$ implies a first-order condition of $P = MRS = G^a Y^{-b} Z^{c-d}$, or $G = P^{1/a} Y^{b/a} Z^{(d-c)/a}$, which is the log-linear form of the demand function. Diminishing marginal utility implies $a < 0$ and $b < 0$; thus the expected signs of the exponents are negative for price $(1/a)$ and positive for income $(b/a)$.

sure of giving. It might be more desirable to measure units of final "output" provided by charitable organizations as a result of an individual's contributions. Like expenditures in education and other areas of service delivery, contributions measure the cost of inputs, not output. Neither the relative cost nor the productivity of inputs is accounted for in that dollar measure, in large part because the output of the nonprofit sector is so heterogenous and knowledge about production relationships is so limited. On the other hand, one may argue that the dollar value of contributions is the most appropriate measure of giving when individuals typically have only vague notions of how their gifts are translated into the provision of services. While some contributors may have a rough idea about the proportion of an organization's budget devoted to administration and fund raising, for example, most lack the time and expertise to assess and compare unit costs of service provision. In any case, the form in which data are available dictates that giving will be measured by the monetary value of contributions.

There are two basic sources for contributions data used in econometric studies of individual giving. The most readily available information is that based on the returns of taxpayers who itemize their deductions. Because the charitable deduction is a tax feature of long standing—and potential tax savings—it is widely utilized among itemizing taxpayers. More important, it is a deduction with relatively few constraints: for itemizers it is neither subject to a floor, like the medical deduction, nor dependent on other taxpayer characteristics, like the deductions for taxes and interest. There are, however, two principal weaknesses of the contributions data based on itemized deductions. First, no data are available for taxpayers who elect to take the standard deduction. The result is that econometric studies using tax return data are necessarily based on itemizers only. If the behavior of taxpayers who itemize is different from that of other taxpayers, the resulting estimates will, of course, not be representative of the latter. More important, equations based on samples of itemizers may be subject to sample selection bias if the decision to itemize is itself a function of contributions. This possibility is discussed below in section 2.5 of this chapter. A second potential weakness of contributions data based on tax returns is the possibility of systematic overstatement. Not only is there an incentive for taxpayers to remember "too much," the incentive to overstate gifts rises with the marginal tax rate, leading to a potential confounding of giving and cheating effects. Available data on reporting suggest that the aggregate amount of overstatement is relatively small for contributions (Clotfelter 1983b, appendix). The possibility of confounded price effects is discussed further in section 2.5 below.

The second major source of data on individual contributions is information from household surveys. Although the accuracy of survey responses may be less than information given on tax returns, surveys have the advantage of including nonitemizers as well as itemizers. One possible bias would remain, however, if nonitemizers—because they have no reason to keep records of gifts for tax purposes—tend to underreport their giving in household surveys. There is, unfortunately, no evidence on the existence or extent of this bias, nor is there a way to test this possibility with available data. It is worth noting, however, because such differential reporting rates could provide at least a partial explanation for differences in reported giving based on itemization status.

*Price*

Based on the discussion above of an ideal measure of giving, the price of giving would be defined as the foregone consumption to an individual of providing a unit of output to a given recipient. To the extent that factors such as exemption from the property tax or the use of volunteer labor (or the payment of below-market wages) reduces the cost of providing such a unit, the price of giving would be reduced. In addition, the price would depend on the level of output if the "supply curve" of charitable services is upward sloping. For example, the cost of providing counseling services could rise as the number of users increases. Due to the difficulty of defining outputs and identifying relevant production functions, however, these kinds of variations in output price are ignored in defining the price of giving. In particular, the supply curve for services is assumed to be horizontal.[36]

Following Vickrey (1962) and Schwartz (1970a) virtually all of the econometric studies of contributions use as the basic measure of the price the after-tax foregone consumption per dollar of giving. In the presence of an income tax with marginal rate $m$, the basic price of giving is simply $(1-m)$. In practice, however, the calculation of the price can involve considerable complexity. To begin with, the federal income tax code contains a number of special features that can affect marginal tax rates. Rather than simply calculating taxable income and referring to the appropriate tax schedule, a complete calculation of marginal tax rates usually requires calculation of tax liability at two levels of contributions and then calculating the slope. Further complications arise from such special features as income averaging, the alternative tax on capital gains, the maximum tax on earned income, the minimum tax, and tax surcharges. For example, income averaging has the effect of reducing an individual's marginal tax rate below what it would otherwise be on a given amount of taxable income. Because its calculation is based on previous years' tax return data not recorded on tax files used in empirical studies, it is necessary to use iterative methods to construct the necessary information.[37] Hence, some amount of programming is required to obtain a precise measure of the marginal

36. See also Schwartz (1970a, p. 1270) for a discussion of this point.
37. Studies accounting for the effect of income averaging on marginal tax rates include Feldstein and Taylor 1976; Clotfelter 1980b; and Clotfelter and Steuerle 1981.

tax rate.[38] Such subtleties are usually forgotten, however, in studies using aggregated data. The usual approach in that case is to calculate the taxable income and corresponding marginal tax rate for the average income value in a given income class.[39]

A second complication in the calculation of the price of contributions arises in the case of gifts of appreciated assets. As Schwartz (1970a) and Feldstein (1975a) have noted, the net cost of contributing a dollar of appreciated assets, when compared to present consumption, is

$$(7) \qquad\qquad P_a = 1 - m - m_c g,$$

where $m$ is the marginal tax rate on ordinary income, $m_c$ is the tax rate on capital gains income, and $g$ is the asset's ratio of capital gains to market value. Where the marginal tax rate is 50 percent on ordinary income and 20 percent on capital gains and gain-to-value ratio is one-half (following the example given in section 2.2), $P_a = 0.4$, compared to a price of 0.5 for giving cash.[40] If the alternative to contributing assets is not immediate consumption, however, the price cannot be stated as simply as in (7). As Feldstein and Taylor (1976, p. 1203) discuss, the expected present value of the tax is reduced due to deferral and the possibility that the gain might never be realized and taxed as income to the individual. Thus the opportunity cost of giving an asset in the present is understated by (7) when there exists the option of holding the asset. In order to incorporate this reasoning, they modify (7) by redefining $g$ as the gain-to-value ratio multiplied by the present value of a dollar's worth of tax payment.[41] Since there are no data on either component of this variable, Feldstein (1975a), Feldstein and Clotfelter (1976), and Feldstein and Taylor (1976) employ a maxi-

---

38. Two other provisions affecting marginal tax rates are worth noting: the maximum tax on earned income and the minimum tax. Under the maximum tax, taxable income is allocated to "earned" and "unearned" income, with the former facing a maximum rate of 50 percent and the latter "stacked" on top of the former. This allocation rule has the effect of reducing the top marginal tax rate below the statutory maximum of 70 percent. For further discussion of this provision, see Lindsey 1981. Chap. 3 discusses its effect on the price of contributions in 1980.

The minimum tax, imposed in several forms in recent years, attempts to ensure that some minimum amount of tax is paid by high-income taxpayers. Legislation in 1982 required taxpayers to pay the greater of the normal tax or an alternative minimum tax, calculated as 20 percent of an alternative taxable income over an exemption. Since contributions were allowed as a deduction, the price of giving for the small group of taxpayers coming under this provision was 0.80. Whether this represented an increase or decrease is unclear, however, since many of these taxpayers paid little normal tax and thus faced low marginal tax rates to begin with. See U.S. Congress, Staff of the Joint Committee on Taxation 1982, pp. 7–9; *Internal Revenue Code* 1982, sec. 55; and U.S. Congress 1982, sec. 201.

39. See, for example, Feldstein 1975a.

40. Note that the price of giving assets could be negative. Where the top marginal tax rate on ordinary income is 0.91, as it was in the 1950s, a value of $g$ of 0.5 implies $P_a = -0.14$.

41. This could be modified to account for the possibility that no taxes will be paid by letting $g$ be the *expected* present value.

mum-likelihood approach to select a value for $g$. The first two studies find that a ratio of 0.5 yields the best fit, while the third obtains both higher and lower values but assumes 0.5 for the purpose of estimation (Feldstein and Taylor 1976, pp. 1205–6).

The ambiguities of defining the price of giving assets aside, it is not obvious how that price should be used in explaining contributions. One could enter both the price of giving cash and the price of giving assets, but, as Feldstein and Taylor note (p. 1204), these measures would tend to be highly collinear. The approach adopted by Feldstein (1975a) and in subsequent studies is to form a weighted average of both prices, the weights being the proportion of gifts in cash and in asset form by income class.[42]

Because contributions are deductible in calculating state income taxes, state tax rates are another complicating feature in the calculation of the net price of giving. In 1977, thirty-two states plus the District of Columbia had income taxes providing a deduction or a credit for contributions. For taxpayers with incomes of $30,000, effective state marginal tax rates ranged as high as 14 percent (Feenberg 1982, p. 11). These rates cannot simply be added to the federal rate, however, because of the interactions between state and federal taxes. Since state taxes as well as contributions are deductible in calculating the federal income tax, the inclusion of state income taxes makes the price of giving

$$(8) \qquad P = 1 - (m_f(1 - m_s) + m_s),$$

where $m_f$ and $m_s$ are, respectively, the applicable federal and state marginal income tax rates.[43] The only indication in the published literature as to how much difference the inclusion of state taxes makes is Feldstein and Taylor's (1976, p. 1204n) comment on the similarity of estimates for 1970 with and without them. As Feenberg emphasizes, however, state taxes provide a source of variation in net prices that is quite independent of income. This independence takes on considerable importance in assessing the statistical properties of estimated price effects in equations explaining contributions. This point is discussed in section 2.5 below.

In considering the various tax provisions that determine the net price of giving, it becomes obvious that a precise determination of the price requires individual data rich in tax information as well as data on state of residence. In the face of these interacting and sometimes complex tax provisions, one question that arises is whether individuals actually are cogni-

42. As Feldstein and Taylor point out (1976, p. 1204), using the actual breakdown between cash and noncash gifts actually made by an individual would introduce simultaneity into the definition of the price. One alternative treatment to a weighted average is Schwartz's (1970a, p. 1271) inclusion of capital gains in equations explaining contributions, but the ambiguity of this specification makes it less desirable than the weighted average.

43. See, for example, Reece 1979, p. 145.

zant of the price of giving they actually face. To test taxpayers' awareness of their marginal tax rates, Morgan, Dye, and Hybels (1977, p. 178) included a question in the Survey Research Center's National Study of Philanthropy intended to measure the marginal tax perceived by respondents. According to the authors, only 21 percent of the taxpayers in the sample gave "conceivably correct" answers, defined as rates equal to or below the maximum rate for the taxpayer's income and not lower than the minimum rate of 14 percent. Morgan, Dye, and Hybels conclude that this finding "casts doubt on the efficacy of deductibility as a major spur to charitable activity" (p. 231). For taxpayers with incomes over $30,000, however, the "conceivably correct" rate was over 43 percent (p. 178). In addition, the test for acceptable answers appears to have been quite strict. It is possible, for instance, that taxpayers' rough estimates of their marginal tax rates are unbiased, but subject to variation. While individuals may guess too high or too low, they may be correct on average. Certainly at middle and upper incomes, the source of most charitable gifts, there is considerable sophistication about taxes and tax rates.[44]

A final point relating to the calculation of the net price of giving arises from the dependence of the price on the amount that is contributed, an attribute resulting from the nonlinearity of the budget set. The approach adopted by Feldstein (1975a) and most succeeding studies was to calculate the price of giving the first dollar of contributions. Although this "first-dollar" price is clearly independent of the contributions decision, it may be a poor measure of the marginal price in some cases. As table 2.10 above suggests, however, the first-dollar price is probably a very close approximation of the marginal price in most cases. The correspondence between these two price definitions is analyzed using a sample of taxpayers in section 2.5 below.

*Income*

Demand theory clearly implies that income is a determinant of demand (except in the unlikely case that the income elasticity is everywhere zero), but it is often less clear how, exactly, income comes into play. In terms of the simple model presented in section 2.3, disposable income would be the appropriate measure. Accordingly, most empirical studies define income as gross income less the federal income tax. (In order to make this an exogenous measure of income, the tax is usually calculated as if no contributions were made.) The federal-tax definition of adjusted gross income (AGI) is usually used for gross income because of its easy availability, al-

---

44. A front-page "Tax Report" item in the *Wall Street Journal* is illustrative: "Try to delay deductions, such as charitable gifts, from years when the alternative tax will kick in to years when you will pay the regular tax" (*Wall Street Journal*, "Tax Report," 9 February 1983, p. 1).

though it is flawed by the omission of important income sources, such as excluded and unrealized capital gains and interest on state and local bonds.

Two principal alternatives to the use of disposable income are permanent income and relative income. Developed by Friedman (1957), the theory of permanent income is based on the notion that a household's consumption depends on its normal or "permanent" level of income, not on actual income received in any given year. If permanent income is the correct income measure, the use of annual income will tend to result in a downward bias in the estimated-income coefficient due to the presence of the transitory component in annual income. Several studies of charitable giving include some measure of permanent income. Feldstein and Clotfelter (1976) used a two-year average of income to represent permanent income, and Clotfelter (1980b) employed a fitted value based on trend lines fitted for each individual. In both cases, a measure of the transitory component of income was also included.[45]

The use of relative income is suggested by the theory of interdependent utility, discussed in section 2.3. For each income class in each year of his sample, Schwartz (1970a) measured own income as the average disposable income for that class and other income as the average disposable income in excluded classes. His equations were estimated with and without the other-income variable (see section 2.5 below). Reflecting much the same relative income effect, other studies have included as explanatory variables measures of the income distribution (Hochman and Rodgers 1973; Long and Settle 1979), the incidence of poverty (Dye 1978), and lower-quintile income (Reece 1979), all defined for the donor's community.

Following the simple consumer-demand model presented in section 2.3, empirical models of contributions implicitly assume that labor supply is fixed, and thus that gross income is exogenous. Menchik and Weisbrod (1981, p. 168) argue, however, that this assumption is invalid, leaving models of contributions misspecified. In order to account for the choice between work, volunteering, and other uses of time, they argue for the inclusion of the net wage in models of monetary giving. While such a general model would certainly be desirable, currently available data sets do not offer the kind of information on wages for working individuals and shadow wages for nonworking individuals necessary to estimate a complete model. Instead, one must assume that the labor-supply effects of the charitable deduction are not of sufficient magnitude to create significant bias in estimates of the income elasticity of charitable giving. This assumption does not seem unreasonable.

45. Other studies that use measures of permanent income, without a transitory component, are Schwartz 1970a and Reece 1979.

*Other Variables*

Besides price and income, variables have been included in models of giving in order to reflect the possible effects of personal, social, or demographic characteristics of donors. Age has been used and consistently found to be an important factor in explaining differences in personal giving propensities. Other personal variables that have been employed include marital status, wealth, education, dependents, and past giving. Community characteristics include measures of relative income and poverty, as noted above, as well as measures of government programs intended to benefit potential recipients, the idea being that government programs may reduce contributions. Like the relative-income hypothesis, the notion that public spending may crowd out private giving is an implication of interdependent utility functions.

### 2.4.2    Data and Estimation

Table 2.12 presents a summary of sixteen econometric analyses of charitable contributions in the United States. The studies utilize a variety of data sets, variables, and model specifications. The table gives information for each study on the data source, income limits, estimated price and income elasticities, variables other than price and income, and sample size. The elasticities shown are illustrative of basic estimates, but because these studies typically present estimates based on several different specifications, the estimates shown are not intended as a complete summary of findings.

Following at least thirty years of speculation as to the effect of the tax on giving, Taussig (1967) provided the first econometric study seeking to separate the effects of income and tax rate on giving. Using data on individual tax returns for 1962, Taussig found contributions generally to be insensitive to variations in tax rates. For income classes less than $100,000, marginal tax rates were statistically insignificant. For classes above $100,000, tax rates had a small but significant effect, implying price elasticities ranging from $-0.04$ to $-0.10$. Estimated income elasticities, on the other hand, were large and statistically greater than 1.0. As for the price effect of the income tax, Taussig's basic finding is that "the incentive effect of the deduction for charitable contributions is, in the aggregate, weak" (p. 16). This conclusion, of course, supported the speculations of Vickrey (1962) and others who had argued that any price effect on giving was bound to be small.

Taussig's conclusion has not been borne out, however, in subsequent empirical studies of taxes and giving, although much of his methodology has been adopted. Using aggregate data on contributions in several broad income categories between 1929 and 1966, Schwartz (1970a) found considerably larger price elasticities than those implied by Taussig's work. Schwartz's estimates of the price elasticity ranged from $-0.41$ to $-0.76$.

**Table 2.12    Summary of Econometric Studies of Individual Contributions**

| Study | Data Source | Income Group ($ thousands) | Estimated Elasticities — Price | Estimated Elasticities — Income | Other Explanatory Variables | Sample Size |
|---|---|---|---|---|---|---|
| Taussig 1967 | Tax file, 1962 | 0–25 | — | 1.31 (0.04) | | 15,400 |
| | | 25–100 | — | 1.99 (0.05) | | 16,285 |
| | | 100–200 | −0.10[a] | 3.10 (0.06) | | 10,450 |
| | | 200–500 | −0.06[a] | 2.54 (0.09) | | 4,508 |
| | | 500+ | −0.04[a] | 1.75 (0.12) | | 1,035 |
| Schwartz 1970a | *Statistics of Income,* time series, 1929–66 | 0–10 | −0.69 (0.49) | 0.28 (0.16) | Trend, war years, pre-standard deduction years | 31 |
| | | 10–100 | −0.76 (0.20) | 0.92 (0.16) | | 31 |
| | | 100+ | −0.41 (0.10) | 0.45 (0.09) | | 31 |
| Feldstein 1975a | *Statistics of Income,* pooled, 1948–68 | 4–100 | −1.24 (0.10) | 0.82 (0.03) | | 117 |
| Feldstein and Clotfelter 1976 | Federal Reserve Board Survey, 1963 | 1.721+ | −1.15 (0.20) | 0.87 (0.14) | Age, marital status, wealth | 1,406 |

**Table 2.12 (continued) Summary of Econometric Studies of Individual Contributions**

| Study | Data Source | Income Group ($ thousands) | Estimated Elasticities | | Other Explanatory Variables | Sample Size |
|---|---|---|---|---|---|---|
| | | | Price | Income | | |
| Feldstein and Taylor 1976 | Tax file, 1962 | 4+ | −1.09 (0.03) | 0.76 (0.02) | Age, marital status | 13,770 |
| | Tax file, 1970 | 4+ | −1.28 (0.06) | 0.70 (0.02) | | 15,291 |
| Boskin and Feldstein 1978 | National Study of Philanthropy, 1973 | 1–30 | −2.54 (0.28) | 0.69 (0.06) | Age, marital status | 1,621 |
| Dye 1978 | National Study of Philanthropy, 1973 | 1–50 | −2.25 (0.27) | 0.53 (0.06) | | 1,780 |
| Abrams and Schmitz 1978 | Statistics of Income, pooled, 1948–72 | 4–100 | −1.10 (0.08) | 0.81 (0.02) | Transfers | 136 |
| Reece 1979 | BLS Consumer Expenditure Survey, 1972–73 | — | −1.19[b] | 0.88[b] | | 537 |
| Long and Settle 1979 | National Study of Philanthropy, 1973 | all[d] | −2.10[b] | 0.23 | Relative income, age, wealth, race, income distribution, AFDC, unemployment rate | 1,231 |
| Clotfelter 1980b | Seven-year panel of taxpayers (1972–73 shown) | 2–50 (AGI; 1970 dollars) | −1.34 (0.65) long run short run | 0.67 (0.17) | Age, marital status, dependents, lagged giving | 3,456 |

| Study | Data source | | | | | N |
|---|---|---|---|---|---|---|
| Clotfelter and Steuerle 1981 | Tax file, 1975 | 4+ | −0.49 (0.23) | 0.24 (0.06) | Age, marital status, dependents | 26,397 |
| Feenberg 1982 | Tax file, 1977; 10% subsample | up to 200 | −1.27 (0.05) | 0.78 (0.02) | Age, marital status, capital income | 7,102 |
| Reece and Zieschang 1982 | BLS Consumer Expenditure Survey, 1972–73 | — | −0.91 | 1.31 | Age, education | 685 |
| Dennis, Rudney, and Wyscarver 1982 | Tax file, 1979 | — | −0.42 | 1.23 | | 45,880 |
| Abrams and Schmitz 1983 | Statistics of Income, 1977, pooled by state | 10+ | −0.95 (0.16) | 0.69 (0.06) | Transfers, poverty | 357 |

Sources: Taussig 1967, p. 6, table 1; Schwartz 1970a, p. 1276, table 2; Feldstein 1975a, p. 37, equation 2; Feldstein and Clotfelter 1976, p. 11, equation 6; Feldstein and Taylor 1976, p. 1206, equations 2.5 and 2.4; Boskin and Feldstein 1978, p. 352, equation 1; Dye 1978, p. 313, equation 3; Abrams and Schmitz 1978, p. 35, model 3; Reece 1979, p. 146, equation 3; Long and Settle 1979, p. 14, table 2; Clotfelter 1980b, p. 333, equation 3.3; Clotfelter and Steuerle 1981, p. 425, equation 3.1; Feenberg 1982, p. 17, equation 7; Abrams and Schmitz 1983, table 2, equation 4; Reece and Zieschang 1982, p. 16; Dennis, Rudney, and Wyscarver 1982, p. 21, table 3.

Note: Numbers in parenthesis are standard errors.

[a]Schwartz 1970a, p. 1280.

[b]Elasticities calculated at means; standard errors not available or not appropriate.

[c]Taxpayers with negative disposable income deleted (Feenberg 1982, p. 16).

[d]Married households only.

The income elasticities obtained by Schwartz, ranging from 0.28 to 0.92, were also strikingly different from Taussig's high values. Feldstein (1975a) used the same aggregate tax return data used by Schwartz, but formed a pooled time-series/cross-section sample, thus increasing the variation in income and price. The resulting estimates in the basic equation were $-1.24$ for the price elasticity and 0.82 for the income elasticity. Three additional studies with others (Feldstein and Clotfelter 1976; Feldstein and Taylor 1976; Boskin and Feldstein 1977) using different samples of individual households yielded similarly large price elasticities ($-1.15$, $-1.09$, $-1.28$, and $-2.54$). In the latter two studies, the price elasticities were significantly greater than one in absolute value, and the income elasticities were significantly less than one.

Before reviewing other studies, it is useful to consider one policy implication of these estimates of the price elasticity. Although the magnitude of the elasticity is obviously important in determining the effect of tax incentives, there is one critical value that is of particular, if partly symbolic importance. An elasticity of $-1$ implies that the increased contributions received by charitable organizations as a result of the present deduction, for example, exactly offsets the loss in tax revenue to the Treasury. For price elasticities larger than one in absolute value, contributions increase by more as a result of the tax incentive than the amount of revenue the Treasury loses. This can be shown by considering a tax-revenue function such as $T = Z - sG$, where $Z$ is the tax calculated without reference to contributions, $s$ is the subsidy rate (equal to the marginal tax rate in the case of a deduction), and $G$ is contributions. Holding $Z$ constant, the change in tax revenues is

$$(9) \qquad dT = s\,dG - G\,ds$$
$$= (P-1)\,dG + G\,dP$$

$$(9') \qquad = P\,dG - dG + G\,dP,$$

where the price of giving is $P = 1 - s$. If the price elasticity of giving is $b$, $dG\,P = b\,dP\,G$. Substituting into $(9')$ yields

$$(10) \qquad dT = (1+b)\,G\,dP - dG.$$

It the elasticity is $-1$, $dT = -dG$, that is, the change in tax revenues is equal and opposite to the change in contributions. If $b < -1$, taxes will fall by less than the increase in giving brought about by a reduction in the price of giving.[46]

---

46. This relationship holds for subsidies arising from tax credits or multiple deductions. Because of the nonlinearity of the tax schedule, however, the relationship does not hold exactly if taxpayers drop into lower tax brackets as the result of the deduction. Nor does the simple relationship hold for deductions or credits with floors. If there is a floor of $Q$ dollars and a subsidy rate of $s$, for example, the tax function becomes $T = Z - \min[s(G-Q), 0]$, reducing the revenue loss for a given price effect. This entire analysis ignores income effects.

Subsequent studies have generally tended to support the finding of the Feldstein studies that the price elasticity is at least one in absolute value. It is interesting to note that the largest estimates of the price elasticity (Boskin and Feldstein 1977: $-2.54$; Dye 1978: $-2.25$; and Long and Settle 1979: $-2.10$) all are based on the same data set: the National Study of Philanthropy, conducted by the Survey Research Center and the Census Department, covering contributions made in 1973. Clotfelter (1980b), Clotfelter and Steuerle (1981), Feenberg (1982), and Dennis, Rudney, and Wyscarver (1982) used data from tax files for individual itemizers, with sample sizes ranging from about 7000 to over 45,000. Employing a variety of estimating techniques, these studies found elasticities ranging from $-0.42$ to $-1.34$.[47] Much smaller samples taken from the 1972–73 Consumer Expenditure Survey, including both itemizers and nonitemizers, were analyzed by Reece (1979) and Reece and Zieschang (1982). Estimated equations explaining deductible contributions yielded elasticities of $-1.19$ and $-0.91$.[48] Finally, Abrams and Schmitz (1978; 1983) analyzed aggregate tax data on itemized contributions, obtaining price elasticities of $-1.10$ and $-0.95$. In general, econometric estimates based on analyses of aggregate tax return data appear to be less reliable, being subject to considerable variation associated with changes in sample and model specification. In particular, aggregate estimates appear to be particularly sensitive to the inclusion of low-income itemizers. Such taxpayers appear to be unrepresentative of itemizers in general due to their unusually high ratio of itemized deductions to income. As a result, studies using aggregate data have excluded low-income returns in estimation.

A number of the estimated income elasticities in the studies since 1978 fall in the 0.70 to 0.87 range found in the Feldstein studies, but several estimates are well outside of this range. Studies using disaggregated tax return data imply income elasticities ranging from a low of 0.44 (Feenberg 1982) to a set of high values obtained by Dennis, Rudney, and Wyscarver (1982), illustrated in table 2.12 by a value of 1.23 calculated at the sample means. Studies using survey data including nonitemizers imply income elasticities ranging from 0.23, in a study including relative income as well (Long and Settle 1979), to 1.31 (Reece and Zieschang 1982). Abrams and Schmitz obtained elasticities of 0.69 and 0.81 using aggregate data.

Besides price and income, the variable with the most consistent effect on contributions is age. Measured by a continuous variable or by one or more dichotomous variables, age is consistently associated with higher levels of giving. Table 2.13 summarizes results from three studies that em-

---

47. The latter estimate, based on equation 3.3 in Clotfelter 1980b, is the implied long-run price elasticity. The short-run elasticity corresponding to the first-year effect of a price change is -0.49. See section 2.5.1 for a discussion of this model.

48. The measure of contributions in Reece 1979, denoted CONTRIB, includes political contributions.

Table 2.13          Age Effects: Giving as a Percentage of Under-35 Age Group

| Study | Data | Age 35–54 | 55–64 | 65+ |
|---|---|---|---|---|
| Feldstein and Clotfelter | Survey, 1962 | 113 | 128 | 163 |
| Boskin and Feldstein | Survey, 1973 | 158 | 212 | 236 |
| Clotfelter | Tax returns, 1972 | 144 | 182 | 196 |

*Sources:* Feldstein and Clotfelter 1976, p. 8, equation 4; Boskin and Feldstein 1978, p. 352, equation 1; Clotfelter 1980b, p. 329, equation 7.

*Note:* Where the independent variable is the logarithm of contributions and $a_i$ is the coefficient for a given age dummy variable, the proportional increase over the excluded group (under 35) is equal to $e^{a_i}$.

ployed the same age classifications. The numbers in the table express the ratio of contributions in the given class in the under-35 age group, holding constant income and other variables. The three studies imply, for example, that a taxpayer over 65 years of age will give from 63 to 136 percent more than an otherwise similar taxpayer under 35. Each of the three studies, and other studies as well, suggest that giving increases monotonically with age. Reece (1979, p. 147) estimates that the elasticity of contributions with respect to age is 0.38. There are two possible interpretations of this result: either individuals give more generously as they get older or else younger cohorts are, and will remain, less generous than their parents and grandparents were. The former seems more likely but is not proven by these findings. One other finding on age effects presented by Clotfelter (1980b) suggests that, although giving appears to increase with age, it does so at a decreasing rate. Based on changes in the real level of contributions between 1970 and 1972, taxpayers in the 35-to-54 and 55-to-64 age brackets increased their contributions only 88 percent as rapidly as those under 35, holding constant changes in income. Contributions by taxpayers over 65 increased at only 82 percent the rate of the youngest group.

Other explanatory variables have included marital status, wealth, and measures relating to the well-being of potential recipients. The estimated effects of the last of these three is presented below. Married households tend to give more than other similar households. The estimated percentage difference exhibits a large range, from 4 to 85 percent (Clotfelter 1980b, p. 329, equation 7; Feenberg 1982, p. 17, equation 7). Because of the important demographic differences between married couples and other households, some studies have restricted the sample for estimation to under-65 married households.[49] Another possible determinant of giving included in some studies is wealth. Probably the best measure is that

49. See, for example, Feenberg 1982, p. 17.

contained in the Federal Reserve Board's Survey of Financial Characteristics, used by Feldstein and Clotfelter (1976). In that study, wealth has an estimated elasticity of 0.10 (p. 11, equation 6). Dye (1978, p. 313) obtained an elasticity of 0.05 using the National Study of Philanthropy data. Using a proxy for financial wealth based on interest and dividend income, Feenberg (1982, p. 17) obtained an elasticity of 0.08. Whether these low elasticities are the result of poor measures of wealth or indications that wealth influences bequests much more than lifetime giving is unclear.

## 2.5  Behavioral and Econometric Issues in Empirical Studies

Because they relate to the mechanisms by which tax policy affects giving or to the usefulness of alternative econometric techniques in inferring such effects, certain issues have taken on particular importance in the econometric work on taxes and charity. This section distinguishes between issues of behavior and issues of econometrics. The distinction is necessarily artificial to some degree, however, since determination of behavioral relationships involve econometrics, and econometric issues have implications for estimated behavioral parameters. The first part discusses important behavioral questions dealt with in these empirical studies, focusing almost entirely on the mechanism by which the income tax influences individual decisions to contribute. Such behavioral questions, in effect, have to do with exactly how the model of individual giving is to be specified. The second section discusses econometric problems that arise in estimating models of taxes and giving. Although these issues arise out of the theory of statistical inference, they have important implications for estimated behavioral relationships.

### 2.5.1  Behavioral Issues

This section discusses six issues that focus on the mechanism by which tax policy influences contributions. By asking *how* tax policy affects giving, each essentially questions the specification of the basic econometric model of giving. In particular, each implicitly calls into question the assumption embodied in equation (5) that there is one constant price elasticity and one income elasticity.

### *Are Contributions to Different Types of Charities Subject to Different Influences?*

Beyond the basic question of deductibility and the specification of organizations eligible for the limit based on 50 percent of income, the tax law makes no distinction regarding types of charities supported. Moreover, government data on the charitable deduction virtually never include information on the allocation of gifts by type of charitable organization. Nevertheless, the pattern of gifts by donee type is of great importance in assessing changes in the structure of the nonprofit sector. Table 2.5 gives summary data on the pattern of giving to religion and several other major donee groups by income. The large income differences in the distribution of giving suggest the possibility that price and income effects may be different by donee type.[50]

Four empirical studies have estimated price and income effects for contributions to particular types of organizations, and their results are summarized in table 2.14. Two of the studies, by Feldstein (1975b) and Fisher (1977), rely on aggregate data for income classes and include only a few observations. Accordingly, results of these studies must be interpreted with caution. The other two studies, by Dye (1978) and Reece (1979), use survey data providing 1780 and 537 observations, respectively. While the larger sample sizes of the latter studies insure a much greater degree of statistical reliability, the surveys themselves contain relatively few high-income households; hence the estimates may not be applicable at all income levels.[51]

From the standpoint of sheer magnitude, religious gifts are the single most important category of individual contributions. The studies employing disaggregated data on religious gifts both obtained larger price elasticities ($-2.15$ for Dye and $-1.60$ for Reece) and smaller income elasticities (0.42 and 0.40, respectively) than the corresponding elasticities they obtained for aggregate contributions. The low income elasticity is not surprising, given the decline in the relative importance of religious gifts at higher incomes shown in table 2.5. The large price elasticity is unexpected, however, and appears to go against the notion that religious gifts are unaffected by tax considerations. The price elasticity obtained by Feldstein ($-0.49$) is quite different from these, however. Recognizing the problem posed by relying on seventeen observations, Feldstein estimated income elasticities by donee group, holding the price elasticity constant at his basic estimated value of $-1.24$. Under that specification, the implied income elasticity (0.38) is quite close to those obtained by Dye and Reece.

In contrast to those for religious giving, the income elasticities estimated for contributions to educational institutions are all greater than one, ranging in value from 1.22 to 2.31. The estimates of the price elasticity differ markedly, however. While Feldstein and Fisher obtained estimates exceeding two in absolute value, Reece found virtually no price response. Because Reece's sample includes few high-income households—those most likely to make substantial gifts to colleges and universities—his esti-

50. As noted by Zellner (1977, pp. 1519–20), one implication of this would be that aggregate price and income elasticities would be weighted averages of the elasticities applying to particular categories.

51. Dye 1978 excludes the few households in the National Study of Philanthropy sample with incomes over $50,000 in 1973. Reece's sample "consists almost entirely of households with annual incomes under $40,000" in 1972 and 1973 (Reece 1979, p. 149n).

**Table 2.14**        **Price and Income Elasticities of Giving, by Selected Donee Group**

| Type of Organization | Estimated Elasticities | |
| --- | --- | --- |
| | Price | Income |
| *Religious organizations* | | |
| Feldstein 1975b | | |
|   Unconstrained | − 0.49 | 0.63 |
| | (0.08) | (0.03) |
|   Constrained price elasticity[a] | — | 0.38 |
| | | (0.03) |
| Dye 1978 | − 2.15 | 0.42 |
| Reece 1979 | − 1.60 | 0.40 |
| *Educational institutions* | | |
| Feldstein 1975b | | |
|   Unconstrained | − 2.23 | 1.22 |
| | (0.54) | (0.19) |
|   Constrained price elasticity[a] | — | 1.54 |
| Fisher 1977 | − 2.31 | 2.31 |
| | (0.91) | (0.24) |
| Reece 1979 | − 0.08 | 1.64 |
| *Helath and welfare organizations* | | |
| Feldstein 1975b | | |
|   Unconstrained | − 1.19 | 0.85 |
| | (0.12) | (0.04) |
|   Constrained price elasticity[a] | — | 0.83 |
| | | (0.02) |
| Reece 1979[b] | − 0.98 | 1.43 |

*Sources:* Feldstein 1975b, U.S. Internal Revenue Service, *Statistics of Income, Individual Income Tax Returns*; Fisher 1977, aggregate contributions by income class in Michigan, 1974–75; Dye 1978, p. 315, National Study of Philanthropy; and Reece 1979, Bureau of Labor Statistics Consumer Expenditure Survey, 1972–73.

*Note:* Sample sizes were Feldstein (17); Fisher (18); Dye (1780); and Reece (537).

[a]Price elasticity constrained to be − 1.24, the value estimated in Feldstein 1975a.

[b]Includes contributions deducted from pay plus "contributions to charities such as the United Fund, Red Cross, etc., which were not deducted from pay" (Reece 1979, pp. 144–145).

mates must be interpreted with caution. Finally, Feldstein and Reece present comparable equations for contributions to health and welfare organizations. The price elasticities are reasonably close ( − 1.19 and − 0.98, respectively), but Reece's estimate of the income elasticity (1.43) is considerably larger than Feldstein's (0.85 and 0.83).

A speculation offered by Taussig (1967, p. 19) is that contributions can be separated into two distinct categories—religious and secular—that respond differently to changes in income and price. While religious gifts are relatively unresponsive, elasticities for secular giving are larger. The findings summarized in table 2.14 provide partial support for Taussig's hypothesis. The estimated income elasticities for religious gifts are certainly smaller than those for other categories. However, the evidence regarding the price elasticity does not, on the whole, support the notion that religious giving is less price-sensitive than giving for other purposes.

### Does the Price Elasticity of Giving Vary by Income Class?

Whether taxpayers in lower and middle income classes are as responsive to tax incentives as those in the upper brackets is a question of substantial importance for tax policy and one that has received a good deal of attention. Not only are there large absolute differences in average contributions over the income scale, but also the distribution of gifts by donee classes varies by income. Since tax incentives typically differ as to their impact over the income distribution, the level and distribution of gifts resulting from each incentive are also likely to differ. This fact makes it important to know if incentive effects differ by income level. One provision of the 1981 tax act—the extension of the charitable deduction to non-itemizers—illustrates the importance of information on how the incentive effect varies by income. Because the provision applies largely to low- and middle-income taxpayers, estimates of the revenue impact and the effect on contributions depend on what the price elasticity is in the lower part of the income scale.[52]

The prevailing view among economists before 1975 appears to have been that there was little if any price sensitivity at lower incomes. According to Aaron (1972, p. 211), marginal tax rates applying to taxpayers making less than $15,000 were so low that they "cannot possibly be a major incentive to charitable giving." Taussig's (1967) study, of course, gave added weight to this notion by suggesting that tax rates had no effect on contributions by taxpayers with incomes under $100,000 (see table 2.12). As noted above, estimation problems cast doubt on these results. Other evidence by Taussig appeared to corroborate this conclusion, however. Comparing the marginal tax rates of big givers and small givers (as measured by percentage of income contributed), he showed that only in the income classes above $100,000 did big givers have higher average tax rates than small givers (Taussig, 1967, p. 10).

Schwartz's (1970a) finding of significant price effects at all income levels—with the elasticity actually falling with income—was the first evidence contradicting the general view that there was little incentive effect in the lower income classes (see table 2.12). Table 2.15 summarizes subsequent estimates of the price elasticity by income class, along with the corresponding income elasticities. All of the studies included in the table used data from tax returns for itemizers, with all but Feldstein (1975a) relying on Treasury tax files for various years. Each study uses constant elasticity equations estimated separately by income class. In the results for incomes

---

52. For a discussion of these issues, see U.S. Congress, Senate 1980.

**Table 2.15**          **Price and Income Elasticities by Income Class Based on Separately Estimated Constant Elasticity Models**

| Income Class[a] | Year | Source | Estimated Elasticities[b] | |
|---|---|---|---|---|
| | | | Price | Income |
| $4000–20,000 | 1962 | [3] | – 3.67 (0.45) | 0.53 (0.07) |
| | 1970 | [3] | – 0.35 (0.52) | 0.80 (0.10) |
| $4000–10,000 | 1948–68 | [2, eq. 6] | – 1.80 (0.56) | 0.68 (0.06) |
| | 1975 | [1] | – 0.95 (0.66) | 0.39 (0.21) |
| $10,000–20,000 | 1948–68 | [2, eq. 7] | – 1.04 (0.76) | 0.85 (0.23) |
| | 1975 | [1] | – 1.35 (0.32) | 0.62 (0.09) |
| $20,000–100,000 | 1948–68 | [2, eq. 8] | – 1.13 (0.25) | 0.91 (0.17) |
| $20,000–50,000 | 1962 | [3] | – 0.97 (0.26) | 0.61 (0.19) |
| | 1970 | [3] | – 0.85 (0.31) | 0.89 (0.16) |
| | 1975 | [1] | – 1.66 (0.11) | 0.36 (0.67) |
| $50,000–100,000 | 1962 | [3] | – 1.10 (0.19) | 1.90 (0.20) |
| | 1970 | [3] | – 1.12 (0.22) | 0.87 (0.20) |
| | 1975 | [1] | – 1.36 (0.14) | 0.67 (0.14) |
| $100,000 or more | 1948–68 | [2, eq. 9] | – 0.29 (0.11) | 1.38 (0.06) |
| | 1962 | [3] | – 1.29 (0.04) | 1.02 (0.04) |
| | 1970 | [3] | – 1.74 (0.08) | 1.03 (0.04) |
| | 1975 | [1] | – 1.78 (0.12) | 1.09 (0.05) |

*Sources:* [1] Clotfelter and Steuerle 1981, p. 428, table 4; [2] Feldstein 1975a, pp. 89–90; [3] Feldstein and Taylor 1976, p. 1213, table 3.
[a]Income ranges for [2] are in 1967 constant dollars; other income ranges in current dollars.
[b]Standard errors in parentheses.

below $20,000 there is substantial variation in price-elasticity estimates, ranging from Feldstein and Taylor's (1976) estimate of – 0.35 for their 1970 sample to – 3.67 for their 1962 sample. Among the six estimates in this income class, only the largest permits rejection of the hypothesis that the elasticity is in fact greater than one in absolute value, and three are not significantly different from zero. In short, the price-elasticity estimates in this range lack precision. The main reason for this lack of precision appears to be the very small degree of variation in the prices faced by lower-income taxpayers. Incomes appear to vary more than marginal tax rates in this range, resulting in much smaller standard errors for income terms. Therefore, although the median estimate of the price elasticity for taxpayers, below $20,000 is greater than one in absolute value, these studies leave considerable uncertainty regarding the price response among lower-income households.

Among the equations estimated for the $20,000 to $50,000 income class, two of the three estimated price elasticities are less than one in absolute value, although all are significantly different from zero. The four equations covering incomes up to $100,000, however, all imply point estimates for the price elasticity that are greater than one in absolute value. In general, the standard errors of the estimated coefficients tend to decline with income level due to the increasing variation in price among taxpayers. As for the income elasticity estimates in the $20,000 to $100,000 class, five of the seven are in the range of 0.61 to 0.91.

Four sets of estimates are available in the highest income class—$100,000 and above. The three studies using disaggregated tax return data yield large price elasticities, ranging from $-1.29$ to $-1.78$, and all are significantly different from $-1$. The estimate based on aggregate data is quite small at $-0.29$, but this can be explained by the inherent lack of precision in calculating marginal tax rates for the highest income group when variations among taxpayers in deductions, type of income, and special tax provisions must be ignored. The income elasticities obtained in the three analyses of disaggregated data are remarkably similar. Even though the standard errors are quite small, none is significantly different from 1.0. These separate estimates thus suggest a profile of taxpayers at the upper end of the income scale who are quite sensitive to tax-induced changes in price and to changes in after-tax income.

Another way of allowing for variations in price responsiveness is by estimating more flexible forms of the basic giving equations, forms that allow price and income elasticities to vary by income level. Estimates using three such flexible models for 1975 tax return data are shown in table 2.16. The first is a basic log-linear equation with an interaction term added. It takes the form:

$$(14) \qquad \ln G = A + a \ln Y + (b + c \ln Y) \ln P.$$

The implied price elasticity is

$$(15) \qquad \frac{\partial \ln G}{\partial \ln P} = b + c \ln Y,$$

which varies with income if $c$ is nonzero. In the equation for 1975, on which the first column is based, the estimate of $c$ is negative, implying that the price elasticity grows larger and more negative as income rises. When calculated at the mean values for each income class, the implied elasticity rises from $-0.38$ in the $4,000 to 10,000 class to $-1.67$ for incomes over $100,000. At income levels below $3119, the implied price elasticity is positive. Feldstein and Taylor (1976, p. 1213, equation 4.1) present a similar equation with interaction term for 1970; the results also imply a price elasticity that rises with income. They reject this specification, however, because of the implication of positive price elasticities for incomes below $7455, stating that "the attempt to fix such a smooth and monotonic rela-

**Table 2.16**    **Income Variation in Price and Income Elasticities Implied by Single Equation Models**

| Income Class and Variable | Model | | |
|---|---|---|---|
| | Interaction Term[a] | Translog[b] | Constant Income Elasticity |
| **$4,000 under 10,000** | | | |
| Price | − 0.38 | − 0.42 | − 2.17 |
| | (0.07) | (0.13) | (0.27) |
| Income | 0.55 | 0.55 | 0.72 |
| | (0.02) | (0.05) | (0.02) |
| **$10,000 under 20,000** | | | |
| Price | − 0.66 | − 0.73 | − 1.39 |
| | (0.06) | (0.12) | (0.12) |
| Income | 0.59 | 0.58 | —[c] |
| | (0.02) | (0.04) | — |
| **$20,000 under 50,000** | | | |
| Price | − 0.91 | − 0.97 | − 1.26 |
| | (0.06) | (0.09) | (0.07) |
| Income | 0.65 | 0.65 | —[c] |
| | (0.02) | (0.03) | — |
| **$50,000 under 100,000** | | | |
| Price | − 1.27 | − 1.25 | − 1.14 |
| | (0.05) | (0.06) | (0.06) |
| Income | 0.82 | 0.83 | —[c] |
| | (0.02) | (0.05) | — |
| **$100,000 or more** | | | |
| Price | − 1.67 | − 1.51 | − 1.51 |
| | (0.56) | (0.06) | (0.06) |
| Income | 0.90 | 0.91 | —[c] |
| | (0.02) | (0.02) | — |

*Source:* Clotfelter and Steuerle 1981, p. 428, table 4.

[a]Elasticities calculated at class means, based on the estimated equation:

$$\ln G = 3.39 \ln P + 0.48 \ln Y - 0.42 \ln Y \ln P + \ldots$$
$$(0.26) \qquad (0.02) \qquad (0.02)$$

[b]Elasticities calculated at class means, based on the estimated equation:

$$\ln G = 4.31 \ln P - 0.25 (\ln P)^2 + 0.71 \ln Y - 0.014 (\ln Y)^2$$
$$(0.63) \qquad (0.12) \qquad (0.27) \qquad (0.013)$$

$$- 0.54 \ln Y \ln P + \ldots$$
$$(0.07)$$

[c]Single income elasticity estimated for all classes.

tion between price and income is not appropriate. In order to fit the observations well at high income levels, the functional form is forced to be inappropriate at low levels" (p. 1213). In contrast, Brittain (1981, p. 443) argues that such "varying functions of price seem entirely appropriate, given the strong relationship between P and Y."

An alternative functional form that does not constrain the price elasticity to vary smoothly with income is the translog form:

(16)    $\ln G = a \ln Y + (b + c \ln Y + g \ln P) \ln P + h (\ln Y)^2,$

where the price elasticity is

(17)    $$\frac{\partial \ln G}{\partial \ln P} = b + c \ln Y + 2 g \ln P.$$

Elasticities based on an estimate of the translog form for 1975 are shown in table 2.15. They reveal much the same pattern as shown in model with a simple interaction term: the implied price elasticity rises in absolute value with income, although not quite as steeply. The range is from $-0.42$ in the lowest income group to $-1.51$ in the highest. The income elasticities, almost identical to the interaction model, rise from 0.55 to 0.91—from lowest to highest income class.

The third single-equation model estimated for the 1975 data assumes a constant income elasticity but allows for separate estimates of the price elasticity by income class. The single income elasticity 0.78 corresponds to other income elasticities estimated using aggregate data. The pattern of estimated price elasticities in this model is strikingly different, however, in that low-income taxpayers are shown to be most price sensitive. Price elasticities vary from $-2.17$ in the lowest income class to $-1.51$ in the highest. It is curious that all of these estimates are larger than the overall price-elasticity estimate of $-1.27$ obtained for the 1975 sample reported in table 2.11; there is no easy explanation for the pattern of estimates since each was allowed to vary independently.

A final single-equation model, estimated for the 1979 tax file, is Dennis, Rudney, and Wyscarver's (1982) linear expenditure form.[53] This model rejects not only the assumption that the income and price elasticities are the same for all income groups, but also the notion that they are constant at all income levels for a given individual. The model is based on the notion that utility depends on expenditures above some minimum amount in each spending category. One interpretation of the model is that the elasticities applying to "discretionary" income differ from those applying at lower income levels. Estimates imply price elasticities that rise from about $-0.25$ for taxpayers in the $20,000 to $30,000 income class to $-0.98$ for taxpayers making more than $200,000. Corresponding income elasticities are 1.27 and 1.04. One apparent reason for the variation in elasticities over the income scale is the linear nature of the estimating model itself. That a linear form may be improper is strongly suggested by

---

. 53. Although the linear-expenditure model is a system in name, in practice it implies the estimation of a single equation when there are only two "goods." See Dennis, Rudney, and Wyscarver 1982, p. 10.

one implication of the estimates: utility is a function of contributions over $495 and other expenditures over $17,354.[54] Since a large proportion of taxpayers neither give the former nor make the latter, the validity of the linear form is suspect.

The evidence summarized here provides no firm conclusion regarding the important issue of variation in the price elasticity by income level. The best evidence comes from separately estimated equations, and these estimates strongly suggest that price elasticities at upper incomes are larger than one in absolute value. Estimates for income groups between $20,000 and $100,000 suggest elasticities around $-1$, but these estimates are subject to greater variability. For households with incomes below $20,000, the estimates based on the tax returns of itemizers provide variable and imprecise results. These estimates may be compared to those reported in table 2.12 applying largely to low- and middle-income taxpayers: $-2.54$ (Boskin and Feldstein 1977), $-2.25$ (Dye 1978), $-1.19$ (Reece 1979), $-1.34$ (Clotfelter 1980b), and $-0.91$ (Reece and Zieschang 1982). Differences in estimation techniques aside, this set of estimates leaves a very murky picture indeed regarding the price responsiveness of taxpayers at the lower end of the income scale. In choosing which estimate of this group to rely on, one must choose between the precise data of a self-selected group (in studies using tax data for itemizers) or the imprecise data of a randomly selected group (in surveys)—a dilemma that does not apply at income levels where most people are itemizers. Some of the associated estimation problems are discussed below in part 2.5.2. In summarizing the variation in the price elasticity by income class, Zellner's (1977, p. 1519) conclusion is apt: "Simply put, the price elasticities for different income groups have not been determined very precisely."

*Is There an Independent "Itemization Effect"?*

The basic model of contributions embodies the maintained assumption that a given change in the net price has the same effect whether it arises out of a change in marginal tax rate or a shift into or out of itemization status. An alternate view is that taxpayers respond quite differently to a change in itemization, compared to other changes in net price. As Dye (1978) notes, this explanation is consistent with the observation that, while many taxpayers do not know their marginal tax rates, they usually know if they itemize their deductions. Boskin and Feldstein (1977) and Dye provide tests of this possibility using the National Study of Philanthropy. Dye shows that a dummy variable for itemization status performed as well in explanatory power as the conventional price term. Among the subsample of itemizers, the price term was not significant. From this he concludes

54. The implied utility function is $U = .0275 \ln(G - 495) + .9725 \ln(X - 17,354)$, where $G$ is contributions and $X$ is other consumer expenditures. See Dennis, Rudney, and Wyscarver 1982, p. 19.

that the "price effect is really an itemization effect misspecified as a constant elasticity" (p. 313). This assessment does not account, however, for the significant price effect estimated for samples made up exclusively of itemizers.

To test for an independent itemization effect, Boskin and Feldstein (p. 354) modified the basic equation by allowing the intercept to vary between itemizers and nonitemizers. The resulting estimates are not significantly different, giving no support for the existence of an independent itemization effect. This is the strongest test of the hypothesis, but because it relies on only one data set its negative conclusion should be interpreted with caution.

### Are There Lags in Adjustment in Giving Behavior?

Like other kinds of economic behavior, charitable giving may adjust incompletely to changes in price and income. Schwartz (1970a, p. 1271) notes a "possible desire on the part of donors to sustain a pattern of giving." Vickrey (1975, p. 157) observes "a tendency to establish a steady level of gross support, particularly for ongoing activities, that may persist for a considerable time in face of substantial changes in the tax incentives." And to the extent that donations are stimulated by solicitations, the intensity of which may depend on past giving, levels of donations may be relatively slow to change. Such behavior is suggested by Lamale and Clorety (1959, p. 1310), who note a tendency for retired people to give to religious organizations "at a level which reflects their giving habits before retirement." Similarly Morgan, Dye, and Hybels (1977) observe that taxpayers who had recently begun to itemize their deductions tended to give less than long-standing itemizers, as shown in table 2.17. By the same to-

Table 2.17    **Ratio of Actual to Average Giving by Itemization Status**

| Itemization Status | Ratio of Actual to Average Giving in Income Class (and Age Group for Incomes over $50,000) | |
| --- | --- | --- |
| | Unadjusted | Adjusted[a] |
| Never itemized | 0.71 | 0.71 |
| Started itemizing during last five years | 0.80 | 0.99 |
| Always itemized | 1.42 | 1.37 |
| Stopped itemizing during last five years | 0.88 | 0.79 |

*Source:* Morgan, Dye, and Hybels 1977, p.194, table 25.
[a]Adjusted by regression for correlation with other variables.

ken, they found that taxpayers who had recently stopped itemizing gave more than taxpayers who had never itemized.

Such behavior has important implications for the dynamics of charitable giving and for the usefulness of estimated coefficients for simulating the effects of tax policies. In general, the effects of changes in tax policy will tend to be smaller in the short run than in the long run. It may not be appropriate, therefore, to apply estimates for cross-section equations in simulating the dynamic effects of tax changes.

One model that explicitly recognizes the possibility of lags in adjustment is an incomplete-adjustment model with an exponential coefficient of adjustment $s$:

$$(18) \qquad G_1/G_0 = (G_1^*/G_0)^s$$

where $G_1$ and $G_0$ are levels of contributions in period 0 and 1 and $G_1^*$ is the long-run level of giving, determined by income, price, and other variables:

$$(19) \qquad G_1^* = AY^aP^be^{gx}.$$

A value of $s$ less than one implies that personal giving does not adjust completely in the first period after a tax-induced change in price or net income. Only when $s$ is close to one will long-run equations be accurate in predicting short-run changes in giving. Combining equations (18) and (19) and taking logarithms yields the estimable equation:

$$(20) \qquad \ln G_1 = C + sa \ln Y + sb \ln P + sg X + (1-s) \ln G_0,$$

where $C$ is a constant term. From this equation it is possible to infer the short-run income and price elasticities, $sa$ and $sb$, as well as the long-run elasticities $a$ and $b$.

Table 2.18 presents estimates based on equation (20) using panel data of U.S. taxpayers. Instrumental-variables estimation is used because of the lagged dependent variable. Two of the equations are based on a two-year adjustment period while the last is based on a one-year interval. The estimates of the adjustment coefficient imply that contributions do not adjust right away to the new long-run level as a result of changes in price and income. The coefficient of 0.609 implies, for example, that about 60 percent of the expected long-run change will occur in two years and about 84 percent in four years. Roughly the same adjustment process is implied by the one-year coefficient of 0.371. The estimated coefficients for 1968–70 and 1972–73 imply long-run price and income elasticities on the order of estimates from cross-section equations: $-1.5$ and $-1.3$ for price, respectively, and 0.7 for income. The equation for 1970–72 implies a higher income elasticity and a lower income elasticity. All of the estimates of the price elasticity in this study are subject to relatively large standard errors, however. These estimates appear to support other evidence that taxpayers

**Table 2.18**   Price and Income Elasticities Based on Incomplete Adjustment Model

| Period | Short Run | | Long Run[a] | | Coefficient of Adjustment |
| --- | --- | --- | --- | --- | --- |
| | Price | Income | Price | Income | |
| 1968–70 | −0.938 | 0.423 | −1.549 | 0.698 | 0.609 |
| | (0.302) | (0.061) | (0.511) | (0.115) | (0.049) |
| 1970–72 | −0.241 | 0.466 | −0.450 | 0.870 | 0.540 |
| | (0.301) | (0.068) | (0.559) | (0.151) | (0.052) |
| 1972–73 | −0.487[b] | 0.243[b] | −1.337 | 0.667 | 0.371[b] |
| | (0.231) | (0.055) | (0.649) | (0.173) | (0.050) |

Source: Clotfelter 1980b, p. 333, table 3.

[a]Approximate long-run elasticities. See Clotfelter 1980b, p. 333, table 3.

[b]Short-run elasticities and coefficients for 1972–73 sample refer to a one-year adjustment period and are thus not strictly comparable to parameters based on a two-year time period.

do not adjust to changes in tax policy immediately, resulting in smaller effects in the short run than in the long run.

## *What Is the Form of the Income Effect?*

Another important question regarding the specification of the model of contributions concerns the form in which income enters in the determination of giving. The simple theory of giving discussed in section 2.3 implies that an individual's income will, in general, affect contributions. Income will have a positive effect if, as is thought to be the case, giving is a normal good. As is the case in demand analysis, income is normally measured net of taxes. Several alternatives have been suggested, however, for the use of current, or annual income as the basic measure of income. They include permanent income, discretionary income, and relative income.

As noted in the discussion of variable definitions, permanent income may be defined as an average of annual incomes or as a "fitted" value based on an individual's own personal trend income. Studies that use one of these measures to compare estimates of income elasticities based on permanent and current income conclude that permanent income yields the larger elasticity. Feldstein and Clotfelter (1976, p. 9), using a two-year average of disposable income, found a permanent-income elasticity of 0.87, compared to an elasticity of 0.84 for current income. The difference is well within the associated standard error, however. Cross-section equations for 1972 presented by Clotfelter (1980b, p. 329) show a larger, though still insignificant, difference between elasticities for current disposable income and a permanent-income measure based on the trend in gross income. The elasticity for current net income is 0.53, compared to 0.61 for permanent gross income. A measure of the transitory income component, entered along with permanent income, also has a positive effect on current contributions: if current exceeds permanent income by 10 percent, the equation implies that contributions will rise by an additional 1.7 percent. The available estimates, then, do not allow one to determine whether current or permanent income is the correct income measure. Subject to the difficulties in measuring permanent income, both give similar results. The statistical significance of transitory income suggests, however, that current gifts are not wholly a function of permanent income.

Related to the notion of transitory income, a second variant for the income effect emphasizes the role of "discretionary" income. This explanation of giving implies that an individual's propensity to contribute out of discretionary income—income over that which is required or already committed for other purposes—may be quite different from the propensity to contribute out of other income. A problem in testing this theory lies, of course, in identifying which income is "discretionary." Dennis, Rudney, and Wyscarver (1982) present evidence consistent with this notion by estimating a function that allows such variation in giving propensities.

Another test of this hypothesis is provided by my analysis (Clotfelter 1980b) of changes in giving behavior over time. If increases in income are assumed largely to be increases in discretionary income, one implication of the discretionary-income hypothesis is that contributions should be more responsive to changes in income than the level of giving is to income. In three equations examining changes in contributions, I found (p. 331) elasticities associated with changes in the transitory component of income to range from 0.23 to 0.37, lower than most estimated income elasticities. In addition, the individual's trend in income has a higher elasticity than the transitory component in two of the three equations. While these estimates do not support the discretionary-income hypothesis, they represent only a rough test. In particular, the assumption that all changes in income represent changes in discretionary income is certainly open to question.

A third hypothesis regarding the effect of income is that giving depends on the income of others, including potential recipients, as well as the donor's own income. As Schwartz (1970a) shows, this hypothesis implies the inclusion either of relative income or the income of others along with own income. Where $Y$ is own income and $Y_0$ is the income of others, the basic log-linear model can be written:

$$(21) \qquad\qquad G = AY^a Y_0^c P^b.$$

This is equivalent to estimating

$$(22) \qquad\qquad G = AY^{a+c}(Y/Y_0)^{-c}P^b,$$

where $(Y/Y_0)$ is a measure of relative income. As Schwartz notes, however, $Y$ and $(Y/Y_0)$ are highly correlated, making equation (21) a preferable form for estimation. The implications of relative and absolute income effects are quite different. A general increase in incomes will increase giving if own-income is the determining factor, but would not affect giving if relative income is important. As Schwartz (1970a, p. 1274) suggests, the omission of relative income can lead to an overestimate of the own-income effect because of the correlation between the two income measures. Such omission may of course bias the estimated price effect as well. Schwartz's estimates using models with and without relative income are shown in table 2.19. Other income is measured by average disposable income for those not in the sample being examined. For each income class the estimated elasticity for own income is smaller when other income is included in the equation, which is consistent with the possibility of bias due to the omitted variable. Schwartz concludes from this that relative income is more important than own income (p. 1286), but these results seem too thin for a definitive conclusion.

Other studies have obtained mixed results with regard to the effect of relative income on contributions. In an equation with no price variable, Hochman and Rodgers (1973) found that income dispersion had a posi-

**Table 2.19**    **Estimated Elasticities for Price, Own Income, and Other Income, 1929–66 Aggregate Data**

|  | Income Class | | |
|---|---|---|---|
|  | $0 under 10,000 | $10,000 under 100,000 | $100,000 or more |
| Excluding other income | | | |
| Price | − 0.69 | − 0.78[a] | − 0.41[a] |
| Own income | + 0.28 | 0.92[a] | 0.45 |
| Including other income | | | |
| Price | − 0.85[a] | − 0.79[a] | − 0.38[a] |
| Own income | + 0.19 | 0.76[a] | 0.40[a] |
| Other income | − 0.53[a] | − 0.43 | − 0.38 |

*Source:* Schwartz 1970a, p. 1276.

*Note:* Estimates based on logarithmic specification. Other variables included trend, World War II dummy, dummy for years before standard deduction. $N = 31$.

[a]Coefficients with t-statistics greater than two in absolute value.

tive effect on the level of contributions, thus supporting the interdependent-utility hypothesis. Dye (1978) reports a positive and significant effect for the percent poor in a donor's community, also adding support for the hypothesis. Long and Settle (1979) obtained both positive and negative coefficients for their relative-income variable, and Reece (1979) found no significant effect for the lower-quintile family income. Abrams and Schmitz (1983) found that contributions in 1979 increased with the percentage of the state's population in poverty.

Schwartz argues that the omission of relative income will be more serious in cross-section data, where relative income varies greatly (but collinearly with absolute income). There is, unfortunately, no way to separate the own-income and relative-income components in most estimated income coefficients. When predicting the effects of income changes independent of changes in the incomes of others, this is of no practical importance. It is only in predicting the effects of general increases in income on giving that this distinction is relevant. If, for example, relative income is a significant component underlying income elasticities on cross-section data, such elasticities will tend to overstate the effect of secular increases in national income on giving.[55]

55. For a general discussion of the dynamic properties of cross-section estimates, see Kuh 1959, p. 212.

### Does Government Spending "Crowd Out" Private Charity?

If donors are concerned ultimately about the well-being of potential recipients, donations may be affected by government programs providing aid in the same way they might respond to increases in relative income. Donors may, in short, be able to see through the "veil" of government programs to assess the need by charitable organizations for contributions. Abrams and Schmitz (1978) tested this hypothesis by adding to Feldstein's (1975a) pooled data three alternative measures of expenditures on health, education, and welfare functions. Although the coefficients are of the expected (negative) sign, the omission of a trend variable leaves open the possibility that these variables merely reflect a previously estimated negative trend effect.[56] In order to remove any trend effect from the measure of government expenditures, I estimated equations using a similar data set composed of pooled time-series and cross-section observations spanning the period 1948 to 1980.[57] The estimates are presented in table 2.20. Equation (2) is of the form used by Abrams and Schmitz, including the logarithm of per capita federal expenditures on welfare and related functions

| Table 2.20 | Regressions Explaining Logarithm of Contributions, with Measure of Federal Welfare Expenditures Included | | |
|---|---|---|---|
| | 1 | 2 | 3 |
| Log price | − 1.656 | − 1.665 | − 1.660 |
| | (0.090) | (0.090) | (0.090) |
| Log income | 0.621 | 0.618 | 0.620 |
| | (0.030) | (0.030) | (0.030) |
| Time trend | − 0.00813 | | − 0.00376 |
| | (0.00136) | | (0.00546) |
| Log of expenditures | | − 0.0988 | − 0.0547 |
| per capita | | (0.0165 | (0.0661) |
| Intercept | − 0.070 | 0.225 | 0.090 |
| | (0.250) | (0.248) | (0.316) |
| $R^2$ | .938 | .938 | .938 |

*Note:* The method of estimation was weighted least squares. The sample was restricted to classes with an average income of $4000 and above for the years 1948 to 1980, leaving 337 observations.

56. See Abrams and Schmitz 1978, p. 37, footnote 11, and Feldstein 1975a equation (3), p. 88.

57. A description of this sample is given in Appendix A.

but no trend. As in their study, the estimated coefficient is negative and significant. When the trend was included in addition, however, the government-expenditure variable became insignificant, making it impossible to reject the hypothesis that factors other than crowding out were responsible for the previous negative coefficient. This result casts doubt, of course, on the original Abrams and Schmitz (1978) test of crowding out. In another test, Dye (1978, p. 315) obtained insignificant and wrong-signed estimates using per capita local-government expenditures. It seems quite possible, however, that the redistributive element in local-government programs is lost in any measure of aggregate expenditures. Recently, Abrams and Schmitz (1983) have presented more convincing evidence of a crowding-out effect. Using pooled aggregate data for states, they obtained a negative effect for state-government transfer payments. As with other estimations based on aggregate data, however, these results may be sensitive to variations in sample specification and thus should be interpreted with caution.

### Are Individual Giving Levels Related to Each Other?

Related to the notion of crowding out by government expenditures is the possibility that one individual's donations are affected by the donations made by others. One reason why individuals' giving decisions may be mutually dependent arises out of the same interdependence of utility functions underlying the potential effect of government programs: if donors care about recipients' well-being, contributions made by others can substitute for an individual's own giving. As in the case of government crowding out, this reasoning suggests a negative relationship between an individual's contributions and contributions by others. Another source of interdependence in giving, however, suggests an effect in the opposite direction. The example of others' giving behavior may stimulate one's own giving, either by fueling the altruistic urge or by exerting peer pressure. Furthermore, it is possible that such influences are asymmetric, with gifts by those with more income affecting those with less income, but not vice versa.

The net effect of these possible influences on the interaction of individual giving is uncertain. However, the existence of a significant interaction would have important implications for the interpretation of estimated tax effects on contributions. For example, Steinberg (1982) discusses the interpretation of estimates of the price elasticity based on cross-section data when the true model of contributions is of the form:

$$(23) \qquad G_s = f(P, Y, G_0),$$

where $G_s$ is an individual's own contributions and $G_0$ measures the contributions of others. The full effect of a change in price (holding income constant), for example, is composed of a direct price effect and an indirect effect through the price effect on the contributions of others:

$$(24) \qquad \frac{dG_s}{dP}\bigg|_{dY=0} = \frac{\partial G_s}{\partial P} + \frac{\partial G_s}{\partial G_o}\frac{dG_o}{dP}.$$

If giving by others is constant, as in a cross-section model, the estimated price effect corresponds to the partial derivative $\partial G_s/\partial P$. However, economywide changes in tax policy will affect the giving of others, and the total price effect on giving will differ from the estimated effect if $\partial G_s/\partial G_o$ is not zero. If the substitution effect of others' giving dominates and $\partial G_s/\partial G_0 < 0$, the actual price effect will be smaller in absolute value than the estimated effect. If the peer effect dominates, the actual effect will be larger in absolute value.

The most explicit examination of interactions in giving is presented by Feldstein and Clotfelter (1976). To measure the contributions of others, they added the variable

$$(25) \qquad g_i^* = (\sum_j W_{ij} \ln \overline{G_j}) / (\sum_j W_{ij}),$$

where $\overline{G_j}$ is the mean giving for income class $j$, $W_{ij}$ is a weight assigned to income class $j$ depending on individual $i$'s closeness in the income scale: $W_{ij} = (Y_i/Y_j)^\phi$, and the summation is carried out only for income classes at or above an individual's own class. The range of values for $\phi$ that minimized the residual sum of squares was 10 or more, suggesting that giving only in an individual's own income class matters. Furthermore, the coefficient of $g_i^*$ was not significantly different from zero in an equation explaining giving by individuals. This is by no means a definitive test of the interdependence hypothesis, however, because the interactive effects of giving would be expected to be much stronger at the local level than at the national level, as these comparisons are stated.

### 2.5.2   Econometric Issues

Because of the policy importance of empirical estimates of models of giving, considerable attention has been devoted to the econometric techniques researchers have used. This section discusses some of the questions that have been raised concerning econometric theory and technique. Admittedly, the econometric issues discussed here have behavioral implications, just as the issues of specification discussed in part 2.5.1 have direct implications for the econometric properties of estimated models.

#### Identification of Price and Income Effects

Any tabulation of average contributions by income shows a strong positive relationship. Since marginal tax rates also rise with income, the positive correlation between contributions and income is a combination of an income effect and a price effect. The problem of identifying what portion of the effect, if any, is due to the tax-defined price has been recognized by researchers for some time,[58] but not until the application of multiple-regression estimation techniques was there a reasonable prospect of disentangling the price and income effects. The problems caused by attempting to estimate the separate effects of two highly correlated variables—that is, multicollinearity—are well known. The most important result is a reduction in the precision with which either effect can be estimated, indicated by relatively large standard errors for coefficients. The correlation between net income and price in econometric studies of contributions have, indeed, been large and negative.[59] Despite this fact, estimated standard errors in the cross-section studies have generally not been excessive, especially when micro data have been used.

The problem of separately identifying the price and income effects goes beyond mere multicollinearity, however. Because the tax rate is related by law to income, it is possible that conventional measures of multicollinearity are not sufficient. As Feldstein and Taylor (1976, p. 1208) note, "the problem of collinearity is limited to *linear* dependence. It is possible, however, that the association between price and economic income implies a more fundamental problem of nonlinear under-identification." In other words, it might be impossible to identify price and income effects if the postulated structural model of giving (usually log linear) is not correct. The relationship between price and net income is, of course, not even an exact nonlinear function; only taxable income and the marginal tax rate are exactly linked, and only then within the several tax-filing-status groups. The dependence of price on net income is disturbed by variations in itemization status, deductions, and exemptions. Still, the relationship is uncomfortably close, and it is useful to examine ways in which price and net income vary independently. Besides itemization status, the two most important sources of independent variation are differences in state income tax rates and changes in federal tax rates over time.

Because state income tax rates differ and not all states have income taxes, accounting for the state-tax treatment of contributions adds an important source of independent variation to the price variable. As Feenberg (1982, p. 11, table 1) shows, the combination of state and federal taxes caused the price of contributions for a hypothetical household making $15,000 in 1977 to vary from 0.80 to 0.70. At $30,000 the price varied from 0.68 to 0.58.[60] To illustrate the degree of variation in price and net

58. See, for example, Kahn 1960 and Vickrey 1962.

59. For example, the correlation in the 1975 tax file of itemizers used by Clotfelter and Steuerle 1981 was - 0.39 between net income and price (P50) and - 0.87 for the corresponding log values. The correlation was - 0.63 in Reece's (1979, p. 145) sample of itemizers and nonitemizers. The correlation for time-series data may be quite different, as illustrated by Schwartz's (1970a, p. 1279) positive correlations, ranging from + 0.62 to + 0.95.

60. Federal marginal tax rates for each income level were 0.2 and 0.32 ($T_f$) and maximum state subsidy rates ($T_s$) were 0.12 and 0.14, respectively. The combined price is $1 - T_s - T_f + T_s T_f$.

income that results from differences among individuals in deductions, exemptions, and state tax rates, table 2.21 shows the distribution of prices by net income for married taxpayers under 65 in 1970. Although any average of the price certainly declines with net income, there is some degree of variation at each income level.

Rather than using the price based directly on federal and state tax rates, Feenberg (1982) formed an instrument for the combined price in order to remove dependence of the price on personal characteristics such as marital status or other deductions. Such dependence, he argues, would tend to result in omitted-variable bias if some characteristics are not included in the estimating equation. The instrument is based on calculations of state tax subsidy rates evaluated for fixed income and deductions. Using this procedure Feenberg obtained price-elasticity estimates close to those obtained in earlier studies, but his ordinary least squares estimates are unusually small, making it difficult to be sure about the general effect of this estimation procedure.

A second method of obtaining independent variation in the price variable is to calculate prices over periods in which federal tax rates have changed. Effective tax rate schedules may be changed either by legislation or by inflation-induced bracket creep. Any use of contributions, tax, and income data over time—including Schwartz's (1970a) time-series analysis and Feldstein's (1975a) pooled analysis—would capture some of this kind of independent variation. Feldstein and Taylor (1976) sought more specifically to measure independent changes in the price of giving by aggregating data for 1962 and 1970 into classes with constant real incomes. For each of sixteen income classes they found that prices rose and contributions fell between 1962 and 1970, implying arc elasticities with a median of $-1.92$.[61] In order to account for shifts over time unrelated to price changes, they estimated equations of the form:

$$(26) \qquad \ln (\overline{G_1}/\overline{G_0}) = a + b \ln (\overline{P_1}/\overline{P_0}) + u,$$

where $\overline{G_0}$ and $\overline{G_1}$ are average contributions for a constant-income class in the earlier and later year, respectively, and $\overline{P_0}$ and $\overline{P_1}$ are the corresponding average price terms, and $u$ is an error term. Using data for 1962 and 1970, Feldstein and Taylor were able to take advantage of changes in tax law, in particular the 1964 reduction in tax rates, to capture independent changes in prices. As shown in table 2.22 this approach yielded price elasticities very much in the range of estimates using disaggregated data: from $-1.34$, for unweighted regressions using the price that reflects gifts of assets and dropping the lowest three income classes, to $-1.58$ for weighted regressions using all sixteen observations. However, when this same meth-

61. Values for the highest income class were not counted for this calculation. Arc elasticities were calculated as $(\ln G_{70} - \ln G_{62})/(\ln P_{70} - \ln P_{62})$. See Feldstein and Taylor 1976, p.1211, table 2.

**Table 2.21    Distribution of Returns by Net Income and Price, Married Itemizers under 65, 1970**

| | | | Net Income | | |
|---|---|---|---|---|---|
| Price | Under $10,000 | $10,000– 20,000 | $20,000– 50,000 | $50,000– 100,000 | $100,000– or More |
| 0.31 | 0 | 0 | 0 | 260 | 3,041 |
| 0.31–0.37 | 0 | 0 | 0 | 2,508 | 2,224 |
| 0.37–0.46 | 0 | 0 | 1,410 | 5,845 | 2,387 |
| 0.46–0.61 | 0 | 0 | 6,045 | 2,099 | 1,652 |
| 0.61–0.72 | 1 | 2,480 | 5,334 | 308 | 329 |
| 0.72–0.75 | 0 | 5,302 | 769 | 37 | 59 |
| 0.75–0.78 | 251 | 6,126 | 321 | 26 | 41 |
| 0.78–0.81 | 2,716 | 2,414 | 109 | 20 | 37 |
| 0.81–0.86 | 2,716 | 256 | 70 | 20 | 82 |
| 0.86–1.00 | 709 | 55 | 58 | 37 | 137 |

*Source:* Feldstein and Taylor 1976, p. 1209, table 1.

*Note:* Price reflects federal and state taxes. Net income is adjusted gross income minus federal tax liability with no contributions.

Table 2.22          **Price Elasticities Based on Changes in Contributions and Price for Constant-Income Classes, Selected Periods**

| Specification and Sample | 1962–70 | 1970–75 | 1962–75 |
|---|---|---|---|
| Price reflecting gifts of cash and assets | | | |
| Unweighted regressions | −1.39 (0.19) | 0.56 (0.68) | −0.81 (0.06) |
| Weighted regressions | −1.58 —[a] | −1.09 (0.29) | −0.63 (0.38) |
| Unweighted regressions dropping bottom 3 classes | 1.34 —[a] | 0.43 (0.74) | −0.97 (0.29) |
| Price reflecting gifts of cash | | | |
| Unweighted regressions | −1.54 (0.21) | 0.48 (0.74) | −0.84 (0.26) |

*Source:* 1962–70: Feldstein and Taylor 1976, p. 1212; 1970–75 and 1962–75: Clotfelter and Steuerle 1981, p.434, table 6.
*Note:* Standard errors are in parentheses.
[a]Not reported.

odology was applied using 1975 data (Clotfelter and Steuerle 1981), the implied elasticities were closer to zero and were generally subject to larger standard errors. As table 2.22 shows, for example, the weighted regression for 1970–75 implies an elasticity of −1.09, and the corresponding regression for the entire 1962–75 period yields an estimate of −0.63. The corresponding standard errors are 0.29 and 0.38. The large standard errors for the 1970–75 period may result from the comparatively small change in effective marginal tax schedules over the period. Rough as they are, the results in table 2.22 do lend general support for a negative price elasticity, but they add little to the precision of that estimate.

Using a panel of taxpayer returns, I applied this same methodology to the giving of individuals over time. For any one individual, changes in the price of giving over time result from changes in personal variables—income, deductions, marital status—and changes in the effective marginal tax schedule. The former source of variation does nothing to alleviate the potential identification problem, but the latter does. The basic logarithmic form of the giving equation implies that the ratio of giving will be related to the ratios of individual variables that change over time:

$$(27) \qquad \frac{G_1}{G_0} = A\left(\frac{Y_1}{Y_0}\right)^a \left(\frac{P_1}{P_0}\right)^b e^{cx+v};$$

where $A$ is a constant reflecting a time trend, $c$ is a vector of coefficients, $x$ is a vector of variables measuring changes in individual variables or characteristics for which growth rates in giving may differ, $a$ and $b$ are elasticities, and $v$ is an error term. To the extent that omitted variables such as religion and community characteristics remain relatively constant over time, a model such as (27) mitigates the possible bias resulting from their omission. After taking logarithms, I estimated the model of changes in giving for 4105 taxpayers who itemized deductions in 1968 and 1970, using the Treasury's Seven-Year Panel of Taxpayers. Because of new features embodied in the 1970 tax law (increased exemptions, a low-income allowance, and a significantly reduced tax surcharge), changes in the price of giving during this period were largely affected by exogenous influences, thus enhancing the opportunity to identify the price effect. Adding $10 to all reported giving yielded the following estimated equation:

(28) $\ln (G+10)_{70} - \ln (G+10)_{68} = 0.122 + 0.449 (\ln Y_{70} - \ln Y_{68})$
$\qquad\qquad\qquad\qquad\qquad\quad (0.041)\quad (0.053)$

$\qquad - 0.388(\ln P_{70} - \ln P_{68}) + 0.037\ MRD + 0.0065(D_{70} - D_{68})$
$\qquad\quad (0.269)\qquad\qquad\qquad\quad (0.037)\qquad\quad (0.0197)$

$\qquad - 0.129(\text{age } 35\text{--}54) - 0.183(\text{age } 55\text{--}64) - 0.216(\text{age } 65+),$
$\qquad\quad (0.029)\qquad\qquad\quad (0.037)\qquad\qquad\quad (0.053)$

$\qquad R^2 = 0.059,$

where contributions and net income are expressed in 1970 dollars, $D$ is the number of dependents, and there are dummy variables for married couples *(MRD)* and age of taxpayer.[62] Both the implied income elasticity (0.449) and the price elasticity ($-0.388$) are smaller than most estimates in cross-section studies. The standard error for the price term is especially large, implying a 95 percent confidence interval on the elasticity of 0.139 to $-0.915$. The age dummies suggest that rate of increase in giving drop with age.

These estimates are similar to those based on changes for aggregate income classes in that the estimated price elasticities are smaller than typical cross-section estimates and the standard errors are relatively large. The similarity of these two sets of results strongly suggests that our knowledge about the price elasticity of giving is not as precise as most cross-section analysis would suggest. The lower point estimates implied by the analysis of changes in individual giving are roughly consistent with the aggregate elasticities presented in table 2.22, but there are several alternative expla-

62. Price and income elasticities from this equation are presented in Clotfelter 1980b, p. 331, table 2.

nations for those estimates. First, the sample used for estimating the individual change model included only low- and middle-income itemizers, for whom the true price elasticity may be smaller in absolute value.[63] Second, lags in the adjustment of giving behavior to changes in price and income would tend to show up as lower estimated elasticities. Other estimates of the adjustment coefficient suggest that the two-year span covered by equation (28) would not be long enough to accommodate most of the adjustment in giving.[64] Finally, the smaller point estimates implied by the change equations may result from an errors-in-variables problem arising from the failure of actual changes in price to measure "perceived" changes, where the latter is the correct variable. That smaller price elasticities are estimated in change equations for shorter intervals supports this hypothesis, but it is also consistent with the lagged-adjustment hypothesis.

In summary, the statistical identification of the price and income effects on giving lies at the heart of econometric work to assess the impact of tax policy on contributions. Tests to verify the effect of price involve maximizing the amount of independent variation in tax rates. While they tend to leave more doubt about the precise price elasticity, these tests strongly support the existence of an independent tax-defined price effect on charitable giving.

*Endogeneity of Tax Variables*

Another important econometric problem encountered in empirical analysis of charitable contributions is that the policy variables of interest—price and tax liability—are dependent on the amount of contributions made. As figure 2.4 above shows, the budget set facing the household typically is nonlinear. For itemizers, increased contributions may decrease the marginal tax rate and thus increase the price of giving at the margin. In addition, taxpayers whose contributions cause them to itemize their deductions experience an inframarginal decline in price. Similar effects apply to total tax liability and thus to net income. Including actual values of price and income as explanatory variables in a regression explaining contributions would lead to simultaneity bias, and resulting estimates would be inconsistent.[65] In order to obtain consistent estimates, the measure of price must be made independent of the amount contributed. Three basic approaches have been used to achieve consistent results: use of a "first-dollar" price of giving, use of instrumental variables for the

---

63. See section 2.5.1 for a discussion of variations in the price elasticity.
64. See section 2.5.1 for a discussion of a partial-adjustment model of giving.
65. See Theil (1971), pp. 361–64) for a discussion of consistent estimates. See Feldstein 1975a and Fedlstein and Taylor 1976 for discussions of this bias in models of charitable giving.

marginal price, and a nonlinear procedure that accounts for the entire schedule of prices relevant to an individual.

The first-dollar price is defined as the price applying to an individual's first dollar of giving, and it corresponds to the slope of the budget set in figure 2.3 at the y-axis.[66] Although it provides an exogenous measure of price, it differs from the marginal price for some taxpayers. Obviously, the greater the difference, the less reliable the first-dollar measure of price. For the majority of taxpayers—those who do not itemize—the first-dollar price is exactly the marginal price. A difference is possible only for those who itemize deductions. The illustrative budget set displayed in table 2.11 for an itemizer with average income in 1980 suggests that the contribution required to cause the first-dollar and marginal price to vary more than 10 percent would be very large—on the order of seven times the average contribution for that class, or about $5860.

A more direct test of the accuracy of the first-dollar price is given in table 2.23, which compares calculated prices for a random sample of itemizers in 1970. For the purpose of analyzing the pattern of prices, itemizers are divided into several classes. The most numerous group of itemizers are those who would owe tax and itemize their deductions whether or not they had charitable deductions. This, of course, is the usual case represented by a convex budget, such as that set shown in figure 2.3. In the 1970 sample of itemizers, the first-dollar price was a very accurate measure of the marginal price. Whereas the average marginal price faced by this group was 0.782, the average first-dollar price was 0.779. Obviously the vast majority of such taxpayers reach an equilibrium point on the first segment of their convex budget set. Similarly, the first-dollar price and marginal price are within one percentage point for three other groups of itemizers: those who itemize even though it appears to be advantageous not to (line 3),[67] those whose returns are nontaxable in any case (line 4), and the few for whom contributions make the difference between nontax status and nonitemization (line 6). For two groups of itemizers, however, the first-dollar price is not a very accurate measure of the marginal price. For the few taxpayers whose contributions reduce taxes to zero (line 5), the first-dollar price understates the marginal price. Much more important are those taxpayers who would not find it advantageous to itemize without their charitable contributions (line 2). These taxpayers face nonconvex budget sets, as illustrated above in figure 2.7. Such borderline itemizers face a marginal price (0.787) slightly higher than that faced by itemizers in group 1

---

66. In the first-dollar approach, both price and income are calculated as if no contributions are made. Because it is defined analogously, income is not discussed further in this section.

67. These taxpayers may itemize because of state tax considerations or because of requirements covering married couples filing separately.

**Table 2.23**     Average First-Dollar Price ($P_1$) and Marginal Price ($P_2$) for Itemizers, 1970

| Description | Percentage of Itemizers | Average Values | | |
|---|---|---|---|---|
| | | $P_1$ | $P_2$ | $(P_1 - P_2)$ |
| *Taxable returns* | | | | |
| 1. Excess itemized deductions positive with or without contributions | 88.1 | 0.779 | 0.782 | −0.003 |
| 2. Excess itemized deductions positive with contributions, not without contributions (borderline itemizers) | 6.7 | 0.993[a] | 0.787 | +0.206 |
| 3. Excess itemized deductions negative (itemization is not advantageous for federal taxes alone) | 1.3 | 0.823 | 0.824 | −0.002 |
| *Nontaxable returns* | | | | |
| 4. Nontaxable with or without contributions | 3.0 | 1.000 | 1.000 | 0.000 |
| 5. Nontaxable with contributions, but taxable without | 0.8 | 0.859 | 0.987[b] | −0.128 |
| 6. Nontaxable with contributions; without contributions taxable and negative excess itemized deductions | 0.0[c] | 1.000 | 0.991[b] | +0.009 |
| TOTAL ($N = 7063$) | 100.0 | | | |

*Source:* Seven-Year Panel of Taxpayers; see Clotfelter 1980b, p. 326, table 1.

*Note:* Excess itemized deductions are defined as itemized deductions minus the greater of the standard deduction and the low-income allowance.

[a]For a few taxpayers at the margin of itemization, the $10 of contributions used to calculated tax price was sufficient to change that status and thus result in a price not equal to one.

[b]For a few taxpayers, actual tax liability was under a dollar; thus the marginal tax rate was a small positive number, although reported tax was zero. Most of these taxpayers had tax credits which most likely would have covered all tax liability.

[c]Less than 0.05.

(0.782), but their first-dollar price greatly overstates that marginal price (+ 0.206).

These calculations show that the first-dollar price of giving gives a very close approximation to the marginal price in most cases. The major error to which the first-dollar measure is susceptible is overstatement of the marginal price in the case of borderline itemizers. This has two important implications for econometric studies using a first-dollar measure of price. First, in samples containing both itemizers and nonitemizers, it is incorrect to assume that the itemization decision is exogenous with respect to contributions. For itemizers who chose that status only by virtue of the contributions they made, the correct first-dollar price is one. Since these taxpayers are more likely to be relatively generous givers, assuming that their itemization is exogenous and assigning them a price less than one will impart a negative bias to the price elasticity.

The effect of assuming that itemization is exogenous can be illustrated using the National Study of Philanthropy. Boskin and Feldstein (1977 and 1978), like Dye (1978), took itemization status to be exogenous. Their estimated price elasticity of − 2.54, shown in table 2.24, is comparatively large. In order to examine the possible effect of their assumption, I reesti-

**Table 2.24**    **Alternative Treatment of Borderline Itemizers from the National Study of Philanthropy**

| | | Reestimation | | |
|---|---|---|---|---|
| | Boskin-Feldstein (eq. 1) | Replication of Boskin-Feldstein Equation | Price = 1 for borderline itemizers (N = 30) | Borderline Itemizers Omitted |
| Equation | (A) | (B) | (C) | (D) |
| Log of net income | 0.69 | 0.73 | 0.79 | 0.73 |
| | (0.06) | (0.06) | (0.06) | (0.06) |
| Log of price | − 2.54 | − 2.69 | − 2.20 | − 2.55 |
| | (0.28) | (0.27) | (0.27) | (0.27) |
| Age 35–54 | 0.46 | 0.42 | 0.43 | 0.44 |
| | (0.07) | (0.07) | (0.07) | (0.07) |
| Age 55–64 | 0.75 | 0.69 | 0.71 | 0.71 |
| | (0.09) | (0.09) | (0.09) | (0.09) |
| Age 65 + | 0.86 | 0.90 | 0.90 | 0.91 |
| | (0.09) | (0.09) | (0.09) | (0.09) |
| Intercept | − 2.54 | − 2.33 | − 2.88 | − 2.40 |
| | (0.28) | (0.53) | (0.53) | (0.53) |
| N | 1621 | 1691 | 1691 | 1661 |
| $R^2$ | 0.30 | 0.31 | 0.30 | 0.31 |

*Source:* Boskin and Feldstein 1977, p. 352.

*Note:* Household incomes of between $1000 and $30,000. Dependent variable is ln $(G + 10)$.

mated their equation using the same data set. I calculated federal taxes and marginal tax rates from data on income, mortgage and house value, and exemptions. Other deductions were based on averages for each income class. Taxpayers were classified as borderline itemizers if their contributions made the difference between itemized deductions exceeding or being less than the applicable standard deduction for the household.[68] Equation (B) represents an attempt to replicate the Boskin-Feldstein sample and specification. Probably because of differences in tax-calculation algorithms, the samples and estimates differ slightly. The reestimated price elasticity assuming exogenous itemization status is − 2.69. The last two equations reflect two methods of mitigating the sample selection bias problem. In equation (C) borderline itemizers were assigned the correct first-dollar price of one. The estimated price elasticity is − 2.20, a value significantly different from that in equation (B). Equation (D) was estimated without borderline itemizers in the sample. The estimates from this equation are not significantly different from those in the replication equation, however. Because it includes the entire sample, the preferred equation is (C), the estimates of which support the notion that the incorrect treatment of borderline itemizers leads to a negative bias in the price elasticity. The resulting estimate of this price elasticity is still quite large relative to other empirical work on this question.

The second implication of the problem for borderline itemizers is that there is a sample selection bias in any sample restricted to itemizers, such as samples of tax returns. Any sample of itemizers includes some taxpayers who are in the sample only because their contributions were large enough to put their total deductions over the allowable standard amount. As an illustration of the sample-selection-bias problem, consider the true giving equation $G = XB + u$, where $X$ is a vector of explanatory variables, $B$ is a vector of coefficients, and $u$ is an error term. For this model the conditional expectation of giving for the population is $E(G_i \mid X_i) = X_iB$. However, the comparable expectation for itemizers only is

$$(29) \qquad E(G_i|X_i, I_i > S_i) = X_iB + E(u_i|I_i > S_i),$$

where $I_i$ is an individual's possible itemized deductions and $S_i$ the maximum of the standard deduction and the low-income allowance. For borderline itemizers, contributions will tend to be unusually large given their first-dollar price of one due to the fact that such itemizers, in essence, are included in the sample by virtue of these relatively large contributions. At the same time, similar taxpayers making smaller contributions and thus choosing not to itemize would be excluded from the sample. The result of

68. For a futher description of the sample and tax calculation method, see Appendix A. Out of the 1691 households included in table 2.24, equations B and C, 30 were classified as borderline itemizers.

including all itemizers would then be a positive correlation between the first-dollar price and the error term. This sample selection problem can be dealt with by techniques specifically designed for the purpose or by eliminating them from the sample.[69]

A second approach to the problem of endogeneity in the tax variables is the use of instrumental variables. Feenberg's (1982) instrumental-variables procedure using state tax rates, discussed above, is one such approach. Although it is open to the possibility of underidentification discussed by Feenberg, a more conventional procedure would be simply to use the first-dollar price as an instrument for the true marginal price. When this approach was taken for a sample of itemized returns for 1970, the point estimates of the ordinary least squares and instrumental-variables equations were quite close, which is consistent with the similarity of first-dollar and marginal prices suggested by table 2.21.[70]

A third approach to obtaining consistent estimates is a nonlinear technique that embodies the nonlinearity of budget constraints. Following the work of Hausman and others in estimating models of labor supply,[71] Reece and Zieschang (1982) have estimated the effect of taxes on contributions using nonlinear budget constraints. Their approach recognizes that the amount of contributions an individual makes depends on the entire budget set. When the individual is on any given segment of the set, he behaves just as if he were facing a proportional income tax with the same rate, but with a credit added. This credit, or "rate structure premium," arises from the fact that the actual tax differs from the hypothetical proportional tax, in that not all dollars are taxed at the same proportional rate.[72] Explicit utility functions are then derived by applying Roy's identity to a simple linear demand function for giving. The utility-maximizing consumption point can then be found on the budget set. For convex budget sets, which apply to those who would itemize in any case, this is a fairly straightforward matter of comparing slopes. For nonconvex budget sets, including the case of borderline itemizers, explicit utility calculations must be made. The estimation routine is a nonlinear maximum-likelihood method patterned after Hausman's work. Although the complexity of this approach virtually dictates the use of a simplistic linear demand function, the approach deals explicitly with borderline itemizers and yields consistent estimates. Using a sample of 685 households from the Survey of Con-

69. See Heckman 1979 for a discussion of estimation in the presence of sample-selection bias.

70. For a sample of 4492 itemizers, the ordinary-least-squares estimates for the price and income elasticities were -1.68 (S.E. = 0.29) and 0.505 (S.E. = 0.063). The instrumental variables estimates were -1.72 (S.E. = 0.31) and 0.500 (S.E. = 0.064), respectively.

71. See Hausman 1981 for a description of this work.

72. Actual net income plus this rate-structure premium is the amount comparable to Hausman's "virtual income."

sumer Expenditures, Reece and Zieschang (1982) obtained estimates implying at mean values a price elasticity of $-0.91$ and an income elasticity of 1.31. Compared to conventional Tobit estimates obtained by Reece (1979) for a similar sample and dependent variable, the price elasticity for this nonlinear method is smaller in absolute value ($-0.91$ compared to $-1.19$), and the income elasticity is larger (1.31 compared to 0.88). Given the sensitivity of estimates in other models to sample and variable specifications, it is impossible to determine how much of the difference is attributable to the estimating techniques used and the differences in calculating elasticity values.[73]

### Systematic Reporting Errors

Estimates of aggregate contributions based on amounts reported by donors consistently exceed estimates based on gifts received by charitable organizations, strongly suggesting that donors tend to overstate their contributions. Furthermore, there is some reason to believe that the tendency to report too much may vary by itemization status and tax rate. Vickrey (1962, p. 50), for example, suggests that itemizers may be more careful in recording gifts than nonitemizers. Such differences in memory or record keeping would bias survey findings and imply that at least part of observed differences in giving, such as those shown in table 2.9, are not attributable to a price response. Differences in tax rates may also affect reporting. Since the tax benefit from overreporting is comparable to that obtained from actual increases in giving, it is possible that estimated price elasticities of giving embody an overreporting effect as well as an effect on actual contributions.[74]

In order to explore this possibility, I estimated simple logarithmic equations explaining reported contributions before and after IRS audits.[75] Table 2.25 presents the estimated price and income elasticities for both measures of contributions and four broad income classes. Although reported contributions in each income class are indeed higher than the amounts allowed by auditors, the estimated price and income elasticities are quite close and well within the corresponding standard errors in every case. These results suggest that the tendency to overstate contributions does not rise with the marginal tax rate and that the use of reported contributions does not lead to systematic bias of the price effect.

73. Elasticities in Reece 1979 are based on the percentage change in expected contributions, while elasticities calculated by Reece and Zieschang 1982 are based on changes in giving by a representative household.
74. Kahn (1960, p. 67) suggests that taxpayers might have overstated gifts in the 1940s and 1950s due to high tax rates. Schwartz (1970a, p. 1269) also notes the possibility of biased estimates from overreporting.
75. I am indebted to Eugene Steuerle for discussions on this topic. The data were taken from the 1969 Taxpayer Compliance Measurement Program and were analyzed as a part of a Treasury Department contract on tax administration. For a description of the data, see Clotfelter 1983a.

**Table 2.25**     **Estimated Price and Income Elasticities Using Reported and Corrected Contributions**

| Income Class | Sample Size | Mean of Contributions | | Price Elasticity | | Income Elasticity | |
|---|---|---|---|---|---|---|---|
| | | Reported | Corrected | Reported | Corrected | Reported | Corrected |
| $3,000 to 20,000 | 21,789 | 227 | 211 | 0.06 | −0.06 | 1.39 | 1.39 |
| | | | | (0.37) | (0.36) | (0.06) | (0.06) |
| Over $20,000 to 50,000 | 11,952 | 1,417 | 1,377 | −1.11 | −1.09 | 1.62 | 1.59 |
| | | | | (0.14) | (0.14) | (0.11) | (0.10) |
| Over $50,000 to 100,000 | 4,336 | 4,869 | 4,720 | −1.43 | −1.42 | 1.08 | 1.07 |
| | | | | (0.12) | (0.12) | (0.15) | (0.15) |
| Over $100,000 | 1,020 | 49,351 | 47,890 | −1.60 | −1.59 | 1.08 | 1.10 |
| | | | | (0.16) | (0.16) | (0.11) | (0.11) |

*Source:* 1969 Taxpayer Measurement Compliance Program file. See Clotfelter 1983a for a description of the data set.
*Note:* Other included variables were dummy variables for age, region, and marital status. Standard errors are in parentheses.

*Other Issues*

Several less significant issues have come up in the estimation of econometric models of giving. Three discussed briefly below are the modifications of the logarithm of giving, the problem of heteroskedasticity, and the omission of age in equations using aggregate data. In studies of individual contributions, observations of zero contributions present a special problem. Where such observations represent a sizable portion of the sample, such as in Reece's (1979) sample, a technique that accounts for the zero constraint like Tobit is called for. Where only a small porportion of the sample gives nothing, ordinary least squares is appropriate, but the zero observations make it impossible to take logarithms directly. Transformations to allow a logarithmic form include adding $1 or $10 to all giving amounts or setting a minimum contribution, based in part on convenience and in part on the idea that virtually everyone gives something. Because of the steepness of the logarithmic function in the vicinity of one, Boskin and Feldstein (1977) opted for adding $10. In other words, the constant elasticity function becomes less plausible when proportional changes in any variable become too large. Over the range of contributions values examined in econometric studies, even for samples dominated by low- and middle-income households, the differences between these alternative forms do not appear to be large.[76]

A second issue, raised by Hood, Martin, and Osberg (1977), is heteroskedasticity in the errors in models using aggregated data. Because some observations in the samples used by Feldstein (1975a) and Abrams and Schmitz (1978), for example, are based on many more returns than others, the variance of the error term may not be constant. In order to obtain consistent estimates, it is necessary to apply a generalized least-squares weighting of the observations. Another closely related problem, discussed by Feldstein (1975a), is the likelihood that itemizers with very low incomes are unusual. His solution was to exclude observations with average incomes below a given level.[77] In order to examine the sensitivity of estimates based on pooled aggregate data to adjustments such as these, a data set similar to that used by Feldstein was used to obtain new estimates.[78]

---

76. Boskin and Feldstein (1977, pp. 1444–45) report price-elasticity estimates based on three forms of the dependent variable (standard errors shown in parentheses): $\ln (G + 10)$: $- 2.405 (0.259)$; $\ln (G10)$: $- 2.506 (0.266)$; and $\ln (G1)$: $- 2.872 (0.371)$, where $G10$ and $G1$ are equal to the greater of reported giving and $10 and $1, respectively.

77. In most equations Feldstein also excluded taxpayers with incomes over $100,000 on the basis that their economic incomes were poorly measured by adjusted gross income and that the opportunities of giving through other mechanisms such as trusts made it difficult to calculate their price of giving (Feldstein 1975a, p. 86).

78. For a description of the data, see the Appendix A.

Equations of a basic logarithmic form were estimated weighted and unweighted and for different income ranges. The weighting factor used in the weighted regressions was the square root of the number of taxpayers. The estimated price and income elasticities are shown in table 2.26. Of those shown, equation (E) is the same basic equation and sample as that employed by Feldstein (1975a), except that the income limits are expressed in 1972 dollars rather than 1967 dollars. The estimated elasticities are quite close: − 1.18 (compared to − 1.24) for price and 0.76 (compared to 0.80) for income. For each pair of equations, the effect of weighting the observations is to decrease the income elasticity and increase the size of the price elasticity in absolute value. These changes are by far the greatest in equations (C) and (D). In contrast, the effect of limiting the sample at the lower level or at both the top and bottom is to reduce the absolute value of the price elasticity and to increase the estimated income elasticity. Except for equation (C), the estimates are reasonably well clustered. Yet the differences are still much greater than would be suggested by the relatively small estimated standard errors. Compared to estimates using individual data, these estimates appear less robust. Taken together, however, these results do appear to be consistent with other estimates. On the basis of consistency of estimation and avoidance of bias by the inclusion of low-income itemizers, equations (D) and (F) would seem to be preferred.

Table 2.26    **Estimated Price and Income Elasticities of Giving, Pooled Aggregate Data, 1948–80**

| Equation, Sample and Estimation | Estimates | | | Sample Size |
|---|---|---|---|---|
| | Price Elasticity | Income Elasticity | Trend | |
| Full sample | | | | 483 |
| (A) OLS | − 1.42 | 0.75 | 0.0093 | |
| | (0.07) | (0.03) | (0.0026) | |
| (B) Weighted | − 1.69 | 0.51 | − 0.0027 | |
| | (0.07 | (0.02) | (0.0013) | |
| $Y > \$4,000$ | | | | 393 |
| (C) OLS | − 0.73 | 1.16 | − 0.0020 | |
| | (0.06) | (0.03) | (0.0021) | |
| (D) Weighted | − 1.42 | 0.67 | − 0.0077 | |
| | (0.08) | (0.03) | (0.0012) | |
| $\$100,000 > Y > \$4000$ | | | | 317 |
| (E) OLS | − 1.18 | 0.76 | − 0.0051 | |
| | (0.21) | (0.02) | (0.0012) | |
| (F) Weighted | − 1.34 | 0.60 | − 0.0078 | |
| | (0.08) | (0.02) | (0.0010) | |

Not only do they yield similar estimates, but their elasticities are also close to that implied by equation (E), the basic equation used by Feldstein (1975a).[79]

## 2.6  Individual Giving in Foreign Countries

An important step towards a more complete understanding of the effect of fiscal policies on charitable contributions is to extend the econometric analysis of giving beyond the United States. In so doing, it would be possible to observe much wider variations in the tax treatment of contributions, the level of government services, and private institutional arrangements than is possible in analyzing one country alone. In this vien, the present section presents some available international comparisons of contributions by individuals. One fact that becomes quite clear is that available data on charitable giving in other countries is much less complete than is the case for the United States. The present section deals in turn with certain institutional differences relevant to charitable giving among selected Western countries and then with econometric studies of individual contributions for two countries.

### 2.6.1  Private Giving and Institutional Differences

For the purpose of comparison, it is useful to summarize available information on contributions and institutional characteristics for various countries. Attention is focused on three countries—Britain, Canada, and the Federal Republic of Germany—and additional information on tax laws is presented for other countries. In Britain, the tax law allows deductions for some charitable gifts, but the law differs in three notable respects from the U.S. treatment. First, the gifts must be in the form of a "deed of covenant," whereby the taxpayer agrees to make payments to a charitable organization for at least seven years. Although the amount of the gift is

---

79. A final issue also relevant to the estimation of contributions equations with aggregate data is the effect of omitting age variables in estimating price and income elasticities. As shown by all of the work with individual data on contributions, age is an important influence, with contributions rising steadily with age. In aggregate cross sections of giving, measures of age have been omitted. Since age and income are strongly, albeit not linearly, related, the omission of age in these equations could bias the income or price elasticities. In order to examine what, if any, effect this omission might have, I added a measure of the age distribution of each income class to the pooled equation presented above. For the years 1968 to 1980, it was possible to measure the ratio of over-65 exemptions to taxpayers exemptions, giving the approximate proportion of adults over 65. When this measure was added to the aggregate giving equation, the income elasticity rose from 0.35 to 0.98 and the price elasticity fell in absolute value from -2.62 to -0.07, the latter being insignificant. The relatively small variation in tax schedules tended to make the estimates from this sample quite unstable, however, and it is thus hard to know what to make of this result. In addition, the studies of giving based on disaggregated data all include age variables without having a similar effect on the price elasticity.

fixed in advance, the taxpayer may retain some flexibility as to the ultimate recipient by directing contributions in the covenant to an umbrella organization such as the National Council on Social Services and later specifying the precise donee. Second, contributions have not always been deductible at the top marginal tax rate, as is the case in the United States. From 1946 to 1981 covenanted gifts were deductible only at the lower basic tax rate, but they are now deductible at the surtax rate as well. Finally, the mechanics of the tax subsidy are more direct than in the United States, with the government sending checks directly to charities for the subsidy portion of contributions. The taxpayer deducts from his contribution the tax on the gift, and the government pays to the charity the amount of that saving.[80]

The Canadian and German tax provisions both allow for a direct deduction of contributions in calculating taxable income. Contributions are generally limited to 5 percent of income in Germany and 20 percent in Canada, although there is no limit for some institutions in Canada (Bird and Bucovetsky 1976, especially pp. 16–23; Paqué 1982a, p. 3). The most notable differences from U.S. tax treatment occur in Germany. First, the German law allows contributions to some political organizations to be deducted. Second, members of organized religious bodies—the vast majority in Germany—pay a "church tax" calculated as a percentage of regular tax liability (Paqué, 1982a). Needless to say, these differences would be expected to have an impact on the amount and composition of deductible contributions.

Deductions for contributions are also allowed in Australia, France, and Japan. In Japan contributions to the Community Chest Society are deductible subject to both a floor and a percentage limitation. By contrast, contributions are generally not deductible in Italy and Sweden. One study of tax differences across countries concluded that "direct and indirect governmental support of the private philanthropic sector varies inversely with the involvement of government itself in providing social services" (Arthur Andersen and Company 1977, p. 2975).

The differences in tax law and the size of government are reflected in differences in private giving among countries. In comparison to the United States, these countries have significantly lower levels of charitable giving and, correspondingly, less dependence on private contributions. Although differences in data and definitions make precise comparisons difficult, it is possible to estimate giving as a percentage of personal income for the United States and three other countries. Personal contributions were about 0.2 percent of personal income in Britain in 1975. The compa-

80. Descriptions of British tax law regarding contributions were taken from Owen 1964, pp. 337–38; Culyer, Wiseman, and Posnett 1976, pp. 36, 44–46; Obler 1981, pp. 27–28; and correspondence by the author with E. B. Butler, Inland Revenue, 18 May 1982.

rable figure in Canada for 1979 was about 0.5 percent. In Germany, non-religious giving in 1974 was 0.2 percent of gross income, and the church tax raised another 1.5 percent, for a total of 1.7 percent of income directed toward charitable organizations. Contributions in the United States, in comparison, have been about 2 percent of personal income.[81] At the same time, it is clear that government expenditures provide a large share of support in these countries, whereas these functions are heavily dependent on private support in the United States. For example, the Canadian government provides the support for most of the country's Catholic parochial schools, and Canadian universities receive very little private support other than from fees (Bird and Bucovetsky 1976, p. 5). Similarly, the government provides substantial support in the areas of health, education, welfare, and the arts in Britain and Germany. In addition, the rise of government activity has been accompanied by declines in private giving. Falush (1977, p. 41) notes, for example, that the ratio of giving to personal income in Britain fell by half between 1934 and 1975, a period of substantial growth of government. Although their effects may not be precisely measurable, such differences in tax laws and government activity should be considered in evaluating econometric studies of giving in other countries.

### 2.6.2  Econometric Analysis

Two econometric studies of charitable giving have been undertaken for other countries, one for Canada and one for Germany. Both employed published data from tax returns to yield a pooled time-series/cross-section sample of class averages. Hood, Martin, and Osberg (1977) used annual data on itemized deductions for various income classes covering the period 1968 to 1973. Taxable and nontaxable returns were entered separately, and taxpayer classes with incomes over $100,000 were omitted. With a sample of 248 observations, the resulting estimated equation is:

$$(29) \quad \ln G = -7.99 + 0.521 \ln Y - 0.862 \ln P$$
$$\phantom{(29) \quad \ln G = } (0.757) \quad (0.038) \phantom{\ln Y -} (0.201)$$

$$+ 0.462 \ln K - 0.065 \text{ Trend} - 0.810 \ RF,$$
$$(0.051) \phantom{\ln K} (0.050) \phantom{\text{ Trend} -} (0.222)$$
$$\overline{R}_2 = 0.88,$$

where $G$, $Y$, and $P$ are average values of contributions, net income, and price, as previously defined; $K$ is the percentage of income from capital

---

81. Sources for calculations were: Britain: Falush 1977, p. 331, which gives a ratio of 0.224 percent for personal disposable income; Canada: Canada 1981, table 2, based on total income of $177,577 million and contributions of $885 million; Germany: Paqué 1982a, pp. 5, 7 and unpublished information provided by Karl-Heinz Paqué; and U.S.: Giving U.S.A. 1981, p. 36, and U.S. Council of Economic Advisers 1983, p. 185. For the U.S. the ratio of individual giving to personal income was 2.0 percent in 1970 and 1.9 percent in 1982.

for the class; and *RF* is a dummy variable for the postreform years 1972 and 1973. The estimated income elasticity is 0.52, somewhat below most estimates for the United States. The implied price elasticity, $-0.86$, is also smaller than those implied by most studies, but the large standard error implies a 95 percent confidence interval of $-0.47$ to $-1.26$, making it impossible to reject the hypothesis that the price elasticity is in fact $-1$.[82] Considering the important differences between Canada and the United States in the sources of support for certain nonprofit institutions, the similarity between these estimates and others obtained for the United States is striking.

In a second econometric study, Paqué (1982a) analyzed a similar pooled sample of contributions in the Federal Republic of Germany for five years between 1961 and 1974. After eliminating the six lowest income classes for each year, he obtained a sample of forty observations. Using weighted least squares, he estimated the equation (Paqué 1982a, p. 16, table 1, equation 5):

$$(30) \quad \ln G = -12.48 + 1.274 \ln Y - 1.378 \ln P + 0.308\ YL,$$
$$\qquad\qquad\qquad\ \ (0.018)\qquad\quad (0.128)\qquad\quad (0.044)$$

where *YL* is national income per employee. The implied income elasticity of 1.27 is much larger than most comparable estimates, and the price elasticity is somewhat larger than the median of estimates from previous work. Paqué's explanation (p. 25) is that these differences reflect the virtual exclusion of religious giving from the German contributions data by virtue of the separate "church tax." Given the lower income elasticity of religious giving obtained in the studies cited elsewhere in this chapter, this hypothesis seems quite reasonable.

In a companion study Paqué (1982b) examined the crowding-out hypothesis for Germany, using public-welfare expenditures as a measure of government activity. His results provide no evidence that crowding out had occurred, which is consistent with the findings presented in section 2.4 for the pooled sample with a time trend. It is interesting that such tests for single countries reject the crowding-out hypothesis while, at the same time, there seems to be such a strong negative correlation between contributions and size of government across countries.

---

82. The authors appear to disregard this wide confidence range in contrasting their results with previous estimates in the range of "-1.15 to -1.17" and in stating that an elastic demand curve in the case of contributions "strains credulity" (Hood, Martin, and Osberg 1977, pp. 660–61).

# 3      Contributions by Individuals: Simulating the Effects of Tax Policies

One obvious use for the econometric models of charitable giving discussed in chapter 2 is to predict the effects of changes in tax rules, income, and effective tax rates on the level of contributions. By replacing actual values of price and tax liability by values implied by a given tax rule it is possible to use estimated equations to give "predicted values" of giving. Not only are such simulations useful in assessing the impact of projected changes on the nonprofit sector, they may also be used to estimate the revenue effects of tax proposals affecting the treatment of charitable giving. This chapter discusses simulation methods and results as applied to contributions by individuals. In its assessment of various tax policies, the chapter is positive rather than normative. Issues such as the comparative social worth of expenditures by charities and government are deferred to chapter 8. Section 3.1 describes various tax rules that have been proposed or discussed in recent years. Section 3.2 summarizes previous simulations showing likely effects of some of these rules on contributions. The next section discusses the major methodological issues confronted in performing simulations of charitable giving. Section 3.4 presents new simulations of individual giving in 1983 under a variety of possible tax regimes. The results are compared to previous simulations. The final section of this chapter presents two sets of simulations for contributions over time. The first of these is historical and focuses specifically on the effect of the expansion of the standard deduction on giving. The second is prospective, focusing primarily on the effect of inflationary bracket creep on real giving over time.

## 3.1   Policy Alternatives

Two kinds of tax policies can have a significant influence on individual giving. Most obvious are policies dealing directly with the charitable deduction or charitable giving. Also of potential importance, however, are general tax changes that affect incomes and tax rates.

### 3.1.1   Provisions Explicitly Related to Contributions

Before dealing with specific proposals to modify the itemized deduction for contributions, it is useful to note two principal pillars of support for this deduction. The first is the argument that since income contributed by a family cannot be consumed, contributions are a proper deduction in calculating taxable income. As put forth by Andrews (1972), this view supports the existence of a deduction but not a tax credit for contributions. A second argument takes the view that, while contributions are a discretionary use of income, they merit public support through some kind of tax incentive. By this view, deductions or credits may be desirable, depending on the incentive effects involved. According to Break (1977, p. 1523), the political support that the deduction has enjoyed over the years is due in large part to the combined appeal of these quite different justifications.

The variety of proposals that have been made to change the charitable deduction can be understood as efforts either to rectify perceived inequities or to increase incentives to give. Because the deduction tends to diminish the effective progressivity of the income tax as a whole (Pechman 1977, p. 72), those who view contributions as a consumption item often object to the deduction's distributional consequences. Those who favor incentives for giving, on the other hand, may favor increasing those incentives beyond what is created by the deduction. Not surprisingly, such extensions would imply revenue losses. Other proposals accept the role of incentives in the income tax but seek to restructure them by replacing the deduction with a tax credit.

### *Expansion of the Charitable Deduction*

One of the most important alternatives for encouraging contributions is to expand the present deduction. For example, the Commission on Private Philanthropy and Public Needs (1977) proposed that itemizers at certain income levels be permitted to deduct a multiple of their actual contributions to provide an added incentive to give. Such a multiple or "amplified" deduction would have a significant impact on the price of giving and some income effect as well. The commission's proposal limited the coverage of this multiple deduction, allowing a double deduction for taxpayers with incomes less than $15,000 and a 150 percent deduction for taxpayers with $15,000 to $30,000 in income.[1] There is no limit, of course, to the variety of rate schedules that could be used for a multiple-deduction

---

1. An alternative sliding scale was also suggested. See Commission on Private Philanthrophy and Public Needs 1977, pp. 4–7.

plan. All such multiple deductions would tend to reduce tax revenue unless tax rates were increased, however.

Another possibility for expanding the charitable deduction is to extend the deduction to nonitemizers. Often referred to as the "above-the-line" deduction because it would take the form of an adjustment to gross income rather than a deduction in calculating taxable income, this plan was proposed and actively discussed beginning in the late 1970s.[2] Then, as a part of the 1981 tax act, a schedule for phasing in an above-the-line charitable deduction was adopted. Beginning with a deduction limited to 25 percent of the first $100 in 1982 and 1983, the provision is scheduled to take full effect in 1986.[3] This long phase-in period seemed designed to put off the inevitable revenue losses as far as possible into the future. By allowing all taxpayers to deduct charitable gifts, an above-the-line charitable deduction would nullify the effect of changes in the standard deduction on contributions. To the extent that the expansion of the standard deduction since 1941 has reduced contributions, such a plan thus would have the effect over time of returning contributions to the level they would have been if the standard deduction had not been introduced.

### Limitation of the Charitable Deduction

Concern for equity in taxation has inspired the call for limiting, rather than expanding, the deduction. In the extreme, this view implies eliminating the deduction altogether. For example, the Treasury's model comprehensive income tax released in 1977 argued that contributions constitute a discretionary form of consumption and that no deduction should be allowed in an ideal income tax (U.S. Treasury Department 1977, p. 95). This view is also implicit in recent broad-based flat-tax proposals that would allow few if any deductions from gross income. Even groups interested in support for nonprofit organizations have raised questions about the charitable deduction's detrimental impact on overall tax progressivity. The Donee Group, a group opposed to many of the recommendations of the Commission on Private Philanthropy and Public Needs, implied that the charitable deduction should be eliminated or significantly altered as a part of "basic tax reform."[4] It is fair to add, however, that support for the

---

2. Bills sponsored by Representatives Fisher and Conable and by Senators Moynihan and Packwood were the subject of hearings and debate in 1979 and 1980. See U.S. Congress, Senate 1980.

3. The deduction was to increase to 25 percent of the first $400 in 1984 and 50 percent without limit in 1985.

4. In its report, the Donee Group (1977, pp. 71–72) stated:

In discussing changes in the tax laws affecting charity, we must first state that the Donee Group favors basic tax reform to restore the progressivity of the income tax and to eliminate those preferences and other devices which allow great disparities to continue. We do not, however, believe that if tax reform is gradual and piecemeal, as it is first to go. We believe that there are far more unfair and costly tax preferences than the charitable deduction.

abolition of the charitable deduction is still quite limited. For the most part, the deduction is justified on the basis of its presumed incentive effect.[5]

While the deduction itself appears to retain strong support, incremental limitations on it have periodically been proposed and enacted. As described in chapter 2, percentage-income limitations have been adjusted from time to time, as has the deductibility of gifts of appreciated assets. One limitation that is currently applied to gifts to private foundations, and one that could conceivably be applied in the future to other contributions, is the constructive realization of capital gains in gifts of appreciated property. Such a provision would make it necessary for donors to include as income the capital gains associated with donated property. If 40 percent of long-term gains are included as taxable income, a taxpayer donating property worth $1000 of which $500 is capital gains would have to pay tax on $200. Since this treatment is equivalent to realization and contribution of proceeds, the effect would be to raise the price of contributions to that applying to gifts of cash.

Another method of limiting the deductibility of gifts of appreciated assets is to allow only the cost basis of such gifts to be deducted. As Break (1977, pp. 1525–7) shows, however, this would cause some taxpayers to prefer to make cash contributions, whereas constructive realization would leave donors indifferent between giving assets and giving the cash proceeds.

Finally, any charitable deduction may be limited by allowing only those contributions that exceed some floor to count in reducing taxable income. Floors may be stated as a percentage of income, as in the case of the medical deduction, or as an absolute amount. The primary reason for imposing a floor is to limit the revenue loss associated with a given provision, although floors may also offset adverse distributional effects of a deduction.

### Tax Credit for Contributions

One widely proposed alternative to the charitable deduction is a charitable tax credit. Instead of subsidizing contributions at a rate that varies with a taxpayer's marginal tax rate, as under the deduction, a tax credit would subsidize all taxpayers at the same rate. In this connection Musgrave and Musgrave (1980, p. 362) comment on the current deduction, "A philosopher-economist might observe that the opportunity cost of virtue falls as one moves up the income scale." Citing the "great inequity" inherent in differing rates of subsidy, the Donee Group objected to the proposals of the Commission on Private Philanthropy and Public Needs calling for the preservation and augmentation of the charitable deduction. As an

---

5. The Treasury report noted this justification in listing a charitable deduction as one "optional method" of treating contributions (U.S. Treasury Department 1977, p. 95). Another justification, supported by Andrews (1972), is the argument that contributions are not properly counted in income.

alternative to the deduction, this group proposed a 30 percent tax credit (Donee Group 1977, pp. 72–73). Whether it is justified on the basis of equity in treatment of taxpayers at different income levels or on the basis of efficiency in the subsidization of all gifts, the idea of a tax credit appears to have sustained support as an alternative to the deduction as a means of encouraging charitable giving.[6]

### 3.1.2  Proposals Not Directly Related to Contributions

Tax changes not directly targeted at contributions may nevertheless have a sizable impact on giving. Any proposals that cause significant shifts in after-tax income, restructuring of marginal tax rates, or changes in the proportion of taxpayers who itemize deductions can influence the incomes and prices affecting donor contributions. Moreover, tax schedules that are not indexed to the rate of inflation generally will change over time in real terms, with much the same effect as legislated schedule changes. For example, an unindexed progressive tax schedule will yield increasingly progressive effective rate schedules in the presence of inflation.[7] Whether they are intentional or not, therefore, quite general changes in effective tax schedules can have important effects on charitable contributions.

Significant effects are most likely from two kinds of tax changes. First, movements in the real level of the standard deduction—due to legislation or inflation—will influence the number of itemizers and, accordingly, the number of taxpayers facing prices of giving less than one. As shown above in table 2.7, the proportion of taxpayers who itemize has tended to vary inversely with the constant dollar value of the maximum-allowed standard deduction. Second, any restructuring of the tax rate schedule itself will also affect prices and net incomes. Thus, the choice between a tax schedule that is indexed for inflation and one that is fixed in nominal terms is relevant to the prices and net incomes affecting giving. Other things equal, inflation will push taxpayers into higher tax brackets as well as increase the number of itemizers, thus lowering the price of giving for many taxpayers. The effects on giving of changes over time in tax rates, the standard deduction, and the price level are analyzed below in section 3.5.

### 3.2  Previous Simulations

Before discussing in detail some of the methodological issues confronted in simulating the effects of tax changes, it is useful to review some of the results of previous simulation exercises. The first full simulation based on

---

6. See chapter 8 for an analysis of the efficiency aspects of subsidy rates under a deduction and a credit.

7. See, for example, Clotfelter 1984.

an econometric model of charitable giving was presented by Feldstein (1975a). In it he estimated that the elimination of the deduction in 1968 would have caused giving to fall by 34 percent (p. 96). More elaborate simulations appear in Feldstein and Clotfelter (1976) and Feldstein and Taylor (1976).

Table 3.1 presents simulated changes in contributions and tax revenues for a wide variety of tax provisions, based on the Feldstein-Taylor model and the 1970 file of individual tax returns. In these simulations a price elasticity of -1.285 and an income elasticity of + 0.702 were employed. As indicated by the simulated changes in tax revenues, no adjustment was made in tax rates to keep revenues constant. Tax credits of 25, 30, and 50 percent show increasingly large gains in giving compared to actual 1970 levels. According to these simulations, the 25 percent tax credit would yield contributions closest to the actual level, just 4 percent above actual contributions. Allowing taxpayers to choose between a tax credit or a deduction would retain the high rates of subsidies for upper-income taxpay-

**Table 3.1**     **Simulated Effects on Contributions of Alternative Tax Provisions, 1970**

| Tax Provision | Change in Contributions | | Change in Revenues |
|---|---|---|---|
| | $ Billions | Percentage | $ Billions |
| Tax credit | | | |
| 25 percent[b] | + 0.7 | + 4 | − 0.7 |
| 30 percent[b] | + 2.3 | + 13 | − 2.1 |
| 50 percent[a] | + 12.8 | + 74 | − 11.0 |
| Optional tax credit | | | |
| 25 percent[a] | + 2.1 | + 12 | − 1.8 |
| 30 percent[b] | + 3.4 | + 20 | − 3.0 |
| 30 percent (itemizers only)[b] | + 1.5 | + 9 | − 1.3 |
| Extend deduction to nonitemizers[b] | + 1.2 | + 7 | − 1.0 |
| Constructive realization of gifts of appreciated assets[b] | − 0.5 | − 3 | + 0.3 |
| Floor on deduction | | | |
| $100[a] | − 1.2 | − 7 | + 0.9 |
| $500[a] | − 3.0 | − 18 | + 2.4 |
| 2 percent of AGI[a] | − 3.0 | − 17 | + 2.3 |
| 3 percent of AGI[b] | − 3.5 | − 20 | + 2.7 |
| Eliminate deduction[b] | − 4.6 | − 26 | + 3.5 |

[a]Simulations provided by Martin Feldstein using the 1970 tax file Break. 1977, pp. 1532, 1535, and 1537.
[b]Feldstein and Taylor 1976, p. 1218, table 6.

ers while providing the tax credit for nonitemizers and those with low marginal rates. At the 25 percent rate, making the credit optional would raise the predicted increase in contributions from 4 to 12 percent; at the 30 percent rate the increase in giving would rise from 13 to 20 percent. Of the 20 percent gain under the 30 percent optional credit, about half (9 percent) of the increase is attributable to increased giving by itemizers whose marginal tax rates are lower than the tax credit rate. Extending the charitable deduction to nonitemizers is predicted to increase total gifts by 7 percent, an amount that is less than the optional 25 percent credit because of the low marginal tax rates of most itemizers. In general, the simulations suggest larger changes in contributions than in revenues, as would be expected with an elasticity value greater than one in absolute value.

Among the simulations of proposals that would restrict the deductibility of contributions, the constructive realization of capital gains on asset gifts is predicted to reduce total gifts by 3 percent. Larger declines in giving would result from the imposition of floors of $100 or more in the deduction. The predicted reduction is 7 percent for a $100 floor and 18 percent for a $500 floor. There is little difference in effect between floors of 2 and 3 percent of gross income, for which contributions are predicted to fall 17 and 20 percent, respectively.

The least favorable simulation is the complete elimination of the deduction. The Feldstein-Taylor simulations for 1970 using micro data imply a reduction of 26 percent in contributions. This result compares to a predicted 34 percent reduction for 1968 based on pooled aggregate data (Feldstein 1975a, p. 96) and a 26 percent reduction for a sample of households in 1963 (Feldstein and Clotfelter 1976, p. 22) using similar models. While the first two simulations are for itemizers only, the last is based on a sample of all taxpayers. Not surprisingly, the biggest impact of eliminating the deduction is felt at upper income levels, where the increase in the price of giving is greatest. To indicate what this distributional effect implies for gifts to various donee groups, Feldstein and Taylor used the 1962 distribution of gifts to predict giving by organization type. Table 3.2 shows the simulation results for the elimination of the deduction. Giving to educational institutions and hospitals was predicted to fall the most, owing to the dependence of those organizations on gifts from upper income taxpayers.

### 3.3    Methodological Issues in Simulation

The starting point in simulation models of charitable giving is the basic single-equation model discussed at length in chapter 2. Using the log-linear form, this model can be written:

(1)            $\ln G = a + b_1 \ln P + b_2 \ln Y + cX + u,$

Table 3.2    **Simulated Effects of Eliminating the Charitable Deduction by Donee Type, 1970**

| Donee Group | Percentage Change in Contributions |
|---|---|
| Religious organizations | $-22$ |
| Other charitable organizations | $-27$ |
| Educational institutions | $-48$ |
| Hospitals | $-46$ |
| Other organizations | $-33$ |
| TOTAL | $-26$ |

*Source:* Feldstein and Taylor 1976, p. 1218 table 4. Note that the "health and welfare organizations" category used by the authors is renamed in accordance with the data source—U.S. Internal Revenue Service, *Statistics of Income—1962, Individual Income Tax Returns* 1964, p. 6, table E—"Other charitable organizations."

where $G$ is contributions, $P$ is price, $Y$ is after-tax income, $X$ is a vector of other variables included in the equation, $u$ is an error term representing the effect of unmeasured characteristics and errors in model specification, and $a$, $b_1$, $b_2$, and the vector $c$ are true parameters. For any given values of the independent variables (say $P_0$, $Y_0$, and $X_0$), the predicted value of the logarithm of giving is given by

(2)    $$\ln \hat{G}_0 = \hat{a} + \hat{b}_1 \ln P_0 + \hat{b}_2 \ln Y_0 + \hat{c}X_0,$$

where $\hat{a}$, $\hat{b}_1$, $\hat{b}_2$, and $\hat{c}$ are estimated coefficients. Adding the error representing the deviation of the actual from the predicted value, denoted $\hat{u}$, yields

(3)    $$\ln G_0 = \hat{a} + \hat{b}_1 \ln P_0 + \hat{b}_2 \ln Y_0 + \hat{c}X_0 + \hat{u}.$$

The basic relationship used in simulation models is obtained by combining an equation such as (3) with the corresponding equation using the price and net income variables that would be observed under an alternative tax regime. For example, suppose a given tax regime would yield first-dollar price and income values of $P_1$ and $Y_1$. Assuming there is no change in $X_0$, that equation is:

(3′)    $$\ln G^s_1 = \hat{a} + \hat{b}_1 \ln P_1 + \hat{b}_2 \ln Y_1 + \hat{c}X_0 + \hat{u},$$

where $\ln G^s_1$ is the predicted value for the logarithm of giving. Subtracting (3) from (3′) and rearranging yields:

(4)    $$\ln G^s_1 = \ln G_0 + \hat{b}_1 (\ln P_1 - \ln P_0) + \hat{b}_2 (\ln Y_1 - \ln Y_0),$$

or

(5)    $$G^s_1 = G_0 \left(\frac{P_1}{P_0}\right)^{\hat{b}_1} \left(\frac{Y_1}{Y_0}\right)^{\hat{b}_2}.$$

Only those variables whose simulation values differ from their base values—typically only those affected by tax rules—appear in this expression.[8] If only one tax-defined variable is affected by a tax change, the other term drops out. If a tax change affects neither the price of giving or net income, the simulated value $G^s_1$ would be equal to the base value $G_0$. It is useful to emphasize in this context that tax variables are the only ones to appear in the simulation equation only because they are the only variables assumed to change. It is unlikely that there are more than a few individuals, if any, for whom taxes constitute the most important reason for making charitable gifts. By focusing on changes in tax variables, the model seeks to predict the effects of a change in tax policy. Models such as this do not, as has been suggested, " ' [presume] that philanthropy is governed primarily or principally by tax considerations' " (Ketchum 1982, p. 2).

It is important to note that the estimated-error term $\hat{u}$ drops out of the expression for the simulated value of giving. Whatever omitted factors that cause an individual's contributions to diverge from the predicted value in the base period are assumed to operate in the same way if the alternative tax regime were adopted. The resulting simulated value thus differs from the actual value only in the combined predicted effects of independent variables that change as a result of a change in tax rules. The error with which any estimated equation predicts a given individual's contributions arising simply from the error term $\hat{u}$ is thus typically ignored for the purpose of simulation.[9]

As an application of prediction within the context of an estimated econometric model, this simple framework for simulating the effects of tax changes on charitable giving is relatively straightforward. It is important, however, to give attention to several methodological issues that arise. The first of these relates to the statistical error associated with all predictions. The other methodological issues relate more specifically to the case of charitable contributions.

### 3.3.1  Statistical Errors in Prediction

Two kinds of statistical errors are relevant to the prediction of charitable giving using an estimated econometric model. First, there is an error associated with each individual observation. As denoted by $\hat{u}$ in equation (3), this error measures the deviation of the actual observed value from the value that is predicted by the regression equation. It may reflect unmeasured individual characteristics or specification errors. As discussed above, this error is not considered in simulating the effect of tax changes; such individual error terms are assumed to operate the same under any tax regime. The second kind of error is the statistical sampling error associ-

---

8. See, for example, Feldstein and Clotfelter 1976, p. 20n.
9. See, for example, Feldstein and Taylor 1976, p. 1216.

ated with the parameter estimates. The coefficients $\hat{b}_1$ and $\hat{b}_2$ in equation (5) will inevitably be estimated with less than perfect precision. The standard errors of these estimates may be used to indicate the statistical precision of the predicted value. If coefficients are estimated with large errors, the predicted value correspondingly is imprecise; if coefficients are estimated with little error, predicted values are relatively precise. In his review of econometric studies of charitable contributions, Zellner (1977, pp. 1515–6) emphasizes the importance of providing measures of precision with predictions. Previously published simulations have not included such measures, however.

For the general linear regression of the form $Y = a + \Sigma b_i X_i + u$, the prediction error is given by:[10]

$$(6) \qquad s^2{}_P = s^2/N + \sum_i (X'_i - X^0{}_i)^2 \, \text{Var} \, (\hat{b}_i)$$

$$+ 2 \sum_{j<i} (X'_j - X^0{}_j)(X'_i - X^0{}_i) \, \text{Cov} \, (\hat{b}_j, \hat{b}_i),$$

where $s^2$ is the estimated variance of the estimate, $N$ is the sample size, $X'_i$ is the value of $X_i$ used for simulation, and $X^0{}_i$ is the actual or base value of $X_i$. In general, the size of the error will vary with two factors. The larger the standard errors of the relevant coefficients (as indicated by Var $(\hat{b}_i)$), the less precise will be the resulting predictions. This fact is of course a major reason for the interest shown both in the academic literature and public debate regarding the reliability of the estimated price elasticities in econometric models of giving.[11] The second important element determining the prediction error is the degree to which the values posited for simulation $(X'_i)$ differ from the observations that serve as the basis for the estimates. The more the hypothetical values used in simulation differ from observed values, the less reliable the prediction will be. For example, there would tend to be more error associated with a prediction regarding a major change such as the elimination of the charitable deduction than a minor change in the tax law. Variables for which no change is contemplated affect neither the prediction nor the prediction error.

### 3.3.2 Revenue Effects of Tax Changes

Virtually any change in tax law, including changes in the treatment of charitable contributions, will have some impact on revenues and thus net income. In order to eliminate any aggregate income effect, as well as to reflect the kind of changes that might conceivably be enacted, it is desirable to perform simulations under the assumption of constant tax revenues. Feldstein (1975a) and Feldstein and Clotfelter (1976) used a proportional

10. See, for example, Kmenta 1971, p. 375. The prediction error differs from the forecast error in that the latter also includes the variance of the individual error terms. The latter error terms drop out for the purpose of prediction (see (5)).

11. See, for example, Zellner 1977, p. 1517 or U.S. Congress, Senate, 1980, p. 227.

adjustment of tax rates to equalize revenues under various tax rules, a procedure followed in the present chapter.[12] Two other effects need to be accounted for in making revenue adjustments. First, proportional adjustment in tax rates will affect the price of giving if there is a deduction for contributions. If revenues are adjusted through a 2 percent increase in rates, for example, the price of donating under a deduction rule will fall, thus affecting donations. Second, the level of contributions will itself influence revenues under various tax rules. This interaction calls for an iterative procedure in which estimated contributions are used to recalculate tax variables, which in turn can be used to estimate contributions again.

In the model presented in the next section, the effect of changed tax rules, contributions behavior, and revenue adjustment are reflected in the recursive procedure summarized in expressions (7)–(15) where TAX is tax liability, as defined for any simulated tax regime, $G$ is giving, $P$ is the price of giving, $R_0$ is tax revenue under the actual or baseline tax regime, $\alpha$ is a proportional revenue adjustment parameter, and $f$, $h$, $j$ are functions in the revenue adjustment process.

(7)  $$\text{TAX}_1 = \text{TAX}(G \mid G = O),$$

(8)  $$P_1 = P(G \mid G = O),$$

(9)  $$G_1 = G(\text{TAX}_1, P_1),$$

(10)  $$\text{TAX}_2 = \text{TAX}(G_1),$$

(11)  $$P_2 = P(G_1),$$

(12)  $$\alpha = f(\text{TAX}_2, R_0),$$

(13)  $$\text{TAX}_2{}^* = h(\text{TAX}_2, \alpha),$$

(14)  $$P_2{}^* = j(P_2, \alpha),$$

(15)  $$G_2 = G(\text{TAX}_2{}^*, P_2{}^*).$$

Initial values for tax liability and price in (7) and (8) are first-dollar amounts, calculated using actual values of all tax parameters except contributions. An intermediate value of contributions is calculated in (9) using $\text{TAX}_1$ to determine net income. This equation corresponds to the basic prediction equation given in (5). Equations (10) and (11) repeat the first two steps with this new value of contributions. In (12) an adjustment fac-

---

12. By contrast, Feldstein and Taylor (1976, p. 1215n) made no revenue adjustment, noting the relatively small percentage change in net income.

tor is calculated based on the total revenue generated under the simulated tax regime as compared to the original tax regime. In the simple case in which the simulated tax regime has no effect on tax credits, this adjustment function is simply

$$(12') \qquad \alpha = R_0/\text{TAX}_2,$$

and tax liabilities in (13) are adjusted proportionally. In this case, (14) becomes

$$(14') \qquad P_2{}^* = 1 - \alpha(1 - P_2).$$

This adjustment process must be modified when tax credits are affected by any proposed tax change.[13] Finally, the adjusted values obtained in (13) and (14) are used in (15) to obtain a final estimate of giving.

### 3.3.3   Itemization Status

Needless to say, a taxpayer's itemization status is one of the most important pieces of information available in predicting the effect of a change in tax treatment. Before 1981 only itemizers were allowed to deduct gifts. General tax rate changes affected the price faced by itemizers, while a charitable tax credit or a deduction extended to nonitemizers might cause a significant decrease in the price faced by nonitemizers. In simulating contributions for some hypothetical tax regimes, therefore, it is necessary to determine whether a given taxpayer will be an itemizer or not. It is useful to distinguish between changes in itemization status that are largely independent of the tax treatment of contributions from those that occur because of changes in that tax treatment.

*Exogenous Changes in Itemization*

The more important reason for changes in itemization status is the change from year to year in the standard deduction (now the "zero-bracket amount") relative to the increase in the nominal value of households' deductible expenditures. When expenditures rise faster than the standard deduction—as, for example, when the standard deduction does not change during an inflationary period—more taxpayers find that their deductible expenditures exceed the maximum allowable standard deduction. Accordingly, the number of itemizers rises. Although contributions are one part of these deductible expenditures, taxes and interest represent the bulk of such items for most taxpayers. In simulating the tax changes over time or tax changes involving an adjustment of the standard deduction, it is necessary to provide for a change in itemization status for some taxpayers.

---

13. Where tax credits are affected, for example, the proportional adjustment is applied only to tax liability before credits so that credit rates and price are unchanged.

Modeling the itemization decision of a rational taxpayer involves a straightforward comparison between the allowable itemized deductions that he could report ($ID_i$) and the applicable standard deduction ($SD_i$). If $ID_i > SD_i$, the taxpayer has a smaller tax liability by itemizing deductions, and the simple model predicts that he would be an itemizer. If $ID_i < SD_i$, the taxpayer would not itemize. In a micro data set with information on all potential itemized deductions for all taxpayers, this simple model would be quite appropriate for use in simulations involving changes in itemization. Where deduction data are available only for itemizers, however, it is not possible to utilize this approach without first generating hypothetical deductions data for nonitemizers, a method necessarily dependent on arbitrary allocations.[14]

A model of itemization using aggregate data relates the ratio of gross income and the standard deduction to the probability of itemizing, using a logistic function. Where $I$ is the probability of itemization, $AGI$ is adjusted gross income, and $SD$ is the maximum standard deduction, the function is

$$(16) \qquad \frac{I}{1 - I} = a \left( \frac{AGI}{SD} \right)^{\gamma}$$

The constant $\gamma$ is the elasticity of the odds in favor of itemizing with respect to the income–standard deduction ratio. An equation of this form was estimated for a pooled time-series/cross-section sample of aggregate tax return data covering 1973 to 1980 and even years from 1948 to 1972.[15] Taking logarithms and adding a time trend yields the following equation, estimated by ordinary least squares:

$$(17) \quad \ln \frac{I}{1 - I} = \underset{(0.02)}{1.24} \ln \frac{AGI}{SD} + \underset{(0.004)}{0.020} \ (\text{Year-1947}),$$

$$R^2 = 0.90, N = 483,$$

where $AGI$ is mean income and $I$ is the proportion of taxpayers who itemize by income class. As illustrated in table 3.3 for 1980, the regression's predicted values closely track the actual proportion of itemizers. For the purpose of predicting changes in the proportion of itemizers, it is useful to use equations (16) and (17) to write an expression relating new values of income, the standard deduction, and the itemization proportion (denoted by primes) to the observed values:

$$(18) \qquad \frac{I'}{1 - I'} = \frac{I}{1 - I} \left( \frac{AGI'/SD'}{AGI/SD} \right)^{1.24}.$$

14. See Feldstein and Lindsey 1981 for simulations using data of this type.
15. See Appendix B for a description of this data set.

Table 3.3    **Actual and Predicted Percentage of Taxpayers Who Itemized in 1980, by Income Class**

|  | Percentage with Itemized Deductions | |
| --- | --- | --- |
| Income | Actual | Predicted |
| $0 under 5,000 | 2.3 | 6.8 |
| $5,000 under 10,000 | 7.3 | 21.4 |
| $10,000 under 15,000 | 18.0 | 33.9 |
| $15,000 under 20,000 | 32.4 | 43.9 |
| $20,000 under 25,000 | 50.8 | 51.7 |
| $25,000 under 30,000 | 65.0 | 57.8 |
| $30,000 under 50,000 | 81.7 | 66.6 |
| $50,000 under 100,000 | 93.3 | 79.9 |
| $100,000 under 200,000 | 96.1 | 90.6 |
| $200,000 under 500,000 | 98.1 | 96.1 |
| $500,000 under 1,000,000 | 98.9 | 98.6 |
| $1,000,000 or more | 99.2 | 99.7 |

*Source:* Actual percentage: U.S. Internal Revenue Service, *Statistics of Income—1980, Individual Income Tax Returns* 1982, p. 41, table 1.3; p. 57, table 2.1. Predicted percentage: see text.

To illustrate the magnitude of the estimated itemization elasticity of 1.24, consider a 10 percent increase in the ratio of income to the maximum standard deduction, caused, for example, by a 10 percent increase in income with no change in the standard deduction. For a class with 40 percent of taxpayers itemizing, this change would imply an increase in the percentage itemizing to 45.5. For a class with 95 percent itemizing already, however, the percentage would increase only to 96.0. In summary, although the logistic relationship between the probability of itemization and the income-standard deduction ratio does not directly model a taxpayer's choice between allowable itemized and standard deductions, by accounting for the relationship between nominal income and the maximum standard deduction it does provide predictions regarding changes in itemization.

### Endogenous Changes in Itemization and Deduction Floors

For the purpose of simulating the effects of most tax changes, a less important cause of changes in taxpayers' itemization status is the treatment of contributions itself. As outlined in chapter 2, the itemization decision is a function of contributions behavior for a relatively small group of taxpayers. For these taxpayers the standard deduction acts as a floor for the deductibility of contributions, and the taxpayer faces a nonconvex budget set. The choice of contribution level, and thus itemization status, depends on the shape of the individual's indifference curves. Similarly, an explicit floor for the deductibility of contributions (e.g., as a percentage of income or an absolute amount) also creates a nonconvex budget set with similar behavioral implications.

In order to simulate giving in the presence of nonconvex budget sets, Feldstein and Lindsey (1981, p. 14) employed an explicit direct utility function in the manner of Hausman (1981) and Reece and Zieschang (1982) to make comparisons among points on the budget line for individuals who might be either above or below the deduction floor. The functional form they chose implies constant price and income elasticities of $\mu$ and $\beta$, respectively:

$$(19) \qquad V_i\,(P,Y) \;=\; -k_i\;\frac{P^{1+\mu}}{1+\mu}\;-\;\frac{Y^{1-\beta}}{1-\beta}$$

Substituting previously estimated price and income elasticities, they obtained a value of $k_i$ for each individual as the value that made observed giving equal the utility-maximizing amount. From this they were able to allow for taxpayers switching itemization status. Their calculations imply that about 6 percent of itemizers would stop itemizing if charitable deductions were eligible for a separate deduction.[16] In the simulations presented in the section 3.4, such endogenous shifts in itemization are not considered. Only shifts due to changes in the income–standard deduction ratio are allowed for.

### 3.3.4 Dynamic Considerations

The effects of tax changes on charitable giving may vary over time. One possible dynamic pattern would result from the existence of lags in people's adjustment to tax changes. If such lags are at work, tax changes would tend to have less immediate impact than after the passage of time. Another possibility is that taxpayers may attempt to time their contributions so that their tax liabilities are minimized. It is well known that estimates obtained in regressions using cross-section data may not be appropriate for simulating changes through time.[17] As applied to the simulation of tax effects on contributions, it is useful to consider simulation models that deal specifically with dynamic effects of tax policy. The first model deals with lags in adjustment, and the second takes into account the possibility of timing gifts.

### Lags in Adjustment

The incomplete-adjustment model discussed in chapter 2 provides an explicit form for distinguishing short-run and long-run effects of tax changes on giving. This model may be written:

$$(20) \qquad\qquad G_t \;=\; G^{*\phi}\,G_{t-1}^{1-\phi},$$

---

16. See Feldstein and Lindsey 1981, pp. 14–16.
17. See, for example, Morgan, Dye, and Hybels 1977, p. 174; Nelson 1977a, p. 1505; or Zellner 1977, pp. 1518, 1520.

$$(21) \qquad\qquad G_{t+1} = G^{*\phi} G_{t}^{1-\phi},$$

$$(22) \qquad\qquad G_{t+k} = G^{*\phi} G_{t+k-1}^{1-\phi},$$

where $\phi$ is a constant coefficient of adjustment and $G^*$ is the simulated, or long-run, value of contributions resulting from a given tax regime.[18] If the long-run level of giving $G^*$ differs from the initial level $G_t$, and $G^*$ does not change, actual giving will tend to approach but not reach long-run giving. The time path for giving in response to a hypothetical tax change is illustrated in table 3.4. The time path of charitable contributions by nonitemizers is simulated for the institution of a full charitable deduction in year 1, assuming initial contributions of $12.1 billion, an average marginal tax rate of 0.2 for nonitemizers, and a price elasticity of -1.2. The long-run level of contributions implied by the constant-elasticity model is $15.8 billion.[19] Based on the adjustment coefficient of 0.37 estimated in Clotfelter (1980b, p. 333), contributions by nonitemizers after one period are calculated to be $13.4 billion ($15.8^{0.37}$ $12.1^{1-0.37}$), an increase of $1.3 billion. The revenue loss from the deduction, approximated as the marginal tax rate (0.2) multiplied by actual giving of $13.4 billion, is $2.7 billion. Given these parameters, the increase in giving due to the deduction would not exceed 90 percent of the long-run increase before the sixth year. In addition, the increase in giving would not exceed the revenue loss before the fifth year, even though the (long-run) price elasticity is greater than one in absolute value. If the parameter estimates are assumed to be valid, this suggests that the full effects of tax policy are unlikely to be felt immediately. This simulation casts little light, however, on the effect of tax rules that are phased in slowly or whose effective date is delayed after passage of legislation. For example, the 1981 Economic Recovery Tax Act, which was signed in August 1981, provided for a deduction for nonitemizers that would become fully available only in 1986.

*Timing Effects*

An itemizing taxpayer who expects to face different marginal tax rates in successive years can reduce his total tax liability by increasing the proportion of gifts he makes in the high-tax year. More generally, there is an incentive for making deductible expenditures in tax years in which the net-of-tax price is least. The potential for timing charitable contributions is especially great because giving tends to be more discretionary than most deductible expenditures. One obvious manifestation of timing behavior in charitable giving is the tendency for a major change in tax rates to be accompanied by an acceleration of giving to take advantage of low prices in the old law or a deceleration if the new law offers lower prices.

---

18. See equation (19) in chapter 2.
19. $G^* = (P_1/P_0)^{-1.2} G_0 = (0.8)^{-1.2} 1.2 = 15.8.$

**Table 3.4**  **Simulated Time Path of Contributions and Revenue Losses, Ten-Year Period Following Enactment**

| Year | Long-Run Giving Level ($G^*$) | Actual Giving ($ billions) | Increase in Giving from Year 0 | Revenue Loss | Increase in Actual Giving as Percentage of Increase in Long-Run Giving (percent) |
|---|---|---|---|---|---|
| 0 | 12.1 | 12.1 | — | — | — |
| 1 | 15.8 | 13.4 | 1.3 | 2.7 | 34 |
| 2 | 15.8 | 14.2 | 2.1 | 2.8 | 57 |
| 3 | 15.8 | 14.8 | 2.7 | 3.0 | 72 |
| 4 | 15.8 | 15.1 | 3.0 | 3.0 | 82 |
| 5 | 15.8 | 15.4 | 3.3 | 3.1 | 89 |
| 6 | 15.8 | 15.5 | 3.4 | 3.1 | 93 |
| 7 | 15.8 | 15.6 | 3.5 | 3.1 | 96 |
| 8 | 15.8 | 15.7 | 3.6 | 3.1 | 97 |
| 9 | 15.8 | 15.7 | 3.6 | 3.1 | 98 |
| 10 | 15.8 | 15.8 | 3.7 | 3.2 | 99 |

*Note:* Assumptions: (1) Long-run price elasticity is $-1.2$. (2) Where $G_t$ and $G^*$ are actual and long-run giving levels in year $t$, $\phi$ is a coefficient of adjustment equal to .37, $G^* = (0.8)^{-1.2}(12.1)$, $G_t = (G^*)^{\phi}(G_{t-1})^{1-\phi}$.

Timing behavior might also be important if a floor were placed under deductible contributions, giving taxpayers the incentive to "bunch" their gifts over time. For example, consider a $200 deduction floor. A taxpayer who faces a 25 percent marginal tax rate and who plans to give $1000 over two years would reduce his taxes by $200 if he made all his gifts in one year, compared to a saving of only $150 if he gave equal amounts each year. Feldstein and Lindsey (1981) analyze bunching behavior in a simulation of various deduction floors. Their basic model assumes that bunching occurs only within a two-year time horizon and that bunching is an all-or-nothing decision. The probability of bunching (PROB) is taken to be a function of the after-tax cost of giving if there is no bunching ($CG$) and the cost if there is bunching ($BCG$):

(23) $$\text{PROB} = 1 - (BCG/CG)^\rho,$$

where $\rho$ is a positive constant. Using the example given above, in which $CG = \$850$ and $BCG = \$800$, a value of 0.5 for $\rho$ would imply a bunching probability of 0.03 while $\rho = 10$ implies a probability of 0.45. Because there exist no empirical studies of bunching for the case of contributions, Feldstein and Lindsey present results based on a range of values for $\rho$. Table 3.5 presents their simulations of extending deductibility for contributions to nonitemizers in 1977. Whereas they project an increase in giving of $4.5 billion and a revenue loss of $4.1 billion with no floor, the addition of floors reduces both changes.[20] The effect of bunching is to lessen the changes, but, as Feldstein and Lindsey note, wide variation in the bunching assumption makes little difference.[21]

### 3.3.5  Contributions by Nonitemizers

Because of the difficulty of obtaining data on contributions by nonitemizers, some researchers have employed a modification of the basic simulation model of giving. Feldstein and Lindsey (1981, p. 27) estimated the contributions made by a nonitemizing taxpayer by selecting an itemizing taxpayer with similar demographic characteristics and calculating the predicted quantity, taking into account only the difference in price and income between the taxpayers:

(24) $$G_n = G_i (P_n/P_i)^a (Y_n/Y_i)^b$$

$$= G_i P_i^{-a}(Y_n/Y_i)^b,$$

where $n$ refers to the nonitemizer and $i$ to the itemizer. This approach is based on the assumption that the difference in contributions between

---

20. The principal reason why Feldstein and Lindsey's estimated $4.5 billion increase exceeds the $3.7 billion increase calculated for table 3.2 is their use of a price elasticity of -1.3.

21. A variant of the complete bunching model considered by Feldstein and Lindsey assumed that only a portion of gifts would be subject to bunching. The model and results are similar to those of the complete bunching model.

**Table 3.5    Feldstein-Lindsey Simulations of Changes in Contributions by Current Nonitemizers, 1977 (amounts in billions of dollars)**

| | Full Deductibility | | $300 Floor | | 3 Percent of AGI Floor | |
| | Changes in | | Changes in | | Changes in | |
| | Giving | Taxes | Giving | Taxes | Giving | Taxes |
|---|---|---|---|---|---|---|
| No bunching | + 4.506 | − 4.101 | + 3.608 | − 2.430 | + 3.039 | − 1.944 |
| Bunching[a] | | | | | | |
| $\rho = 0.5$ | —[b] | — | + 3.617 | − 2.442 | + 3.051 | − 1.955 ** |
| $\rho = 2.0$ | —[b] | — | + 3.645 | − 2.447 | + 3.089 | − 1.988 ** |
| $\rho = 10.0$ | —[b] | — | + 3.763 | − 2.605 | + 3.246 | − 2.112 ** |
| $\rho = \infty$ | —[b] | — | + 4.079 | − 2.818 | + 3.686 | − 2.347 ** |

*Source:* Feldstein and Lindsey 1981, p. 36, table 4.

[a]See text for explanation of bunching model.

[b]Bunching not relevant to full deduction.

itemizers and nonitemizers can be attributed entirely to differences in price and income. Because of the strength of this assumption and the availability of survey data on contributions by nonitemizers, estimates of contributions by nonitemizers in the present study are based directly on such survey information.

### 3.3.6   Gifts by Donee Type

Because of its great practical significance, it is quite useful to reflect in simulations the distribution of giving by type of organization. As discussed in chapter 2, however, there is considerably less information regarding the distribution of gifts than in giving in general. The studies attempting to measure separate price and income effects by type of donee typically have been subject to a large degree of uncertainty. An alternative approach taken by Feldstein and Taylor (1976, p. 1217n) and Clotfelter and Salomon (1982), is to simulate tax effects on total giving and then to allocate this total giving to various donee groups using proportions that vary by income level. This approach carries the implicit assumption that the price elasticity does not vary at any income level for gifts to different donee classes. In addition, the use of old distributions, such as those based on 1962 tax returns, is obviously flawed to the extent that the real distribution has changed over time. Despite these drawbacks, the simulations presented in the next section use past distributions modified for changes in the price level in order to suggest how tax policy may affect gifts to different types of nonprofit organizations.

### 3.3.7   Simulation and the Validity of Econometric Models of Giving

Finally, it is useful to note a more general methodological issue that relates to simulation using any estimated econometric model, including those estimated for charitable giving. The econometric model underlying a simulation exercise inevitably contains implicit maintained hypotheses that may limit the validity of the simulation results. The choices of which variables to include and how to define them affect the validity of the simulations in the same way they affect the validity of the estimates. For example, the incorporation of the effects of itemization and the marginal tax rate into a single price variable embodies the hypothesis that there is no itemization effect apart from the price effect, an issue discussed in chapter 2. Similarly, the inclusion of net income as a variable supposes that an increase of $100 in gross income will have the same effect as a $100 decrease in taxes. In much the same way, it is typically assumed that labor supply and thus earnings are independent of the tax provisions being examined. To the extent that such assumptions are incorrect, simulations based on them will also be flawed.

Some possible influences on giving are excluded from estimating models because little or no information or variation has been observed. For example, the basic model of charitable giving allows no role for charitable organizations' financial condition or solicitation activity. Charities are implicitly assumed to be passive recipients of contributions. As implied by Zellner (1977, p. 1518), as well as some of the discussion of charitable giving following the Reagan cuts in federal aid, individuals may respond to the financial plight of charities by increasing their contributions compared to what they would have given otherwise. According to Butler (1981, p. 9), "If the flexible patterns of the past are any guide, the structure of giving will shift in favor of these organizations hurt by the cuts and seen by the public as socially valuable." Charities themselves may respond to hard times by stepping up solicitation efforts.

It is therefore necessary to understand simulation results as being a ceteris paribus exercise in predicting outcomes in response to a hypothetical policy. They can reflect the effects of changes only in variables included in the model; other influences have to be assumed to be constant. Because estimated models have been unable to reflect some possible "systems responses," the resulting simulations obviously cannot take such effects into account. The simulations are thus predictions about the outcomes of certain policy changes, other things equal.

## 3.4    Simulations of Individual Giving for 1983

In order to provide current projections of charitable contributions under different tax regimes, a simulation model using aggregate data is presented. This section describes the data and special features of the simulation program and then presents a variety of simulations for 1983.

### 3.4.1    Basic Data

The primary source of data for this simulation exercise is the 1980 *Statistics of Income*, which gives aggregate tax return information by income class. While disaggregated data have a number of important advantages over aggregate data in estimation of charitable giving models, there are advantages to aggregate data in simulation. The identification of separate price and income effects is a central concern in estimation, and disaggregated data are usually better able to distinguish these effects by producing more precise parameter estimates. For most simulations of charitable giving, however, the effects of tax changes are proportional in nature. The result is that simulations of major policy changes using both kinds of data sets produce quite similar results. Only for behavior involving discontinuities such as "bunching" is disaggregated behavior clearly superior. As noted above, changes in itemization status could be simulated easily using an appropriate disaggregated data set, but existing data sets do not provide adequate information on potential itemized deductions by nonitemizers. Finally, the use of aggregate tax return data for the current study provided the most recent available data on income, taxes, and contributions as well as comparable data that could be analyzed over time.

In order to reflect important differences among taxpayers, four types of taxpaying units are defined for each income class given in the *Statistics of Income*: single itemizers, single nonitemizers, joint itemizers, and joint nonitemizers. The comparatively few returns that were not single or joint were allocated between one of these two tax-status groups.[22] Exemptions other than for dependents were allocated to single and joint returns in each class according to the distribution of adult taxpayers.[23] Dependent exemptions were allocated so that the number of dependents per return in joint households would be a constant multiple of that in single households.[24]

In order to obtain appropriate 1983 levels of variables, income, deduction, and tax-credit data were assumed to grow at the predicted rate of per capita national income. The number of taxpayers was assumed to grow at the average rate of population growth between 1980 and 1983.[25] In order to estimate the number of taxpayers at each income level who itemized their deductions, the 1980 proportions for each income class were adjusted to take into account the growth in nominal income in relation to the (stationary) zero-bracket amount. For this purpose, equation (8) was used with an itemization elasticity of 1.24.

The basic *Statistics of Income* data for 1980 provides information on charitable contributions by itemizers and income for all taxpayers as well as all information needed to calculate taxes and tax rates. Data on contributions by nonitemizers were based on modified tabulations from the National Study of Philanthropy, adjusted so as to correspond to the 1980 income brackets used for all other data.[26] The percentage distribution of

22. In 1980 42 percent of taxpayers filed single returns and 48 percent filed jointly, leaving only 10 percent who fell into other tax-status groups.

23. This includes the blind, over-65, and taxpayer exemptions. Where $J$ and $NJ$ are joint and nonjoint returns in an income class, the proportion of adult exemptions assigned to joint returns in that class was $(2J/(2J + NJ))$.

24. Joint returns in 1980 had an average of 1.34 dependent exemptions while single returns had 0.33, for a ratio of 4.1 (U.S. Internal Revenue Service, *Statistics of Income—1980, Individual Returns* 1982, p. 70 table 2.4). Where $DJ$ and $DNJ$ are dependents in joint and nonjoint returns, the assumption that the ratio of dependents per return in joint households is 4.1 that in single households can be written: $(DJ/J)/(DNJ/NJ) = 4.1$. This implies $DJ = D/((NJ/4.1J) + 1)$, where $D$ is the total number of dependents in the class.

25. Nominal GNP was $2633 billion in 1980 and $3262 billion in 1983 (U.S. Council of Economic Advisers 1983, p. 163; U.S. Office of Management and Budget 1983, pp. 2–9), for a ratio of 1.293. Population grew at an expontential rate of 1.064 percent annually between 1978 and 1981; $P(t) = P(0) \exp(gt)$, where $g = 0.01064$. For 1980–83, this implies $P(1983)/P(1980) = 1.032$. Thus, per capita GNP growth was $1.239/1.032 = 1.201$.

26. See Morgan, Dye, and Hybels 1977, p. 193. Because of the small number of nonitemizers in higher income classes, averages in the top four income classes were smoothed. Average giving for nonitemizers by income class in 1973 dollars was assumed to be: under $4000: $69; $4000 under 8000: $89; $8000 under 10,000: $117; $10,000 under 15,000: $201; $15,000 under 20,000: $329; $20,000 under 50,000: $354; $50,000 under 200,000: $2003; $200,000 and over $6946. These figures were then inflated and prorated to correspond to 1980 income classes.

gifts to various kinds of donee organizations by income class is based on the 1962 *Statistics of Income* data used in previous studies. Again, the data were interpolated so as to yield the appropriate 1980 income classes.

### 3.4.2 Calculation of Taxes and Contributions

With four taxpayer types in each of twelve income classes, each simulation consists of separate calculations for forty-eight representative households, each representing a different number of actual taxpayers. In order to calculate taxes and tax rates, the actual or hypothetical tax law was applied to data on average income, exemptions, and deductions for each representative household. Tax liability calculated in this manner for 1980 using actual values of contributions yielded an estimate of total revenue of \$250.2 billion, compared to actual revenues of \$249.1 billion. For the purpose of simulating taxes or standard price and income effects on charitable giving, therefore, an aggregated model appears to perform quite adequately. Revenues calculated under the first-dollar assumption of zero contributions were \$260.2 billion in 1980. Calculated tax revenues under this assumption using the 1983 law were \$279.6 billion. In order to make comparisons among constant revenue alternatives, tax rates under other hypothetical tax laws were adjusted proportionally so as to yield that same revenue for 1983. In all cases, adjustments were made so that tax credits and tax-credit rates were unaffected. The adjustment process thus affects tax liabilities before credits as well as marginal tax rates.

Because it was the latest available year with data for contributions by itemizers, 1980 was used as the base year for simulating changes in contributions. The various price and income values implied by hypothetical tax policies were compared to the actual 1980 values of price and income according to the basic simulation expression:

$$(25) \qquad G_{83} = G_{80} (P_{83}/P_{80})^a (Y_{83}/Y_{80})^b,$$

where both income measures and 1980 giving are expressed in 1983 dollars.

One special feature of the 1980 tax law that makes an important difference in calculation of $P_{80}$ is the "maximum tax on earned income" that applied in that year. This feature had the effect of reducing the marginal tax rate applicable to deductions for most taxpayers in tax brackets over 50 percent. Thus the price difference brought about by the reduction in maximum rates from 70 to 50 percent in 1981 was not as great as it would first appear.

In order to calculate the effective marginal tax rate under the maximum tax, it is necessary to consider the provision's allocation of taxable income into "earned" and "unearned" portions. Under the maximum tax, the latter was "stacked" on top of the former so as to be taxed at the same rates that would have applied in the absence of this provision. Where $\epsilon$ is the proportion of adjusted gross income accounted for by earned income (salaries plus certain business income), $TI_{50}$ is the maximum taxable income subject to the 50 percent tax rate, $TI$ is total taxable income, and TAX ( ) is the income-tax-schedule function, the tax liability under the maximum tax was

(26)      $\text{TAX}(TI_{50}) + .50\,(\epsilon TI\text{-}TI_{50}) + [\text{TAX}(TI) - \text{TAX}(\epsilon TI)].$

Differentiating (26) with respect to charitable contributions shows that the decrease in taxes due to an additional dollar of deductions—that is, the effective marginal tax rate—is:

(27)                    $m - (m_e - .50)\epsilon,$

where $m$ is the marginal tax rate on total taxable income and $m_e$ is the marginal tax rate on earned taxable income. This rate was calculated for applicable high-income taxpayers using the average proportion of earned income for the class.[27]

The price of giving is defined as a weighted average of the price of making cash gifts and the estimated price of giving appreciated assets:

(28)      $P_{ij} = \phi_i(1 - m_{ij}) + (1 - \phi_i)(1 - m_{ij} - 0.5\,mc_{ij}),$

where $\phi_i$ is the proportion of contributions made in the form of cash by the income class, $m_{ij}$ and $mc_{ij}$ are the marginal tax rates on ordinary and capital gains income, respectively, and $0.5$ represents the expected present value of the realized gains per dollar of asset value.[28]

Two alternative sets of estimated parameters are used in the simulations. The first, based on the constant-elasticity model estimated for the 1975 tax file, uses a constant-price elasticity of -1.27 and an income elasticity of 0.78. The second estimated model is the translog variable-elasticity form, which allows both the price and income elasticities to vary by income level. Calculated at the means of rather broad income classes, as shown in table 2.16, the price elasticity varies from -0.42 to -1.51 while the income elasticity varies from 0.55 to 0.91. The variation in incomes in the 1980 data base used in the current chapter is greater, resulting in a positive implied price elasticity at the very lowest income level. In the simulations based on this model, therefore, the price elasticity is constrained to have a maximum value of zero.

### 3.4.3   Simulation Results

Before presenting a comparison of alternative proposals, it is useful to begin by examining the base years used for comparison. Table 3.6 pre-

27. Using the maximum rates allowed by the provision, the model calculated earned income as wages plus 30 percent of the sum of income from small businesses. See Lindsey 1981 for a thorough treatment of the effect of this provision on tax rates.

28. For further discussion of the definition of the price of contributing appreciated assets, see chapter 2, especially equation (7).

Table 3.6        Comparison of Itemization Rate, Price of Giving and Contributions
                 between 1980 and 1983

|  | 1980 Actual | 1983 Estimated | |
|---|---|---|---|
| Percentage itemizing | 31.0 | 34.0 | |
| Price of giving | | | |
| Itemizers | 0.69 | 0.74 | |
| Nonitemizers | 1.00 | 1.00 | |
| Total | 0.90 | 0.91 | |
|  | | Constant Elasticities | Variable Elasticities |
| Contributions ($ billions, 1983 dollars) | | | |
| Total | 47.2 [a] | 45.1 | 45.2 |
| Top 5 income classes[b] | 11.2 | 9.2 | 8.6 |

[a]$38.7 billion in 1980 dollars.
[b]Over $50,000 in 1980.

sents aggregate data on itemization, the price of giving, and contributions for 1980 and the corresponding simulated values for 1983. Three major changes occurred between these years to influence contributions: the proportion of taxpayers who itemized deductions went up, the top marginal tax rates were substantially cut, and real incomes fell. One major result was that the average price faced by itemizers increased from 0.69 to 0.74—reflecting sharp increases at upper incomes—and the overall average price rose from 0.90 to 0.91. Based on the projections of incomes and prices, total contributions measured in 1983 dollars are estimated using constant elasticities to fall from $47.2 billion in 1980 to $45.1 billion in 1983, a decline of 4 percent. The decline is slightly greater using the variable-elasticity model. Due to the steep price increases at upper income levels, contributions made by taxpayers in the top five income classes (over $50,000 in 1980) are projected to decrease by a substantially greater degree. Using the constant-elasticity model, the estimated decrease in giving by this group was 18 percent, to $9.2 billion; the decrease was 23 percent, to $8.6 billion, using variable elasticities. The simulation of changes in giving over time, including changes in the 1980–83 period, is discussed in more detail in the following section. The simulations discussed in the remainder of this section use 1983 values—corresponding to two sets of elasticity assumptions—as a basis for comparison among alternative tax rules.

*Aggregate Giving*

Table 3.7 presents the aggregate simulation results for 1983. For the 1983 law and each of nine proposed variants, the table gives estimated aggregate contributions under the alternative assumptions regarding price and income elasticities. The table also shows the adjustment factor necessary to obtain revenues equal to the 1983 tax law as well as the average price of giving faced by itemizers and nonitemizers under each proposal. As noted above, the average price of giving in 1983 was 0.74 for itemizers. Nonitemizers could deduct 25 percent of gifts up to $100, but the price of contributions above this level was 1.0. Since average contributions by nonitemizers would have exceeded $100 without the deduction even in the lowest income class, this limited deduction had very little effect at the margin. Thus the price for nonitemizers was set at 1.0.

Three proposals involve possible extensions of the basic charitable deduction. The most generous of these is a 150 percent multiple deduction. Because it would entail a significant drop in taxable incomes, it would require a 7 percent across-the-board increase in tax rates in order to raise revenue equal to the 1983 law. The estimated increase in giving, to $63.8 billion under the constant-elasticity assumption, indicates the strength of this price incentive, especially at upper incomes. A more likely multiple-deduction scheme would be one that extends the added incentive primarily to low- and middle-income taxpayers. The graduated multiple deduction shown in table 3.7, recommended by the Commission on Private Philanthropy and Public Needs, would allow a 200 percent deduction for those with incomes under $15,000 and a 150 percent deduction for those with incomes between $15,000 and $30,000. If applied in 1983 this deduction rule would cause an increase in contributions of $1.8 billion or $0.9 billion, depending on the elasticity assumption. Because the constant-elasticity model implies a larger price responsiveness for lower-income taxpayers, that model produces bigger changes for policies with their primary impact at lower levels. The third possible expansion of the deduction is its extension to nonitemizers, without limit, as provided in the 1981 tax act for 1986. This change reduces the average price of giving faced by nonitemizers from 1.0 to 0.86. The overall increase in giving is $5.7 billion or $3.4 billion, depending on the elasticity assumption used. In order to maintain the level of revenues, tax rates would have to be increased by about 1 percent under the graduated deduction and about 2 percent under the extension to nonitemizers.

Proposals to limit the charitable deduction range from the elimination of the special treatment of gifts of appreciated assets to the outright elimination of the deduction. The constructive realization of capital gains on donated assets would cause a small increase in the price of giving for itemizers (0.739 to 0.744) and a decline in total giving of less than $1 billion. Eliminating the deduction altogether would have a sizable impact on total giving, however. Under the constant-elasticity assumption, contributions would fall by $11.8 billion, from $45.1 to $33.3 billion. This 26 percent drop is the same percentage predicted by Feldstein and Taylor (1976) and

**Table 3.7    Simulation Totals for 1983: Revenue, Price of Giving, Contributions**

| Tax Law or Proposal | Revenue Adjustment | Average Price of Giving[a] | | Contributions (billions) | |
|---|---|---|---|---|---|
| | | Itemizers | Nonitemizers | Constant Elasticities | Variable Elasticities |
| 1983 law | — | 0.74 | 1.00 | $45.1 | $45.2 |
| *Expansion of the charitable deduction* | | | | | |
| 150 percent multiple deduction | 1.07 | 0.62 | 1.00 | 63.8 | 66.8 |
| Graduated multiple deduction | 1.01 | 0.69 | 1.00 | 46.9 | 46.1 |
| Extension to nonitemizers | 1.02 | 0.74 | 0.86 | 50.8 | 48.6 |
| *Limitation of the charitable deduction* | | | | | |
| Constructive realization on gifts of appreciated assets | 1.00 | 0.74 | 1.00 | 44.3 | 44.5 |
| Elimination of deduction | 0.97 | 1.00 | 1.00 | 33.3 | 36.1 |
| *Substitution of tax credit for deduction* | | | | | |
| 20 percent | 1.00 | 0.81 | 0.86 | 43.3 | 42.2 |
| 30 percent | 1.02 | 0.72 | 0.79 | 50.4 | 46.4 |
| *Flat-rate tax* | | | | | |
| On taxable income (20.7%)[c] | — | 0.80 | 1.00 | 39.8 | 40.7 |
| On adjusted gross income plus excluded long-term gains (13.6%)[c] | — | 1.00[b] | 1.00 | 33.0 | 36.0 |

[a]Weighted by number of returns.

[b]There is no distinction between itemizers and nonitemizers under this proposal.

[c]Tax rates shown in parentheses are after revenue adjustment. Original tax rates were 19.5 and 11.8 percent for the last two simulations. Calculated revenue adjustment factors were 1.06 and 1.15.

Feldstein and Clotfelter (1976) using very similar models but disaggregated data. Using variable elasticities, however, the decrease is only $9.1 billion, or about 20 percent. While both declines are certainly large, the difference between these two simulations illustrates the importance of the underlying econometric model.

The results of substituting a general tax credit for the present deduction were simulated using tax-credit rates of 20 and 30 percent. Either change, of course, would reduce the price faced by nonitemizers paying some tax; unless the credit was refundable, the price for nontaxable returns would be one. The prices faced by an itemizer might increase or decrease, depending on his marginal tax rate. Under the 20 percent credit, contributions would fall about 4 percent to $43.3 billion using constant elasticities and 7 percent to $42.2 billion using variable elasticities. Giving under the 30 percent credit would rise, however, by 12 or 3 percent, depending on the model used. The relatively large difference between the two basic models for the tax credits illustrates the importance of the variation in assumed price responsiveness among income classes. The constant-elasticity model—based on an estimate from a sample heavily weighted with high-income taxpayers—implies considerable price responsiveness among low-income nonitemizers. The variable elasticity form, on the other hand, implies a much smaller price response at the lower end. The tax credit highlights this difference because of its effect on the price faced by low-income taxpayers.

The final two simulations shown are for more general tax changes, both in the direction of a "flat-rate" tax. The base for the first is taxable income as defined in 1983. Because this base excludes exemptions ($1000 each) and the zero-bracket amount, this tax would be progressive at lower income levels and nearly proportional at upper income levels. The second tax uses a much broader income base, adjusted gross income plus the excluded portion of long-term capital gains; it would be much closer to a truly proportional levy than the first variant. The flat-rate tax on taxable income would lower the price for those itemizers with marginal tax rates formerly below the new rate (about 21 percent) and would raise the price for taxpayers whose marginal tax rates were reduced.[29] The net effect in 1983 would be to raise the average price faced by itemizers from 0.74 to 0.80. Total contributions would fall to $39.8 billion, using the constant-elasticity assumption. The simulated effect on contributions would be much more extreme if gross income were the tax base, because contributions would lose their deductibility altogether. In this case, total contributions are projected to fall to $33.0 billion or $36.0 billion, depending on the parameter assumption.

---

29. The original rate multiplied by the adjustment rate was $(.195)(1.06) = .207$.

For each of the simulated totals for giving shown in table 3.7, there is an associated prediction error. Table 3.8 gives the 95 percent confidence intervals corresponding to predictions for three tax regimes. Where $s_p^2$ is the prediction error, defined in equation (6) and calculated using the variance-covariance matrix of the estimates underlying the simulations, the 95 percent confidence interval is 1.96 $\sqrt{s_p}$ above and below the point estimate calculated for each representative taxpayer. Since the equations were estimated in logarithmic form, the intervals are slightly asymmetric when converted to dollars. For example, the prediction interval corresponding to the estimate for the elimination of the deduction, based on constant elasticities, is $32.2 billion to $34.5 billion, implying a range about 7 percent the size of the point estimate. The interval corresponding to the variable-elasticity formulation is relatively larger—13 percent of the point estimate. Owing to the smaller changes in prices and incomes implied by the 20 percent tax credit and the graduated multiple deduction, the prediction intervals for these proposals tend to be smaller. Using the constant-elasticity form, the 95 percent confidence interval for the 20 percent tax credit is $41.9 to $44.6 billion, or 6 percent of the point estimate. The interval for the graduated multiple deduction is 4 percent of its point estimate. For comparison, the prediction intervals for the 1983 law are given also. These intervals are the smallest of all because of the similarity of the 1983 tax schedule to that of the base year, 1980.

**Table 3.8**        **Prediction Intervals at 95 Percent Level for Selected Simulations**

|  | Total Contributions (billions) | | | Interval as Percentage of Point Estimate |
|---|---|---|---|---|
|  | Point Estimate | Lower Bound | Upper Bound |  |
| *Elimination of deduction* | | | | |
| Constant elasticities | 33.3 | 32.2 | 34.5 | 6.9 |
| Variable elasticities | 36.1 | 33.9 | 38.6 | 13.0 |
| *20 percent tax credit* | | | | |
| Constant elasticities | 43.3 | 41.9 | 44.6 | 6.2 |
| Variable elasticities | 42.2 | 39.9 | 44.6 | 11.1 |
| *Graduated multiple deduction* | | | | |
| Constant elasticities | 46.9 | 45.9 | 47.9 | 4.3 |
| Variable elasticities | 46.1 | 44.7 | 47.5 | 6.1 |
| *1983 law* | | | | |
| Constant elasticities | 45.1 | 44.2 | 46.0 | 4.0 |
| Variable elasticities | 45.2 | 44.1 | 46.4 | 5.1 |

*Distributional Effects*

The various proposals would influence contributions to different degrees throughout the distribution of income. In order to illustrate the potential variation in distributional impact, table 3.9 shows the changes in net income and giving by income class resulting from three proposals. The simulations shown assume constant income and price elasticities. The elimination of the deduction—with the accompanying overall rate reduction—would cause some redistribution of income away from high-income taxpayers. The contributions of all itemizers who pay tax would fall, with those in higher tax brackets having the largest reductions. So great is the implied increase in price at the upper end that contributions for taxpayers making more than about $60,000 would fall by over 50 percent in the long run. There is a similar, but less dramatic, redistribution in giving projected under a flat-rate tax on taxable income. Although this tax would substantially redistribute income from lower- to upper-income taxpayers, the price increases at the top would more than offset these income gains, resulting in decreases of over 35 percent in contributions for taxpayers in the top four brackets. These results, of course, are dependent upon the specific values used for price and income elasticities. A sufficiently large income effect combined with a smaller price effect could imply increases, rather than decreases, in contributions at the highest income levels.

The third policy simulated in table 3.9 is a graduated multiple deduction, allowing itemizers with incomes below $15,000 to deduct twice the amount of their contributions and those with incomes between $15,000 and $30,000 to deduct 150 percent. Of course there is little effect on taxpayers above $30,000, except for the small impact of the increased tax rates made necessary by the change. Increases in contributions for taxpayers making between $6000 and $30,000 are quite large, however. These simulations show that the distributional impact of tax policies may vary markedly. Because donors at different income levels differ in their giving patterns, such distributional effects are central in assessing the effect of tax changes on charitable support for different kinds of organizations within the nonprofit sector.

### 3.4.4   Contributions by Type of Donee

It is possible to combine the aggregate and distributional impact of tax changes to estimate the effect on contributions by type of organization. As discussed above, the patterns of giving to various types of organizations vary significantly by income level. In order to reflect such giving patterns, the percentage distribution of gifts observed in the National Study of Philanthropy, in real terms, was applied to the various simulated outcomes for 1983. Table 3.10 gives the estimated percentage change in total contributions to each donee group based on this distribution. Provisions

Table 3.9 Distributional Effects of Tax Changes: Illustrations for Three Tax Proposals (percentage change compared to 1983 law)

| Income (thousands) | Elimination of Deduction | | Flat Rate on Taxable Income | | Graduated Multiple Deduction | |
|---|---|---|---|---|---|---|
| | Income | Giving | Income | Giving | Income | Giving |
| $0 under 6.1 | 0 | 0 | 0 | 0 | 0 | 0 |
| $6.1 under 12.2 | +0.2 | -3.0 | -3.8 | -0.5 | 0 | +3.0 |
| $12.2 under 18.3 | +0.2 | -9.2 | -3.8 | -0.2 | +0.2 | +13.4 |
| $18.3 under 24.3 | +0.2 | -13.0 | -3.2 | -2.1 | +0.1 | +7.9 |
| $24.3 under 30.4 | +0.1 | -17.5 | -2.7 | -2.7 | +0.2 | +14.3 |
| $30.4 under 36.5 | 0 | -24.3 | -1.6 | -9.0 | -0.1 | -0.1 |
| $36.5 under 60.9 | -0.1 | -33.6 | +0.2 | -14.3 | -0.1 | -0.1 |
| $60.9 under 121.7 | -0.2 | -51.0 | +5.7 | -31.8 | -0.1 | -0.1 |
| $121.7 under 243.4 | -0.1 | -59.5 | +13.1 | -38.0 | -0.2 | -0.2 |
| $243.4 under 608.5 | -0.3 | -62.8 | +17.7 | -38.2 | -0.2 | -0.3 |
| $608.5 under 1217 | -1.0 | -64.5 | +19.7 | -38.3 | -0.2 | -0.3 |
| $1217 or more | -1.5 | -65.4 | +20.9 | -38.2 | -0.2 | -0.3 |
| TOTAL | 0 | -26.1 | 0 | -11.8 | 0 | +3.9 |

Note: Simulations use constant-price elasticity of −1.27 and income elasticity of 0.78.

**Table 3.10   Simulated Long-Run Changes in Giving by Type of Organization, as Percentage of 1983 Levels**

| Percentage Difference from 1983 Law | Total | Religious | Educational | | Combined Appeals | Medical | Cultural | Other |
|---|---|---|---|---|---|---|---|---|
| | | | Higher | Other | | | | |
| 150 percent deduction | +42 | +23 | +154 | +117 | +71 | +73 | +169 | +74 |
| Graduated multiple deduction | +4 | +5 | +1 | 0 | +2 | +3 | 0 | +2 |
| Extension to nonitemizers | +13 | +14 | +8 | +8 | +11 | +11 | +7 | +11 |
| Constructive realization on gifts of appreciated assets | -2 | -1 | -7 | -6 | -3 | -3 | -8 | -3 |
| Elimination of deduction | -26 | -21 | -50 | -52 | -36 | -34 | -58 | -37 |
| 20 percent tax credit | -4 | +2 | -35 | -37 | -16 | -14 | -44 | -18 |
| 30 percent tax credit | +12 | +19 | -24 | -25 | -1 | 0 | -34 | -4 |
| Flat tax on taxable income | -12 | -8 | -30 | -31 | -19 | -18 | -36 | -19 |
| Flat tax on adjusted gross income plus excluded long-term gains | -27 | -23 | -46 | -47 | -34 | -33 | -51 | -35 |

*Note:* Simulations use constant-price elasticity of -1.27 and income elasticity of 0.78.

that affect giving at lower incomes tend to have their major effect on support for religious groups; provisions with large impacts on giving by those at upper incomes show up primarily in support for educational and cultural institutions. For example, the graduated multiple deduction—shown in table 3.9 to produce large increases in giving at incomes below $30,000—increases religious giving by 5 percent, more than the change in any other category. In contrast, eliminating the deduction has its major impact at the top of the income scale. Consequently, giving to higher education is predicted to fall by 50 percent in the long run. These estimates show that the distributional character of tax changes are important, although aggregate effects on giving predominate. A rising tide of giving would tend to lift all boats, though by different amounts.

Needless to say, the assumptions concerning the distributional patterns of giving lie at the heart of such simulations. It is useful, therefore, to compare these results with a similar set using an alternative distribution—that based on the tabulation of contributions made on 1962 tax returns. As shown in table 3.2, these distributions are based on different methods and types of data and yield somewhat different conclusions. Table 3.11 summarizes their implications for the distribution of gifts in 1983 as well as the effects of three tax changes. The allocation of the $45 billion total of giving for 1983 based on the National Study of Philanthropy data shows quite a high estimate of religious giving, but its estimates for giving to educational institutions are much more in line with other estimates of receipts by nonprofit organizations. Considering the separate origins and dates of the two distributions, these distributions are remarkably comparable.[30] In any case, the percentage changes for comparable categories for the two distributions are quite close, which suggests that the general thrust of results like those in table 3.10 will tend to hold up under different specific distributional assumptions.

### 3.5 Simulations of Changes in Giving over Time

One useful application of the simulation techniques discussed in this chapter is to assess the effects on giving of inflation and tax changes over time. Any change that affects marginal tax rates, real net income, or the number of taxpayers who itemize their deductions will tend to affect giving behavior. Thus, contributions may be influenced by legislated revisions in the tax schedule or by inflationary bracket creep. In fact, the ef-

---

30. The estimates of religious giving differ by $5.7 billion. The lower estimate of $28.4 billion is close to the *Giving U.S.A.* estimate of religious giving for the previous year ($28.1 billion) and probably would be nearer the 1983 figure. The education figure based on the 1962 distribution ($1.6 billion) may be compared to the estimate of giving by individuals to higher education in 1981–82 ($2.3 billion). The latter includes a good portion of bequests, but does not include other education (*Giving U.S.A.* 1983, pp. 38, 54).

**Table 3.11    Estimates of Giving Implied by Two Distributions of Giving by Type of Organization**

| | Level of Contributions, 1983 ($billions) | Percentage Change in Contributions from 1983 due to: | | |
|---|---|---|---|---|
| | | Extension of Deduction to Nonitemizers | 20 Percent Tax Credit | Flat tax on Taxable Income |
| *Distribution Based on National Study of Philanthropy* | | | | |
| Religious | $32.89 | +14 | +2 | −8 |
| Educational | | | | |
|   Higher | 1.98 | +8 | −35 | −30 |
|   Other | 0.66 | +8 | −37 | −31 |
| Combined appeals | 2.56 | +11 | −16 | −19 |
| Medical | 2.52 | +11 | −14 | −18 |
| Cultural | 0.60 | +7 | −44 | −36 |
| Other | 3.69 | +11 | −18 | −19 |
| TOTAL | 45.09 | +12 | −4 | −12 |
| *Distribution Based on Tabulation of 1962 Tax Returns* | | | | |
| Religious | 27.89 | +13 | +1 | −9 |
| Other charitable | 6.47 | +13 | −6 | −13 |
| Educational | 1.57 | +9 | −30 | −27 |
| Hospitals | 0.64 | +9 | −30 | −27 |
| Other organizations | 8.47 | +12 | −11 | −16 |
| TOTAL | 45.09 | +13 | −4 | −12 |

fects of such changes may be far more important than the potential impact of provisions specifically directed towards contributions. This section presents two applications of simulation techniques that highlight the effects of inflation and general tax changes. The first is a retrospective look at the period 1948 to 1980 focused on the effect of inflation and changes in the standard deduction on the proportion of taxpayers who itemize their deductions. The second uses the behavioral relationships discussed in this chapter with forecasts of inflation and income growth to predict future giving.

### 3.5.1  Inflation, the Standard Deduction, and Itemization, 1948–80

Since the first debates in Congress over its introduction in the 1940s, the standard deduction has been recognized as a potential threat to charitable contributions. Taxpayers who elect it receive no incremental tax reduction with increases in giving, making the net price of giving equal to one.[31] Concern over the effect of the standard deduction has reemerged in recent discussions of tax policy toward charitable giving. Spokesmen for the nonprofit sector have argued that the extensions of the standard deduction after 1970 and the conversion to a flat, zero-bracket amount in 1978 have significantly reduced the number of itemizers, thus discouraging charitable giving.[32] From 1970 to 1980 the maximum standard deduction for married couples was increased from $1000 to $3400, an increase of 74 percent after inflation. Over the same period the proportion of taxpayers who itemized fell from 48 to 31 percent.[33] What has been the effect of such changes on giving?

In order to assess the importance of changes in the standard deduction, actual rates of itemization and giving are compared to estimates of the corresponding rates that would have been observed had the standard deduction been indexed in real terms. Had the maximum standard deduction been indexed at its 1948 level ($1888 in 1972 dollars), for example, the nominal maximum would have risen from $1000 in 1948 to $3372 in 1980. If the 1970 value ($1093 in 1972 dollars) were the benchmark, however, the maximum-standard-deduction levels would be only 58 percent as large. These two values are used to produce two alternative simulations. For each alternative, the proportion of taxpayers who would have itemized was estimated using the logistical function given in equation (16), with an elasticity of 1.24. Since there is no change in the price and net-in-

---

31. This is of course true for those who owe no tax. Thus changes in exemption levels will affect contributions to the extent that the prices and tax liabilities of taxpayers are changed.

32. See, for example, the statement of Senator Daniel P. Moynihan, a cosponsor of a bill to extend the charitable deduction to nonitemizers. In part he stated: "The problem, of course, is that as fewer and fewer taxpayers 'itemize,' the purpose of the charitable deduction is steadily eroded and its incentive effect attenuated" (U.S. Congress, Senate 1980, p. 21).

33. See table 2.6.

come values facing itemizers and nonitemizers in a given income and family-status category, simulated changes in giving arise only from the proportion of itemizers.[34]

Table 3.12 presents the actual and simulated values for the percentage of itemizers and total giving for even years between 1948 and 1980.[35] The simulations based on the indexed 1948 value show that this large standard deduction would have reduced the number of itemizers in comparison with actual levels in most years. For example, only an estimated 37 percent of taxpayers would have itemized in 1970 had the 1948 standard deduction been maintained in real terms. As a result, contributions in most years would have been smaller than they were in fact. For the low 1970 standard deduction, the reverse is true. Had the 1970 real value been in effect, more taxpayers would have itemized and contributions would have been higher.

These calculations show two clear effects: contributions were stimulated by the erosion in the real value of the maximum standard deduction between 1948 and 1970 and contributions were discouraged by the large increases in the maximum after 1970. The year 1970 marked an historic low point in the value of the maximum standard deduction. If 1970 is used as the point of reference, the tax structure in 1980 appears to be relatively unfavorable toward charitable giving, as suggested by spokesmen for the nonprofit sector. If 1948 is used as the benchmark, however, it can be seen that the maximum standard deduction is virtually unchanged in real terms.

### 3.5.2   Inflation and the Impact of the 1981 Tax Act

In this section the basic behavioral model is used to make projections of giving. The model described here projects values of giving to 1986 based on 1980 basic data, projections of economic variables, and legislated changes in the income tax. This kind of model is probably the most perilous kind of simulation exercise because it produces values of future giving

34. Average contributions by year and income class for itemizers were obtained from reported tax deductions in the *Statistics of Income*. Average contributions by nonitemizers are based on means by income class taken from the National Study of Philanthropy, adjusted for price changes. While itemizers and nonitemizers are by no means homogenous groups, this simulation method recognizes no difference among these in every group. Lags in adjustment, for example, are not taken into account, and this is a drawback where changes in itemization status are particularly rapid.

The appropriate income class was determined by converting average income for the class into 1973 dollars. The average giving obtained in the 1973 survey for the coresponding class was then reconverted into the appropriate year's prices. The 1973 values of average giving for nonitemizers are a smoothed series based on Morgan, Dye, and Hybels (1977, p. 193, table 24). See Clotfelter and Salamon 1982, p. 186, table 3.

35. By way of comparison, the estimates of actual total giving tend to be somewhat higher than estimates of the trade publication *Giving U.S.A.* before 1974 and then slightly lower after that. The estimate of $39.1 billion for total giving in 1980 differs from the figure of $39.9 billion in that publication by about 2 percent (1983, p. 36).

**Table 3.12**     Individual Contributions and Itemization: Actual Levels and Simulations for Indexed Maximum Standard Deductions

| Year | Maximum Standard Deduction in 1972 Dollars | Estimates of Actual Levels | | Simulated Levels Assuming Real Maximum Standard Deduction Fixed at: | | | | | |
| --- | --- | --- | --- | --- | --- | --- | --- | --- | --- |
| | | | | 1948 Level | | | 1970 Level | | |
| | | Percentage Itemizers | Total Giving | Percentage Itemizers | Total Giving | Percentage Difference from Actual | Percentage Itemizers | Total Giving | Percentage Difference from Actual |
| 1948 | 1888 | 16.4 | 4.0 | 16.4 | 4.0 | 0 | 26.8 | 4.6 | +14 |
| 1950 | 1867 | 18.8 | 4.5 | 18.6 | 4.5 | 0 | 29.8 | 5.1 | +14 |
| 1952 | 1726 | 22.1 | 5.6 | 20.4 | 5.5 | −2 | 32.0 | 6.3 | +12 |
| 1954 | 1679 | 27.1 | 6.3 | 24.6 | 6.1 | −3 | 37.1 | 7.0 | +11 |
| 1956 | 1593 | 31.4 | 7.5 | 27.6 | 7.2 | −4 | 40.5 | 8.1 | +9 |
| 1958 | 1514 | 35.5 | 8.3 | 30.3 | 7.9 | −4 | 43.4 | 8.9 | +6 |
| 1960 | 1455 | 39.7 | 9.3 | 33.6 | 8.8 | −5 | 46.7 | 9.8 | +5 |
| 1962 | 1416 | 42.5 | 10.1 | 35.7 | 9.6 | −5 | 48.7 | 10.5 | +1 |
| 1964 | 1374 | 41.4 | 11.2 | 34.2 | 10.6 | −5 | 46.7 | 11.6 | +4 |
| 1966 | 1303 | 40.9 | 12.5 | 32.8 | 11.8 | −5 | 44.9 | 12.8 | +2 |
| 1968 | 1212 | 43.7 | 14.9 | 34.2 | 14.2 | −5 | 45.9 | 15.1 | +1 |
| 1970 | 1093 | 48.0 | 16.4 | 36.9 | 15.4 | −6 | 48.0 | 16.4 | 0 |
| 1972 | 2000 | 35.0 | 19.0 | 36.1 | 19.1 | +1 | 47.0 | 20.4 | +7 |
| 1974 | 1738 | 35.7 | 21.8 | 34.1 | 21.7 | −1 | 44.6 | 22.9 | +5 |
| 1976 | 2115 | 30.8 | 32.8 | 25.7 | 25.7 | +1 | 42.7 | 27.5 | +8 |
| 1978 | 2260 | 28.7 | 30.7 | 31.4 | 31.3 | +2 | 40.4 | 33.2 | +8 |
| 1980 | 1897 | 31.0 | 39.1 | 31.2 | 39.1 | 0 | 40.3 | 41.2 | +5 |

simply on the basis of anticipated statutory and economic variables. No basic changes in behavior—by donors or charitable organizations—is reflected. The results therefore must be viewed as a conditional prediction—an estimate of the likely outcome of tax and economic changes, holding other things constant.

Two steps are involved in this calculation. First, basic data on income and number of taxpayers by tax status are "aged" using economic projections to yield likely levels for each succeeding year. For example, gross income is assumed to grow at the rate projected for per capita GNP. Based on these quantities and the actual or hypothetical tax schedules applying to each year, taxes and marginal tax rates can be calculated. If the price level rises at a faster rate than the growth in tax bracket limits, "bracket creep" will tend to raise marginal tax rates for taxpayers at a given real income. In addition, changes in the percentage of taxpayers itemizing their deductions are projected using the model summarized in (16) above. Based on marginal tax rates and projections of itemization status, the price of giving is calculated. The second basic step in the simulation is to estimate giving using a behavioral model embodying changes in net income and price. The model used is based on the assumption of incomplete adjustment and takes the form of equation (20), where the coefficient of adjustment is 0.37. Desired long-run giving takes the constant-elasticity form summarized in equation (21), where the price elasticity is -1.27 and the income elasticity is 0.78.

The basic data used for this projection model were tabulations for 1980 individual tax returns. Projections of inflation and income growth were taken from the 1984 federal budget. These assumptions are summarized in the first two columns of table 3.13.[36] Taxes and giving were calculated separately for twelve income classes, joint and nonjoint returns, and for itemizers and nonitemizers, resulting in forty-eight separate calculations for each year. The model's simulations reflect four major tax changes: the institution of a 50 percent top marginal tax rate in 1982, a 23 percent proportional reduction in other tax rates over three years, a phased-in charitable deduction for nonitemizers becoming a full deduction in 1986, and a general indexation of tax brackets beginning in 1985. Because the model

36. Gross national product projections were: 2938 (1981), 3058 (1982), 3262 (1983), 3566 (1984), 3890 (1985), and 4232 (1986). GNP deflator projections were: 195.5 (1981), 207.2 (1982), 218.1 (1983), 229.4 (1984), 240.6 (1985), and 251.7 (1986) (U.S. Office of Management and Budget 1983, pp. 2–9, 2–10). Over the period 1980 to 1986 these projections imply an average exponential growth rate of 7.9 percent for national income and 5.7 for prices. Where $p_1$ and $p_t$ are price levels in period 1 and $t$, the exponential rate is $r$ in the expression $p_t = p_0 \exp(rt)$.

An exponential rate of 0.01064 was calculated for population growth from estimates of U.S. population in 1978 and 1981 of 222.585 and 229.805 million, respectively (U.S. Bureau of the Census 1982, p. 2). Taken together, these economic assumptions imply growth in real per capita income of about 1 percent a year.

**Table 3.13**     Simulations of Individual Giving, 1981–86

| Year | Assumed Increase from 1980 in Income | Prices | Percentage Itemizing | Total Contributions (billions) Current Dollars | 1980 Dollars | Percentage Given by Itemizers | Taxpayers with Incomes over $50,000 in 1980 |
|---|---|---|---|---|---|---|---|
| 1980 | — | — | 31.0 | 38.7 | 38.7 | 66.8 | 23.8 |
| 1981 | 11.6 | 9.4 | 32.6 | 42.9 | 39.2 | 67.9 | 22.6 |
| 1982 | 16.1 | 16.0 | 33.1 | 44.9 | 38.7 | 67.6 | 21.4 |
| 1983 | 23.9 | 22.1 | 34.0 | 47.2 | 38.6 | 67.9 | 20.3 |
| 1984 | 35.4 | 28.4 | 35.3 | 50.5 | 39.3 | 68.2 | 19.4 |
| 1985 | 47.7 | 34.7 | 35.7 | 54.6 | 40.6 | 67.4 | 18.6 |
| 1986 | 60.7 | 40.9 | 36.2 | 60.5 | 42.9 | 65.5 | 17.9 |

was designed to project actual levels of giving, no adjustment in revenues or tax rates were made as in the model described in section 3.4. The price of giving is a weighted average of the prices applying to gifts of cash and of appreciated assets, as given in equation (28). As in the previous models presented in this chapter, contributions by nonitemizers were based on data from the National Study of Philanthropy.

Table 3.13 summarizes the basic simulation results as well as the economic assumptions underlying them. The model implies that the percentage of taxpayers who itemize their deductions will rise from 31 percent in 1980 to over 35 percent in 1984, most of this being due to the erosion in the real value of the zero-bracket amount during this period. After 1984 this proportion continues to climb slightly due to growth in real per capita income. In order to reflect the effects of tax changes on the distribution of giving, the last column shows the percentage of gifts made by taxpayers with incomes over $50,000 in 1980—roughly the most affluent 3.4 percent of taxpayers.[37] In the estimates of giving for 1982 and 1983 the effect of the reduction in top marginal tax rates is evident. Total giving drops slightly in real terms, to about $39 billion in both years, and the proportion of gifts made by the top income group falls from 23 to 20 percent over two years.[38] Although the reduction in top rates became effective in 1982, the model's incomplete-adjustment mechanism tends to spread out the effect over several years. For the income groups below the top marginal tax rates, the legislated tax reductions are offset to varying degrees by inflation-induced bracket creep.[39] Beginning in 1984 contributions are projected to increase in real terms, corresponding to the expansion of the charitable deduction for nonitemizers. By 1986, when the full deduction is scheduled to become effective, total giving is projected to rise to $60.5 billion, some 11 percent above the 1983 level in real terms.[40]

In concluding, it is useful to compare these simulations with the most recent data on charitable contributions. Before doing so, though, the uncertain nature of estimates such as these bears reemphasizing. Not only are the estimates subject to the kind of statistical errors described in section 3.3, they are also vulnerable to errors in the projection of basic economic variables that underlie them. It is possible to make a partial assessment of the accuracy of these simulations by examining recent tax return data that became available after the simulations were carried out. According to official data for 1981 and preliminary data for 1982, contributions by itemizers increased from $25.8 billion in 1980 to $26.4 billion and $33.8

---

37. This group comprises the top six income brackets.

38. By comparison, the estimates of total individual contributions in *Giving U.S.A.* are $44.6 and $48.7 billion in 1981 and 1982, respectively (1983, p. 36).

39. See Clotfelter 1984 for a discussion of inflation, tax cuts, and marginal tax rates.

40. A deduction for 25 percent of the first $100 of contributions was allowed for nonitemizers in 1982 and 1983, but this has little effect at the margin since average giving for nonitemizers in every income class exceeded $100.

billion in 1981 and 1982, respectively (U.S. Internal Revenue Service, *Statistics of Income—1981, Individual Income Tax Returns* 1983 p. 54, table 2.1; Epstein 1983–84, p. 19). In comparison, the simulated totals for itemized giving in 1981 and 1982 were $29.2 billion and $30.3 billion, amounts that erred by about 10 percent in opposite directions. Analysis of the difference for 1982 shows that actual income growth was stronger than projected, and the simulated proportion and number of itemizers were about 7 percent lower than actual levels. The projections for contributions in 1982 thus understate the contributions by itemizers and overstate the contributions by nonitemizers, resulting in a probable understatement of the total. As for the pattern of giving by income class, the simulation model appears to have anticipated the effect of the 1981 tax cut quite well. Table 3.14 shows the change in average giving by income level between 1981 and 1982. In contrast to the modest increases in contributions at incomes below $50,000, the average giving rates above the $200,000 income level decreased sharply, revealing the impact of reducing the top tax rate from 70 to 50 percent. While some of this drop in high-income giving may be due to transitory price effects—with taxpayers making some gifts early in order to take advantage of the higher deduction rate—the econometric evidence on charitable giving suggests that the change in tax schedule will have a lasting effect on giving behavior.

Beyond the question of accuracy in projecting total contributions, therefore, simulation models such as that used here are useful in identifying major trends in future giving. The current simulation model suggests that individual contributions will likely increase in real terms between 1980 and 1986, due largely to an expansion in the number of itemizers and

**Table 3.14**     **Average Contributions by Itemizers, 1981 and 1982**

| Income | Average Contributions | | Percentage Change |
| --- | --- | --- | --- |
| | 1981 | 1982 | |
| Under $5,000 | 192 | 192 | 0 |
| $5,000 under 10,000 | 490 | 516 | + 5 |
| $10,000 under 15,000 | 574 | 583 | + 2 |
| $15,000 under 20,000 | 595 | 617 | + 4 |
| $20,000 under 25,000 | 613 | 646 | + 5 |
| $25,000 under 30,000 | 643 | 685 | + 7 |
| $30,000 under 50,000 | 885 | 918 | + 4 |
| $50,000 under 100,000 | 1,709 | 1,689 | − 1 |
| $100,000 under 200,000 | 4,716 | 4,533 | − 4 |
| $200,000 under 500,000 | 14,483 | 12,099 | − 16 |
| $500,000 under 1,000,000 | 50,125 | 33,834 | − 33 |
| $1,000,000 or more | 204,499 | 146,530 | − 28 |

*Source:* U. S. Internal Revenue Service, *Statistics of Income—1981, Individual Income Tax Returns,* 1983, pp. 53–54, table 2.1; Epstein 1984, p. 19, table 1.

the planned introduction of the charitable deduction for nonitemizers. Due to the latter provision as well as to the nature of the tax rate reductions, however, the distribution of giving will be altered with those in upper income classes giving a smaller share of the total. Based on past patterns of contributions by type of charity, these changes suggest that gifts to religious institutions and health and welfare agencies will rise relative to gifts to cultural and educational institutions.

## 3.6  Conclusion

This chapter discusses the application of econometric estimates of charitable giving in simulating the effects of alternative tax provisions. Models have been presented that simulate the effects of hypothetical tax provisions in a given year, the effects of past taxes on past giving, and the effects of legislated changes on future giving. A basic point made in the chapter is that contributions may be influenced either by tax provisions explicitly designed to affect giving or by general characteristics of the tax structure. The models discussed here focus on changes in the tax-defined price and net income of donors. By no means does this imply that taxes are the only or the most important influence on charitable giving, merely that they have some effect. The econometric studies discussed in chapter 2 yield the clear implication that taxes do in fact have a significant effect.

Two kinds of effects can be distinguished in the simulation results presented here. First, tax provisions may affect the level of total giving. For example, eliminating the charitable deduction would cause total giving to fall by about one quarter, assuming tax rates were adjusted to keep revenues constant and donors had sufficient time to adjust to their new levels of giving. A similar effect on total giving is the $1 billion increase in 1983 due to the limited charitable deduction for nonitemizers. A second and equally important effect of these tax provisions is on the distribution of contributions by the income class of donors and by the types of organizations supported. Although a 20 percent tax credit would have a limited impact on total giving, the simulations suggest that contributions to some types of organizations would fall by more than a third. Another case in point is the 1981 tax act. By cutting marginal tax rates of the taxpayers in the highest brackets and extending a deduction to nonitemizers, the law is projected to bring about a marked decrease in the share of contributions made by upper-income taxpayers.

# 4      Volunteer Effort

Pervasive but difficult to quantify, volunteer work has been widely re-garded as a vital component of charitable activity in the United States. Despite the historical trend toward greater professionalism in public and private social-welfare agencies, volunteers have remained an important source of skilled labor in many organizations. A Gallup survey in 1981 es-timated that over half of American adults and teenagers did some volun-teer work during the year, either for an organization or informally (Gallup Organization 1981, p. iv). Based on data from this and one other recent survey, Weitzman (1983) has estimated that the market value of the time spent by volunteers is in the range of $54 to $65 billion in 1980 dollars.[1] Although the proper valuation of volunteer time involves more than sim-ply applying market wage rates, such estimates suggest that the resource cost of volunteering is probably at least as large as aggregate contributions of money, which totaled about $40 billion in 1980.[2]

Recent federal administrations have made a special point to encourage volunteering. From John Kennedy's call for VISTA and Peace Corps vol-unteers to Ronald Reagan's establishment of a Presidential Task Force on Private Sector Initiatives, there has been an implicit understanding that volunteering may serve social goals more effectively or less expensively than government spending programs. President Reagan made this an ex-plicit part of his administration's program: "Voluntarism is an essential part of our plan to give the government back to the people" (*Washington Post,* 8 October 1981).

---

1. $54 billion figure is based on estimates of $31.9 billion for 1973, using the National Study of Philanthropy. The $65 billion figure uses the Gallup survey for 1981. See Weitzman 1983, p. 270, table 1.
2. See, for example, *Giving U.S.A.* 1983, p. 36.

What defines charitable voluntary work? Normally, volunteers receive no pay, although they may receive reimbursement for expenses. Most volunteering is done under the auspices of private nonprofit organizations, but public agencies also make use of volunteers. Surveys of volunteers usually ignore work for unions and professional societies, and some exclude work in religious organizations dealing primarily with worship and religious education. Another distinction is made between work done for organizations and help provided informally, such as helping neighbors. Since it is more difficult to measure precisely, such informal help is sometimes excluded in measures of volunteer effort. Finally, there is no generally accepted minimum amount of time or effort required to be classified as a volunteer.

Despite these inevitable ambiguities, it is possible to get some idea of the extent of volunteering from recent surveys. In 1981 the Gallup organization formulated two measures of volunteer effort for use in household surveys. In a survey taken in September, respondents were asked if they were "involved in any charity or social service activities, such as helping the poor, the sick or elderly." By this measure, 29 percent of adults were volunteers, implying a total force of volunteers, cited above, of at least 40 million Americans ("Americans Volunteer: A Profile" 1982, p. 21). In a March survey, on the other hand, volunteering was defined much more broadly to include all volunteer work for religious organizations as well as informal helping. By this measure 52 percent of adults, some 80 million in all, had volunteered during the previous year (Gallup Organization 1981, pp. i–iv.; Hodgkinson and Weitzman 1984, p. 26). Numbers such as this are often cited to illustrate the importance of voluntary action as an alternative to government in dealing with social concerns.

In recent years, however, there has been a growing concern that the number of volunteers may be on the decline. Established nonprofit organizations have reported reductions in the number of members and volunteers, particularly among women. For example, the League of Women Voters reported a decline of about 8 percent in its membership between 1978 and 1980 (*Washington Post,* 23 May 1980). In the decade between 1969 and 1979, the American Red Cross reportedly lost a third of its over 2 million volunteers.[3] It is impossible to determine with much precision the overall decline in volunteers, however, because comparable survey data over time are not available.

The purpose of this chapter is to examine the effect of the tax structure on volunteer effort. This effect may be direct, for example, through deductions for expenses incurred in volunteering. Or it may be indirect, through the effect of taxation on labor force participation and hours of

3. *Durham Morning Herald,* 2 August 1981. See also McGuire and Weber 1982, p. 5; *Washington Post,* 27 April 1980; and *New York Times,* 16 April 1978.

work. Another possible indirect effect is that the income tax may stimulate volunteering through its encouragement of monetary gifts, which would be the case if contributions and volunteering are "complementary" goods. Section 4.1 presents tabulations on the extent of volunteering and characteristics of volunteers, and section 4.2 describes the federal tax provisions relevant to volunteer activity. Section 4.3 examines the question of the tax effects on volunteering within a simple economic model of individual choice. Sections 4.4 and 4.5 discuss econometric analyses of volunteer work—the former reviewing previous studies and the latter extending this work to look at the volunteer effort of women. The final section discusses the implications of theoretical and empirical work for tax policy.

### 4.1   Extent and Characteristics of Volunteer Effort

There is substantial variation in the kinds of work done and the frequency of volunteering by population groups. Table 4.1 provides detail about the kinds of organizations volunteers worked for during the year 1981, where volunteering is defined broadly to include all volunteer work in religious congregations[4] and informal helping. In fact, informal assistance and religious volunteering are the most frequently cited categories.

Table 4.1    Percentage of Adult Men and Women Who Had Volunteered in the Past Year, by Activity, 1981

| Activity | Women | Men |
| --- | --- | --- |
| Health | 15 | 9 |
| Education | 15 | 8 |
| Justice | 1 | 1 |
| Citizenship | 6 | 7 |
| Recreation | 4 | 10 |
| Social/welfare | 5 | 4 |
| Communication | 6 | 6 |
| Religious | 22 | 16 |
| Political | 6 | 7 |
| Arts and culture | 3 | 3 |
| Work-related | 3 | 8 |
| Informal/alone | 28 | 17 |
| General fund raisers | 7 | 6 |
| None | 44 | 53 |
| Number of interviews | 793 | 808 |

Source: Gallup Organization, 1981, pp. 6–7.
Note: Percentages sum to more than 100 percent because multiple responses were allowed.

4. Religious volunteering may be divided between work done in community and traditional social-welfare projects, and work done in connection with education, administration, and worship activities that are entirely within the religious domain of the congregation. Although the former may be rooted in religious belief, it is often separated from the latter in classifying volunteer work. In table 4.1 both types of work are included.

Informal volunteering, done apart from any organization and including such assistance as helping a neighbor with repairs and baking brownies for a scout group, was cited by 17 percent of men and 28 percent of women. Religious volunteering was next with 16 and 22 percent, respectively. After these activities, women most often cited work in health and education, while men were most likely to work in recreational activities. From this tabulation, it is evident that men and women have somewhat different patterns of volunteer work. For both sexes, however, volunteering for religious groups exceeds that for any other organizational area and corresponds to the predominance of religious giving in individuals' contributions of money.

In order to examine variations in the rate of volunteer work, table 4.2 presents volunteering rates for men and women according to several demographic and economic characteristics. This table is based on a 1965 survey that excluded political, informal, and strictly religious volunteering. The overall rate of 16 percent is below the 29 percent figure for 1981 cited above, but the definitions are not comparable. For men and women, volunteering reaches a peak in the 35 to 44 age bracket. At every age, women volunteer at higher rates, with the difference being greatest in the 25 to 34 age group. Volunteering also varies by marital status, with married adults volunteering the most. The results for occupation reveal that men with high-skill occupations have very high rates of volunteering. In general, volunteering appears to be positively correlated to occupational status for both sexes.

The tabulation for labor force participation in table 4.2 shows that women who are not in the labor force are more likely to volunteer than those who are, but this relationship is reversed for men. A more detailed breakdown of volunteer work by hours of paid work is given in table 4.3. Among men, those working from 1 to 34 hours per week volunteered the most at each age level, with those employed 35 hours or more per week behind them. Men not working volunteered the least. Among women, the pattern was less clear. For women over 35, those without a paying job were the most active volunteers, conforming to the traditional stereotype. For women under 35, those working less than 35 hours volunteered the most, reflecting perhaps the emergence of new patterns of labor force participation. Women working 35 or more hours per week volunteered the least.[5] Indeed, housewives have constituted one traditional source of vol-

5. The squeeze between job and volunteering is described by one woman: "While I work and am paid for 40 hours per week, earning a livelihood involves at least 50 total hours: one hour each midday and one hour daily commuting. In addition, I sleep 56 hours per week, prepare 11 meals weekly averaging one hour each, do minimum housework in 20 hours a week and shop for necessities one to three hours per week. From 168 hours per week I'm down to less than 40 hours of 'disposable time' and haven't hugged my son or husband. It is not true that 'almost everyone has time he can give' " (letter of Jo Ann M. Crane, *Wall Street Journal*, 5 January 1982, p. 30). For another illustration, see the *Washington Post*, 23 April 1980, p. B7.

Table 4.2        Percentage of Adults Volunteering, by Sex and Other Characteristics, 1965

| Characteristics | Women | Men | Total |
|---|---|---|---|
| *All adults* | 18.5 | 13.5 | 16.1 |
| *Age* | | | |
| 14–17 | 18.8 | 11.7 | 15.3 |
| 18–24 | 11.3 | 10.4 | 10.8 |
| 25–34 | 23.3 | 13.8 | 19.0 |
| 35–44 | 27.4 | 21.2 | 24.2 |
| 45–54 | 20.4 | 16.0 | 18.1 |
| 55–64 | 15.3 | 10.0 | 12.8 |
| 65 and over | 9.6 | 7.6 | 8.7 |
| *Marital status* | | | |
| Single | 14.2 | 10.3 | 12.1 |
| Married, spouse present | 22.3 | 15.6 | 19.0 |
| Other | 10.4 | 4.6 | 9.0 |
| *Occupation* | | | |
| Professional, technical | 26.8 | 28.5 | 25.2 |
| Managers, officials, proprietors | 20.9 | 23.2 | 22.8 |
| Clerical | 18.6 | 13.6 | 17.1 |
| Sales | 20.1 | 20.9 | 20.5 |
| Blue-collar | 10.3 | 8.9 | 9.1 |
| Service | 13.6 | 18.5 | 15.2 |
| Farm | 17.7 | 14.2 | 14.8 |
| *Labor force participation* | | | |
| Employed | 17.5 | 15.3 | 16.1 |
| Unemployed | 13.8 | 7.0 | 10.2 |
| Not in labor force | 19.2 | 8.6 | 16.5 |

*Source:* U. S. Department of Labor 1969, p. 6.

*Note:* Excludes political, strictly religious, and informal volunteering. Covers the year ending November 1965.

unteers. This appears to be changing, however, as a result of the recent increase in women's labor force participation as well as hostility in the women's movement to traditional voluntary work.[6] Because of the importance of this shift for overall volunteering, it is useful to consider tax effects on the labor force participation of women.

Two further tabulations covering both men and women in 1981 are presented in table 4.4. They show that volunteering rises with household income and family size. Economic theory suggests that the value of time rises with both income and family size; thus the implicit cost of volunteer-

6. In 1971 and 1974 the National Organization of Women endorsed resolutions against volunteering in preference to paid work for women (*New York Times,* 16 April 1978).

Table 4.3          **Average Annual Hours of Volunteer Work by Employment, Age and Sex, 1973**

| Age and Sex | Unemployed or Not in Labor Force | Employed 1 to 34 Hours per Week | Employed 35 or More Hours per Week |
|---|---|---|---|
| *Women* | | | |
| 35 and under | 68.5 | 84.8 | 37.1 |
| | (275) | (115) | (252) |
| 36 to 50 | 128.4 | 79.6 | 49.1 |
| | (361) | (138) | (210) |
| Over 50 | 93.4 | 79.6 | 55.6 |
| | (614) | (92) | (167) |
| *Men* | | | |
| 35 and under | 31.8 | 68.3 | 48.1 |
| | (31) | (70) | (419) |
| 36 to 50 | 38.1 | 148.2 | 93.9 |
| | (17) | (34) | (602) |
| Over 50 | 58.1 | 129.6 | 90.8 |
| | (271) | (91) | (542) |

*Note:* Numbers of observation are given in parentheses. Volunteering was defined as unpaid work for religious and other charitable organizations.
*Source:* Tabulations from National Study of Philanthropy. See Morgan, Dye, and Hybels 1977 for a description of the data.

ing would go up with both. Other forces may work in the opposite direction, however. If volunteering is a normal good, demand for it will rise with income. The evidence in table 4.4, which is consistent with other findings that memberships in voluntary associations rise with social class,[7] suggests that this income effect outweighs the increase in the value of time. Similarly, volunteering appears to rise with family size despite the increase in the value of time, suggesting strongly that at least some volunteer work has the effect of providing services to a family's own children as well as to others.

In addition to tabulations by other variables, it is instructive to examine the variation in volunteering among households. Since hours of the day are distributed a good bit more equally than income, one would expect more uniformity in volunteering than in the giving of dollars. It is by no

7. Data reported by Warner and Lunt (1941, pp. 323–33) in their study of an American community they called Yankee City suggest that membership in voluntary associations rose with social class. The percentages of each class belonging to three or more associations were: lower-lower: 7.2; upper-lower: 12.1; lower-middle: 20.1; upper-middle: 37.9; lower-upper: 47.1; and upper-upper: 49.1.

Table 4.4          Adult Volunteers by Income and Household Size, 1982

|  | Percentage of Adults Who Volunteered | |
|---|---|---|
|  | During the Year | More Than 36 Hours in the Previous 3 Months |
| *Household income* |  |  |
| Under $4,000 | 40 | 5 |
| $4,000 – 6,999 | 36 | 13 |
| $7,000 – 9,999 | 35 | 16 |
| $10,000 – 14,999 | 46 | 14 |
| $15,000 – 19,999 | 53 | 15 |
| $20,000 and over | 63 | 24 |
| *Household size* |  |  |
| One | 41 | 15 |
| Two | 47 | 15 |
| Three | 55 | 19 |
| Four or more | 59 | 21 |

*Source:* Gallup Organization 1981, pp. 19–21.
*Note:* Definition of volunteering includes informal helping as well as work for organizations.

means obvious, however, whether the propensity to volunteer is more or less equally distributed than the propensity to give out of income. In order to describe how the extent of volunteering differs among households, table 4.5 presents the cumulative percentages for volunteer hours and number of households based on a weighted sample of 2436 households in 1973 classified by amount of volunteering. Over 40 percent of households contributed no volunteer time at all. At the other end, the 8 percent of households volunteering the most hours accounted for over half of all volunteer hours. Figure 4.1 presents the corresponding Lorenz curve, which plots the cumulative percentage of households against the cumulative percentage of volunteering. Shown by the solid line, this curve illustrates the unevenness of volunteering in the population. For comparison, the comparable distribution of monetary contributions by income is also plotted, using a dotted line. Based on the available data, these curves show that the propensity to contribute out of income varies less over the population than the propensity to volunteer. The coefficients of equality calculated from these data are 0.30 for contributions and 0.23 for volunteering.[8] Because incomes differ, of course, the distribution of actual contributions by households is much less equal.

---

8. "The coefficient of equality" is defined as the ratio of the area under the curve to the area of the complete triangle that contains it. The higher the value of the coefficient of equality, the more even the distribution. Perfect equality would be signified by a coefficient value of 1.0.

**Table 4.5**            **Distribution of Volunteer Hours by Households, 1973 (percentage)**

| Volunteer Hours per Year | Unweighted Number of Households | Weighted Percentage of Households | Weighted Percentage of Volunteer Hours |
|---|---|---|---|
| None | 1028 | 42.2 | 0 |
| 1–29 | 317 | 13.0 | 1.1 |
| 30–59 | 139 | 5.7 | 1.7 |
| 60–99 | 136 | 5.6 | 3.0 |
| 100–199 | 272 | 11.2 | 10.7 |
| 200–299 | 160 | 6.6 | 10.9 |
| 300–499 | 180 | 7.4 | 20.0 |
| 500–999 | 153 | 6.3 | 29.9 |
| 1000+ | 51 | 2.1 | 22.6 |
| TOTAL | 2436 | 100.1 | 99.9 |

*Source:* Tabulations from the National Study of Philanthropy.

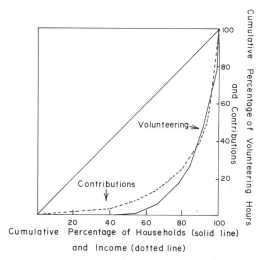

**Fig. 4.1**            Distribution of volunteering hours and contributions, 1973.
*Source:* tables 2.3 and 4.5.

A final empirical issue that can be addressed with simple tabulations is whether contributions of money tend to go with volunteering. The notion that "money follows involvement,"[9] or the reverse, concerns the complementarity of the activities of contributing and volunteering. If people tend to do them together, stimulating one will also stimulate the other. If, on the other hand, contributions of time and money are substitutes, the en-

9. See James E. Kemper, *Wall Street Journal,* 22 December 1982, p. 20.

couragement of one would tend to come at the expense of the other. The possibility of a complementary relationship appears to be supported by surveys that have found that giving money and time do in fact appear to go together. The Gallup survey in 1981 using the broader definition of volunteering found that 91 percent of those who volunteered also gave money, compared to only 66 percent among those who did not volunteer (Gallup Organization 1981, p. 23). More detail is available in the 1973 Michigan survey of philanthropy, which included questions about contributions of time and money. Table 4.6 is a tabulation from that survey showing average hours of volunteer work for husbands and wives according to the couple's ratio of contributions to income. With few exceptions, the table shows that households contributing larger proportions of their income also volunteered more.[10] In addition, this effect appears to be stronger for men than for women. Whereas husbands average fewer volunteer hours in the bottom four classes, their volunteering exceeds that of wives in the next four. While these results suggest that contributions of time and money are complementary, they are by no means definitive since other variables are not held constant. The issue of complementarity is addressed below in considering the effect of income taxation on volunteering.

Table 4.6    Average Annual Volunteer Hours by Ratio of Contributions to Income, Married Couples, 1973

| Ratio of Monetary Contributions to Income[a] | Wife | Husband | Total | N |
|---|---|---|---|---|
| 0 | 24 | 20 | 44 | 85 |
| 0–.02 | 43 | 38 | 81 | 798 |
| .02–.04 | 87 | 73 | 160 | 370 |
| .04–.06 | 119 | 98 | 217 | 200 |
| .06–.08 | 143 | 125 | 269 | 87 |
| .08–.10 | 138 | 151 | 289 | 80 |
| .10–.15 | 171 | 224 | 396 | 101 |
| .15–.20 | 169 | 181 | 350 | 45 |
| .20–.30 | 173 | 151 | 324 | 27 |
| .30–.50 | 227 | 205 | 432 | 19 |
| Greater than .50 | 155 | 246 | 401 | 39 |
| TOTAL | | | | 1851 |

Source: Tabulations from the National Study of Philanthropy.
Note: Intervals are inclusive of the upper limit.

10. Morgan, Dye, and Hybels (1977, p. 174) present other tabulations supporting the same conclusion.

## 4.2   Tax Treatment of Volunteer Services

Two sets of provisions in the federal income tax relate to the contribution of volunteer time: First, the tax provisions concerning deductions for charitable contributions affect the attractiveness of money contributions—the alternative to volunteering—and refer specifically to volunteer services. As outlined in chapter 2, the charitable deduction was available before 1982 for taxpayers who itemized their deductions but was extended to nonitemizers beginning only in 1983. The tax code explicitly excludes the value of services contributed to charitable organizations in describing deductible items. Contributions of blood are also excluded (*1980 U.S. Master Tax Guide* 1979, sec. 1141, p. 414). Most expenses incurred in volunteering are, however, deductible as part of the charitable deduction. These include unreimbursed costs of transportation, telephone, meals, and lodging in connection with volunteer work. In contrast to deductions for business expenses, neither depreciation nor insurance costs are eligible for the charitable deduction. In addition, the mileage allowance is less than that allowed for business travel.[11]

Second, the tax treatment of volunteering is affected by more general provisions of the income tax, including the tax-rate schedule, the definition of taxable income, and special provisions for secondary earners. To the extent that volunteer activity is an alternative use of time to other nonmarket activities and work, the definition of taxable income and the schedule of tax rates are relevant to volunteering because they determine the income and substitution effects underlying a household's allocation of time. Special provisions for secondary earners, in particular, may affect household decisions about volunteering. Congress included in the 1981 tax cut a deduction for married couples for part of the second earner's income. Beginning in 1983 the deduction is scheduled to be 10 percent of the earned income of the spouse with lower income up to $30,000 (U.S. Congress, Staff of the Joint Committee on Taxation 1981, p. 35). Because this provision will in many cases cause the tax rate faced by the secondary earner to diverge from the tax rate at which contributions of money may be deducted, this special provision will tend to favor money gifts over contributions of time. In order to illustrate this and other tax effects on volunteering, it is useful to consider a simple example of a household's choice between money contributions and volunteering.

In assessing the tax treatment of volunteering, one question that can be raised concerns the neutrality of the tax system on treating gifts of money and time. That the tax law allows deductibility of the former but not the latter has been criticized by some.[12] Long (1977) demonstrates, however, that this traditional tax treatment is neutral, at least for itemizers. An ex-

11. In 1982, 8¢ per mile.
12. See, for example, Baird 1972.

ample will serve to illustrate this point. Consider a taxpayer who can make $10 by working another hour or can do an hour of volunteer work worth $10 to a charitable organization. Under these circumstances the charity will receive $10 worth of services whether the taxpayer volunteers for an hour or works an hour and contributes the proceeds. Neutrality would require that the tax treatment leave the taxpayer as well-off in one situation as in the other. Table 4.7 summarizes the tax treatment of gifts of time and money. In all cases, volunteering has no effect on taxes or disposable income since it is neither taxed nor deducted. For taxpayers who itemize their deductions, as shown in line (a), contributing one's earnings leaves taxes unchanged, the same as for volunteering. Thus the basic tax treatment of itemizers is neutral, which is Long's (1977) central argument.

The income tax was not neutral, however, in its treatment of contributions by taxpayers who did not itemize their deductions. Because contributions were not deductible against earnings at the margin, the tax made volunteering more advantageous, other things equal. In order not to lose

**Table 4.7     Tax Treatment of Giving Money and Volunteering**

| | Change in Household's Tax Liability (in dollars) | | |
| --- | --- | --- | --- |
| | Tax Increase Due to Additional Earnings | Tax Decrease Due to Gift | Tax Change |
| Tax treatment of earning and contributing $10; 30 percent marginal tax rate. | | | |
| *Pre-1982 law* | | | |
| (*a*) Itemizer | + 3.00 | − 3.00 | 0 |
| (*b*) Nonitemizer | + 3.00 | 0 | + 3.00 |
| Full charitable deduction for nonitemizers and deduction of 10 percent for second-earner income (itemizers and nonitemizers) | | | |
| (*c*) Primary earner works extra hour and contributes $10 | + 3.00 | − 3.00 | 0 |
| (*d*) Secondary earner works extra hour and contributes $10 | + 2.70 | − 3.00 | − 0.30 |
| Tax treatment of volunteering one hour | 0 | 0 | 0 |

income, a taxpayer at the 30 percent tax bracket, for example, could choose between volunteering an hour or working an hour for $10, contributing $7 and keeping the remaining $3 to cover the increased taxes.[13] When the above-the-line deduction for nonitemizers is fully implemented, this distortion will be eliminated. The actual effect of this new deduction will depend, of course, on whether volunteering is encouraged more by the complementarity effect through the price of money gifts than it is discouraged by the end of this distortion.[14]

The new partial deduction allowed for the second earner will introduce a different distortion at the same time the itemizer/nonitemizer distortion disappears. If the primary earner works an additional hour and contributes the proceeds, the income tax will be neutral between gifts of time and money, as in line (a). If the gift comes from the secondary earner, however, giving money will be favored over volunteering. This distortion will not be large, of course, because the difference between spouses' marginal rates is small, being no higher than 5 percent when the basic tax rate is 50 percent.

## 4.3    Theory of Volunteer Work

The theories of helping and charitable behavior discussed in chapter 2 apply in much the same way to the contribution of time as to material gifts. In analyzing the kinds of volunteer work typically observed in American communities, it is not uncommon to discover elements of enjoyment, altruism, and self-interested consumption of family services and training underlying that work. Table 4.8 summarizes the responses to a survey of adult volunteers taken in 1981. When asked why they first became involved in volunteering, volunteers were most likely to say they wanted to help others or do something useful. Manifestations of this impulse range from the almost missionary fervor of the early March of Dimes to the pragmatic "we do it because it needs to be done."[15] The next most frequent response given by volunteers in 1981 was that they had an interest in the work (35 percent). Twenty-nine percent said they felt needed or thought they would enjoy the work. Indeed, some volunteer activity appears to include a not unsubstantial component of socializing and other

---

13. It is worth noting that the example assumes that the taxpayer can choose to spend an additional hour working. In addition, actual choices between earning-giving and volunteering would be affected by the taxpayer's productivity in a marginal hour spent in each pursuit. In general, the benefit to the charity from volunteering and giving money must be compared along with the change in tax liability. The definition of neutrality, however, is independent of either of these assumptions.

14. The theoretical analysis of this question is taken up in the next section.

15. See Sills 1957, p. 241, and *Raleigh News and Observer,* 13 December 1981. A New York man who does health-related volunteer work expressed a similar sentiment: "I do all this to help people in trouble. I couldn't pass anyone having a problem without doing something about it" (*New York Times,* 29 January 1977).

Table 4.8          Adults' Stated Reasons for Volunteering

| Reasons | Percentage of Volunteers |
|---|---|
| Wanted to do something useful; help others; do good deeds for others | 45 |
| Had an interest in the activity or work | 35 |
| Thought I would enjoy doing the work; feel needed | 29 |
| Had a child, relative, or friend who was involved in the activity or would benefit from it | 23 |
| Religious concerns | 21 |
| Wanted to learn and get experience; work experience; help get a job | 11 |
| Had a lot of free time | 6 |
| Thought my volunteer work would help keep taxes or other costs down | 5 |
| Other | 1 |
| Don't recall | 5 |
| Number of interviews | (843) |

*Source:* Gallup Organization 1981, p. 28.
*Note:* Adults in this survey were asked: "For what reasons did you first become involved in this volunteer activity?" Percent total exceeds 100 because more than one response per question was allowed.

enjoyment. For example, in a study of charitable activity in an English village, Obler (1981, p. 36) observes that

> private giving is an integral part of public, social life in Penridge. Hardly a week goes by when there is not a coffee morning, whist party, village fete, fashion show, concert, wine and cheese party, show and sell stall or an open garden day to raise money for some cause.

The historical social-class homogeneity of most voluntary associations may be a further indication of the social aspect of some volunteering.[16] Twenty-three percent of the 1981 sample of volunteers had a child, relative, or friend involved in the activity or would benefit from it, suggesting a somewhat different consumption motive for volunteering. Twenty-one percent expressed a religious motivation, which could certainly be related to the most frequently given response described above. The final response named by more than 10 percent of the sample was a desire to obtain work

16. Warner and Lunt (1941, pp. 118, 303–33) found that most voluntary associations in Yankee City were homogenous in social-class composition, with upper-class women dominating the membership rolls of charitable organizations.

experience (11 percent). Some volunteer coordinators have said that career aims are important for a growing number of volunteers, particularly women who have been outside the labor force (*New York Times,* 29 January 1977).

There are, in short, several distinct classes of motivations for engaging in voluntary work. They may be summarized as *a*) giving, *b*) consuming, and *c*) investing. The giving component has much in common with contributions of material gifts, but the form of the gift may take on special significance, as noted below.

Volunteering may have a consumption aspect to the extent that it provides personal or family services or offers contact with others, camaraderie, and interesting experiences. It may have an investment aspect to the extent that it offers experience that can be useful in the job market. Needless to say, it is no more feasible to quantify these components than to distinguish them from altruistic motives in observing actual volunteer behavior. That volunteering may be enjoyable or useful, however, suggests that theoretical models need to incorporate these possibilities.

An individual often has the choice between contributing money or volunteering in support of a charitable organization's programs. The analysis of volunteering thus raises the question of what determines the form in which giving is carried out. To explain why individuals choose to volunteer, two kinds of reasons may be offered. One is that, for some people, the very motivation for giving may be tied to a desire to be personally involved to at least some extent with that giving. Such individuals would not be indifferent between contributing ten hours to a worthy cause and making a monetary contribution that would buy the equivalent amount of work. Quite a different explanation is suggested by the "new home economics," a body of theory that analyzes work in the home analogously to production in a firm, with home production being the function of material inputs and the time of at least one household member. According to this view, volunteering and donations of money can be viewed as inputs in the nonmarket production of the good "giving and helping," or "charity." By implication, households derive satisfaction from the final "output" of the production process, not from the hours of volunteer work or from the dollars of contributions. While a desire for personal involvement—the first explanation—would seem to place a lower limit on the amount of volunteering that an individual would find acceptable, the home-production model implies that a family's mix of donations and volunteering will depend only on its relative efficiency in volunteering and the value of time of household members.

### 4.3.1   Models of Taxes and Volunteering

As in the case of monetary contributions, it is useful to analyze the effect of taxes on volunteering in the context of a simplified economic model. Using this model, it is possible to distinguish several effects of an income tax with a deduction for charitable contributions. Several issues are then dealt with in more detail, including the notion of "home production" of charity and the interaction between the time allocations of husband and wife.

### Volunteering in a Simple Model of Giving

It is straightforward to extend the basic neoclassical model of consumer behavior to explain contributions of money and volunteering. The individual may be viewed as choosing the desired amount of contributions, volunteering, and leisure subject to an exogenous wage rate and the total amount of time available. Appendix C presents such a model, in which the individual values contributions, volunteering, leisure, and purchased commodities. The individual in this model will volunteer until the valuation of a marginal hour of that activity equals the after-tax wage rate, the same condition applying to the allocation of time for leisure.

This analysis implies that taxes can affect volunteering in several ways. First, any income effect of taxes will affect the marginal utility of income. A tax increase lowers net income and raises the marginal utility of income, thus reducing the equilibrium amount of volunteering. This implies that empirical work should account for the effect of total tax liability on net income. Second, changes in the marginal tax rate influence volunteering by changing the shadow price of time. An increase in the marginal tax rate reduces the opportunity cost of volunteering and thus tends to increase volunteering. Finally, tax rules may affect the marginal utility of volunteering. One important way of doing this is by reducing the price of making donations of money. If donations and volunteering are *complementary* goods in the economic sense, reducing the price of one of them will tend to increase demand for the other.

The question of complementarity takes on central importance in considering whether U.S. tax laws have encouraged or discouraged volunteering. Since, on the one hand, the charitable deduction makes contributions of money less expensive relative to volunteering, one might suppose that volunteering would be discouraged, as compared to what they might have been without the deduction. But complementarity raises the opposite possibility. If contributions of money and time are complementary activities, the stimulation of the former through the charitable deduction would also encourage the latter.

### Donations and Volunteering as Inputs to "Charity"

One important distinction to be made with regard to this general model is whether individuals place a value on the hours of volunteering they do, or whether they simply value the resulting charitable services that result. If one is willing to assume that individuals do not place such a value per se on the form of charity, it is possible to simplify the preceding model by viewing donations and volunteering simply as two inputs used in producing the composite commodity, "charity." In this model the choice between donations and volunteering is assumed to be separated from other allocation decisions.[17] In the absence of the charitable deduction, the budget line is *KL,* with slope $(1-t)w$, as shown in figure 4.2. Allowing a full deduction for money donations changes the slope of the budget set from $w(1-t)$ to $w$. Clearly there is a substitution effect in favor of donations, shown here by the decrease in volunteering between points *a* and *b*. This is the detrimental effect of the deduction on volunteering. However, the income effect may outweigh this effect. If the amount of full income spent on charity remains a constant, the budget line becomes *JL*. If the deduction causes the individual to increase his total outlay for charity, however, the budget line would shift further out, say to *J' L '*. As drawn, this income effect dominates the substitution effect, and volunteering increases as a result of the deduction. Whether the income effect outweighs the detrimental substitution effect in general will be determined by two aspects of preferences: the "complementarity" of donations and volunteering, as shown by the curvature of the indifference curves, and the income elasticity of volunteering. If donations and volunteering were perfect substitutes, with indifference curves being straight lines, the deduction could cause the individual to switch entirely from volunteering to donations. Or, if volunteering were an inferior good (or had zero income elasticity), the

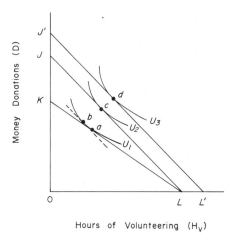

**Fig. 4.2**    Deductibility of contributions and individual volunteering. *KL*: no deductibility; slope $= w(1-t)$. *JL*: deductibility; slope $= w$. *J' L '*: deductibility with increase in budget for charity.

17. Separability implies that the marginal rate of substitution between volunteering and donations is not affected by the amount of other goods consumed. See Appendix C.

deduction would decrease volunteering. In general, however, the effects of the deduction are unclear in theory, and it is necessary to turn to empirical work to assess the effect of the charitable deduction on volunteering.[18]

## Volunteering in a Model of the Household

One important feature missing from models of individual behavior is the possibility of interactions in volunteering among household members. Gronau (1973) presents a model in which husband and wife maximize household utility subject to time constraints. Where production is of the fixed-proportion form and each spouse has marginal cost functions depending on their shadow wage and the price of purchased inputs, the household's optimal allocation involves letting the lower-cost spouse do the production of a given household good. Gronau distinguishes between households in which both spouses work in the market and those in which only the husband works in the market. Because of the complexity of the various combinations of work, leisure, and home production, I focus here and in part 4.4 of this chapter on the important case in which only the husband works in the market. One reason for doing this is that it allows a straightforward test of the complementarity hypothesis. By observing nonworking wives in households with different prices for donations, it is possible to estimate the cross-price effect on the amount of volunteering.

If one views volunteering as one form of home production, Gronau's analysis (p. 641) implies that the effect of an exogenous increase in household income on the family's allocation of time between leisure, volunteering, and other home production will depend on the time-intensity of each activity, the income elasticity of each activity, and the substitutability of each spouse's leisure and volunteering, home production, and market goods. The increase in income will increase the value of the wife's time, but the net effect on her time allocation is uncertain.

## Simultaneous versus Sequential Time Allocation

The neoclassical theory of the allocation of time described in this section pictures the individual or household making simultaneous decisions about how much time to spend in work, volunteering, home production,

---

18. A similar model is suggested by the theory of "home production." In this framework, volunteering—like other uses of nonworking time—is merely an input in the production of "homemade" commodities. Following Gronau's (1973) formulation, the household might value goods $Z_1, \ldots, Z_n$, each of which is subject to production functions of the form $Z_i = Z_i(X_i, H_i)$, where $X_i$ is a market good and $H_i$ is hours devoted to home production of $Z_i$. Gronau assumes fixed-proportions technology so that the marginal cost of producing $Z_i$ is $MC_i = a_i P_i + b_i w^*$, where $P_i$ is the price of $X_i$, $w^*$ is the shadow price of time, and $a_i$ and $b_i$ are constants. Applying this assumption to the production of charity gives the marginal cost as $MC = aP + bw^*$, where $P$ is the tax-defined price of making monetary donations. The assumption of fixed-proportion technology is, of course, the extreme of complementarity and was used only to highlight the possibilities for intrafamily allocations of time. In any case, the notion of home production of charity implies separability.

and leisure as well as how to spend money earnings. It is worth noting a sequential model in which some of these decisions are made before others. Specifically, it may be that the household first chooses the hours of market work, and only then decides how to allocate nonmarket work time between leisure, volunteering, and home production. To the extent that these nonmarket activities are similar to each other and hours of market work are often inflexible, this may be a reasonable model. If so, it highlights the importance of income taxation on labor supply as a determinant of volunteer effort. This model is considered further in section 4.5.

## 4.4  Empirical Analysis Related to Volunteer Work

In terms of the neoclassical model of time allocation, income taxation has three distinct effects on the supply of volunteer behavior by households. First, the income tax obviously affects disposable income and thus the demand for leisure and other forms of consumption. Second, the marginal tax rate has a substitution effect which affects the relative attractiveness of another hour spent in working, volunteering, or some other activity. Together, these effects may be quite important in determining whether individuals will participate in the labor market and how much they will work. These decisions obviously bear directly on the time available for volunteering. Whether they are made prior to or jointly with decisions to volunteer is unclear, however. Third, the deductibility of contributions of money and the marginal tax rate together determine the price of such contributions relative to consumption expenditures. What effect this price has on volunteering depends in part on whether contributions of time and money are complements or substitutes.[19]

Since market work is a principal competitor for the time available to individuals, this section begins with a brief review of empirical evidence on the effect of income taxes on labor supply. It then proceeds to a description of empirical work focusing directly on volunteering.

### 4.4.1  Taxes and Labor Supply

The effect of income taxation on labor force participation and work effort has been a topic of great importance in public finance long before the emergence of "supply-side" economics. The theory underlying most empirical work embodied three principal assumptions: individuals have preferences for "leisure" (nonworking time) and market goods, they may work any number of hours within their time constraint, and they respond the same to a change in the net wage whether it is caused by a change in the gross wage or the tax rate. In the empirical work on labor supply, attention has been focused on labor force participation and hours of market

19. See section 4.3 for an explanation of these terms.

work. Little attention has been paid to the allocation of time not spent in market work—the amalgam labeled "leisure." Following the economic theory of an individual's choice between leisure and other consumption, an income tax is shown to have an income effect and a substitution effect. Since leisure is a normal good, increasing the tax lowers disposable income and tends to increase work effort. The substitution effect, by lowering the net wage, goes in the opposite direction, discouraging market work.[20] Which effect dominates depends, of course, on the nature of preferences and the structure of the income tax. Empirical estimation is required.

In an early study, Break (1957) concluded that taxes had little effect on the labor supply of men. Increasingly sophisticated analyses since then have yielded much the same conclusion. Kosters (1969), for example, obtained very small estimates of the uncompensated labor supply for men—in the range of -0.04 to -0.09. Hausman's (1981) recent work also implies an uncompensated labor-supply elasticity for men around zero, although Hausman's findings imply larger income and substitution effects than those of previous studies. In contrast, most empirical analysis of the labor supply of women implies a relatively high degree of sensitivity to income taxes. Hausman, for example, finds uncompensated wage elasticities on the order of + 0.5 for female heads of households and + 1.0 for wives, implying a much greater importance for income taxation. The potential income effect of taxation on the labor supply of married women with children is illustrated in table 4.9, which shows market participation rates for women as a function of husband's income and education. In general, as the incomes of husbands rise, the proportion of wives who work in the labor force declines markedly. Although this suggests nothing about the division of time spent outside of the labor force, it certainly demonstrates that important differences exist in the amount of time available for volunteer work.

### 4.4.2   Empirical Analysis of Volunteering

In assessing explicit analyses of volunteering, it is useful to relate theoretical models of individual behavior to empirical analysis, discuss the data and models used in previous analyses, and describe the results of those analyses.

---

20. The effect of a proportional income tax can be written:

$$\frac{dL}{dt} = wS - y\,\frac{\partial L}{\partial y}$$

where $L$ is hours of work, $t$ is the tax rate, $S$ is the income-compensated wage effect on labor, $w$ is the gross wage, and $y$ is total income. The first term on the right-hand side corresponds to the substitution effect of the tax, and the second to the income effect. See, for example, Atkinson and Stiglitz 1980, pp. 23–61.

Table 4.9      **Labor Force Participation Rates of Married Women with Children under 18, by Years of Schooling Completed and Income of Husband, 1978**

| Husband's Income, 1977 | Total[a] Participation Rate | Years of School Completed by Wife | | |
|---|---|---|---|---|
| | | 0 to 11 | 12 | 16 |
| Under $3,000 | 49.2 | 36.1 | 56.0 | —[b] |
| $3,000 to 4,999 | 50.8 | 41.6 | 55.8 | —[b] |
| $5,000 to 6,999 | 50.6 | 42.9 | 56.1 | —[b] |
| $7,000 to 9,999 | 54.9 | 48.6 | 56.8 | 75.6 |
| $10,000 to 12,999 | 56.7 | 49.4 | 56.4 | 68.5 |
| $13,000 to 14,999 | 54.6 | 44.3 | 54.9 | 58.2 |
| $15,000 to 19,999 | 51.3 | 39.8 | 51.7 | 55.2 |
| $20,000 to 24,999 | 46.1 | 36.4 | 44.6 | 49.5 |
| $25,000 to 34,999 | 40.3 | 33.3 | 34.4 | 48.5 |
| $35,000 to 49,999 | 26.7 | —[b] | 35.8 | 46.8 |
| $50,000 or more | 26.7 | —[b] | 23.7 | 24.6 |

*Source:* U.S. Bureau of Labor Statistics 1979, pp. A33–A34, table 14.
*Note:* Labor force is given as percentage of population.
[a]Total includes wives with other amounts of schooling than shown separately.
[b]Base is less than 75,000 persons.

## Models for Estimation

Based on the theoretical discussion in section 4.3, an empirical model for estimating the effect of taxes on volunteering is given by:

(1)      $H_v = f(w^*(1-t), P, Y_f - T, Z)$,

where $H_v$ is hours of volunteer work, $w^*(1-t)$ is the net-of-tax wage rate, $P$ is the net price of giving a dollar in contributions, $Y_f$ is "full income," $T$ is taxes, and $Z$ is a vector of household characteristics such as age, family composition, and education. This function is interpreted as a supply function for volunteer effort. It can be estimated from available data without reference to demand by assuming that the demand for volunteer service is perfectly elastic at the going price of zero.

Two "prices" are important in this supply function. To the extent that individuals can choose the number of hours they work, the net-of-tax wage represents the opportunity cost of spending an hour doing (unpaid) volunteer work. For those who are not working at all, $w^*$ in this ideal model is the gross "reservation wage" necessary to entice them to work. Since giving money is obviously a substitute for giving time, the price of money gifts $P$ is included to reflect the cross-price effect on volunteering while $w^*(1-t)$ is the "own-price" of volunteering.

Full income measures potential income for some given amount of work effort and so is not a function of the amount of labor supplied. Previous empirical work on the supply of labor suggests that leisure is a normal good. This finding provides no guidance, however, as to how the demand for volunteer activity changes when income changes. Finally, a model of volunteer work should contain a set of variables designed to account for demographic characteristics likely to influence the desire or ability to do volunteer work. The information presented at the beginning of this chapter suggests, for example, that volunteering varies by age, sex, and family composition as well as income. As in any econometric analysis, it is important to account for other potentially important variables in order to isolate as much as possible the independent effect of the variable of interest—in this case, taxes.

### Econometric Problems

The estimation of this ideal model is difficult in practice owing to the complexity of the allocation process within households and shortcomings in available data. One of several alternative models might be used to explain the allocation of time within a household. In its most general form, a model might allow for the simultaneous determination of hours of work and volunteering for each member of a household, or at least each adult member.[21] In order to estimate such a model, it would be necessary to have not only the hours of work and volunteering for each adult but also a wage rate for each. In practice, wage rates of working couples are often not recorded separately for both spouses, and reservation wages are, by their nature, unobserved. As has been spelled out in the recent econometric literature, restricting the sample to those with observed wages will introduce sample selection bias into the estimates.[22] Even the observed wage may not be a wholly appropriate measure of the potential wage. As Lewis (1969) has pointed out, the wage may be a function of the number of hours worked, making wages earned by part-time workers suspect. In addition, wages may reflect conditions of the workplace, making a determination of the potential wage or full income problematic.

One simplification that can be made in this general model is to assume a recursive structure, whereby decisions to work or not precede the decisions about how much to work and whether and how much to volunteer. In this model taxes would be a determinant of the number of hours worked, leaving remaining hours to be divided between volunteering and other activities that can be lumped together as "leisure," though the latter includes household work. Since neither volunteering nor leisure provide monetary income, the marginal tax rate (through the net wage) would not affect the choice between them. The price of cash gifts would, however, affect volunteering through its cross-price effect, as above. In this recur-

21. For models of household decision making, see Becker 1974.
22. For a discussion of this problem, see Heckman and MaCurdy 1980.

sive model, the primary influence of taxes on volunteering would be seen in the determination of hours of work. How the nonwork time is split between volunteering and leisure depends on the income elasticity of each and the cross-price effect between the price of donations and volunteering.

### Data on Volunteer Work

Household surveys provide the most important source of data on volunteer activity. Since 1965 several national surveys (U.S. Department of Labor 1969; Gallup Organization 1981) have been performed with the primary objective of estimating the amount and kind of volunteer work performed in the United States. Questions on volunteering have also been included in other surveys.[23] As reflected in the first section of this chapter, however, these surveys have differed in many respects, including the very measure of volunteer activity. Respondents were asked whether they participate in certain volunteer activities and how many hours they spend. The surveys differed, however, in both the time period covered and the kinds of activities counted as volunteering. The time period covered ranges from the previous week to the previous year. As for the definition of volunteer activity, surveys differ in their inclusion of volunteering for religious organizations and informal volunteering, such as helping a neighbor move.

The data set with the most complete information on tax-related variables is the National Study of Philanthropy undertaken by the Census Bureau and the University of Michigan's Survey Research Center.[24] The sample included over 2800 households, selected so as to oversample households with high incomes. The survey asked about volunteer activity of husband and wife during the year 1973, and this activity was broken down by type of organization served. Data on labor force participation, household income, and tax status are included, but it is impossible to identify the wage rates of both spouses in two-earner couples.

A major advantage of the National Study of Philanthropy is the information available on income taxes. Since respondents were asked whether or not they itemized, it is possible with some reliance to calculate the price of giving for almost all the sample. The only major problem is those taxpayers who are on the "borderline" between itemizing and not itemizing and who would, in fact, not have found it advantageous to itemize if their charitable contributions had been zero. The presence of these taxpayers requires special attention. With the exception of the study by Mueller discussed below, all of the econometric studies of volunteering done to date have employed this data set.

---

23. See, for example Morgan, Dye, and Hybels 1977.
24. For a full description, see Morgan, Dye, and Hybels 1977.

*Econometric Studies*

Three previous econometric analyses of volunteering have been identi-fied and are described here. The first is that of Mueller (1975).[25] The data were based on a 1963 survey of 310 women who had graduated from Co-lumbia between 1945 and 1951. Although the survey contained no ques-tions about taxes, important social and economic information was avail-able. In particular, information on the respondent's current or last market wage, husband's income, age of children, religion, and size of community was included. In addition, Mueller added two variables intended to ac-count for volunteer work done in anticipation of gaining useful job-related skills. One is the average comparable market wage for the kind of volun-teer work being done, and the other is a dummy variable signifying the re-spondent's desire to look for a job. Using ordinary least squares, Mueller estimated equations explaining total hours of volunteer work and hours of volunteer work other than for professional societies. Neither the hus-band's income nor the gross wage are significant in explaining volunteer hours. These results suggest that volunteering is unlike leisure, which is re-sponsive to the wage and income elastic. Instead, Mueller argues, the re-sults suggest that women engage in volunteering because it will give them valuable skills rather than because it is enjoyable. Supporting this notion, Mueller found that women volunteered more if they performed jobs with high market wages and if they planned to return to work. These findings could merely suggest, however, that interesting volunteer jobs elicit more effort and that volunteer jobs meet similar personal needs as market jobs. Taken together, these findings suggest that the potential for strong tax ef-fects through income or wage rates is limited.

Among the other explanatory variables, identifying with a major reli-gious faith was positively associated with volunteer work. Whether reli-gious women volunteer more in nonreligious organizations is unclear, however. Size of community also had a significant effect. Women in small towns and rural areas volunteered the most. The number of children or the presence of young children were not significant variables.

The second study of volunteer effort, by Dye (1980), was the first to ex-amine explicitly the effect of taxes. By including the price of giving money as an explanatory variable, Dye was able to focus on the question of whether volunteering is a substitute or a complement for contributions of money. This empirical question is one of the most important in evaluating the effect of taxes on volunteering.

25. Havrilesky, Schweitzer, and Wright (1973) analyzed some aggregate data on volunteers for environmental groups. Data on income and wages were not included, and no variables were significant at the 95 percent level in explaining median hours of volunteered time. The authors did find, however, that volunteering was greatest in areas with the poorest environ-mental quality.

As the first researcher to use the National Study of Philanthropy, Dye was able to calculate the net price of giving using data for individual households. Equations were estimated in two stages. The first explains whether households volunteered at all, and the second explains hours of volunteering by the household. While this procedure is not ideal from an econometric point of view, [26] it points up two rather distinct components to the volunteering decision, comparable to the participation and hours of work components in labor supply. In his basic equations Dye considers volunteering for the entire household together, though he notes that similar results were obtained from individuals. In both stages volunteering is explained by the logarithm of the price of money gifts, net income, and wealth and by dummy variables for education, age, and marital status. Dye found that volunteering increases with education and wealth, is higher for married couples, and is lower for those over 65.

Volunteering in Dye's equations is negatively associated with the price of giving money, suggesting that volunteering and monetary contributions are gross complements. Taken together, his equations imply a cross-price elasticity of -0.83. If correct, this finding would imply that policies lowering the price of contributions will encourage volunteering. In other words, the tendency for both kinds of contributions to be done together outweighs any tendency to substitute one form for another. As strong as this complementarity appears to be, however, one weakness in Dye's empirical model is the absence of a net wage. As noted above, the measurement of the net wage for households is greatly complicated by the fact that wages cannot be observed for those who do not work. Nonetheless, the omission of this variable may bias the cross-price effect. For example, if the price of contributions is positively correlated to the net wage, the negative effect for the price of contributions may result partly from an omitted net wage that would have had a similar negative effect if included. If price and the net wage are negatively related, the estimated price effect would, in absolute value, be an underestimate.

In the third econometric study, Menchik and Weisbrod (1981; 1982) used the same survey data to estimate a more complete model of volunteer work. By including the net wage as an explanatory variable, they are able to reflect the choice between market work and volunteering. Since the net wage is the opportunity cost of volunteering, a straightforward model such as that described in Appendix C predicts that a rise in the net wage will discourage volunteering as long as the substitution effect dominates the income effect. The addition of the net wage required a restriction in the sample used, however. Since the Michigan survey data does not pro-

---

26. As Dye suggests, Tobit would be appropriate, as would logit or probit for the first stage and some method that accounts for sample selection in the second.

vide separate data on the wages of working spouses, wages could be approximated from family income only for households with one earner.[27] Consequently, Menchik and Weisbrod analyzed the volunteer activity of working adults in single-earner households. Volunteering by spouses not in the labor force as well as by two-earner households was not considered in the study.[28]

A second important feature of the Menchik-Weisbrod study is the replacement of reported income by "full income," the income that would have been earned if the earner had worked full-time. Because it is independent of the labor supply of the worker, it is considered an exogenous variable. The tax and marginal-tax-rate variables are also calculated using full income. The only drawback to this procedure is that it assumes that participation decisions—specifically, the decision of nonworking spouses not to work—are independent of taxes. The importance of the bias introduced by such treatment is, however, unclear.

Menchik and Weisbrod also include a variety of explanatory variables measuring characteristics of the household and local area. Their 1982 study reports Tobit estimates of equations explaining hours of volunteering as a function of the net wage, the price of contributing money, and full income as well as local government expenditures, sex, marital status, the presence of children in the household, age entered quadratically, and dummy variables for size of community, parental characteristics, and informal helping activity.

Table 4.10 summarizes their basic estimates for total volunteering. The sample used for estimation excludes households with incomes over $50,000. The most striking finding is that the net wage has a positive and significant coefficient, contrary to the expected negative effect. Menchik and Weisbrod (1982, p. 24) explain this by noting the possibility that volunteering is undertaken primarily as an investment in human capital, not as a "consumption" activity like leisure. If the return to this kind of investment is correlated with the net wage, volunteering could rise with the net wage. They find further support for the investment model in the insignificant sign of full income; a positive effect would be expected under the consumption model of volunteering.[29] The price of making monetary donations is insignificant. Thus no support is provided either for Dye's con-

27. They approximated the hourly wage by
$$w = (Y - \sum_i r_i A_i) / H,$$
where $Y$ is total income, $A_i$ is the holding in asset of type $i$, $r_i$ is that asset's rate of return, and $H$ is approximate annual hours of work. Savings accounts and bonds were assigned a rate of return of 7 percent, while stocks and other assets were assumed to have a rate of 3 percent.

28. Menchik and Weisbrod (1981, p. 169n) also note that this sample selection rule may introduce statistical bias as well as to the extent that workers are systematically different from those not in the labor market.

29. This expectation assumes volunteering to be a normal good.

Table 4.10          Menchik-Weisbrod Equation Explaining Hours of Volunteer Work

| Explanatory Variables | Estimated Coefficients |
|---|---|
| Constant | 0.413 |
| Net wage | 76.5[a] |
| Price of contributions | 29.8 |
| Full income | 0.007 |
| Local-government expenditures | −0.32 |
| Female | 12.07 |
| Married | 222.2 |
| Young child | 262.0 |
| Other children | 375.0[a] |
| Age | −59.9[a] |
| Age squared | 0.566[a] |
| Large city | −38.6 |
| Suburb of city | −100.9 |
| Medium-sized city | 34.2 |
| Small city | −300.6[a] |
| Parents contributed | −91.0 |
| Parents attended religious services | −281.4 |
| Father completed high school | 37.5 |
| Hours of informal helping | 0.484 |

*Source:* Menchik and Weisbrod 1982, p. 25.

*Note:* The sample included 816 observations of households with incomes of $50,000 or less. The method of estimation was Tobit.

[a]Significant at 95 percent level.

clusions that giving time and money are complementary or for the alternative hypothesis that they are substitutes.

## 4.5 Further Analysis: Explaining Volunteering by Women

This section extends previous empirical work by focusing on volunteering by women. As shown in tables 4.1 and 4.2, women volunteer more often than men. Yet analysis on working adults in single-earner households, such as the Menchik-Weisbrod study, virtually ignores the volunteer behavior of women. An important drawback to this approach is that, for most women in the philanthropy survey, neither wages nor potential wages can be approximated.[30] Therefore, it is impossible to apply the neoclassical model of simultaneous time allocation, described above in section 4.3.

---

30. For a description of Menchik and Weisbrod's (1981) method of approximating wages for single-earner households, see their section D and footnote 27. Because income is not reported separately for spouses, it is impossible to obtain wage estimates for two-earner households.

A sequential variation of the full neoclassical model is, therefore, adopted in this section. It is assumed that, for women, the labor-force-participation decision is made prior to the parceling up of nonmarket work time between "home production," volunteering, and leisure. As a consequence, the allocation of time by women becomes a recursive process, with the volunteering decision following the labor-force-participation decision. In this model taxes have two important effects on volunteering: the effect on participation and the effect on time allocation given the participation decision. A more restrictive form of this model would be that hours of work are also determined prior to the allocation of nonwork time, but this assumption will be used only as one alternative in this section. The assumption that the participation decision comes prior to the volunteering decision does not seem unreasonable, given the large number of women who choose to remain out of the labor market for long periods during their lives. Still, the recursive model used here is largely an assumption of convenience, made necessary by the lack of appropriate labor market data for most women.

Equations explaining the decision to volunteer as well as the number of hours of volunteering per year for women were estimated using the same National Study of Philanthropy. Equations (A) and (C) in table 4.11 give the estimated coefficients of a set of explanatory variables measuring household net income, net price of making donations, age, the presence of children, education, family background, and newness in the neighborhood. Equation (A), which explains volunteering as a dichotomous variable, is estimated by the logit maximum-likelihood procedure. Corresponding to the tabulation in table 4.2, volunteering rises and then falls with age in equation (A). Volunteering is higher for women with more children under 18 at home, suggesting that a mother's involvement with child-related activities increases the likelihood that she will become a volunteer. The estimated coefficients of the education terms suggest, as has previous analysis, that women's volunteering increases with education. Finally, the negative effect of the net price of donations supports the hypothesis of complementarity between donations and volunteering.

Equation (C), explaining hours of volunteer work, is estimated by the Tobit maximum-likelihood method. It shows significant coefficients only for the presence of a small child (negative) and college education (positive). The coefficient of price is negative, but not significantly different from zero at the 95 percent level ($t = 1.0$). The point estimate of the coefficient implies a cross-price elasticity of $-0.25$ for expected hours of volunteering, calculated at the mean number of hours.[31] These equations

---

31. The elasticity is $F(z)$ $(b/H)$, where $F(z)$ is the predicted probability of positive hours of volunteering (0.499), $b$ is the coefficient of the price term ($-52.3$), and $H$ is the mean number of hours of volunteering (103.4).

Table 4.11    **Volunteering by Women**

|  | Volunteering (dichotomous) | | Annual Hours of Volunteer Work | |
|---|---|---|---|---|
|  | Logit | | Tobit | |
|  | (A) | (B) | (C) | (D) |
|  | Women | | Women | |
| Explanatory | Not | All | Not | All |
| Variable | Employed | Women | Employed | Women |
| Log of net income | − 0.00241 | − 0.0388 | 18.1 | 3.90 |
| Log of price | − 0.966[a] | − 0.895[a] | − 52.3 | − 79.6[a] |
| Age | 0.105[a] | 0.188[a] | 14.4 | 24.9[a] |
| (Age)$^2$ | − 0.00113[a] | − 0.00190[a] | − 0.149[a] | − 0.241[a] |
| Children under 18 | 0.181[a] | 0.226[a] | 18.4[a] | 24.5[a] |
| Children under 5 | − 0.138 | 0.162 | − 64.8[a] | − 1.77 |
| High school graduate | 0.879[a] | 0.773[a] | 104.[a] | 94.1[a] |
| College graduate | 1.71[a] | 1.44[a] | 191.[a] | 169.[a] |
| Parents contributed | 0.201 | 0.155 | 8.01 | − 3.44 |
| New in neighborhood | − 0.266 | − 0.256 | 7.90 | − 1.82 |
| Hours of market work | — | − 0.00688[a] | — | − 1.27[a] |
| Intercept | − 3.43[a] | − 5.06[a] | − 649[a] | − 783.[a] |

*Source:* National Study of Philanthropy 1973.
*Note:* The sample size was 1122 in equations (A) and (C) and 2323 in equations (B) and (D). The predicted probability of observing volunteering ($F(z)$) was 0.499 and 0.314 in equations (C) and (D), respectively.
[a]Significantly different from zero at 95 percent level.

provide only mixed support for the hypothesis of a complementarity effect of the charitable deduction on volunteering. To reiterate, both equations (A) and (C) rest on the assumption that participation decisions are made prior to volunteering decisions, thus making it possible to restrict the examination to those not in the labor market. While the behavior of this sample may differ from that of working women, this assumption, if correct, would imply that there is no simultaneity bias due to the endogeneity of the participation decision.

The much stronger assumption that hours of market work are predetermined is embodied in equations (B) and (D), which include women both in and out of the labor force. The estimated effects in general are similar to those in equations (A) and (B). In addition, the hours of market-work variable exerts a negative and significant effect on volunteering. The point estimate in equation (D) implies that volunteer hours will be reduced about eight hours for every ten additional hours of market work, suggesting that volunteering will take most of the brunt of increases in women's hours of market work. Because adequate wage data are not available for most women, however, it is impossible to estimate a complete model that accounts for simultaneous choice of hours of volunteering and market work. The price of contributions is significant in both equations. In equation (D), the cross-price elasticity is $-0.35$.[32] This point estimate implies that a 10 percent decrease in the price of giving, say from .60 to .54, would cause a 3.5 percent increase in the expected amount of volunteering.

### 4.6  Conclusion

In summary, the income tax appears to influence volunteering by affecting both participation choices and the division of nonmarket work time. The hypothesis that giving time and giving money are complementary activities receives some support in each analysis of the National Survey of Philanthropy. While the findings are not everywhere statistically significant and are based on only one data set, the findings are reasonably consistent with each other. If correct, these findings suggest that the tax system has a much more pervasive effect on behavior than what can be observed in contributions alone. They suggest that the tax system indirectly encourages involvement in charitable organizations by providing an explicit incentive for only one form of involvement. The work of religious and charitable organizations appears to use people's time and money together. While the proportions obviously vary from person to person and from organization to organization, neither alone is as useful as both together. If the United States is, as de Tocqueville observed, a nation of joiners and voluntary associations (de Tocqueville 1835), then the tax system, through its deductions for charitable contributions, appears to foster that quality. It is not unreasonable to suppose that the extension of the deduction to nonitemizers will further encourage involvement in and volunteer work for charitable organizations. Informal volunteering and helping behavior may be encouraged as well.

---

32. The elasticity is again calculated at the mean number of annual hours of volunteering for the sample which is 71.3.

# 5    Corporate Contributions

In 1980 corporations in the United States contributed an estimated $2.3 billion to charitable organizations, or about 0.8 percent of their pretax net income.[1] Although this amount appears small in relation to aggregate individual giving, considerable importance has been attached to corporate contributions. Because of corporations' visibility in political and economic activities, corporate gifts are viewed as a barometer of business sentiment and, to some extent, as a model for individual giving. President Reagan focused particular attention on corporate giving in 1981 when he called on corporations to lead private philanthropy in making up for reductions in federal expenditures for social programs.[2]

Despite the present importance of corporate giving, the propriety of such corporate behavior has been debated vigorously over the past several decades. As president, Franklin Roosevelt opposed the practice on the grounds that corporations should not be able to "purchase" goodwill and that charitable contributions were properly the domain of shareholders ("Corporation Gifts to Charities" 1935, p. 540). Similarly, current critics have argued that philanthropy and other manifestations of "social responsibility" that sacrifice profits constitute improper behavior by corporations.[3] In spite of these arguments, however, the view that corporations

---

1. U.S. Internal Revenue Service, *Statistics of Income, 1980—Corporation Income Tax Returns* 1983, p. 36, table 3. This figure is based on corporations with positive net income only. As noted in the text, the percentage limitation on the deductibility of corporate contributions makes this restriction necessary.

2. For a discussion of the pressure brought by this call, see Butler 1981, p. 12.

3. See, for example, Friedman 1962, chap. 8; Lindley Clark, "The Business of Business Isn't Charity," *Wall Street Journal,* 2 February 1982, p. 31; or Paul MacAvoy, "The Business Lobby's Wrong Business," *New York Times,* 20 December 1981, p. F3. MacAvoy states: "Unless social and charitable activities reduce long-run marginal costs or increase consumer demand then they divert resources from the social goals inherent in maximum production."

do have such responsibility appears to be widely held. In some communities, for example, corporations are active in supporting urban development and other community projects though membership in "5 percent clubs," signifying contributions equal to 5 percent of net income.[4] One prominent business organization explicitly recognizes such social responsibility in its official statement on corporate philanthropy:

> The Business Roundtable believes that corporate philanthropy, primarily through corporations, is an integral part of corporate social responsibility. All business entities should recognize philanthropy both as good business and as an obligation if they are to be considered responsible corporate citizens of the national and local communities in which they operate.[5]

A recent survey of corporate officers involved in philanthropy (Siegfried and McElroy 1981, p. 19) revealed that corporate responsibility was the most important reason for making contributions, followed by a desire to improve conditions in the community. Contributions may, of course, have more pragmatic motives as well. Siegfried and McElroy report that over a quarter of their sample of corporate officers thought that an improved public image was a "very important" reason for making corporate contributions. In fact it appears to be a common practice for corporations to make at least some contributions with an eye to improving its public image.[6]

This chapter examines corporate charitable contributions, with particular emphasis on the influence of the federal corporate income tax. The first section describes the size, composition, and growth in corporate giving. The next section briefly describes the major tax provisions related to contributions. The third section discusses several theories to explain corporate giving and note the implications of each for empirical analysis. The fourth section describes previous empirical studies of corporate contributions. A principal objective of such studies is to determine the effect of the corporate tax on the level of giving. As in the case of individuals, the tax affects a corporation's after-tax net income as well as its price of giving, so this section focuses particularly on the influence of income and price on

4. See, for example, Kathleen Teltsch, "Minnesota a Model of Corporate Aid to Cities," *New York Times,* 27 July 1981, pp. A1, A11. See also Andrews 1952, p. 17.

5. Business Roundtable, "Business Roundtable Position on Corporate Philanthropy," March 1981.

6. A representative of a southern power company reportedly told Franklin Roosevelt that his company's policy was to make the first contribution to each local charity drive in cities and towns in its area ("Corporation Gifts to Charities" 1935, p. 540). Similar reasoning based on marketing research underlies Horvitz's (1974) explanation of the legal aspects of gifts that bring benefits to the firm. The connection between self-interest and social responsibility is made by one business executive: "One of the important duties of each citizen, whether a corporation or an individual, is to work in a multitude of ways for the betterment of society. In the long run this is a self-interested proposition, in no way inconsistent with a corporation's duties to its shareholders" (Atwater 1982, p. 17).

giving. The final section of the chapter presents new evidence on the effect of taxation on corporate giving using data on tax returns from 1936 to 1980. The implications of these findings are also considered.

## 5.1 Growth and Distribution of Corporate Contributions

The $2.55 billion of corporate giving in 1980 is only about one-fifteenth the size of individual giving. Since virtually no corporate giving goes to religious organizations, however, it may be more meaningful to compare corporate giving to nonreligious individual giving. By this measure, corporate giving is about a sixth the size of individual giving. If contributions of individuals and corporations are expressed as a percent of income available to each, the ratios are comparable. Whereas corporations contributed about 0.8 percent of their aggregate net income in 1980, contributions by individuals as a percent of personal income amount to 1.8 percent for all contributions and 0.7 percent for nonreligious contributions only.

Table 5.1 traces the growth of corporate contributions since 1936. Expressing amounts in 1972 constant dollars, total corporate giving rose from $91 million in 1936 to $2.32 billion in 1980, an increase of fourteen times. During the same period, corporate net income increased to five times its 1936 level, and there were eight times as many corporations with assets and net income. Contributions as a percentage of net income increased from 0.28 percent in 1936 to 0.79 percent in 1980. By any measure, therefore, corporate contributions have grown in absolute and relative importance over this period. The table also shows the variation in corporate tax payments over the period, with the average tax rates rising to their highest levels during World War II and the Korean War. Although the correlation is not exact, it appears that the contributions-to-income ratio tends to be highest in those years of highest tax rates, suggesting that corporations are sensitive to the net-of-tax price of contributions in much the same way that individuals are.

### 5.1.1 Contributions by Industry and Income

At any one time, the level and distribution of contributions vary by industry and firm size. Table 5.2 presents contributions as a percentage of net income for eleven major industries and selected minor industries in 1980. In general, the contributions ratio tends to be relatively highest in industries with more direct contact with consumers—for example, banking, retail trade, and food products. The lowest ratios, for holding companies and mining, are for industries with little direct contact with consumers. These ratios may, of course, vary for a number of reasons, including differences in profitability, but one factor that appears to be important is the potential usefulness of contributions in creating a favorable public image.

**Table 5.1    Corporate Contributions: Returns with Net Income and Assets, 1936–80 (dollar amounts in thousands of dollars)**

| Year | Contributions | Net Income | Contributions as Percentage of Net Income | Taxes as Percentage of Net Income | Number of Returns |
|---|---|---|---|---|---|
| 1936 | $ 25,657 | $ 9,101,973 | .28 | 11.0 | 188,533 |
| 1937 | 29,029 | 9,391,521 | .31 | 11.4 | 178,935 |
| 1938 | 22,826 | 6,368,559 | .36 | 13.3 | 159,056 |
| 1939 | 29,023 | 8,708,642 | .33 | 14.0 | 187,920 |
| 1940 | 36,761 | 11,068,395 | .33 | 22.8 | 207,270 |
| 1941 | 56,496 | 17,796,797 | .32 | 39.7 | 246,195 |
| 1942 | 95,197 | 23,785,152 | .40 | 51.0 | 249,668 |
| 1943 | 156,073 | 28,398,598 | .55 | 55.5 | 260,341 |
| 1944 | 230,441 | 26,879,959 | .86 | 54.9 | 266,615 |
| 1945 | 261,487 | 21,944,924 | 1.19 | 48.8 | 281,244 |
| 1946 | 208,161 | 26,680,636 | .78 | 32.6 | 334,042 |
| 1947 | 235,213 | 32,789,713 | .72 | 32.9 | 357,041 |
| 1948 | 233,594 | 35,790,976 | .65 | 32.9 | 370,056 |
| 1949 | 217,066 | 30,157,558 | .72 | 32.1 | 360,243 |
| 1950 | 247,569 | 43,704,379 | .57 | 39.3 | 400,914 |
| 1951 | 338,809 | 44,902,623 | .75 | 48.8 | 414,856 |
| 1952 | 393,474 | 40,085,418 | .98 | 47.4 | 418,174 |
| 1953 | 487,881 | 41,440,712 | 1.18 | 47.5 | 418,150 |
| 1954 | 306,840 | 39,137,178 | .78 | 42.6 | 419,679 |

| Year | | | | | |
|------|-----------|-------------|------|------|-----------|
| 1955 | 406,742 | 49,821,123 | .82 | 43.2 | 489,592 |
| 1956 | 409,868 | 49,818,409 | .82 | 42.6 | 537,275 |
| 1957 | 410,239 | 48,337,857 | .85 | 42.3 | 550,665 |
| 1958 | 380,137 | 43,061,174 | .88 | 43.3 | 586,746 |
| 1959 | 469,530 | 51,194,875 | .92 | 43.6 | 650,035 |
| 1960 | 472,860 | 49,397,433 | .96 | 44.0 | 658,227 |
| 1961 | 501,894 | 51,981,781 | .97 | 42.4 | 703,160 |
| 1962 | 588,634 | 55,889,041 | 1.05 | 42.6 | 772,503 |
| 1963 | 649,350 | 60,958,152 | 1.07 | 42.9 | 795,436 |
| 1964 | 721,211 | 68,316,387 | 1.06 | 40.6 | 844,783 |
| 1965 | 771,731 | 80,161,530 | .96 | 39.2 | 900,442 |
| 1966 | 796,498 | 86,838,441 | .92 | 39.3 | 923,913 |
| 1967 | 814,666 | 85,939,311 | .95 | 38.5 | 971,793 |
| 1968 | 984,577 | 94,045,273 | 1.05 | 41.7 | 983,345 |
| 1969 | 1,044,608 | 92,784,603 | 1.13 | 42.2 | 1,029,660 |
| 1970 | 786,951 | 83,036,167 | .95 | 39.8 | 991,660 |
| 1971 | 854,488 | 95,967,034 | .89 | 38.8 | 1,046,052 |
| 1972 | 996,310 | 112,018,071 | .89 | 38.0 | 1,119,422 |
| 1973 | 1,163,718 | 137,421,249 | .85 | 37.9 | 1,178,250 |
| 1974 | 1,186,374 | 170,185,222 | .70 | 38.6 | 1,184,177 |
| 1975 | 1,184,321 | 168,526,861 | .70 | 39.0 | 1,199,848 |
| 1976 | 1,464,686 | 209,086,024 | .70 | 39.6 | 1,248,794 |
| 1977 | 1,756,504 | 243,212,774 | .72 | 39.4 | 1,400,910 |
| 1978 | 2,063,129 | 272,789,622 | .75 | 39.3 | 1,495,398 |
| 1979 | 2,664,449 | 319,488,771 | .83 | 37.3 | 1,562,549 |
| 1980 | 2,320,850 | 294,222,899 | .79 | 35.4 | 1,568,535 |

Table 5.2              Corporate Contributions by Industry: Returns with Net Income, 1980

| Industry | Contributions as Percentage of Net Income | |
|---|---|---|
| Agriculture, forestry, and fishing | 0.53 | |
| Mining (total) | 0.47 | |
| *Selected minor industry*[a] | | |
| Oil and gas extraction | | 0.38 |
| Construction | 0.95 | |
| Manufacturing (total) | 0.84 | |
| *Selected minor industries* | | |
| Food and kindred products | | 1.10 |
| Chemicals and allied products | | 0.97 |
| Petroleum and coal products | | 0.47 |
| Primary metal industries | | 0.93 |
| Fabricated metal products | | 0.92 |
| Machinery, except electrical | | 0.82 |
| Electrical and electronic equipment | | 1.02 |
| Motor vehicles | | 0.91 |
| Transportation | 0.80 | |
| Communication | 0.78 | |
| Electric, gas, and sanitary services | 0.74 | |
| Wholesale trade | 0.59 | |
| Retail trade | 1.16 | |
| Finance, insurance, and real estate (total) | 0.66 | |
| *Selected minor industries* | | |
| Banking | | 1.77 |
| Other credit agencies | | 0.93 |
| Security, commodity brokers and services | | 0.72 |
| Insurance | | 0.75 |
| Real estate | | 0.68 |
| Holding companies | | 0.10 |
| Services | 0.84 | |
| All industries | 0.79 | |

*Source:* U.S. Internal Revenue Service, *Statistics of Income—1980, Corporation Income Tax Returns 1983,* pp. 36–43, table 3.
[a]Minor industries with over $50 billion in assets each.

One relationship that has interested researchers is that between contributions and corporate income. Whether it is seen as a measure of company scale or capacity to make gifts, net income is often taken as a quantity by which firm contributions can be compared. Figure 5.1 displays contributions as a percentage of pretax net income by asset class in 1940,

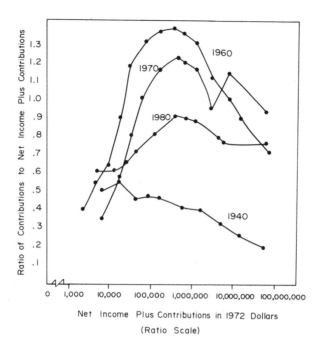

**Fig. 5.1**    Contributions ratio as function of net income, selected years.
*Source:* U.S.Internal Revenue Service, *Statistics of Income, Corporation Income Tax Returns.*

1960, 1970, and 1980. Since the asset size of corporations tends to rise with net income, the resulting patterns show the combined effect of both measures of firm scale. Except in 1940, the ratio of contributions to net income rises with average income and then falls. Maximum contribution ratios were 1.4 percent at $278,000 (1972 dollars) in 1960, 1.2 percent at $369,000 in 1970, and 0.9 percent at $358,000 in 1980. In 1940 the contribution ratio fell throughout the range except for the peak of 0.6 percent at $175,000. Each distribution suggests that, among the largest firms, the contribution ratio falls with increased size. Besides this similarity, the striking characteristic of figure 5.1 is the overall dissimilarity among the distributions over time. This suggests the importance of careful econometric analysis of corporate giving in order to disentangle the effects of taxes, profits, and other economic conditions in explaining these differences.

### 5.1.2    Size Distribution of Corporate Gifts

When one looks beyond average values, one of the striking features of corporate giving is the dramatic unevenness of giving among corporations. It goes without saying that corporations vary greatly in size. Thus it is to be expected that the scale of virtually all expenditure items will also vary between large and small corporations. But, as table 5.3 shows, corporations differ widely in their propensity to make contributions at all. Whereas over 90 percent of corporations with assets over $1 billion made some contribution in 1977, only 15 percent of those with positive assets less than $25,000 made contributions at all. (Six percent gave over $500 in 1977.) Overall, only 35.5 percent of active corporations in 1977 made contributions.[7] Since these figures are based on annual data, it is difficult to guess how many of these corporations refrain from making contributions over a longer period. Combining their greater incomes and higher rate of contributions, one can readily see that large corporations account for the lion's share of total corporate giving. As shown in table 5.3 the largest 0.2 percent of firms accounted for over three-quarters of all corporate contributions.

Table 5.3        Proportion of Firms Making Contributions by Asset Size: Active
                 Corporations, 1977

| Asset Size | Percentage of All Firms | Percentage of All Contributions | Firms Making a Contribution as Percentage of Firms in the Class |
|---|---|---|---|
| Zero assets | 1.7 | .0 | 18.9 |
| $1 under 25,000 | 17.5 | .1 | 14.6 |
| $25,000 under 50,000 | 13.1 | .1 | 27.0 |
| $50,000 under 100,000 | 15.9 | .3 | 29.8 |
| $100,000 under 500,000 | 34.0 | 2.4 | 38.9 |
| $500,000 under 1,000,000 | 7.9 | 1.7 | 54.1 |
| $1,000,000 under 5,000,000 | 7.2 | 4.4 | 65.3 |
| $5,000,000 under 10,000,000 | 1.0 | 2.1 | 73.7 |
| $10,000,000 under 25,000,000 | .8 | 3.8 | 78.5 |
| $25,000,000 under 100,000,000 | .6 | 9.0 | 83.2 |
| $100,000,000 under 1,000,000,000 | .2 | 20.6 | 83.8 |
| $1,000,000,000 or more | .04 | 55.5 | 91.5 |
| TOTAL | 99.9 | 100.0 | 35.5 |

Source: Rosen 1981, table 11.

7. It is possible that the presence of corporate foundations, which may make grants while the company itelf makes no contributions, tends to understate the proportion of contributing firms. Yet foundations are used predominantly by the largest corporations, where the proportion of contributors is greater, so this factor is probably not of great importance. The use of foundations is discussed below.

As the preceding tables suggest, propensities to contribute out of net income vary significantly. Table 5.4 shows just how much this propensity does vary, by ordering corporations by the proportion of net income contributed. The contributions measured in this table are deductible contributions; thus very few contributions in excess of 5 percent of net income are included.[8] The table again suggests that the distribution of giving is very unequal even when differences in corporate income are taken into account. Firms in the bottom three classes account for 55 percent of all corporate net income but only 6 percent of contributions. At the other end, fully a quarter of all corporate gifts are given by corporations with only 3 percent of all net income.

The degree to which corporations differ in their propensities to contribute can be illustrated by a Lorenz curve of contributions by net income, as shown in figure 5.2. As in the cases of individual contributions and volunteering, considerable inequality exists in corporate gifts. In fact, the Gini coefficient is 0.31 for corporate contributions, almost the same as the 0.30 index calculated for all individual contributions. Among individuals and corporations alike, contributing units representing only 10 percent of total income made over 50 percent of all contributions of each type.

**Table 5.4**    **Corporate Contributions by Percentage of Net Income Contributed: Active Corporations, 1977**

| Contributions as Percentage of Net Income | Percentage of Net Income | Percentage of Contributions |
|---|---|---|
| 0.0 | 16.2 | 0.0 |
| 0.0–0.2 | 27.4 | 1.7 |
| 0.2–0.4 | 11.4 | 4.6 |
| 0.4–0.6 | 9.3 | 6.2 |
| 0.6–0.8 | 10.4 | 10.2 |
| 0.8–1.0 | 6.7 | 8.5 |
| 1.0–1.2 | 3.4 | 5.2 |
| 1.2–1.4 | 1.8 | 3.3 |
| 1.4–1.6 | 1.7 | 3.5 |
| 1.6–1.8 | 1.2 | 2.8 |
| 1.8–2.0 | 1.2 | 3.3 |
| 2.0–2.5 | 2.1 | 6.4 |
| 2.5–3.0 | 1.6 | 6.0 |
| 3.0–4.0 | 1.3 | 6.3 |
| 4.0–5.0 | 1.2 | 7.3 |
| 5.0+ | 3.1 | 24.7 |
|  | 100.0 | 100.0 |

*Source:* Rosen 1981, table 7.

8. For a discussion of the 5 percent rule, see section 5.2.

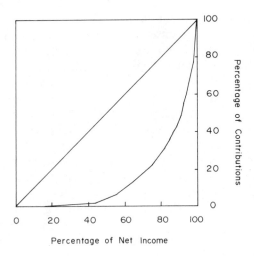

Percentage of Net Income

**Fig. 5.2**    Distribution of corporate contributions by net income, 1977. *Source:* Table 5.4.

### 5.1.3 Recipients of Corporate Contributions

As with the case of individual contributions, it is impossible to analyze fully the economic effect of corporate contributions—or of tax laws affecting such contributions—without knowing the uses to which the gifts are put. The most obvious difference between the giving patterns of individuals and corporations concerns religious giving. While virtually no corporate gifts go to religious organizations, almost 60 percent of individual gifts are religious in nature.[9] Among the secular beneficiaries of corporate giving, the most important categories are health and welfare and education. Table 5.5 gives comparable distributions of corporate giving between 1955 and 1982 based on surveys of large corporations by the Conference Board. During this period corporate gifts to civic and cultural organizations grew (from 3.2 to 23.1 percent of the total) while gifts in the health and welfare group declined in relative importance (from 50.7 to 31.0 percent). By 1982 the most important category of corporate giving was education, which accounted for over 40 percent of the total; health and welfare organizations received about a third, and civic and cultural organizations claimed about a tenth each.

9. See chapter 2.

Table 5.5           **Percentage Distribution of Corporate Giving**

|  | 1955 | 1965 | 1970 | 1975 | 1980 | 1982 |
|---|---|---|---|---|---|---|
| Health and welfare | 50.7 | 41.5 | 38.6 | 41.2 | 34.0 | 31.0 |
| Education | 31.3 | 38.4 | 37.6 | 35.1 | 37.8 | 40.7 |
| Culture and art | } 3.2 | 2.8 | 5.3 | 7.5 | 10.9 | 11.4 |
| Civic activities | | 5.8 | 8.1 | 10.3 | 11.7 | 11.7 |
| Other | 14.8 | 9.2 | 8.1 | 5.8 | 5.6 | 5.2 |
| TOTAL | 100.0 | 100.0 | 99.9 | 99.9 | 100.0 | 100.0 |
| Number of firms | 180 | 540 | 401 | 796 | 732 | 534 |

*Sources:* Nelson 1970, p. 41; Troy 1977, pp. 28–29; 1983, p. 10; 1984, p.11. Also see *Corporate Support of Higher Education 1980*, 1981, p. 5.

In table 5.6 distributions of contributions by donee groups are given for various industries, suggesting in several cases that gifts are made to donees with mutual interests to the industries. For example, the highest concentrations on civic activities tend to be among firms in service industries, many of which are likely to contain firms closely identified with particular cities. Education receives the largest shares in manufacturing industries, which appear most likely to benefit from advances in knowledge and technical training. These patterns are by no means clear, however, and the distributions themselves also vary somewhat from one year to the next.

Siegfried and McElroy (1981, p. 27) present complementary evidence on the effect of firm size on the distribution of gifts by donee. In their sample of corporations in medium-sized cities, they found, not unexpectedly, that the larger the firm (measured by number of employees), the larger the average share of gifts made to national causes. In addition, larger firms gave more to the educational and arts and cultural groups of organizations. The donee group that suffers a relative decline as firm size increases is health and welfare—a group likely to contain many organizations with a local focus. For their sample as a whole, Siegfried and McElroy found that local causes dominated national causes by a ten-to-one ratio (p. 16) and that the share of contributions made to a corporation's headquarters city varied directly with the share of the firm's employees there (p. 28). Thus, there is some reason to suppose that corporations seek to support charitable activities that benefit the geographical areas where their employees or customers live. Whether this is a manifestation of corporate social responsibility or plain good business sense is not obvious, but it does at least lay the groundwork for constructing models of corporate giving.

Table 5.6     Distribution of Corporate Contributions by Donee Group; 786 Large Corporations Classified by Industry, 1980

| Industrial Classification | Number of Companies | Total Giving ($ thousands) | Health and Welfare | | Education | Culture & Art | Civic | Other |
|---|---|---|---|---|---|---|---|---|
| | | | Federated Campaigns | Other | | | | |
| Chemicals | 45 | $ 99,205 | 13.8% | 13.4% | 44.3% | 8.7% | 11.9% | 8.0% |
| Electrical machinery | 48 | 104,191 | 22.5 | 14.1 | 47.5 | 7.4 | 6.2 | 2.4 |
| Fabricated metals | 22 | 20,287 | 16.1 | 14.2 | 24.3 | 6.4 | 16.9 | 22.1 |
| Food, beverage & tobacco | 40 | 70,583 | 12.3 | 26.1 | 33.5 | 13.1 | 9.2 | 5.9 |
| Machinery, nonelectrical | 48 | 52,672 | 18.4 | 10.8 | 48.7 | 7.8 | 8.1 | 6.2 |
| Mining | 8 | 5,832 | 5.7 | 19.9 | 46.1 | 10.2 | 14.6 | 3.4 |
| Paper | 25 | 34,768 | 14.0 | 15.0 | 34.9 | 10.4 | 20.3 | 5.5 |
| Petroleum & gas | 33 | 228,867 | 7.9 | 11.2 | 42.6 | 18.4 | 14.5 | 5.3 |
| Pharmaceuticals | 18 | 41,880 | 9.1 | 28.5 | 33.7 | 6.4 | 7.4 | 14.9 |
| Primary metals | 27 | 38,795 | 19.8 | 20.0 | 39.2 | 9.9 | 8.2 | 3.1 |
| Printing & publishing | 17 | 15,415 | 10.2 | 17.2 | 37.1 | 20.4 | 10.7 | 4.4 |
| Rubber | 12 | 6,512 | 30.7 | 20.0 | 35.7 | 5.4 | 7.2 | 1.1 |
| Stone, clay, & glass | 15 | 18,693 | 12.7 | 19.0 | 32.8 | 18.2 | 9.3 | 7.9 |
| Textiles | 23 | 13,226 | 11.5 | 28.2 | 30.5 | 5.0 | 13.9 | 11.0 |
| Transportation equipment | 22 | 71,889 | 22.0 | 13.6 | 38.4 | 9.6 | 8.5 | 8.0 |
| TOTAL MANUFACTURING | 403 | 822,815 | 14.2 | 15.5 | 40.7 | 12.0 | 11.1 | 6.5 |

| | | | | | | | | |
|---|---|---|---|---|---|---|---|---|
| Banking | 88 | 75,848 | 25.9 | 16.0 | 25.1 | 13.6 | 14.9 | 4.5 |
| Business services | 24 | 10,424 | 15.2 | 20.6 | 34.0 | 17.5 | 9.0 | 3.8 |
| Engineering & construction | 9 | 10,960 | 20.2 | 25.5 | 30.8 | 10.5 | 5.0 | 8.0 |
| Finance | 15 | 12,026 | 13.1 | 18.0 | 27.3 | 19.3 | 11.8 | 10.6 |
| Insurance | 99 | 63,751 | 22.8 | 15.8 | 29.5 | 11.1 | 16.0 | 4.7 |
| Merchandising | 26 | 48,017 | 33.2 | 20.5 | 18.4 | 13.1 | 10.3 | 4.6 |
| Telecommunications | 25 | 66,591 | 29.4 | 15.3 | 32.1 | 9.7 | 8.8 | 4.8 |
| Transportation | 11 | 16,688 | 15.7 | 14.8 | 33.3 | 7.5 | 23.1 | 5.7 |
| Utilities | 88 | 43,568 | 29.6 | 14.8 | 25.2 | 10.6 | 13.9 | 6.0 |
| TOTAL NONMANUFACTURING | 385 | 347,873 | 26.1 | 16.7 | 27.2 | 11.9 | 13.0 | 5.2 |
| TOTAL ALL COMPANIES | 788 | 1,170,688 | 17.7 | 15.9 | 36.7 | 11.9 | 11.7 | 6.1 |

*Source:* Troy 1983, p. 30.

## 5.2    Tax Treatment of Corporate Contributions

Charitable gifts and contributions have been deductible since 1936.[10] Until 1981 the major limitation was that deductible contributions could not exceed 5 percent of net income, calculated without regard to contributions and several other items.[11] Contributions actually made in a year that exceeded this 5 percent limit could be carried forward for up to five years, with the carry-overs being subject to the 5 percent limit in later years as well. The Economic Recovery Tax Act of 1981 increased this percentage limit from 5 to 10 percent. Because the increased depreciation allowances in that bill will have the effect of reducing reported net income, however, it is possible that for some companies the new 10 percent rule could place a lower absolute ceiling on contributions than the 5 percent limit did under previous law.[12]

As in the case of the personal income tax, the tax savings available to companies that make contributions are proportional to the marginal tax rate on net income. Where $t$ is the marginal tax rate on corporate income, a company that contributed $G$ dollars effectively reduces its tax liability by $tG$ dollars if the ceiling on contributions has not been reached.[13] In any one year this marginal tax rate varies by size of corporate income because of the progressive rate structure of the tax, although in recent years the rates have leveled off at fairly low incomes. Over time this marginal tax rate has varied widely, due largely to wartime excess-profits taxes. Figure 5.3 indicates the variation in tax rates from 1936 to 1980 by showing the average tax rate for corporations with assets and net income and the top marginal tax rate for each year.

Corporate gifts may be made in cash or property, though most are in cash form. Siegfried and McElroy (1981, p. 7) found in their survey, for example, that about 12 percent of the value of corporate giving was made in kind rather than in cash. Before 1969 the fair market value of goods could be deducted for contributions out of inventory. As Johnson (1966, p. 496) notes, this rule made it advantageous for certain companies to

10. See Freemont-Smith (1972, pp. 9–13) for a history of judicial rulings concerning the legality of corporate contributions.

11. The rule applied to taxable income computed without regard to the charitable deduction, net operating loss carry-backs, capital loss carry-backs, and certain special deductions. (*Internal Revenue Code* 1982, sec. 170(b)(2), pp. 201–2).

12. As Horvitz (1974) explains, it is possible for a corporation to extend the percentage limitation in practice by showing a business motive for some gifts and classifying them as regular business expenses.

13. A small number of corporations (less than 1 percent in 1980) were subject to a corporation minimum tax that had the effect of changing the price of making contributions. The tax was 15 percent of the excess of preferences (which did not include contributions) over the greater of the normal tax paid and $10,000. For corporations subject to this tax and with normal tax over $10,000, the price was reduced from $t$ to $(1 - 0.15)t$. See *Internal Revenue Code* 1982, sec. 56 and 57, and U.S. Congress, Staff of the Joint Committee on Taxation 1982.

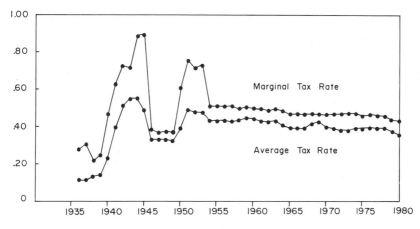

**Fig. 5.3**        Average and marginal tax rates for corporations, 1936–80.

contribute goods out of their own inventories. Since the deductible basis for goods was defined as their usual selling price, companies with relatively low production costs and high distribution costs may bear little or no cost when donating their own products.[14] The current law now limits contributions of inventory to the cost basis of the goods for most kinds of gifts, thus eliminating this incentive.[15] Finally, corporations may also contribute the volunteer services of their employees. As in the individual income tax such volunteer work receives no special deduction, but the wages of such employees remain fully deductible.

### 5.2.1   Corporate Foundations

The tax law allows corporations to set up foundations for the purpose of receiving and distributing contributions. Contributions from a corporation to its foundation are deductible like other contributions and are subject to the percentage ceiling, but grants made by foundations are not subject to the ceiling. In part because of the flexibility this allows, many larger corporations have established such foundations. According to Nelson (1970, p. 11) most corporate foundations were established during the Korean War, when high tax rates encouraged giving. Nelson estimates that between 1955 and 1965 foundations accounted for a quarter of all

14. Where $t$ is the firm's marginal tax rate and $v$ is the portion of marginal cost due to distribution, it was advantageous under previous treatment to contribute such goods when $t > 1 - v$.

15. The general rule is given in *Internal Revenue Code* 1982, sec. 170(e)(1)(A). For contributions of scientific research property or inventory used by charitable organizations to benefit the ill, the needy, or infants, the deduction is reduced by one-half of the difference between market value and cost, and the deduction can be no more than twice the cost. See sec. 170(e)(3) and 170(e)(4).

corporate contributions. In interpreting data on corporate contributions, it is useful to consider the role played by these corporate foundations. Foundations could play one of two possible roles in the distribution of donations. First, they could act to "smooth out" contributions over the business cycle. Corporations desiring to maintain a given level of support to a donee, for example, may choose to have the foundation make rather constant contributions while the firm itself makes contributions to the foundation that vary with tax and profit considerations. Siegfried and McElroy (1981, p. 25; McElroy and Siegfried 1982a, p. 24) found that a majority of their corporations with foundations use them to stabilize the flow of support to donees. In this case, contributions from the firm would be expected to fall relative to foundation grants during low-profit years and exceed foundation giving during periods of high profits. While this balance might be expected to vary from year to year, one would expect a net outflow from corporate foundations during recessions and the reverse during periods of economic growth. A second role that corporate foundations might play is that of permanent endowment to support the corporation's giving. Rather than making regular contributions to it, the parent firm in this model would make only one or several initial contributions to set up the foundation's endowment. In any given year thereafter, grants made by a corporate foundation would normally exceed contributions received from the corporation.

Table 5.7 presents information on payments to and by the foundations in a sample of large corporations. The numbers of corporations with positive entries for each item are shown in parentheses. In 1980, for example, there were 353 corporate foundations that made contributions out of a sample of 732 corporations with company or foundation gifts. In 1978 and 1979 corporate foundations received more than they paid out in contributions, but this relationship was reversed in 1980. In fact, 1980 was the first year since 1975 that corporate foundations in the Conference Board's sample paid out more than they received (*Corporate Support of Higher Education* 1981, p. 5). In that 1975 and 1980 were both recession years and corporate profits were correspondingly low, this finding is consistent with the hypothesis that foundations are used to smooth out corporate giving over time. One implication of this smoothing-out model is that contributions made by companies (counting grants to their own foundations) will tend to be more highly correlated to annual net income than the total flow of corporate (company and foundation) gifts to charities would be. While total corporate gifts may be related to a firm's normal level of profits, deductible company contributions will tend to be more highly correlated to current profits. Thus the income effects estimated from data on annual net income and total contributions would reflect a permanent rather than a current net-income effect. The figures in table 5.7 also to some extent support the endowment model in that the number of grants from foundations exceed the number of contributions received from par-

**Table 5.7**  **Structure of Corporate Contributions (millions of dollars)**

|  | 1980 | | 1979 | | 1978 | |
|---|---|---|---|---|---|---|
| Total company contributions | $994.7 | (709) | $855.7 | (763) | $834.4 | (759) |
| Less grants to company foundations | 381.4 | (249) | 372.1 | (291) | 418.7 | (249) |
| Other company contributions | 563.3 | (661) | 483.6 | (722) | 415.7 | (696) |
| Plus contributions by company foundations | 431.3 | (353) | 351.9 | (352) | 277.5 | (329) |
| Total corporate contributions | 994.6 | (732) | 835.5 | (786) | 693.2 | (759) |

Source: *Corporate Support of Higher Eductation 1980* 1981, p. 5.
Note: Numbers in parentheses are counts of nonzero answers.

ent firms. For example, in 1980 foundations for 353 corporations made contributions while only 249 foundations in the sample received contributions from their related corporation. Table 5.8 presents survey data only for corporations with foundations, giving the relative frequency of positive and negative balance between payments to and by foundations. That payouts exceed payins for a majority of firms in both years suggests that the role of foundations goes somewhat beyond simple smoothing, although the smoothing model is probably appropriate for most corporations.

## 5.3  Models of Corporate Giving and the Role of Taxes

The prospect of companies giving money away seems at first glance to fly in the face of the profit-maximization model. Indeed, such behavior appears to demand a theory of firm behavior that stresses factors other

**Table 5.8**  **Flow of Funds into and out of Company Foundations, 1978 and 1981**

|  | 1978 | | 1981 | |
|---|---|---|---|---|
|  | Number of Companies | Percentage of Total | Number of Companies | Percentage of Total |
| Payins equal to payout | 26 | 7 | 14 | 4 |
| Payins less than payouts | 178 | 52 | 232 | 64 |
| Payins greater than payouts | 141 | 41 | 115 | 32 |
| Total | 345 | 100 | 361 | 100 |

Sources: Troy 1981, p. 17; 1983, p. 17.

than profits. The purpose of this section is to consider two basic models of firm giving behavior and to trace out their implications for the effect of taxes on giving. The first model is simple profit maximization, and the second focuses on utility maximization by managers.

### 5.3.1 Profit Maximization

If a company is managed so as to maximize profits, the only possible reasons for making contributions would be if such expenditures increased revenues or reduced costs. Revenues may be increased if contributions perform a public relations function, and this possibility has not escaped the attention of students of corporate giving. One commentator cites as a benefit of contributions "better public acceptance of the company's products and a higher regard for it and its managers as citizens of the community."[16] By the same token, profits are increased if contributions serve to reduce the cost of operations by more than the amount contributed. One way costs may be reduced is if contributions have the effect of making a community a more desirable place in which to live and work and if this reduces the level of wages the company must pay.[17] Or a company's good public image may reduce other costs, for example, by making zoning changes easier or reducing the costs of vandalism.

Because of the nature of these benefits to firms, it is difficult to assess their importance empirically. One may, however, consider implications of this model. One implication is that, if such effects are important for any firm, they will tend to be most important for firms whose sales or market share may be sensitive to public perceptions. Another implication is that firms would tend to make contributions in the communities where they are located. Regarding the first, Johnson (1966) argues that firms in competitive or monopolistic industries stand to gain little from influencing public opinion, whereas firms in oligopolistic industries do. His analysis (Johnson 1966, pp. 496–504) suggests indeed that firms in rival industries contribute more than do firms in competitive and monopolistic industries. Patterns of giving by industry as shown above in table 5.2 indicate that the industries with the highest rates of giving tend to contain firms that depend on a favorable public image. Along the same lines, the empirical work reported in the next section shows that high rates of contributions are correlated with high rates of advertising. As for the location of contributions, survey data suggest that corporations make most of their gifts within their home states (Andrews 1952, p. 63), although this fact could also suggest utility maximization on the part of managers. In sum-

---

16. G. Clark Thompson quoted in Andrews 1952, p. 17. Martin Segal states: "Increasingly, corporations believe that good public relations resulting from support for the arts are an appropriate advertising and marketing expense ("Business Can Benefit by Giving to the Arts," *Wall Street Journal*, 1 January 1982, p. 26).

17. See Schwartz 1968, p. 480.

mary, there is good reason to believe that at least some portion of a corporation's contributions have a profit-related motive attached to it, much of it serving to improve the company's public image. As Andrews states (pp. 95–96), "Corporations seldom hide their philanthropic light under a bushel, and it is no accident that their contributions committees usually include the director of public relations."

What is the effect of an income tax on contributions if the management's objective is to maximize after-tax profits? Consider a firm with production function $Q(X,G)$, where $G$ is contributions and $X$ is other inputs. Where $t$ is the tax rate, $r$ is the output price, and $s$ is the price of the composite input $X$, net profit is

$$N = [rQ(X,G) - sX - G] (1 - t),$$

assuming that contributions are fully deductible. The first-order condition determining the demand for contributions is the usual condition for derived demand in competitive markets, $rQ'(G) = 1$, the value of the marginal product being equal to the before-tax price of giving a dollar. The income tax in this case has no effect on the company's optimal contributions.[18] The result is qualitatively the same if the price of inputs is also made a function of contributions, $s(G)$. In this case the optimality condition is

(1) $$rQ'(G) - s'(G)X = 1,$$

or that the marginal increase in profit (due to increased revenues and reduced costs) is equal to marginal cost, again with taxes not coming into play.

One can modify this profit-maximization model by relaxing the assumption that contributions have a contemporaneous effect on output. Suppose, instead, that contributions build a kind of goodwill that lasts over a period of years. For simplicity, consider a two-period model in which revenue is a function of total contributions in the two years. Where $h$ is a discount factor that expresses year-two amounts in terms of year-one dollars and where total contributions for the two years are a fixed amount $G^0 = G_1 + G_2$, the present value of net profits for both years is:

(2) $$V_n = (rQ(X_1,G^0) - sX_1 - G_1)(1 - t_1) + h[rQ(X_2,G^0)$$

$$- sX_2 - (G^0 - G_1)] (1 - t_2).$$

The profit-maximizing solution is simply to take the deduction in the year in which the present value of the deduction is greater. The net cost of the contribution will be $(1-t_1)G^0$ in the first year and $h(1-t_2)G^0$ in the second. Where the net price of giving is $P = 1 - t$, this implies taking the deduction

18. See also Schwartz 1968, p. 481.

in year two if $hP_2 < P_1$. Thus profit maximization is consistent with the timing of contributions according to variations over time in marginal tax rates if contributions have more than a contemporaneous effect on revenues.[19] Not only is it reasonable to believe that contributions do in fact have a more sustained effect, corporate foundations act to reinforce this sustained effect by smoothing out gifts over time.

### 5.3.2   Utility Maximization

A second general explanation for corporate giving rests on utility-maximizing behavior by managers or owners of the corporation. If either managers or owners derive utility from making contributions, the corporate tax may affect the amount of corporate giving.

Adopting Williamson's (1964) model of discretionary behavior suggests that a company's charitable contributions may enter the utility functions of managers. Accordingly, the management may choose to sacrifice profits in order to make such contributions. Suppose, for example, that management values two "goods": after-tax profits and corporate contributions. Whether they view corporate giving as a substitute for personal gifts, personal consumption, or certain forms of corporate conspicuous consumption, managers may place special value on or receive special credit for contributions made by their companies.[20] Contributions may be profitable over some range, but beyond some point their marginal profit is negative. Figure 5.4 shows excess profits as a function of contributions and indifference curves for management. Contributions in this case will exceed the profit-maximizing point $G_1$ and will be at a point such as $G_2$.

In order to determine the effect of taxes on contributions, consider a manager who maximizes utility as a function of contributions and net profit. Where $G$ and $N$ are contributions and net profit, respectively, utility is $U(G,N)$. Defining net profit as before, with $s$ exogenous, utility is

(3)              $$U[G,(1 - t)(rQ(X,G) - sX - G)].$$

Where $U_g$ and $U_n$ are marginal utilities, the first order condition is:

(4)              $$U_g + U_n (1 - t)[rQ'(G) - 1] = 0, \text{ or}$$

(4')              $$U_g/U_n (1 - t)[1 - rQ'(G)].$$

19. Although Schwartz (1968, p. 481n) refers to the possible response to transitory tax changes, his analysis takes the observation of a significant price effect to imply "that corporate giving is philanthropic rather than profit-oriented" (p. 492).

20. Managers in closely held corporations especially may take this kind of personal role in contributions, as is discussed below. See Nelson 1970, pp. 32–33. For further discussion and a test of whether corporate contributions are a source of utilitiy for managers, see Goldberg 1979.

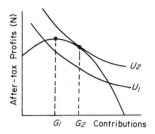

**Fig. 5.4**            Managerial preferences for contributions.


Taxes clearly are important. Only in the special case in which the manager has no interest in the level of contributions per se ($U_g = 0$) does the tax rate drop out; this case is simply that of profit maximization, which implies the condition analyzed above, $rQ'(G) = 1$. If the production function is quadratic in $G$, $Q(G) = a + bG - cG^2$, and if units are defined so that $r = 1$, the first-order condition becomes

(5)            $U_g/U_n = (1 - t)[1 - b + 2cG]$, or


(5')            $G = (U_g/U_n)/[(1 - t)2c] + (b - 1)/2c.$

The effect of a change in the tax rate on contributions can be seen by differentiation:

(6)            $$\frac{\partial G}{\partial t} = (U_g/U_n)/[(1 - t)^2 2c],$$


which is positive. Thus an increase in the corporate rax tax rate is expected to increase the company's contributions when the management values contributions directly. Whereas the profit-maximization model implies that taxes will affect only the timing of contributions, this utility-based model implies that taxes can affect the permanent level of contributions made by a company.

    A special case of managerial utility maximization arises in closely held corporations in which the owner or owners can choose between making contributions through the corporation or making personal contributions out of profits. When the alternative to corporate contributions is declaring dividends and making personal contributions from them (as opposed to, say, paying bigger salaries to the owners), the corporation income tax will generally make it attractive to contribute through the corporation. In terms of foregone after-tax dividends, the price of giving a dollar through the corporation is $(1 - t)(1 - m)$, where $t$ is the marginal corporate rate and $m$ is the relevant marginal rate in the personal income tax. When the corporation is subject to tax, this price is less than the price of $(1 - m)$ applying to personal contributions. Where the corporation has appreciated assets available to give, the advantage of contributing through the corporation may be even greater. The advantages of owners making contributions through corporations are not limited to closely held corporations, but the mechanism for owner control of gifts is problematic where the number of owners is very large.[21]

### 5.3.3   Rules of Thumb

A third model by which corporations may decide the level of contributions is by using rules of thumb based on industry norms, past behavior, or percentage of income. Because such behavior in the short run might be consistent with the long-run maximization of profits or utility, this notion does not necessarily constitute a separate theory of corporate giving. To the extent that rules of thumb are part of a "satisficing" approach whereby managers seek only a satisfactory level of profit, however, rules of thumb can be part of a distinctly different model of corporate behavior. Most of the corporate officers interviewed by Siegfried and McElroy (1981, p. 70) said their companies used a rule of thumb in determining contributions. Most respondents said their companies calculated contributions as a percentage of net income, while over a quarter based it on the previous year's giving. Fewer than 10 percent said they aimed for an absolute level of contributions.

Depending on its importance, such rule-of-thumb behavior may have one or two effects on observed patterns of corporate gifts. First, the prevalence of contribution rules based on a percentage of net income obviously would make the income elasticity near one, to the extent that the percentages used by corporations were similar. Second, if a firm's gifts are based, even in part, on the previous year's giving, an autoregressive model will result, making it necessary to correct for serial correlations in estimation.

### 5.3.4   The Price of Corporate Contributions

The models discussed in this section examine the effect of the corporate income tax rate on contributions under a rule of full deductibility. Schwartz (1968, p. 481) observes that, under this rule, the appropriate price to use for corporate gifts is $(1 - t)$ because the relevant alternative to corporate gifts is consumption of retained earnings. Implicitly, this assumes that contributions are strictly a form of corporate consumption,

---

21. One corporation, Berkshire Hathaway, allows shareholders to designate gifts in proportion to their holdings of shares. See Bill Richards, "Berkshire Hathaway Pleases Shareholders by Letting Them Earmark Corporate Gifts," *Wall Street Journal*, 26 April 1983. The advantage of giving through a corporation also underlies a proposal by Robert Sproull (1982) to allow shareholders to have the before-tax profit corresponding to some portion of their dividends to be contributed to a charity of their choice.

that is, that contributions do not increase revenues. This approach ignores the possibility, however, that an important alternative to contributions might be other expenditures, such as advertising. This possibility would become more important if the full deductibility rule were modified. Partial deductibility rules, such as the separate taxation of contributions as a "preference item," would change the *relative* cost of inputs, however. Neither these simple models nor empirical observation under the full deductibility regime would be directly appropriate for inferring the effects of such a rule.[22] If the deductibility of contributions were modified in this way, the relative attractiveness of contributions and advertising would be affected along with the relative attractiveness of contributions and consumption. Thus neither the simple models discussed in this section nor empirical observation of behavior under the full deductibility regime are directly appropriate for inferring the likely effects of a partial deductibility rule.[23]

### 5.4    Empirical Studies of Corporate Giving

Given the important role of firms in the study of economics as well as the interesting theoretical questions surrounding corporate philanthropy, it is not surprising that economists have devoted attention to empirical investigations of such behavior. Corporate contributions have, however, received less attention than giving by individuals. This difference may be due to the relatively small size of corporate giving. In addition, there appear to be fewer sources of data on contributions by corporations than by individuals. Table 5.9 summarizes the data and models used in the published studies of corporate contributions. The studies include time-series as well as cross-section analyses, using for the most part data collected from corporate tax returns. This section reviews the econometric analyses of corporate giving, discussing the sources of data, the definition of variables, and the specification of models.

### 5.4.1    Sources of Data

Virtually all the data used in econometric studies of corporate philanthropy are based on information from federal corporate income tax returns. These data are tabulated by the Internal Revenue Service in the published *Statistics of Income* series and in the unpublished "Source Book of Statistics of Income." The former provides annual data on income, assets, contributions, and other tax-related items as reported on corporation tax returns based on a large sample of returns selected each

22. See Clotfelter 1983b.
23. For an analysis of partial deductibility for the case of travel and entertainment, see Clotfelter 1983b.

**Table 5.9**      **Summary of Empirical Studies of Corporate Contributions**

| Study | Data Source | Corporations Excluded from Sample | Contributions Measure | Income Measure | Price Measure | Other Variables | Functional Form |
|---|---|---|---|---|---|---|---|
| Johnson 1966 | SBSOI,[a] 1936–61 | Zero assets; nonpositive net income | Ratio of contributions to net income | Net income | — | Concentration, asset size | — |
| Schwartz 1968 | SOI[b] time series, 1936–61; cross section by minor industry, 1948, 1959, 1960 | None | Average contributions | Net income after taxes  Cash flow after taxes | Weighted average based on tax rates (price = 1 for corporations with no net income) | Time series: trend; cross section: advertising expenditures | Linear; linear with lags; logarithms; first differences |
| Nelson 1970 | SOI, time series, 1936–63; SBSOI, 1954–1957 (4-year averages for 121 industry classes) | Nonpositive net income | Total contributions | Net income after taxes, before contributions (time series); net income before taxes (cross section) | Weighted average based on average tax rates | Time series: trend, expectations, net worth  Cross section: Net worth, employment, number of corporations | Log-linear |
| Levy and Shatto 1978 | SOI 1971, 56 aggregate industries; SOI, 1946–76 | —[c] | Total contributions | Net income | Average tax rate | Cross section: investment, advertising; time series: dividends | Log-linear  Linear |

| Study | Data source | Exclusions | Dependent variable | Income variable | Other variables | Independent variables | Functional form |
|---|---|---|---|---|---|---|---|
| Bennett and Johnson 1980 | *SOI*, 20 aggregate manufacturing industries, 1967 and 1971 | —[c] | Total contributions | Net income | — | Investment, advertising, unionization, concentration | Linear |
| Maddox and Siegfried 1981 | *SBSOI*, asset and minor industry classes, 1963 | Zero assets | Average contributions | Net income | — | Relative size, concentration ratio (4-firm), advertising, R&D | Linear |
| McElroy and Siegfried 1982a[d] | Authors' survey of 229 corporations | Zero contributions; no financial data | Direct contributions of firm and foundation | Net income | State tax credit dummy | Contributions by other firms; government expenditures; population | Liear, logarithms |
| McElroy and Siegfried 1982b | *SBSOI*, asset and minor industry classes, 1972, 1976. | Zero assets; assets less than $10 million | Total contributions, weighted; average contributions (log-linear) | Net income | — | — | Linear; quadratic, log-linear |

[a]U.S. Internal Revenue Service, "Source Book of Statistics of Income."

[b]U.S. Internal Revenue Service, *Statistics of Income, Corporation Income Tax Returns*.

[c]Information not given.

[d]Also presents illustrative regressions using data in McElroy and Siegfried 1982b.

year. With some variation from year to year, this information is tabulated by the size of corporate assets and by major industrial groups. Tabulations typically are presented separately for corporations with positive profits as well as for all corporations. The "Source Book" provides a more detailed tabulation, consisting of a two-way classification of firms by industry and asset size, making it attractive for cross-section analysis. Besides this tax return information, the only other data that have been used in an econometric analysis of corporate giving is a survey of companies conducted by McElroy and Siegfried (1982a; 1982b). Not only do survey data of this kind allow the examination of behavior by individual firms, but they also allow considerably more detail in the examination of nontax influences on contributions. While these other influences are of great interest, they are likely not to be of central importance in assessing the effect of the corporate tax in philanthropy.

The most important limitations of the Internal Revenue Service data, which are used in all but one of the analyses discussed in this section, have to do with the possible mismeasurement of contributions and economic profits.[24] The reported amounts for "contributions or gifts" counts only those contributions that are deductible. Deductibility is limited by the nature of the expenditure itself and its amount. Only contributions to approved nonprofit or philanthropic organizations are deductible, and qualifying contributions by law cannot be placed in some other expenditure category. Several studies have alluded to this problem, noting the possibility that tax return data may understate true contributions.[25] Some information on the likely extent of this understatement is given by Andrews (1952, p. 252), who cites a 1950 survey suggesting that incorrectly reported contributions were 7.6 percent the size of underreported contributions.[26] According to Johnson (1966, p. 494), however, a court case in 1951 established the principle that contributions must be reported as such. Combined with what Johnson sees as a growing acceptance of corporate contributions, this would suggest that misreporting may have declined since the introduction of the charitable deduction. Based on the findings for 1950, however, the extent of misreporting was probably never great.

24. A third limitation, not relevant to the analysis presented here, is the classification of firms by industry according to the major activity rather than a recognition of different industries represented by a single firm.

25. Tax rulings relevant to the distinction between charitable contributions and regular business expenses are discussed in Horvitz 1974. Despite the distinction between these classes of expenses, it appears in practice that contributions are often not fully separated from public relations and similar expenses on corporate returns due to the accounting cost of doing so and because there are no tax consequences for firms below the contributions limit. Johnson (1966, p. 494) suggests that gradual acceptance of corporate contribution may be reducing this classification problem over time. McElroy and Siegfried (1982b, p. 10) state, however, "Since contributions are a tax-deductible expense like any other business expense, there is no incentive to classify them in a separate budget." This ignores the legal incentive cited by Johnson 1966, p. 494n.

26. Also see Nelson 1970, p. 32.

The limitation on the amount of the charitable deduction is also an important consideration in studying giving behavior. Before 1981 contributions made during a given year amounting to more than 5 percent of income were not deductible in that year. Firms exceeding the limit could carry such deductions forward for five years. Deductible contributions in any one year therefore include currently deductible gifts and any past gifts that exceed the limit.[27] The available data provide little definitive information either on the amount of contributions that exceed the limit or the amount of the deductions accounted for by carry-overs. For firms with no positive net income, however, few if any contributions are deductible, so tax returns are a very incomplete measure of actual contributions for these firms.[28] As shown in table 5.10, corporations with no net income in 1980 accounted for over 40 percent of corporate returns but only 1.2 percent of contributions. Because of their profit situation and because most of their contributions are not deductible, it is not surprising that giving by these firms is very low. Clearly, the problem is that deductible giving may be only a fraction of total giving. The inclusion of firms without positive net income is therefore a source of downward bias in the measure of contributions. If, furthermore, the net price for such firms is taken to be one—thus ignoring the possibility of taking the deduction in future

**Table 5.10**    **Returns and Contributions by Corporations by Net Income and Assets, 1980**

|  | Returns | | Deductible Contributions | |
|---|---|---|---|---|
|  | Number | % | Amount | % |
| Firms with net income |  |  |  |  |
| Without assets | 28,402 | 1.0 | 7,728 | 0.3 |
| With assets | 1,568,590 | 57.9 | 2,323,204 | 98.5 |
| Firms with no net income |  |  |  |  |
| Without assets | 50,206 | 1.9 | 2,638 | 0.1 |
| With assets | 1,063,700 | 39.2 | 24,984 | 1.1 |
| Total | 2,710,538 | 100.0 | 2,358,554 | 100.0 |

Source: U.S. Internal Revenue Service, *Statistics of Income—1980, Corporation Income Tax Returns* 1983, pp. 44–46, tables 4, 5.

27. Carryovers were also subject to the 5 percent limitation. See, for example, *1980 U.S. Master Tax Guide* 1979, section 1147, p. 418.

28. Firms with no net income may nevertheless have some deductible contributions because the 5 percent rule is based on a slightly different definition of income. As noted above, the rule applies to taxable income computed without regard to the charitable deduction and other items. Thus firms with zero or negative taxable income might be able to deduct some contributions in the same year. See, for example, U.S. Internal Revenue Service, *Statistics of Income—1977, Corporation Income Tax Returns* 1981, p. 141.

years—a negative bias is imparted to the correlation of price and giving since giving is understated and price is overstated. Among the studies reviewed here, only Schwartz (1968) and Maddox and Siegfried (1981) include firms with no net income. How serious the bias is, of course, depends on the number of such firms and the extent of the two measurement errors.

The second problem with the IRS tax data is general mismeasurement of economic variables. This problem is particularly apparent regarding the definition of corporate income. The divergence between depreciation allowances permitted by the tax code and "true" economic depreciation is well known.[29] Depletion allowances present a similar problem in the measurement of income. Reported net income may also diverge from the economic definition of profit in closely held corporations where part of what conceptually should be "return to capital" may be paid in the form of compensation to corporate officers. Nelson (1970, pp. 63–66) has suggested that this last problem probably causes profits to be more seriously understated for small corporations than for large ones, thus inflating the measured ratios of contributions to net income in lower income and asset classes. To illustrate, contributions as a percentage of net income falls from 4.38 to 0.55 from the second to the highest asset classes in 1957. When income is defined to exclude taxes and include officers' compensation, however, this proportion *rises*, from 0.20 to 0.90 (Nelson 1970, p. 62).

### 5.4.2   Explanatory Variables

As in the case of contributions by individuals, tax policy influences corporate giving in two important ways: by affecting the net price of giving a dollar of contributions and by affecting the after-tax income available to managers. Other characteristics such as industry structure and advertising have also been examined, and although they are not directly related to tax policy, these other factors are noted as well in this section.

*Price*

There is little disagreement in the empirical literature that the net cost to a firm of making another dollar of corporate contributions generally is $1(1 - t)$, where $t$ is the marginal tax rate on net income. (Where the 5 percent ceiling has been exceeded, of course, the price will be more, depending on the likelihood of carrying over the excess deduction to future years.) The methods of approximating the marginal tax rate have varied, however. Schwartz (1968) based his price measure on the average tax rate, letting average price be a weighted average of the complement of the average rate and one, where the weights are donations by taxable and nontaxa-

29. See, for example, Samuelson 1964.

ble firms.[30] Since firms with no net income have very few deductible contributions, this measure is quite close to the simple complement of the average tax rate.[31] Nelson (1970), in contrast, calculated an aggregate net price based on marginal tax rates. In years with wartime excess-profits taxes, he computed a weighted average of income tax and excess-profits tax rates. In other years his estimate of the marginal tax rate is simply the maximum marginal rate.[32] There is no account taken for the declared-value excess-profits tax which was in force between 1936 and 1945, nor for the surtax on undistributed net income in 1936 and 1937. The marginal tax rate implicit in Nelson's estimates are given in Appendix G. For comparison, Appendix F summarizes the marginal tax rates embodied in the various components of the corporate tax since 1936. Appendix G compares the average tax rate and Nelson's estimate of the marginal tax rate. Clearly, Nelson's marginal tax rate does show more variation over time, as one would expect given the progression in corporate taxes. Nelson's measure has three weaknesses, however. First, it ignores the declared-value excess-profits tax that was imposed from 1936 to 1945 on net income amounting to more than 10 percent of capital stock. Since many firms of all sizes earned more than a 10 percent rate of return over this period, this tax added to the marginal tax rate on net income. The Nelson calculations also omit the undistributed profits surtax of 1936 to 1938, which featured marginal tax rates up to 22 percent. Finally, the Nelson calculations do not account for the deductibility of some portions of the tax in calculating other portions. Because of these interactions, it is inappropriate to calculate the total marginal rate by simply summing the components.

Two other aspects of the price of contributions are the relative cost of making gifts in various years and the relative cost of contributing goods versus money. Because of changes in tax laws and a firm's net income over time, marginal tax rates may change. This opens up possibilities for the timing of gifts so as to minimize tax liability. Particularly striking changes in tax rates occurred at the beginning and end of the wartime excess-profits taxes, in 1940, 1945, 1950, and 1953. Nelson (1970, pp. 47–48) has focused on the effect of anticipated tax changes, noting that each of these years witnessed unusually high contributions, presumably caused by firms' bunching gifts into the higher-tax year. Such timing effects are important to distinguish from the effects of "permanent" changes in net prices. For the sake of predicting the effects of permanent changes in the

30. Where $t_a$ is the average tax rate, $D_t$ and $D_{nt}$ are donations by taxable and nontaxable corporations, the price variable is $P = [(1 - t_a)D_t + D_{nt}]/(D_t + D_{nt})$ (Schwartz 1968, p. 482).

31. In 1977, for example, returns with no net income had only 1.4 percent of total deductible contributions. The complement of the average tax rate for firms with net income was 0.608, and the Schwartz weighted average was 0.613 (U.S. Internal Revenue Service, *Statistics of Income—1977, Corporation Income Tax Returns* 1981 pp. 43, 45).

32. For a description and illustration of this calculation, see Nelson 1970, Appendix B. Appendix E compares the Schwartz and Nelson analyses.

tax structure on corporate contributions, it is necessary to know this permanent price effect, and not the transitory price effect. In order to reflect the anticipation of changes in tax rates, Nelson (1970, p. 48) included in some estimated equations a qualitative variable that takes on the value of zero in years before adoption or following the end of wartime excess-profits taxes—two in the first and last years of such taxes, and one otherwise.

Corporations may contribute goods as well as cash. Formerly, such contributions were deductible at "fair market value." Johnson (1966, p. 496) notes that corporations with low production costs and high distribution costs could benefit from contributing manufactured goods since both would be deductible but only the former would be borne. Johnson found that industries which produce usable products (for example, manufacturing and construction) contributed at higher rates than industries with few usable products (for example, finance and mining) (p. 497). The benefit from contributing inventory is now limited in most cases, however, as noted in section 5.2 of this chapter.

*Income and Scale*

The variable most often used in these empirical studies to measure the income or scale of a corporation is net income before tax. Not only is it readily available for all years, net income also seems to correspond to the economic definition of profit, at least gross profit. As noted in the previous discussion of data, however, the net income quantity defined by the tax law may not necessarily be the same as the economic one. In particular, depreciation allowances may diverge from true economic depreciation, and the degree of this divergence may be expected to change over time with the enactment of various accelerated depreciation allowances. Thus net income as defined in the tax law may be a misleading measure of economic profit. One alternative to the use of net income is cash flow income, which is net income plus depreciation and other amortization. Its use may be justified on the basis that depreciation allowances ought to be included in a variable intended to measure a corporation's ability to contribute. Or it may be viewed, given the wide fluctuations in allowable depreciation treatment, as simply a more consistent proxy for economic profit than net income would be. Among previous econometric studies of corporate giving, only Schwartz (1968) used cash flow income. It is worth considering what the likely effect will be of using net income as the measure of capacity when a variable such as cash flow is more appropriate. In this case, net income could be viewed as an imprecise measure of cash flow, presenting a simple case of errors in variables. The result would be a downward bias in the estimate of the scale effect, implying that the elasticity for the cash flow variable would tend to be larger than that for the income variable.

A second important drawback to the use of net income is that it does not reflect the impact of corporate tax liability on a corporation's capacity to contribute. The only study to examine after-tax income is Nelson's (1970) time-series analysis in which after-tax net income is the capacity variable. Although the choice between net income and cash flow income is not clear, since neither are perfect measures of economic profit, it does seem clear that after-tax quantities are preferable to before-tax ones.

*Industry Structure*

Several of the cross-section studies include some measure of industry structure to explain corporate contributions. Johnson (1966) examines two related hypotheses. The first is that corporations with more monopoly power demonstrate more social responsibility by making larger contributions. Using concentration as one measure of economic power, Johnson shows that contributions in fact *fall* as industry concentration increases. Johnson's second hypothesis regarding industry structure is more compelling. Johnson distinguishes "rival," or oligopolistic firms from purely competitive and monopolistic ones. Rival firms may use contributions "to seek a comparative advantage over each other" (p. 497). In contrast, by this hypothesis, competitive firms cannot afford to do this and monopolistic firms have no need to. Johnson then shows that the contributions-to-income ratios tend to be highest in industries characterized by "rivalry" (p. 499). Johnson also uses this argument to explain the hump shape of the contributions-to-income ratio as a function of asset size, arguing that the middle-asset classes display the highest degree of rivalness (p. 501). In contrast, Maddox and Siegfried (1981), using aggregated data by minor industry for 1963, found that contributions tended to rise with concentration ratios.

*Trend*

As in other analyses of changes over time, it is possible that models will not measure all of the effects occurring over time. In the case of corporate contributions, time trends usually indicate a secular increase in contributions over time. Johnson (1966, p. 494) argues that there has been a "gradual acceptance" of corporate contributions over time by management and stockholders. Another reason might include changes in the industrial composition of U.S. corporations.

*Other Variables*

Among the other variables used to explain contributions, advertising is intriguing as well as ambiguous in its probable effect. Because contributions may serve a purpose similar to that of advertising, advertising expenditures presumably reflect the extent to which corporations may use contributions for public relations purposes. As Schwartz (1968, p. 482) implies, however, no sign can be predicted unambiguously. Firms that advertise may also find it useful to give contributions, but for a given firm the two items may well be substitutes. Levy and Shatto (1978) use investment as an explanatory variable, but it is unclear why. McElroy and Siegfried included relative firm size, research development expenditures, population, and contributions by other firms in the city in analyses of two different data sets (Maddox and Siegfried 1981; and McElroy and Siegfried 1982a).

### 5.4.3  Findings

The findings of previous econometric studies of corporate contributions are summarized in tables 5.11 and 5.12. The more aggregative time-series analyses provide the only evidence on the effect of the tax-defined net price on corporate giving. The estimated elasticities are generally greater than one in absolute value, implying, as in the case of personal contributions, that charities receive more in contributions as a result of the deduction than the Treasury loses in revenue. The magnitude of the estimated elasticity appears to be sensitive to functional form and variable definitions. Schwartz, using logarithms of pretax net income and price based on average tax rates to explain the logarithm of average contributions, obtained a price elasticity of $-2.00$. Nelson, using after-tax net income and lagged price based on marginal tax rates, obtained an elasticity of $-1.03$ in his logarithmic equation explaining total contributions. The estimates for the income elasticity vary similarly, from 0.53 to 1.43 among the equations summarized in table 5.11. Schwartz's equations suggest that the use of cash flow yields higher income elasticities than net income while the use of the logarithmic form yields larger price elasticities. The use of lagged price variables yields results similar to those obtained with current price. The inclusion of a trend variable appears to make little difference. The trend is negative but insignificant in Schwartz's regressions. Nelson obtains a positive and significant trend effect, but this may reflect growth in the number of firms over time.

Among the cross-section studies, the only common point of comparison is the income elasticities. These estimates vary less widely than in the time-series studies. Leaving aside an estimate of 0.03 obtained in an equation also containing investment, by Levy and Shatto (1978), these estimates range from 0.44 for Schwartz's (1968) equation with net income and advertising to 1.17 for McElroy and Siegfried's (1982) quadratic equation. Because income can vary greatly in a cross-section sample while other variables are constant, these cross-section estimates are probably more dependable than those for the time-series studies. Taken as a whole, the cross-section equations imply that contributions probably rise less than proportionally with corporate income. Regarding the estimated ef-

Table 5.11    Summary of Time-Series Results

| Study | Form and Sample | Price Elasticity | Income Elasticity | Other Variables (sign if significant) | Sample Size |
|---|---|---|---|---|---|
| Schwartz 1968 | Actual values | -1.36 | .63 | — | 26 |
| | Logarithms | -2.00 | .63 | — | 26 |
| | Actual values: net income, lagged price, and income[a] | -1.52 | .53 | trend | 25 |
| | Actual values: cash flow | -1.06 | 1.33 | — | 26 |
| | Logarithms: cash flow | -1.68 | 1.34 | — | 26 |
| Nelson 1970 | Logarithms: net income, lagged price | -1.03 | 1.05 | trend (+), expectations[b] | 27 |
| | Logarithms: current and lagged net income and price[a] | -1.18 | 1.43 | trend (+), expectations[b] | 27 |

[a]Elasticities shown are sums of current and lagged variable elasticities.
[b]See text for definition of expectations variable.

**Table 5.12**   **Summary of Cross-Section Results**

| Study | Form and Sample | Income Elasticity | Other Variables (sign if significant) | Sample Size |
|---|---|---|---|---|
| Schwartz 1968 | Logarithms: net income | .44 | Advertising (+) | 60 |
| | Logarithms: cash flow | .60 | Advertising (+) | |
| Nelson 1970 | Logarithms | .68 | Number of corporations (+) | 121 |
| | | .52 | Number of corporations (+), net worth | 121 |
| | | .47 | Number of corporations, net worth, employment (+) | 121 |
| Levy and Shatto 1978 | Logarithms | .03 | Investment (+), advertising (+) | 56 |
| Bennett and Johnson 1980 | Logarithms: 1967 | .58 | Net investment, advertising (+) percent union (−), concentration ratio (−) | 20 |
| | Logarithms: 1971 | .53 | Net investment (+), advertising, percent union, concentration ratio (−) | 20 |

| | | | | |
|---|---|---|---|---|
| Maddox and Siegfried 1981 | Linear: positive assets, 1963 | | | |
| | All industries | .47 | Relative size (+), R&D/sales (+) | 2262 |
| | Manufacturing | .48 | Concentration (+), relative size (+), advertising/sales (+), R&D/sales (+) | 1163 |
| McElroy and Siegfried 1982a | Linear | .72 | Other firm contributions (+), population (−) | 162 |
| | Logarithms | .72 | | |
| McElroy and Siegfried 1982 | Weighted, assets $10 million or more, 1976 | | | |
| | Linear, all industries | .90 | — | 371 |
| | Linear, all manufacturing | .87 | — | 480 |
| | Quadratic, all industries | 1.17 | — | 371 |
| | Logarithms | .88 | — | 371 |
| | Linear: weighted, assets $10 million or more, 1972 | .96 | — | 204 |
| | Linear: weighted, positive assets, 1976 | .97 | — | 255 |

fects of other variables, corporations that advertise heavily also appear to make more contributions. Because decisions on both categories of expenditures are made simultaneously, however, it is not clear what the behavioral implication of that correlation is. Bennett and Johnson (1980) confirm Johnson's (1966) initial finding that contributions are inversely related to industry concentration.

A final effect on corporate giving examined in both time-series and cross-section equations by Nelson (1970) is the possible influence of profitability. If, independent of income, more profitable corporations contribute more than less profitable ones, then the inclusion of net income may reflect both scale and profitability components. Where $G$, $P$, $I$, and $K$ are contributions, price, income, and capital stock, respectively, a profitability effect would be measured by $b_3$ in the equation:

$$(7) \qquad \ln G = a + b_1 \ln P + b_2 \ln I + b_3 \ln (I/K).$$

If capital stock is included along with income as an independent variable, the coefficient on $I$ will be a combination of income and profitability effects:

$$(8) \qquad G = a + b_1 \ln P + (b_2 + b_3) \ln I - b_3 \ln K.$$

Nelson included net worth in time-series regressions (not shown in table 5.11) as well as in the cross-section analysis. In the time-series equation (Nelson 1970, p. 55), the coefficient of net worth is indeed negative, as suggested in equation (8). In the cross-section equation, however, the coefficient of net worth is positive but insignificant. While by no means definitive, these results suggest that income may measure both capacity and profitability effects and that, when net worth is omitted, the income coefficient will not be a pure measure of the scale effect. In order to measure accurately any profitability effect, it would be important to correct for taxes as well as for the effect of inflation in the presence of cost-based accounting rules.

## 5.5    Analysis of Corporate Contributions, 1936–80

In order to refine the models discussed in the previous section as well as to take advantage of data for recent years, a new analysis of corporate giving was undertaken in the current study. As in most previous studies the Internal Revenue Service's tabulations of tax return information in the *Statistics of Income* provided the basic data.[33] Two samples of observations were used for the analysis. First, annual tabulations of corporations by asset size were pooled over the period 1936–80 to yield a sample of 506

---

33. Data for the years 1963–68 were obtained from the unpublished "Source Book of Statistics of Income." All other data were taken from the U.S. Internal Revenue Service, *Statistics of Income, Corporation Tax Returns* (various years).

observations. This pooling makes it possible to observe corporations of different sizes over time. Pooled data therefore provide considerably more variation in income and asset size than is possible with aggregate time-series data. In addition, pooling allows for changes over time in the structure of tax rates, which obviously is impossible in cross-section analysis. Unlike the cross-section analyses discussed above, observations in the present analysis are not broken down by industry. If industrial composition changes over time, differences in contribution rates will tend to be reflected in the trend variable. The second sample used in the present study is a time-series of aggregate observations over the same period, 1936–80. Although this sample provides less information than the pooled sample, it is necessary for testing hypotheses regarding the dynamic nature of corporate giving. Because the number of asset classes as well as their real dollar limits change over time, correction for serial correlation and the examination of the response to changes in tax rates was confined to a subset of recent observations.

### 5.5.1  Data and Variables

The data and basic variable definitions from the *Statistics of Income* are described in section 5.4. For the current analysis, corporations with zero assets were excluded from the sample because they are likely to be in unusual or transitional situations.[34] In addition, firms without positive net income were excluded. As discussed in the previous section, such firms have virtually no deductible contributions, due to the limitations on the deductibility of contributions to 5 percent of net income, and only deductible contributions are given in the *Statistics of Income*. While the published data on contributions may understate actual contributions for any firm—due to the 5 percent limitation—the understatement is especially serious in the case of firms with no net income.

### *Income*

The basic measure used to reflect firms' scale or capacity to contribute is after-tax cash flow, defined by:

$$(9) \quad CF = NI + (\text{Depreciation} + \text{Depletion} + \text{Amortization}) - T,$$

where $NI$ is net income calculated without deducting contributions and $T$ is total federal corporate tax liability calculated without the deduction for contributions. The net-income and tax variables are calculated so as to be independent of the size of actual contributions and thus exogenous to the contribution decision. After-tax cash flow measures income available to management in a given year. Although depreciation, depletion, and amor-

---

34. Firms reporting no assets included final returns of liquidating, dissolving, or merging corporations and foreign corporations. Internal Revenue Service, *Statistics of Income— 1977, Corporation Income Tax Returns 1981,* pp. 124–25.

tization refer to costs the corporation has borne or eventually will bear, the amounts allowed for each—particularly depreciation—may bear little relationship to the true pattern of costs.

Given the importance of favorable depreciation features of the tax law, particularly in the last two decades, it is important to examine the effect of such provisions on corporate contributions. If net income as defined by the tax code were the correct measure of firm capacity, then accelerated depreciation schemes would be expected to discourage contributions to the extent that net income falls. If, however, cash flow is the correct measure, then such provisions may have no effect or may stimulate contributions. In order to compare the cash-flow and net-income concepts of income, equations using after-tax net income $(NI - T)$ are also examined. The use of pretax net income seems to have little to recommend it since the income available to management clearly must be net of taxes.

*Price*

As in previous studies, the relative price of contributions is defined as one minus the tax rate on corporation incomes. For decisions at the margin, the correct tax rate is the marginal tax rate. Only Nelson (1970) has attempted to estimate marginal rates as such. As discussed in the previous section, however, his method relies in most years on taking the maximum statutory rate and in all cases produces only one overall rate per year. More detail is required for the present study because it examines corporations of different sizes in each year. To obtain the marginal tax rates applicable to various asset classes in each year involved two steps. First, averages of income and other relevant variables were calculated for each class in each year. Second, the various corporate tax schedules were applied to the tax bases in each class. In this way it was possible to account in some detail for variations in tax schedules over time, progression in rates within a given year, and interactions among the components of each year's corporate tax liability. Over the period studied, these components included the normal corporate income tax, the surtax (1941–78), the undistributed net-income surtax (1936–37), the declared-value excess-profits tax (1936–45), and the wartime excess-profits tax (1940–45, 1950–53).

The first step in calculating the component marginal rates within each asset-class observation was to apply the tax schedules in each year to the means for net income, capital stock, and other relevant variables. since the tax schedules are not linear, rates for the average income may differ from the average of all marginal rates, but comparisons of normal tax liabilities (i.e., before surtaxes) for selected classes show that calculated tax liabilites are generally close to actual figures, suggesting that calculated marginal rates are quite close to the actual. It is likely, however, that the calculated marginal rates will tend to mask some variation in the actual marginal tax rates faced by individual corporations. This problem is probably alleviated to a large extent because the sample used is restricted to corporations with positive net income. In addition, it is necessary to note that the tax calculation method used here omits all but the most important provisions of the tax code for any year. In most calculations, no account is taken, for example, of provisions related to long-term capital gains, carry-overs of unused excess-profits taxes, carry-overs of prior year net operating losses, or for special provisions related to utilities or insurance companies. The similarity of calculated and actual tax liabilities for the basic corporate tax suggest that these provisions are not greatly important for aggregate calculations.

The second step in the calculation of corporate marginal tax rates was to account for the interaction of component taxes. Because some of these taxes were deductible in calculating other taxes, the marginal tax rate on net income is not simply the sum of the marginal rates applicable to each tax base. To take a simple example, the corporate tax in 1939 was the sum of the declared-value excess-profits tax (*DEPT*) and the normal tax (*NT*), where the former is a deduction in calculating the latter. Where *NI* is net income and *CS* is the firm's capital stock, the total tax could be written as

$$(10) \qquad T = DEPT(NI, CS) + NT(NI - DEPT).$$

The marginal tax rate for the total tax is

$$(11) \qquad \frac{dT}{dNI} = \frac{\partial DEPT}{\partial NI} + \frac{\partial NT}{\partial NI}\left(1 - \frac{\partial DEPT}{\partial NI}\right).$$

Where *RNT* and *RDEPT* are marginal rate brackets applicable to a given return, the marginal rate for the total tax is

$$(11') \qquad R = RDEPT + RNT(1 - RDEPT).$$

Besides the basic measure of price based on the marginal tax rate on corporate net income, two variants were tested as well. The first was defined as one minus the average tax rate, where the average rate is the ratio of the total corporate tax liability (normal tax, surtax, and excess-profits taxes) to net income plus contributions. Because no calculation of marginal tax rate for aggregated corporate data can give exact results, it is useful to compare the performance of the price based on the approximate marginal tax rate with that based on the average tax rate. The latter is more straightforward to calculate, although as Fiekowsky (1977) has noted, average tax rates are not without ambiguities of their own.

The final measure of price used separates the marginal price into its permanent and transitory components. Where $P$ is the price based on the marginal tax rate in a given year and $P^N$ is the normal or permanent price faced by corporations, the observed price can be divided into permanent and transitory components:

$$(12) \qquad\qquad P = P^N k,$$

where $k$ is the transitory deviation of price from its normal level. In the current study normal price is defined as the average price faced over the most recent three-year period. As it has been used in other applications, this general formulation[35] makes it possible to distinguish responses to permanent price changes from those to temporarily high or low prices, such as those resulting from wartime excess-profits taxes. The motivation for this specification is much the same as that behind Nelson's (1970, pp. 47–48) use of a qualitative variable for anticipated major changes in tax rates.

### Time Trend

As in the two time-series analyses described in the previous section, the estimated equations in the present study include a linear time trend designed to reflect changes in the level of real giving over time not explained by other explanatory variables. Such a trend may be the result of a number of different effects, including changes in attitudes regarding the legality or propriety of corporate giving and changes in the perceived need for private giving in general.

### 5.5.2    Estimation

Equations explaining corporate contributions were estimated using two samples based on *Statistics of Income* data. First, an aggregate time-series analysis similar to that of Schwartz and Nelson was performed. Second, a pooled time series of cross sections was analyzed in order to combine the advantages of both kinds of data. These analyses are discussed in turn.

### Time-Series Analysis

Annual data on corporate contributions from 1936 to 1980 for corporations with net income and assets were analyzed. Analysis of residuals from preliminary regressions revealed the presence of serially correlated errors. The time-series analysis therefore employs a correction for autocorrelation. For all published data the observations in the time-series analysis are based on the mean aggregate value. For the price of giving, the basic measure is one minus the weighted average of calculated marginal tax rates for each asset class, where net income is used as the weight. This series is given in Appendix G. Alternative measures of price are the top marginal tax rate, given in Appendix F, and the average tax rate. One aspect of price response that cannot be captured in a single measure is the possibility that corporations seek to time their gifts so as to give more in years when tax rates are relatively high. To capture this timing effect, the price was split into permanent and transitory components.

---

35. Friedman's (1957) analysis of permanent income is well known. For an application to tax analysis, see Auten and Clotfelter 1982.

Table 5.13 presents the basic time-series estimates. Equation (A) gives estimated elasticities for the basic measures of price and capacity, based on marginal tax rates and cash flow, respectively. The price elasticity is −0.41, with a standard error of 0.07, and the elasticity for cash flow is 0.54 (standard error = 0.22). The trend is positive, suggesting an average annual growth rate of 3.3 percent in corporate contributions that is not explained by trends in tax rates or after-tax cash flow. A slightly smaller price elasticity is obtained when the basic price measure is replaced by the price corresponding to the top tax rate, in equation (B). Replacing cash flow income by after-tax net income, in equation (D), results in a lower income elasticity (0.40) but almost no change in the estimated price elasticity (−0.43). Using pretax net income results in a drop in the estimated price elasticity to −0.33 and little change in the income elasticity, in comparison to equation (A). The price-elasticity estimates in these equations vary from −0.30 to −0.43, and the income elasticities vary from 0.40 to 0.57. Variants using the lagged price produced similar estimates.[36]

The result most at variance with the basic estimates in equation (A) is the very high price elasticity, −1.70, estimated in equation (C) using price defined in terms of average rather than marginal tax rates. The price- and income-elasticity estimates of −1.70 and 0.50 are much closer to those obtained by Schwartz of −2.00 and 0.63 in his log-linear specification. Because of the divergence in the estimated price elasticities, the choice of price measure is clearly a matter of some significance. While the correct measure of a company's price is based on its marginal tax rate, the issue is whether the average rate or a marginal rate based on average income better reflects marginal rates for all companies. On the one hand, the marginal rate calculated as a function of the average income for a class overstates the actual rates for firms with no net income, implying that the average tax rate may be a better measure of the average of marginal rates than the calculated marginal rate. A weakness of average tax rates as a proxy for marginal rates—besides not being calculated from the tax schedule—is that they may be much more strongly procyclical than marginal rates. In order to correct for this possible bias, the national unemployment rate was added in equations (F) and (G). Both estimated elasticities fall in absolute value, with the price based on the average rate becoming insignificant. At the same time the corporate-income coefficients become insignificant, reflecting the high negative correlation with the unemployment rate. While the procyclical nature of corporate gifts is made clear, the high degree of collinearity in the time-series data makes it impossible to distinguish any income effect.

A final specification used with the time-series data allows for a split in the price variable between permanent and transitory components. Equa-

---

36. Substituting the lagged price yielded price and income elasticities of −0.40 and 0.52.

**Table 5.13**     Estimated Time-Series Equations: Dependent Variable—Logarithm of Aggregate Contributions

| Equation | (A) | (B) | (C) | (D) | (E) | (F) | (G) |
|---|---|---|---|---|---|---|---|
| **Price** | | | | | | | |
| $\ln(1 - R_m)$ | -0.41 (0.07) | | | -0.43 (0.07) | -0.33 (0.06) | -0.16 (0.05) | |
| $\ln(1 - R_l)$ | | -0.30 (0.05) | | | | | |
| $\ln(1 - R_a)$ | | | -1.70 (0.26) | | | | -0.32 (0.27) |
| **Income** | | | | | | | |
| $\ln CFN$ | 0.54 (0.22) | 0.53 (0.21) | 0.50 (0.20) | | | -0.08 (0.15) | -0.11 (0.17) |
| $\ln NIN$ | | | | 0.40 (0.17) | | | |
| $\ln NI$ | | | | | 0.57 (0.14) | | |

| | | | | | | | |
|---|---|---|---|---|---|---|---|
| Unemployment rate | | | | | | $-0.082$ | $-0.084$ |
| | | | | | | $(0.007)$ | $(0.011)$ |
| Trend | 0.033 | 0.036 | 0.026 | 0.041 | 0.035 | 0.046 | 0.045 |
| | $(0.011)$ | $(0.011)$ | $(0.010)$ | $(0.008)$ | $(0.008)$ | $(0.006)$ | $(0.007)$ |
| Intercept | 5.41 | 5.71 | 6.14 | 9.03 | 4.63 | 21.6 | 22.2 |
| | $(5.37)$ | $(5.01)$ | $(4.84)$ | $(4.09)$ | $(3.32)$ | $(3.6)$ | $(4.1)$ |
| $R^2$ | 0.76 | 0.71 | 0.78 | 0.76 | 0.76 | 0.96 | 0.96 |
| Autocorrelation coefficient | 0.75 | 0.83 | 0.78 | 0.75 | 0.83 | 0.51 | 0.47 |

*Note:* There are 44 observations, except in equation (B) (42 observations) and equation (G) (41). The method of estimation is generalized least squares, with a correction for first-order serial correlation.

Variables are defined as: $R_m$ = annual weighted average of class marginal tax rates (see Appendix G, col. 1); $R_a$ = average tax rate (Appendix G, col. 2); $R_t$ = marginal tax rate at highest incomes (see Appendix F);

$R_p$ = normal or "permanent" marginal tax rate = $(R_m(t-1) + R_m + R_m(t+1))/3$;

$CFN$ = cash flow after taxes, before contributions, (net income + depreciation + depletion + amortization + contributions − (taxes + $R_m$ (contributions))), in 1972 dollars (deflation using the GNP price deflator);

$NIN$ = net income after taxes, before contributions, in 1972 dollars;

$NI$ = net income, in 1972 dollars; Trend = year − 1935. Numbers in parentheses are standard errors.

tion (13) shows the estimated equation using prices based on marginal tax rate:

$$(13) \quad \ln G = -0.27 \ln (1 - R_p) - 0.37 [\ln (1 - R_m) - \ln (1 - R_p)]$$
$$\quad\quad\quad\quad (0.16) \quad\quad\quad\quad\quad\quad (0.12)$$

$$+ 0.22 \ln NCF - 0.059 U + 0.039 \text{ Trend}$$
$$\quad (0.24) \quad\quad\quad (0.013) \quad\quad (0.011)$$

$$+ 14.0 , R^2 = 0.89, \rho = 0.46.$$
$$(5.9)$$

The elasticity with respect to the permanent price is $-0.27$ while the transitory tax effect is $-0.37$; these coefficients are not significantly different. The transitory tax effect suggests that corporations as a whole time their gifts to some extent in order to increase the tax savings from contributions. Nelson's results using a qualitative variable to represent anticipated price changes suggests the same sort of timing effect. It is interesting to note that the exclusion of that anticipation variable causes Nelson's estimated price elasticity to change from $-1.0$ to $-0.6$.[37] As in equations (F) and (G) the estimated-income effect is statistically insignificant.

### Pooled Time-Series/Cross-Section Analysis

The second data set analyzed includes annual observations by asset class for firms with net income and assets. This pooling yielded a total of 506 observations with sizable variations in both the size of firms and the price of giving. Two econometric problems often arise in estimation using pooled data such as this: autocorrelation and heteroskedasticity. The

---

37. Nelson (1970, p. 51, table 11) estimated the equation:
$$\log GC = -0.75 + 1.05 \log Y - 1.03 \log P_{-1}$$
$$\quad\quad\quad\quad (0.26) \quad\quad\quad (0.11)$$
$$+ 0.055 E + 0.016 \text{ Trend}, R^{-2} = 0.93,$$
$$\quad (0.028) \quad\quad (0.003)$$

where $GC$ is total giving in (thousands of) 1936 dollars, $Y$ is total net income after taxes and before contributions, $P_{-1}$ is the lagged value of Nelson's price variable, and $E$ is his measure of expectations. I assumed $E = 0$ in 1939, 1946, 1949, and 1954 (years immediately before or after an excess-profits tax) and $E = 2$ in 1940, 1945, 1950, and 1953 (the beginning and ending years of such taxes). Where contributions were measured in 1972 dollars, I obtained the equation:

$$\ln GC = -7.06 + 1.05 \ln Y - 0.99 \ln P_{-1}$$
$$\quad\quad (5.67) \quad (0.24) \quad\quad (0.11)$$
$$+ 0.124 E + 0.040 \text{ Trend}, R^2 = 0.94.$$
$$\quad (0.062) \quad\quad (0.007)$$

Obviously, the estimates are quite close except for the coefficient of $E$, which may oe attributable to an incorrect assignment of that variable in my analysis.

presence of serially correlated errors in the aggregated time-series equations suggests that this may be a problem in the pooled equations as well. Heteroskedasticity may arise because the error associated with class means tends to vary with the number of observations, and the number of firms by asset class in the present data varies greatly. Analysis of residuals showed that residuals did, in fact, tend to increase as the number of firms in each class fell. Accordingly, a generalized least squares procedure was used to account for both autocorrelation and heteroskedasticity. This involved, first, correcting for first-order serial correlation and, second, weighting the resulting observations by the square root of the number of firms in the class.[38] For the present sample, the former was complicated because the dollar values of class limits in the *Statistics of Income* were changed several times over the 1936–80 period, preventing comparison of class averages between certain years.[39] In estimation, transitional years were omitted in order to form comparable lagged values.[40]

Table 5.14 presents the estimates based on the pooled time-series/cross-section sample. The basic model using the price based on marginal tax rate is compared with after-tax cash flow and net-income variables in equations (A) and (B). Although the price elasticities are quite close, the estimated income elasticities differ significantly: 1.1 in (G) and 0.6 in (B). As noted above, if the legal net-income variable is a poorer measure of economic profit than cash flow income, one would expect, as in other cases of errors in variables, that the income coefficient in (B) would tend to be biased toward zero. For this reason, equations using the cash flow definition are presented in the remainder of the table. Equation (C) presents equation (A) corrected for autocorrelation. The estimated value of the autocorrelation coefficient in the equation is 0.85, indicating substantial positive correlation over time in a given class's residuals. While the point estimate of the income elasticity is 1.1 in (A) and (C), the price elasticity falls in absolute value from $-0.47$ to $-0.23$ between the two equations. The most apparent difference between these estimates and those based on the time-series data is that the income elasticities based on the pooled data are considerably larger, with point estimates ranging from 1.05 to 1.14, aside from equation (B). This difference is attributable to the greater vari-

---

38. A similar procedure is suggested by Kmenta 1971, pp. 508–12. For a discussion of weighted least squares, see Theil 1971, pp. 244–49. For a similar application to cross-section data on corporate contributions, see McElroy and Siegfried 1982b.

39. The number of asset classes by year was: 10 from 1936 to 1953; 14 from 1954 to 1961; 7 in 1962; 14 in 1963; 12 from 1964 to 1967; and 11 from 1970 to 1980.

40. Observations for 1954, 1962 through 1964, and 1970 were omitted. Each variable was transformed, e.g., $g^* = g_t - rg_{t-1}$, where $g$ is the logarithm of giving and $r$ is the estimated autocorrelation coefficient. The equations on these transformed variables were then weighted. It is also worth noting the implicaton of inflation for this estimation procedure. Inflation has the effect of changing the real bracket limits of asset classes over time, although inspection of the data over time shows that the distribution of firms among classes changes slowly, so that correcting for first-order serial correlation is not unreasonable.

Table 5.14    Estimated Pooled Equations: Dependent Variable—Logarithm of Average Contributions

| Explanatory Variables | (A) | (B) | (C) | (D) | (E) | (F) | (G) |
|---|---|---|---|---|---|---|---|
| $\ln(1-R_m)$ | -0.47 (0.06) | -0.46 (0.06) | -0.23 (0.03) | | -0.20 (0.03) | | -0.57 (0.25) |
| $\ln(1-R_a)$ | | | | -1.75 (0.15) | | -1.81 (0.17) | |
| $\ln ACFN$ | 1.12 (0.01) | | 1.11 (0.03) | 1.04 (0.03) | 1.14 (0.02) | 1.05 (0.02) | 1.12 (0.04) |
| $\ln NIN$ | | 0.59 (0.76) | | | | | |
| $U$ | | | | | -0.024 (0.006) | -0.001** (0.007) | 0.011** (0.014) |
| Trend | -0.0065 (0.0017) | -0.0077 (0.0018) | -0.020 (0.005) | -0.0082 (0.0040) | -0.015 (0.003) | -0.007 (0.003) | 0.015** (0.013) |
| Intercept | -6.44 (0.12) | -5.56 (0.15) | -0.84 (0.05) | -0.96 (0.50) | -1.30 (0.06) | -1.28 (0.05) | -1.79 (0.14) |
| $R^2$ | 0.96 | 0.96 | 0.77 | 0.84 | 0.87 | 0.89 | 0.92 |
| Autocorrelation coefficient[a] | — | — | 0.85 | 0.83 | 0.78 | 0.78 | 0.89 |
| Sample[a] | 1936–80 | 1936–80 | 1936–80 | 1936–80 | 1936–80 | 1936–80 | 1965–80 |

*Note:* Standard errors are given in parentheses. Coefficients denoted by double asterisks have t-statistics less than 2 in absolute value. Variables are defined for asset classes as follows: $R_m$ = marginal tax rate; $R_a$ = average tax rate (normal tax plus excess-profits taxes as percent of net income); $ACFN$ = average cash flow after taxes, before contributions; $NIN$ = average net income after taxes, before contributions; $U$ = unemployment rate.

[a]The number of observations per year was: 1936–53: 10; 1954–61: 14; 1962: 7; 1963: 14; 1964–69: 12; and 1970–80: 11. Equations (A) and (B) are based on the entire 506 observations. The remaining equations include only years for which the preceding year had the same number of observations. For equations (C) to (F) this was 438 observations. For equation (G) it was 158.

ation in average company size in the cross-section data than in the time-series, and it is similar to the results obtained in previous econometric analyses. The equations suggest that contributions increase at a rate slightly faster than proportional to income or capacity. As in the time-series regressions, the use of alternative income measures made little difference in the estimated income elasticity.[41] As discussed below, the choice between cash flow and net income must rest on the reasonableness of each. In contrast to the positive trend in aggregate giving in the time-series analysis, the trend terms for average giving in the pooled analysis using the full sample are negative.

Regarding the effect of price in the pooled equation, the contrast between the magnitude of the estimated price elasticities based on marginal and average tax rates remains striking. In the basic equation covering the entire sample and employing the correction for autocorrelation (C), the elasticity associated with the marginal price is $-0.23$, compared to $-1.75$ for the average price (the latter being roughly the same magnitude as that in the corresponding time-series equation (C) in table 5.13). In equations (E) and (F) the unemployment rate is included to account for any cyclical effects not measured by net income. In contrast to the time-series sample, where unemployment and corporate income are highly correlated, the addition of unemployment in these pooled equations has little effect on the estimated-income coefficients.

Equation (G) is limited to observations after 1964. The use of this more recent period makes the autocorrelation correction more straightforward since there is only one change in asset-class definitions. In addition, using the recent period allows one to avoid the most difficult problems in measuring marginal tax rates, particularly those associated with excess-profits tax. For this sample the estimated income elasticity is quite close to that obtained in the entire sample, but other coefficients are different. Most apparent, the point estimates of the price elasticity are larger in absolute value for each specification, although the standard errors are considerably bigger, presumably due to the higher correlation between income and price during the post-1964 period. The unemployment rate is insignificant in both equations, and the trend is positive and significant in the last equation.

41. Substituting net income for cash flow in equation (A) yielded an almost identical income elasticity of 1.10 (standard error $= 0.01$), but a smaller absolute price elasticity of $-0.21$ (0.05). The $R^2$ was 0.97. An alternative measure of firm scale, assets, was included along with cash flow in another formulation; estimated elasticities were: price: $-0.42$; cash flow: 0.03; and assets: 0.91. $R^2 = 0.97$. This suggests that assets may be as good a measure of scale as income.

An equation splitting up the price effect into permanent and transitory components was estimated as in the time-series analysis. The equation including the unemployment rate was

$$(14) \quad \ln G = -0.27 \ln (1 - R_p) - 0.14 \, [\ln (1 - R_m) - \ln (1 - R_p)]$$
$$\quad\quad\quad\quad (0.07) \quad\quad\quad\quad\quad (0.11)$$

$$+ \, 1.12 \ln NCF - 0.064 \, U - 0.012 \text{ Trend} - 5.81,$$
$$(0.01) \quad\quad\quad (0.006) \quad\quad (0.002)$$

$$R^2 = 0.97, N = 391.$$

Only the permanent price effect is significantly different from zero at the 95 percent level, with an implied elasticity of $-0.27$. The point estimate of the transitory price effect, $-0.14$, is insignificant.[42]

*Evaluation*

In assessing the findings of the present study, it is important to focus in particular on the income effect and the price effect. The present results regarding the elasticity of corporate giving with respect to measures of income or capacity are generally comparable to those obtained in earlier studies. The equations using cross-section data, in which income shows the most variation, imply an income elasticity slightly above 1.0 when net cash flow is used; the use of net income results in a smaller estimate. The present analysis, however, does not resolve the question of what is the proper measure of income or capacity. Neither pretax net income, after-tax net income, nor after-tax cash flow stands out in terms of explanatory power. Consequently, it appears to come down to which measure is the most reasonable. Pretax net income is commonly used as a measure of firm income, but the exclusion of tax liability causes actual capacity to be measured incorrectly. This is so particularly in the context of "managerial discretion" models of firm behavior in which management maximizes utility subject to a net-profit constraint. Even more dubious is the notion—implicit in any use of the legal definition of net income—that corporate contributions respond to changes in accounting definitions used for tax purposes. There is little reason to believe, for example, that an increase in allowable depreciation charges would itself lower contributions through an income effect unless managers were subject to some sort of accounting illusion. The major attraction of the cash flow definition is that it is unaffected by artificial changes in the accounting definitions of depreciation, depletion, and amortization. These quantities are added back into net income on the assumption that they do not represent current ex-

---

42. Because of the number of lags already involved in the definitions of permanent price, no correction for serial correlation was made for this equation.

penditures that reduce available capacity to make contributions. To the extent that allowable depreciation and depletion allowances exceed the true corresponding magnitudes, the cash flow measure is all the more attractive.

Net income and cash flow income imply quite different results for tax policies providing for liberalized depreciation allowances, such as the Economic Recovery Tax Act of 1981. The most apparent effect of the new depreciation rules will be to reduce net income as defined for tax purposes in the short run. Over the lifetime of any class of capital goods, the major effect of any shortening of accounting lives is to increase depreciation deductions. This increase will last until capital being depreciated under the previous accounting rules is fully depreciated. How this change in depreciation will affect contributions depends crucially on which specification is adopted. In order to illustrate the effect of a liberalization in depreciation such as that embodied in the 1981 tax act, table 5.15 presents a simple example of a firm whose capital stock has a life of five years and is replaced over time. The effect of shortening the accounting life of assets in year 3 is to increase depreciation expenses in the short run, thereby reducing net income (both before and after tax), but *increasing* cash flow. Because the estimated equations presented above suggest that these measures of capacity have similar effects on contributions, these opposite changes also imply opposite effects on contributions. The implications of the act for corporate giving in the 1980s therefore depend on which econometric specification is selected. Since the statistical fits of both models are quite close, one must fall back on the reasonableness of the models. Using this criterion, the cash flow specification seems preferable, implying that the income effect of the act will tend to encourage giving.

Conclusions about the price effect of tax rates on corporate giving are equally unsettled as a result of the present analysis. Although most of the estimates of the price elasticity based on marginal tax rates cluster between $-0.2$ and $-0.4$, estimates using the average tax rate are considerably higher. Because of its theoretical soundness, the marginal-price concept is preferable, but difficulties in measuring marginal tax rates make one cautious about rejecting the average price results entirely. Splitting the price into permanent and transitory components suggests that corporations time their contributions in order to take advantage of temporarily high tax rates. As Nelson (1970) notes, corporate foundations may be used in this connection to smooth out the pattern of gifts over time.

With these reservations in mind, it is nevertheless illuminating to apply the estimated coefficients to project corporate giving under various changes in tax policy. One of the most extreme changes in the present tax structure would be the elimination of the corporate tax. Like previous studies, the present estimates are strictly applicable to changes in price and income variables that are within the range of observed values. Simu-

**Table 5.15    Effect of Shortened Asset Life for Accounting Purposes: An Example of a Change in Year 3**

| Year | Cash Flow Income[a] | Depreciation[b] | Net Income | 50% Income Tax | After-Tax Contributions[c] | | | |
|---|---|---|---|---|---|---|---|---|
| | | | | | Cash Flow | Net Income | Based on Net Income | Based on Cash Flow |
| 1 | 200 | 100 | 100 | 50 | 150 | 50 | 10.0 | 10.0 |
| 2 | 200 | 100 | 100 | 50 | 150 | 50 | 10.0 | 10.0 |
| 3 | 200 | 130 | 70 | 35 | 165 | 35 | 8.1 | 11.1 |
| 4 | 200 | 160 | 40 | 20 | 180 | 20 | 5.8 | 12.2 |
| 5 | 200 | 140 | 60 | 30 | 170 | 30 | 7.4 | 11.5 |
| 6 | 200 | 130 | 70 | 35 | 165 | 35 | 8.1 | 11.1 |
| 7 | 200 | 120 | 80 | 40 | 160 | 40 | 8.7 | 10.7 |
| 8 | 200 | 110 | 90 | 45 | 155 | 45 | 9.4 | 10.4 |
| 9 | 200 | 100 | 100 | 50 | 150 | 50 | 10.0 | 10.0 |
| 10 | 200 | 100 | 100 | 50 | 150 | 50 | 10.0 | 10.0 |

[a]Revenue minus costs other than depreciation and other amortization.

[b]In years 1 and 2, a five-year asset life with straight-line depreciation is used. A constant capital stock of 500 is assumed. In year 3, the allowed asset life is reduced to two years, increasing the allowable depreciation on one year's worth of capital to 50 rather than 20; total depreciation is $80 + 50 = 130$. In year 4, it is $60 + 50 + 50 = 160$; in year 5, $40 + 50 + 50 = 140$; and so on.

[c]Beginning contributions (years 1 and 2) are assumed to be 10. Calculated contributions are calculated assuming variables other than income or cash flow remain constant: $G_t = 10 (N_t/N_1)^b$, where $N_1$ and $N_t$ measure net income or net cash flow in years 1 an $t$ and where the coefficient $b$ is assumed to be 0.6 for net income and 1.1 for net cash flow.

lating the elimination of the corporate tax, of course, involves a much larger change in price and income than what has been observed; thus a simulation based on such estimates must be taken as merely suggestive of the possible impact. Taking the values of after-tax cash flow, taxes, and price for all corporations with net income in 1980 to be $370.7 billion, $62.8 billion, and 0.54, respectively (U.S. Internal Revenue Service, *Statistics of Income—1980, Corporation Income Tax Returns* 1983, p. 36, table 3), and assuming price and income elasticities of $-0.4$ and $1.1$, respectively, corporate giving in the absence of the corporate income tax is estimated to fall by only 7.2 percent. Although the elimination of the tax would cause the price of gifts to rise by about 85 percent, after-tax cash flow would increase by 17 percent, nearly offsetting the price increase.[43] Obviously, larger price elasticities would imply larger reductions in contributions, so a 7 percent decline should probably be taken as a minimum reduction in corporate giving if the tax were eliminated. Assuming the basic validity of the estimates presented here, it seems quite unlikely that the elimination of the corporate income tax would result in an increase in corporate gifts.

A second change in the corporate tax that is less far-reaching would be a limitation on the deductibility of charitable gifts. If, for example, contributions were included as a preference item in the corporate minimum tax, the price of making contributions would be increased for corporations subject to that tax. For a firm facing a 46 percent marginal rate and subject to the minimum tax, including contributions as a preference item at a 15 percent rate would increase the price of giving from 0.61 to 0.76.[44] If there were no cross-price effects between this price and other business expenditures, simulation of the effect using the present model would be straightforward. Based again on figures for 1980, contributions would be projected to fall by about 8.5 percent.[45] Again, larger price elasticities would imply larger declines associated with this change. As noted previously in this chapter, current estimates of the price elasticity of corporate giving may shed little light on the effect of changing the *relative* price of firm's expenditures. If changing the deductibility of contributions caused firms to substitute other expenditures—like advertising—for contributions, simulations based on current estimates will probably understate the reduction in contributions.

---

43. $G_1/G_0 = (1/.54)^{-0.4} (433.5/370.7)^{1.1} = 0.928.$

44. Before the inclusion the price is $(1 - (0.46)(1 - 0.15)) = 0.609.$ Afterwards, it is $(1 - (0.46)(1 - 0.15) + 0.15) = 0.759.$

45. $G_1/G_0 = (.759/.609)^{-0.4} (370.4/370.7)^{1.1} = 0.915,$ where $370.4 = 370.7 - .15(2.33).$

# 6      Charitable Bequests

In 1982 nonprofit organizations received some $5.5 billion in charitable bequests. Though they typically amount to less than a tenth of the size of contributions by living individuals, these bequests have almost always exceeded the total of corporate contributions (see *Giving U. S. A.* 1983, p. 36). In certain areas, notably private foundations and higher education, bequests are an extremely important source of philanthropic support. In contrast to the numerous econometric analyses of individual and corporate contributions, there has been only a limited amount of empirical work to explain charitable bequests. This may have more to do with the limited amount of appropriate data than with any assessment of the relative importance of bequests. In any case, a major objective of this chapter is to discuss previous work as well as to present new findings regarding the effect of federal taxation on bequests.

The first section of the chapter describes the federal tax structure affecting charitable bequests, and the second provides a statistical overview of the extent and distribution of such bequests. The third section describes the methods and results of previous econometric analyses of charitable bequests. The fourth section provides new estimates of the tax effects on bequests using a sample of 1976 estate tax returns. The final section presents a brief discussion of the likely effects of several proposed changes in the estate tax.

## 6.1   The Estate Tax

The present federal estate tax was adopted in 1916, although there were transfer taxes on inheritances and estates at various times in the nineteenth century (Pechman 1977, p. 222). The tax base consists of assets owned by the decedent at time of death plus certain lifetime gifts less funeral and administrative expenses, certain debts, a deduction for certain property passing to the decedent's spouse, and a charitable deduction. This charitable deduction may include some lifetime gifts (to the extent that such gifts are included in gross estate), but charitable bequests make up most of the deduction. Following Sunley (1977, p. 2320), therefore, the amount of this deduction is referred to in this chapter as charitable bequests. Like the charitable deduction in the income tax, the estate tax charitable deduction covers bequests to nonprofit charities, government agencies, foundations, and the like. Unlike the income tax provision, though, there is no limit to the estate tax deduction, and gifts to foreign charities are not disallowed.[1]

In addition to these deductions, the estate tax is reduced by several tax credits, the most important of which is a "unified" credit that in 1977 replaced an exemption of $60,000. From 1943 to 1976, the $60,000 exemption applied to all returns, and the tax rate schedule was fixed in nominal terms, with rates ranging from 3 to 77 percent. Shoup (1966, p. 5) notes that, with the exception of the related gift tax, "the stability of the nominal rate scale and the exemption level of the estate tax over two and a half decades is without parallel in any significant federal, state, or local tax in the same period." The Tax Reform Act of 1976 modified the rate schedule, producing a top rate of 70 percent, and substituted the unified credit for the exemption, providing for it to grow over time (*1980 U. S. Master Tax Guide* 1979, p. 29). The size of this unified credit made it equivalent to a much larger exemption. For example, the minimum estate size required to be subject to the tax doubled in 1977 from $60,000 to $120,667 as a result of the credit. In addition, the credit was increased over time under the 1976 legislation. The Economic Recovery Tax Act of 1981 extended the 1976 act by further increasing the unified credit and again cutting the top tax rate over a four-year period, to 50 percent (*Internal Revenue Code* 1982, sec. 2001, p. 847). In addition, the 1981 act removed the previous limit of 50 percent of the estate that had applied to the marital deduction, making it an unlimited deduction.[2]

### 6.1.1  Effective Tax Schedules over Time

In order to compare the effective rate schedule of the estate tax over time, it is of course necessary to account for inflation. In particular, the stability of the nominal tax schedule between 1943 and 1976 masks a steady erosion in the real value of the exemption as well as an increase in

---

1. See Shoup 1966, pp. 60–61; and Pechman 1977.
2. *Internal Revenue Code* 1982, pp. 846–48. Between 1971 and 1981, the marital deduction was limited by the greater of $50,000 or one-half of the adjusted gross estate (U.S. Internal Revenue Service, *Statistics of Income—1976, Estate Tax Returns* 1979 p. 5).

progessivity, as the real bracket widths diminished over time.[3] Table 6.1 illustrates the effect of inflation on the real exemption level, which is effectively the minimum estate that can be taxed, as well as on the real tax rate schedule. The impact is especially evident over the thirty-four years between 1943 and 1976. During the period prices rose two-and-a-half times. The value of the exemption in 1972 dollars fell from about $166,000 to $45,338 over the period. The 1976 legislation put an end to this deterioration, however, by increasing the real filing level to some $86,000 in 1977 and to almost $90,000 in 1981. The effective exemption level was increased still more by the 1981 act. By 1987 the filing requirement was scheduled to rise to $228,000 in 1972 dollars, well above the 1942 level in real terms. Over the period 1943 to 1987, therefore, inflation and legislation have combined to cause a gradual decline, followed by a steep rise, in the size of the minimum estate subject to the estate tax.

The last three columns of table 6.1 show the marginal tax rate that would apply to estates (after deductions but before the exemption) of given real amounts over time. For example, an estate of $500,000 in 1972 dollars would be $180,700 in 1943 dollars, yielding a taxable estate of $120,700 after the exemption. This taxable estate fell into the 30 percent rate bracket. Over the period of fixed nominal rate schedules, 1943 to 1976, marginal rates for each real estate size rose, the greatest increase being the rise applying to a $5,000,000 estate—45 to 70 percent. The projected trends following the 1976 tax law reveal a more complex pattern. For the $500,000 estate rates are projected to rise from 35 to 43 percent. At the higher estate levels, however, rates will fall, from 53 to 50 percent at $2,000,000 and from 70 to 50 percent at $5,000,000. While the legislation of 1976 and 1981 has the effect of reducing the number of estates covered by the tax, therefore, the marginal rates have not been cut uniformly. For many estates, the marginal tax rates in the 1980s will be as high as at any time since 1943 for estates of equal real value.

A major effect of the erosion in the real exemption level up until 1976 was a gradual expansion in the coverage of the estate tax. As table 6.2 shows, the number of estate tax returns increased from about 14,300 in 1943 to over 200,000 in 1976. As a percentage of all deaths in the country, these returns grew from 1.0 to 10.5 percent over the period. There is little doubt, given the tax legislation of 1976 and 1981, that 1976 will represent a peak in coverage for the estate tax for at least some time to come. In contrast to measures of coverage based on the number of individuals, it is much more difficult to determine the proportion of the total wealth of decedents in any one year represented by the estate tax base. Pechman (1977, p. 225) estimated that before 1977 the taxable portion of the estate tax

---

3. See Clotfelter 1984 for a discussion of the relationship between inflationary bracket creep and progressivity.

**Table 6.1**    Exemption and Unified Credit Levels and Marginal Tax Rates on Given Real Estates, Selected Years, 1943–87

| Year of Death | Exemption | Unified Credit | Equivalent Exemption[a] | Minimum Estate Subject to Tax in 1972 Dollars[b] | Marginal Tax Rate on Constant Dollar Estate (thousands of 1972 dollars)[c] | | |
|---|---|---|---|---|---|---|---|
| | | | | | 500 | 2000 | 5000 |
| 1943 | 60,000 | | | 166,021 | 30 | 35 | 45 |
| 1947 | 60,000 | | | 128,893 | 30 | 37 | 49 |
| 1950 | 60,000 | | | 111,940 | 30 | 39 | 53 |
| 1954 | 60,000 | | | 100,755 | 30 | 39 | 53 |
| 1958 | 60,000 | | | 90,854 | 32 | 42 | 56 |
| 1960 | 60,000 | | | 87,336 | 32 | 42 | 56 |
| 1962 | 60,000 | | | 84,973 | 32 | 42 | 56 |
| 1965 | 60,000 | | | 80,688 | 32 | 42 | 59 |
| 1969 | 60,000 | | | 69,132 | 32 | 45 | 63 |
| 1972 | 60,000 | | | 60,000 | 32 | 45 | 63 |
| 1976 | 60,000 | | | 45,338 | 35 | 53 | 70 |
| 1977 | | 30,000 | 120,667 | 86,160 | 37 | 53 | 70 |
| 1978 | | 34,000 | 134,000 | 86,900 | 39 | 57 | 70 |
| 1979 | | 38,000 | 147,333 | 90,156 | 39 | 57 | 70 |
| 1980 | | 42,500 | 160,563 | 89,880 | 39 | 61 | 70 |
| 1981 | | 47,000 | 175,625 | 89,830 | 39 | 61 | 70 |
| 1982 | | 62,800 | 225,000 | 108,575 | 41 | 65 | 65 |
| 1983 | | 79,300 | 275,000 | 126,088 | 41 | 60 | 60 |
| 1984 | | 96,300 | 325,000 | 141,673 | 41 | 55 | 55 |
| 1985 | | 121,800 | 400,000 | 166,251 | 41 | 50 | 55 |
| 1986 | | 155,800 | 500,000 | 198,650 | 43 | 50 | 50 |
| 1987 | | 192,800 | 600,000 | 228,137 | 43 | 50 | 50 |

[a]Minimum exemption level that would result in zero tax with no unified credit. For 1977 to 1981, *1980 U.S. Master Tax Guide* 1979, p. 29; for 1982 to 1987, calculations from estate tax tables.

[b]Exemption or equivalent exemption deflated by GNP price deflator (U.S. Council of Economic Advisers 1983, p. 166).

[c]Refers to 1972 value of gross estate after deductions but before any exemption. Marginal tax rates were calculated using the nominal value for each real estate size.

base represented less than a quarter of the total wealth of decedents. Other evidence suggests that using the gross estate measure, estate tax returns may account for more than half of the aggregate estate of all decedents.[4] In sum, while fewer than a tenth of all decedents file estate tax returns, these returns account for a significant portion of the total estate being transferred in any one year.

Table 6.2 also shows that the tax's expanded coverage was accompanied by an increase in total reported charitable bequests. Between 1943 and 1976 such bequests grew from $202 million to $3.0 billion, almost four-and-a-half times. The average charitable bequest fell over the period, however, as the tax expanded over time to include less wealthy decedents. In 1972 dollars, the average fell from about $39,000 in 1943 to $11,300 in 1976. As a percentage of gross estate, which corresponds roughly to total assets at death, charitable bequests ranged from a high of 7.8 percent in 1969 to a low of 4.2 percent in 1949.

### 6.1.2   Lifetime Gifts and Trusts

In addition to the tax schedule itself, charitable bequests are also affected by the gift tax and the various tax provisions related to trusts. The gift tax is a progressive levy applied to lifetime (inter vivos) gifts that exceed an annual exemption.[5] Before 1977 the gift tax had a separate schedule, but now the gift and estate taxes are assessed as a unified transfer tax with a single schedule.[6] Since charitable gifts are deductible in the gift tax as are charitable bequests in the estate tax, the major practical importance of the gift tax for charitable giving lies in its role as protector of the estate tax. Without the gift tax, individuals could arrange to dispose of their wealth before death through gifts, thus escaping the estate tax and undercutting any incentive effect of the estate tax's charitable deduction.

Charitable giving is also affected by the tax treatment of trusts, both charitable and noncharitable. The tax treatment of charitable trusts and

4. David and Menchik (1981, table 2) present a sample of estates of husbands between 1947 and 1978, which can be used to give a very rough idea of the distribution of all estates. The percentages of estates in each net estate category were: no estate: 25.2 percent; $0–5,000: 12.7; $5,000–10,000: 14.6; $10,000–20,000: 23.1; $20,000–50,000: 16.7; $50,000 or more: 7.7. A weighted average of wealth was calculated using the midpoints of the first five categories, $50,000 for 0.8 percent of decedents, and $221,425 for the remaining 6.9 percent of decedents (corresponding to the average gross estate for estate tax returns in 1969). By this calculation, estate tax returns accounted for approximately 65 percent of the total estates of decedents.

5. In 1981 the exemption was raised from $3,000 to $10,000 per taxpayer (Sugarman and Feinberg 1981, p. 4).

6. Before 1977 the gift tax rates were generally three-fourths of the corresponding estate tax rates, although the gift tax rates applied to gifts net of the tax whereas the estate tax rates applied to the estate before the tax. In addition, gifts made within three years of death were usually counted as being made "in contemplation of death" in the pre-1977 law, but exceptions were possible (U.S. Internal Revenue Service, *Statistics of Income—1976, Estate Tax Returns 1979*, p. 5). See also Shoup 1966, Pechman 1977, or Sunley 1977.

**Table 6.2**      Estate Tax Returns, Gross Estate, and Charitable Bequests, Selected Years (dollar amounts in billions)

| Year | Estate Tax Returns | As Percentage of Deaths | Gross Estate | Charitable Bequests | Charitable Bequests as Percentage of Gross Estate |
|------|------|------|------|------|------|
| 1943 | 14.3 | 1.0 | 2,908 | 201.9 | 6.9 |
| 1947 | 23.4 | 1.6 | 4,775 | 223.1 | 4.8 |
| 1948 | 24.6 | 1.7 | 4,933 | 296.2 | 6.0 |
| 1949 | 25.9 | 1.8 | 4,918 | 205.9 | 4.2 |
| 1950 | 28.0 | 1.9 | 5,505 | 274.4 | 5.0 |
| 1953 | 36.7 | 2.4 | 7,412 | 354.5 | 4.8 |
| 1954 | 36.5 | 2.5 | 7,467 | 397.8 | 5.3 |
| 1958 | 46.5 | 2.8 | 11,648 | 668.9 | 5.7 |
| 1960 | 64.5 | 3.8 | 14,622 | 950.8 | 6.5 |
| 1962 | 78.4 | 4.4 | 17,007 | 876.0 | 5.2 |
| 1965 | 97.3 | 5.3 | 21,757 | 1,309.5 | 6.0 |
| 1969 | 133.9 | 6.9 | 27,445 | 2,132.1 | 7.8 |
| 1972 | 174.9 | 8.9 | 38,869 | 1,998.1 | 5.1 |
| 1976 | 200.7 | 10.5 | 48,202 | 2,993.9 | 6.2 |

*Source:* U.S. Internal Revenue Service, *Statistics of Income, Estate Tax Returns,* various years; data on deaths from U.S. Department of Health and Human Services 1982, part A, p. 1, table 1.1.

split-interest trusts is discussed in chapter 2. Noncharitable trusts also may have effects on giving. Probably the most important effect that noncharitable trusts can have is to blunt the effect of high statutory estate tax rates, most notably in the "generation-skipping" trust. Because the creation of a trust involves no transfer of property subject to the estate tax until the trust's termination, a trust can be used to avoid estate taxation. By designating his wife and/or his children to receive income as "life tenants" of a trust, a man can allow some of his heirs to receive the income from this property without paying estate tax. Only when the remainder interest is received, possibly by grandchildren, is estate tax paid. Although two generations of heirs benefit from the bequest, there is only one transfer that is subject to estate taxation.[7] Any incentive effect that the estate tax charitable deduction might otherwise have thus tends to be weakened when such trusts are used. Other than this possible blunting of the price effect of the estate tax, it is impossible to identify precisely the effect of trust use on charitable bequests. McNees (1973, p. 82) suggests that charitable bequests and trusts are alternative means of tax reduction and, as such, may be complements or substitutes. To view charitable bequests merely as a tax-reduction device is simplistic, however, since the net estate passed on to heirs is reduced by such gifts. Whatever the exact relationship between charitable bequests and the use of trusts, it seems likely that decisions regarding them are made simultaneously in the process of estate planning, whether or not trusts have charitable interests written into them.

In order to give some idea of the typical composition of trusts, table 6.3 gives the distribution of remainder interests for trusts created by millionaires in 1957. For trusts that provided income to the spouse during his or her life, over half of the dollar value was designated to go to the children following the death of the spouse. By contrast, about 6 percent of the value of such trusts went to charity, and less than 1 percent had both a charitable remainder and a remainder interest for children. For generation-skipping trusts that made the decedent's children the sole life tenants, grandchildren received four-fifths of the total value while charities accounted for about 1 percent. The use of trusts increases with estate size; and among those trusts that are established in lower- and middle-size estate categories, the most common form is that which provides lifetime income to the spouse and the remainder interest to the children (Jantscher 1967, pp. 83, 71). Finally, married or widowed decedents are more likely to employ the trust form than those who are single or divorced (Shoup 1966, p. 173, table B-11).

7. For discussions of the role of trusts, see Shoup 1966, pp. 33–45 or Jantscher 1967.

Table 6.3        **Distribution of Remainder Interests of Trusts Created by Millionaires in 1957 (dollar amounts in thousands)**

| | Type of Trust | | | |
|---|---|---|---|---|
| | Surviving Spouse Sole Life Tenant | | Children Sole Life Tenants | |
| Remaindermen | Amount | Percentage | Amount | Percentage |
| Children only | $ 52,427 | 51.2 | $ 949 | 0.6 |
| Grandchildren only | 3,729 | 3.6 | 121,582 | 79.5 |
| Charity only | 6,495 | 6.3 | 1,418 | 0.9 |
| Children and charity | 609 | 0.6 | — | — |
| Grandchildren and charity | — | — | 513 | 0.3 |
| Other | 39,045 | 38.2 | 28,552 | 18.7 |
| TOTAL | $102,305 | 99.9 | $153,014 | 100.0 |

*Source:* Robert Anthoine, "Testamentary Trusts," in Shoup 1966, Appendix B, pp. 167, 168.

## 6.2 The Distribution of Charitable Bequests

Before turning to econometric analysis of charitable bequests, it is useful to describe the size and distribution of such bequests in general terms. One of the most striking aspects of bequest giving is the tremendous inequality in the size of gifts. Even more than lifetime charitable giving, bequest giving is dominated by a relatively tiny number of wealthy individuals. Not only do a relatively few estates ever get taxed, only a small minority of those whose estates are big enough to be taxed make any charitable bequests at all. At the other end, a few decedents make very large gifts indeed. In 1980 and 1981, for example, the bequests of the largest five donors accounted for 1.0 and 1.2 percent of all bequests nationally. In 1982 the largest five bequests added up to an astonishing 26.5 percent of the total.[8]

Table 6.4 presents summary data based on estate tax returns filed in 1977. For the most part, these were returns for individuals who died in 1976 and whose estates were subject to the 1976 tax law. Since decedents with estates less than $60,000 were not subject to tax, there were no returns for a majority of estates. Of the 200,741 returns that were filed, about 70 percent were taxable. Total charitable bequests amounted to

8. The top five bequests included a gift of $1.3 billion by J. Paul Getty and four gifts totalling $145 million (*Giving U.S.A.* 1983, pp. 18–19; 1981, pp. 12–13; and 1982, pp. 15–16). See Schaefer (1968, p. 27) for a similar point regarding the distribution of bequest giving.

Table 6.4    Charitable Bequests and Estate Tax by Size of Gross Estate, Returns Filed in 1977

| Size of Gross Estate (thousands) | Returns | | Charitable Bequests | | | | Average Tax Rate after Credits[a] |
| --- | --- | --- | --- | --- | --- | --- | --- |
| | Total Number | Percentage with Charitable Bequests | Amount (millions) | As Percentage of Gross Estate | Marginal[a] Tax Rate | | |
| Taxable returns | 139,115 | 12.8 | 2,312.8 | 5.7 | — | | 12.3 |
| $60 under 70 | 3,972 | 5.3 | 0.2 | 0.1 | 3 | | 0.1 |
| $70 under 80 | 8,973 | 8.4 | 1.3 | 0.2 | 7 | | 0.6 |
| $80 under 90 | 8,673 | 7.9 | 1.7 | 0.2 | 11 | | 1.6 |
| $90 under 100 | 7,424 | 10.0 | 3.5 | 0.5 | 14 | | 2.5 |
| $100 under 120 | 11,653 | 9.4 | 6.1 | 0.5 | 18 | | 4.1 |
| $120 under 150 | 20,098 | 9.6 | 12.4 | 0.5 | 22 | | 4.2 |
| $150 under 200 | 24,754 | 11.3 | 28.0 | 0.6 | 28 | | 6.2 |
| $200 under 300 | 23,826 | 13.2 | 58.8 | 1.0 | 30 | | 9.5 |
| $300 under 500 | 16,424 | 17.6 | 109.6 | 1.7 | 30 | | 12.6 |
| $500 under 1000 | 9,078 | 21.8 | 142.0 | 2.3 | 32 | | 15.5 |
| $1000 under 2000 | 3,004 | 29.5 | 158.7 | 3.9 | 37 | | 17.9 |
| $2000 under 3000 | 681 | 42.1 | 98.8 | 6.0 | 45 | | 20.1 |
| $3000 under 5000 | 432 | 43.5 | 121.2 | 7.4 | 49 | | 21.4 |
| $5000 under 10,000 | 213 | 51.6 | 152.9 | 10.6 | 59 | | 23.4 |
| $10,000 or more | 90 | 72.2 | 1,417.7 | 48.0 | 77 | | 16.0 |

| Size of gross estate | Nontaxable | 61,632 | 10.7 | 681.1 | 8.9 | |
|---|---|---|---|---|---|---|
| | — | | | | | — |
| $60 under 70 | — | 10,345 | 10.0 | 12.5 | 1.9 | — |
| $70 under 80 | — | 7,145 | 8.1 | 13.3 | 2.5 | — |
| $80 under 90 | — | 6,793 | 7.6 | 14.8 | 2.6 | — |
| $90 under 100 | — | 5,823 | 8.6 | 17.6 | 3.2 | — |
| $100 under 120 | — | 10,777 | 6.3 | 27.8 | 2.3 | — |
| $120 under 150 | — | 9,455 | 10.7 | 44.2 | 3.6 | — |
| $150 under 200 | — | 5,489 | 17.0 | 89.7 | 9.6 | — |
| $200 under 300 | — | 3,955 | 19.0 | 106.3 | 11.2 | — |
| $300 under 500 | — | 1,483 | 23.7 | 89.4 | 17.1 | — |
| $500 under 1000 | — | 263 | 70.3 | 100.1 | 57.1 | — |
| $1000 or more | — | 104 | 76.0 | 165.4 | 58.1 | — |
| TOTAL | — | 200,747 | 12.2 | 2,993.9 | 6.2 | 10.3 |

Source: U.S. Internal Revenue Service, *Statistics of Income—1976, Estate Tax Returns* 1979, pp. 15–17, table 1.
[a]Based on 1976 law. Average tax rates are based on gross estate.

$3.0 billion, of which $2.3 billion was claimed on taxable returns. The proportion of returns claiming the charitable deduction was 12.2 percent overall and 12.8 percent for taxable returns. The inequality in the size of charitable bequests is amply illustrated in the table. The 90 taxable estates over $10 million, representing only 0.04 percent of estate tax returns, accounted for 47 percent of all reported bequests. In summary, the bulk of charitable bequests come from a relatively small number of large estates.

One of the most striking features of table 6.4 is the tendency for the ratio of charitable bequests to gross estate to rise with estate size. For taxable returns, charitable bequests rose from 5 percent of gross estate in the lowest class to 72 percent in the highest. For nontaxable returns it increased from 10 to 76 percent. This increasing propensity for charitable giving is consistent with the notion that wealthier individuals, being able to provide adequately for heirs with more left over are in a better position to leave bequests to charitable organizations.[9] A survey of married men with net assets over $100,000 produced other corroborating data. The proportion of those men planning to leave their wives with less than half of their estate was highest for those with the largest incomes and presumably the largest estates (Morgan, Dye, and Hybels 1977, p. 184, table 23).

An alternative explanation for the observed increasing propensity to make charitable bequests is that higher marginal tax rates induce more giving. Calculated at the class means, the marginal tax rate for taxable returns increased from 3 to 77 percent, reflecting the progressivity of the rate schedule. To what extent this marginal tax rate has a separate effect on charitable bequests can be determined only by multivariate statistical analysis.

Not only do the amounts contributed differ by estate size, but the distribution of organizations supported by charitable bequests also varies. Table 6.5 presents such a distribution for 1960, the last year for which data by type of organization are available. The types of donees listed are educational, scientific, and literary organizations, broken down by public and private, religious groups, and "other charitable"—a residual category including bequests to private foundations. For all estate tax returns, "other" bequests accounted for 79 percent of all charitable bequests, compared to 9 percent for religious gifts. In a pattern similar to that observed for contributions by living individuals, the relative importance of religious gifts falls as estate size grows. Bequests to religious organizations accounted for two-thirds of total charitable bequests in estates of $60,000 to $70,000, falling to less than 1 percent for the largest estate classes. The proportion of gifts made to educational, scientific, and literary organizations, principally colleges and universities, shows little clear relationship to estate size. Together they made up about 12 percent of charitable be-

9. See Shoup (1966, p. 64) for a statement of this argument.

Table 6.5          Percentage Distribution of Charitable Bequests by Type of
                   Recipient, 1960

|                                      | Type of Organization | | | |
| | Educational, Scientific, and Literary | | | |
| Gross Estate Class (thousands) | Public | Private | Religious | Other Charitable |
|---|---|---|---|---|
| $60 under 70 | 2.1 | 1.4 | 66.0 | 30.5 |
| $70 under 80 | 0.4 | 3.7 | 58.9 | 37.0 |
| $80 under 90 | 0.2 | 7.8 | 53.9 | 38.1 |
| $90 under 100 | 2.0 | 5.7 | 51.6 | 40.6 |
| $100 under 120 | 2.9 | 2.9 | 48.0 | 46.1 |
| $120 under 150 | 1.3 | 6.3 | 35.5 | 56.8 |
| $150 under 200 | 2.9 | 5.9 | 28.3 | 62.9 |
| $200 under 300 | 3.9 | 6.6 | 24.6 | 64.8 |
| $300 under 500 | 4.7 | 7.0 | 20.9 | 67.3 |
| $500 under 1000 | 3.5 | 11.4 | 12.3 | 72.8 |
| $1000 under 2000 | 2.6 | 9.7 | 10.2 | 77.6 |
| $2000 under 3000 | 9.7 | 5.6 | 5.4 | 79.2 |
| $3000 under 5000 | .03 | 8.3 | 11.2 | 80.5 |
| $5000 under 10,000 | 2.9 | 25.4 | 1.1 | 70.7 |
| $10,000 under 20,000 | 2.8 | 2.4 | 0.9 | 94.0 |
| $20,000 or more | 2.8 | 1.5 | 0.3 | 95.5 |
| All returns | 3.4 | 8.5 | 9.4 | 78.7 |

*Source:* U.S. Internal Revenue Service, *Statistics of Income—1960, Estate Tax Returns* 1964, pp. 48–49, table 3.

quests in 1960, most of which went to private institutions. The residual category increased from 31 to 96 percent of charitable bequests. The portion of this category attributable to private foundations is impossible to ascertain, but the table certainly suggests an increasing use of private foundations as estate sizes increase.[10]

## 6.3  Previous Studies

The previous empirical analysis of tax effects on charitable bequests consists principally of four econometric studies: analyses of individual estate tax returns by McNees (1973) and Boskin (1976), an analysis of aggregate tax return data by Feldstein (1977), and a study using probate records

10. Shoup (1966, pp. 62–63) reports that in 1957, 43 percent of the charitable bequests by estates over a million dollars went to "private" charitable organizations, and 41 percent in 1959.

by Barthold and Plotnick (1983). This section describes these studies briefly in order to give background for the new estimates presented in section 6.4. Following a discussion of the economic model of bequest giving, this section describes the data and findings of the previous studies.

### 6.3.1 Economic Models of Bequest Giving

Despite recent work seeking to explain patterns of bequests and wealth transmission,[11] economic analysis of bequest behavior is still a developing area of inquiry. As Boskin (1976) spells out in the most complete discussion of the theory of charitable bequests, the decision to bequeath assets to charity is a complex one, one that is related to an individual's decisions regarding labor supply, savings, consumption, lifetime gifts, lifetime contributions, and noncharitable bequests. Boskin shows that even a simplified utility function, including consumption, lifetime gifts, contributions, and charitable and noncharitable bequests, yields a system of demand equations with a number of tax-determined prices. The equation he obtains for charitable bequests is:

(1)
$$CB = f(K + (WH + rK)(1 - m_y), 1/(1 - m_g), 1 - m_y, q/(1 - m_e), q),$$

where $K$ is initial wealth, $WH$ is labor income, $r$ corresponds roughly to the interest rate, $q$ measures inflation relative to the interest rate, and $m_y$, $m_g$, and $m_e$ are applicable marginal tax rates in the income tax, the gift tax and the estate tax. Charitable bequests are thus seen as a function of labor supply (which Boskin assumed to be fixed for convenience), initial wealth, savings, and the relative prices of gifts, bequests, contributions, and charitable bequests (Boskin 1976, pp. 29–32).

A central variable in studies of charitable bequests is their price. A model such as equation (1) makes it clear that there are a number of different prices, expressed here relative to the "price" of consuming a dollar's worth of goods, namely 1. For example, the relative price of making lifetime gifts versus bequests involves not only the real rate of interest but also the effect of deductibility. A lifetime gift reduces lifetime tax as well as estate tax, whereas a bequest reduces the estate tax only. The models used for estimation focus instead on the price of making charitable bequests relative to that of making certain noncharitable bequests. Specifically, the reference used is to noncharitable bequests other than to the taxpayer's spouse (which is itself subject to a deduction). The typical price variable is thus the ratio of the price of charitable bequests ($q$) to the price of noncharitable bequests ($q/(1 - m_e)$), which is simply $1 - m_e$. Consider an individual whose estate would be taxed at a 30 percent marginal rate. Because of the charitable deduction, a charitable bequest of $10,000 will

11. See, for example, Atkinson and Stiglitz 1980, pp. 85–88; or David and Menchik 1981, or Tomes 1981.

cost the estate $7000 net of tax, while a similar bequest to a son or daughter would cost a full $10,000. The price of the charitable bequest relative to the noncharitable bequest is 0.7, or one minus the marginal tax rate in the estate tax.[12]

Because of the increased number of options as well as the inevitably metaphysical nature of consumption decisions regarding events after one's death, this conception of price is a good deal more complex than that in the case of lifetime contributions. By the same token, however, it should be remembered that gifts and bequests are alternative uses to consumption and contributions during life, so that the price of lifetime giving is in principle more complex than it is usually portrayed. As in other applications, the proper complexity for a given model is dictated in part by the researcher's judgment about the importance of various influences. By this criterion, it seems reasonable to include in studies of both lifetime and bequest giving only the most immediate relative price, although this appears to be a more important limitation in the case of bequests.

The simple model discussed above is quite general as to behavioral assumptions and implied functional form. It implies that charitable bequests are a function of wealth or estate size and the relative price of charitable bequests. It would be as consistent with constant elasticities for price and estate size as it would with variable elasticities. One might imagine more specific behavioral assumptions about bequest giving. One possibility is that an individual has a target amount of wealth that he wishes to pass on to his heirs. Any increase in taxes would come out of planned charitable gifts. Changes in the price of bequest giving would have no effect on noncharitable bequests and thus would affect charitable bequests only through an increase in lifetime savings. Such behavior would imply a large wealth effect but no price effect on charitable bequests. An alternative model of bequest giving might be that individuals have a target instead for charitable giving. If it is measured in terms of the gross dollar gift, then obviously changes in neither wealth nor price would have any effect. If the target is measured in terms of the net cost to the estate, however, a fall in the price would be accompanied by an equiproportionate increase in charitable bequests. Under these circumstances, the price elasticity would be − 1.[13] Models of bequest giving based on such targets are quite stylized and may be totally unrealistic, but it is useful to consider such special cases in evaluating estimated price and estate-size elasticities. The net cost target, for example, would provide a plausible explanation for a unitary price elasticity. The empirical work discussed in the remainder of the chapter embodies no assumptions regarding targets, but instead is based on a general model.

---

12. See Feldstein (1977, p. 1500) for a discussion of the price.
13. See Feldstein and Lindsey (1981) for a discussion of such behavior in the case of lifetime giving.

### 6.3.2 Data and Variables

McNees (1973) and Boskin (1976) employed estate tax files composed of information from individual returns. Both studies employed a sample of 1957 and 1959 returns that had been used in a special study of estate tax returns.[14] Variables on the file include estate size, state of residence, age, sex, marital status, an indirect measure of dependents, the use of trusts, and gift giving. In addition, charitable contributions are broken down for four categories of recipient organizations: (*a*) religious, (*b*) educational, scientific, and literary, (*c*) social welfare and (*d*) other. The 1969 file used by Boskin provided much the same information on estate size, age, sex, and marital status. It also provides more detail on the composition of assets. However, the 1969 file does not break down gifts by type of donee, nor is there information on trusts (Boskin 1976, p. 38). Both files provide ample information from which to calculate the marginal estate tax rate.

The aggregate data used by Feldstein (1977) is sparse in detail, providing only class means for estate size and charitable bequests. Following the procedure he used in his article on individual contributions (1975a), Feldstein calculated marginal tax rates based on class averages for the taxable estate quantity.

The measure of the decedent's estate is a central variable in explaining charitable bequests, and several alternative measures are available. *Gross estate* is defined in the tax law to include "the value of all property to the extent of the interest therein of the decedent at the time of his death" *(Internal Revenue Code* 1982, sec. 2033). In addition, transfers made within three years of death were included in this calculation before the full unification of the estate and gift taxes. The estate generally could be valued as of the time of death or six months later, at the discretion of the estate's executor.[15] Because it takes no account of most debts, gross estate can be a poor measure of economic wealth. This defect is remedied in the *economic estate* measure, which is defined as gross estate minus debts, administrative costs, funeral expenses, and lifetime gifts. Economic estate corresponds most closely with net worth available for disposition at time of death. A further modification can be made to subtract the estate tax liability from the economic estate, leaving *adjusted disposable estate.*[16] McNees used the economic estate measure. Boskin preferred adjusted disposable estate in analyzing the 1969 data. Feldstein, on the other hand, was forced by data limitations to use gross estate minus all deductions other than those for charity and marital bequests.

---

14. See Shoup (1966) for a more complete description of the data.
15. See U.S. 1979 Internal Revenue Service, *Statistics of Income—1976, Estate Tax Returns 1979*, pp. 4–5 for a full description of gross estate.
16. See Boskin (1976, pp. 38–39) for a discussion of estate measures.

Although economic estate is the measure corresponding most closely to net worth at time of death, there is an important drawback to its use when the contributions deduction includes lifetime charitable transfers as well as charitable bequests. As previously noted, such lifetime gifts (generally those made within three years of death) are a small part of the charitable deduction on average. It is also believed that these charitable lifetime gifts are underreported since they have no tax consequence.[17] But for individuals who do make and report large lifetime charitable gifts, the exclusion of lifetime gifts from the measure of estate (as in the economic estate or adjusted disposable estate measures) will understate the relevant net worth while including the lifetime gift in the charitable deduction. A more appropriate measure of net worth is one that includes transfers made in the last three years of life. Accordingly, the basic measure of estate used in the analysis of the 1976 estate tax file presented in section 6.4 is economic estate plus lifetime transfers minus the estate tax, referred to as *net estate*.

The basic price measure used in the studies is the marginal estate tax rate or one minus that rate. McNees, who simply used the marginal tax rate, was careful to specify the rate independently of the amount of charitable bequests in order to obtain consistent estimates (McNees 1973, p. 82). Boskin and Feldstein defined their price terms analogously, except that Boskin was able to obtain information on state as well as federal tax rates in his 1969 sample.

### 6.3.3 Findings

*McNees*

Using the 1957–59 tax file, McNees estimated linear and logarithmic equations for charitable bequests, allowing estate size to enter quadratically. He estimated separate equations for estates above and below a million dollars. His principal finding is that the marginal estate tax rate was significant for the large-estate group, suggesting "a sizable incentive effect of the contributions deduction" (p. 84). The lack of information about the scale used in defining the variables makes it difficult to quantify this tax effect. McNees also found that bequests were strongly related to estate size. Charitable bequests tended to be lower for widows and those who used trusts; for large estates charitable giving tended to be positively related to inter vivos gift giving (McNees 1973, p. 83, table 1).

*Boskin*

As a result of preliminary regressions, Boskin used a simple dichotomous variable for decedents who were not married, rejecting other marital status variables as insignificant. He also used a single dummy variable

---

17. Their effect is to raise gross estate and deductions by the same amount.

for decedents under 65. More importantly, he split the price variable into three pieces, allowing separate coefficients and elasticities for prices below 0.6, between 0.6 and 0.8, and over 0.8. An illustrative regression using the 1969 sample and estimated using the Tobit procedure is given below:

$$(2) \quad CB = 0.326\,ADE - 347\,P(P < 0.6) - 443\,P(0.6 < P < 0.8) \\ - 668\,P(P > 0.8) - 225\,\text{Married} - 245\,(\text{Age} < 65),$$

where $CB$ is charitable bequests, $ADE$ is adjusted disposable estate, and $P$ is the price defined by the marginal estate tax rate.[18] All coefficients are significantly different from zero. The elasticity of charitable bequests with respect to estate size, calculated at the means, is 0.40. The price elasticity varies greatly, for $-0.20$ for decedents with the largest estates ($P < 0.6$) to $-2.53$ for those with smaller estates.

Table 6.6 summarizes the elasticities of charitable bequests with respect to estate size and price for this and other basic specifications. Two specifications for the 1957–59 sample included a single price term. The first, using the economic estate variable, yielded an estate-size elasticity of 0.52 and a price elasticity of $-1.2$, both calculated at the mean values. When adjusted disposable estate was substituted for economic estate, the estate elasticity rose to 1.1. One should be wary of the elasticities based on a simple linear model, however. As Boskin (1976, pp. 34–35) notes, such a model implies that a one percentage point rise in the price will cause the same dollar decrease in bequests in all estates, regardless of size. Breaking

**Table 6.6**    **Estimated Price and Estate Elasticities for Charitable Bequests (Boskin 1976)**

|  | Sample | |
|---|---|---|
|  | 1957–59 | 1969 |
| Economic estate[a] | 0.52 | — |
| Price | $-1.2$ | — |
| Adjusted disposable estate[b] | 1.1 | — |
| Price | $-1.2$ | — |
| Adjusted disposable estate | 0.54 | 0.40 |
| Price < 0.6 | $-0.94$ | $-0.20$ |
| 0.6 < Price < 0.8 | $-1.4$ | $-0.96$ |
| Price > 0.8 | $-1.8$ | $-2.53$ |

*Source:* Boskin 1976: 1957–59, p. 41, table 2, equations (2)–(4); 1969, p. 45, table 4, equation (1).

[a]Gross estate minus debts and expenses.
[b]Economic estate minus taxes that would be paid if there were no charitable bequests.

18. The method of estimation was Tobit. The intercept was not given.

up the price term, as shown in equation (2), is one way to allow this price response to vary over estates of different sizes. The elasticities based on this model are compared in table 6.6 for both samples. Both imply a smaller price elasticity for the biggest estates, but this difference is less in the 1957–59 sample, with elasticities ranging from −0.94 to −1.8. Boskin found similar patterns of price elasticities when he divided charitable bequests according to the type of donee. In average magnitude, the elasticities were largest for the residual category (Boskin 1976, p. 43), suggesting that the creation of private foundations may be especially sensitive to the charitable deduction in the estate tax.

*Feldstein*

Using a pooled time-series/cross-section sample of estate class averages over the period 1948 to 1963, Feldstein estimated models that allowed the price and estate-size elasticities to vary. The ratio of charitable bequests to estate size, or its logarithm, was the dependent variable, and independent variables were transformations of estate size and price. As in the Boskin study, the price was calculated for the first dollar of charitable bequests. State inheritance taxes were ignored by necessity since only national totals were available.[19]

The estimated elasticities showed great variation, as shown in table 6.7. Based on data for all estate-size categories, the basic models (A) and (B) imply price elasticities ranging from −4.0 to −0.1. When an interaction term including the logarithm of the estate size was added, however, all estimated price elasticities using this full sample were positive, and Feldstein rejects them as being unreasonable. The price elasticities based on equations for large estates only do yield uniformly negative elasticities, though the range of variation is still large. In evaluating the results, Feldstein acknowledges "the instability of the parameter estimates and the frequency of implausible estimates" (p. 1497) and concludes that the results provide little firm evidence regarding the magnitude of the price response.[20]

*Barthold and Plotnick*

In the only study not using federal tax return data, Barthold and Plotnick (1984) employed a sample of Connecticut estates probated during the 1930s and 1940s. Gross estate was used as the measure of estate size, and tax price was defined as in earlier studies but including the state as well as the federal tax rate. From probate records the authors obtained information on the decedent's heirs and religion. The authors used a logarithmic

19. Feldstein notes (1977, p. 1487) that inheritance taxes in 1963 were relatively insignificant in comparison to the federal estate tax. He calculated that the tax liability counting the federal estate tax, state transfer taxes, and federal credits was in no state greater than 1 percent more than the federal tax liability calculated without reference to state taxes.

20. For his own assessment of the results, see his conclusion (Feldstein 1977, pp. 1495, 1497).

**Table 6.7**                **Estimated Price Elasticities for Charitable Bequests (Feldstein 1977)**

|  | (A) | (B) | (C) | (D) |
|---|---|---|---|---|
| | *Equations for All Estates* | | | |
| Estate size | | | | |
| $    80,000 | − 4.04 | − 1.96 | 1.50 | 2.01 |
| 120,000 | − 2.06 | − 1.09 | 0.70 | 1.92 |
| 500,000 | − 1.45 | − 0.69 | 0.54 | 2.48 |
| 5,000,000 | − 0.31 | − 0.11 | 0.18 | 2.00 |
| | *Equations for Large Estates* | | | |
| Estate size | | | | |
| $   500,000 | − 2.72 | − 9.50 | − 1.65 | − 1.27 |
| 1,000,000 | − 2.05 | − 6.42 | − 1.40 | − 0.92 |
| 5,000,000 | − 0.58 | − 2.13 | − 0.70 | − 0.19 |

*Source:* Feldstein 1977, table 3 (2.1–2.3, 2.6), p. 1493 and table 7 (6.1–6.3, 6.6), p. 1497.
*Note:* Models are as follows:
(A) $G/E = a + bP + cE$;
(B) $G/E = a + b_1P + b_2P^2 + c_1E + c_2E^2$;
(C) $G/E = a + b_1P + b_2P^2 + c_1E + c_2E^2 + c_3P \ln E$;
(D) $\ln(G/E) = a + b_1P + b_2P^2 + c_1E + c_2E^2 + c_3P \ln E$.
For each model, price is defined as $Pl$, based on taxable estate plus charitable bequests.

functional form and obtained estimates using Tobit. The estate-size elasticity implied by the estimates was 0.4. The estimate also indicated that decedents with a surviving spouse and more heirs tended to leave smaller charitable bequests.

In contrast to most previous work, the tax price was not significant in any equation in the study. Barthold and Plotnick emphasize that the federal and Connecticut estate tax schedules were changed several times during the period covered by the sample, thereby reducing the collinearity between estate size and price. In particular, they note that the Connecticut law underwent a significant change in 1937, a year before a large proportion of the wills in their sample were probated. There were also changes in the federal tax schedule, notably in 1942, covering deaths in 1943 and after. These changes in law pose a problem, however. Unless individuals respond immediately to changes in the estate tax by revising their wills, some bequests will be a function of current tax laws while others will depend on past laws. This is especially serious where changes are large and time intervals are short. The result in this case is that the price term will be measured with error and its estimated coefficient will be biased toward zero. Without further information about the process of estate planning, it is impossible to say how much bias this effect would have had for this particular sample.

## 6.4    Analysis of 1976 Estate Tax Returns

In order to extend the empirical analysis of charitable bequests using more recent data, I analyzed a sample of federal estate tax returns for 1976. The basic data source was the 1976 estate tax file (U. S. Internal Revenue Service 1976) prepared by the Internal Revenue Service, a stratified random sample of all estate returns filed in 1977. Like the 1957–59 and 1969 estate tax files used in earlier analyses, the 1976 file provides information on estate size and composition, charitable gifts, other deductions, age, and marital status. Based on the information provided, it is possible to calculate the federal estate tax and tax rate. A 20 percent random sample of the file was drawn for use in the statistical analysis. A small portion of the returns included in the file in fact represented deaths in 1977, and these returns were excluded. Because the 1976 tax act provided for substantial modifications in the estate tax schedule beginning in 1977, it is quite difficult to guess what effect the new provisions had on bequests by decedents who died early in 1977. Finally, estates smaller than $5000 were excluded in order to focus on decedents with at least a minimum of net worth.[21] The resulting sample consisted of 6621 returns. A second sample consisting of all estates of $1 million or more was used in order to estimate separate behavioral parameters for the wealthiest decedents. This sample contained 2302 returns.

The basic measure of estate size in this analysis is net estate *(NE)*, defined as economic estate plus lifetime transfers minus the estate tax liability calculated without the charitable deduction. Adjusted disposable estate, defined as economic estate minus the tax, is used as an alternative. The new estate measure is preferred because it, like the charitable-giving measure, includes certain lifetime charitable gifts. The price of charitable bequests *(P)* is one minus the marginal estate tax rate that would apply in the absence of bequests. As Feldstein (1977) has emphasized, this price is exogenous with respect to the charitable-bequest decision if other deductions, in particular the marital deduction, are predetermined. In fact, the assumption that a person decides on the amount of the bequest to a spouse, up to half the estate, before deciding on charitable bequests seems reasonable. In practice, married decedents almost always left at least half of their estates to spouses. Previous research suggests that bequests are strongly influenced by both the age and marital status of decedents. The present study employs quite detailed measures of each in order to control for these important effects. Age at death was entered as a set of dichotomous variables for ages 50 to 59, 60 to 69, 70 to 79, and 80 and older. The excluded group consists of those under 50. Marital status was denoted by dichotomous variables for widows and widowers, single individuals, and

---

21. Preliminary analysis showed, however, that there were relatively few estates below this level and that their exclusion had little effect on the estimates.

those divorced or separated, with married individuals being the excluded group.

### 6.4.1    Estimates for All Estates

Table 6.8 gives the mean values for the principal variables employed in the analysis. The mean charitable bequest for the sample was about $32,000. The average gross estate was about $558,000, and the average economic estate was $465,000. Adjusting for lifetime gifts in gross estate and taxes yields net estate, with a mean value of about $407,000. The average net price of making charitable bequests for the sample was 0.77. About 35 percent of the decedents were over 80, and another 29 percent were in their 70s. One-half of the decedents were married and another third were widowed. Only 8 percent were never married.

| Table 6.8 | Means of Selected Variables and Tax Items, 1976 Estate Tax Returns |
|---|---|
| *Full sample* | |
| Charitable deduction, in thousands (*CB*) | 32.3 |
| Gross estate, in thousands | 558.4 |
| Economic estate, in thousands | 465.4 |
| Estate tax if no charitable deductions, after credits, in thousands | 108.6 |
| Lifetime transfers in gross estate, in thousands | 50.6 |
| Net estate, in thousands (*NE*) | 407.4 |
| Net price (*P*) | 0.774 |
| | |
| Age | |
|   Under 50[a] | 0.049 |
|   50–59 | 0.105 |
|   60–69 | 0.205 |
|   70–79 | 0.293 |
|   80 and over | 0.348 |
| | |
| Marital status | |
|   Married[a] | 0.546 |
|   Widow or widower | 0.342 |
|   Single | 0.080 |
|   Divorced or separated | 0.032 |

*By estate size* (in thousands)

| | Price | Net estate | (N) |
|---|---|---|---|
| Less than $250 | .860 | 123.8 | (3887) |
| $250 under 500 | .689 | 382.5 | (1188) |
| $500 under 1000 | .660 | 681.9 | (1059) |
| $1000 or more | .545 | 2134.3 | ( 487) |

*Note:* Sample size was 6621.

[a]Categories omitted in estimation.

Three basic equations explaining the logarithm of charitable bequests are presented in table 6.9. The first two imply constant price and estate-size elasticities while the third allows for variation in the price elasticity. In equation (A) the Tobit coefficient of $-11.8$ for the logarithm of price implies an elasticity of expected charitable bequests with respect to the price of $-1.67$.[22] While this estimate exceeds in absolute value the overall elas-

**Table 6.9        Logarithmic Equations Explaining Charitable Bequests, 1976**

| Explanatory Variables | (A) | (B) | (C) |
|---|---|---|---|
| ln $P$ | $-11.8$ | $-20.4$ | |
| | (2.7) | (2.3) | |
| | [$-1.67$] | [$-2.79$] | |
| ln $P$, $P < .60$ | | | $-12.9$ |
| | | | (2.8) |
| | | | [$-1.77$] |
| ln $P$, $.80 > P \geq .60$ | | | $-17.9$ |
| | | | (3.4) |
| | | | [$-2.46$] |
| ln $P$, $P \geq .80$ | | | $-26.8$ |
| | | | (6.9) |
| | | | [$-2.31$] |
| ln $NE$ | 3.01 | | 2.84 |
| | (0.52) | | (0.53) |
| | [0.42] | | [0.39] |
| ln $ADE$ | | 1.30 | |
| | | (0.41) | |
| | | [0.18] | |
| Age | | | |
| 50–59 | 1.39** | 1.39** | 1.41** |
| 60–69 | 4.53 | 4.55 | 4.53 |
| 70–79 | 6.42 | 6.44 | 6.42 |
| 80+ | 8.82 | 8.85 | 8.79 |
| Marital status | | | |
| Widow | 4.94 | 3.94 | 4.73 |
| Single | 10.94 | 9.88 | 10.67 |
| Divorced | 6.29 | 5.18 | 6.15 |
| Constant | $-41.8$ | $-34.4$ | $-42.6$ |
| $F(z)$ | 0.141 | 0.137 | 0.138 |
| Sample size | 6621 | 6451 | 6621 |

*Note:* The numbers in parentheses are standard errors. All coefficients except those noted by double asterisks were statistically different from zero at the 95 percent level. The numbers in brackets are elasticities of the expected value of the dependent variable with respect to the explanatory variable.

22. Where $b$ is the Tobit coefficient shown, and $F(z)$ is the cumulative normal distribution signifying the predicted probability of observing a positive bequest, the elasticity is $bF(z)$. See, for example, McDonald and Moffit 1980.

ticity obtained by Boskin for the 1957–59 data, it does not appear beyond the bounds of his 1969 estimates. The present estimate also falls well within the spread of values obtained by Feldstein (1977). The estate-size elasticity of 0.42 is quite close to that obtained by Barthold and Plotnick and by Boskin for 1969 and is somewhat smaller than Boskin's estimates for 1957–59. These estimates for the basic equation imply that bequest giving is affected both by estate size and the net price of giving. In addition, the latter effect is quite strong.

Before comparing price and income elasticities implied by various functional forms, it is useful to examine the estimated effects of age and marital status on bequest giving. The size of charitable bequests rises sharply with the age of the decedent. Although there is no significant difference between the gifts of decedents under 50—the excluded group—and those in their 50s, decedents 60 and older gave significantly more. Furthermore, the estimated age effects are monotonic. For example, equation (A) implies that decedents in their 70s gave 30 percent more than those in their 60s, and those over 80 gave 40 percent more than those in their 70s.[23] This increase in charitable giving with age is of course strikingly similar to the age pattern observed in giving by living donors.

The differences in bequest giving by marital status are also noteworthy. The group with the highest expected level of bequest giving is single decedents. Expected bequest giving by this group was over four times as high as that by married individuals. That single decedents give more than those who left spouses is not surprising since these decedents are also likely to have the fewest potential heirs within the family. This result also corresponds to the previous finding, noted above, that single and divorced decedents were least likely to employ trusts, instruments most often designed to provide for family members. Divorced or separated decedents were next highest in giving, averaging 2.4 times the amount donated by married individuals. Widows and widowers, who had no spouse but presumably did have roughly the same number of children as married decedents, gave at twice the rate as those who were married. The age and marital status effects observed in equation (A) are mirrored in the other equations presented below. From these results, it seems quite evident that both age and marital status have important influences on the level of bequest giving.

Equations (B) and (C) are variations of the basic equation. In equation (B) net estate is replaced by adjusted disposable estate. The implied estate-size elasticity is less than half the size of that in equation (A), probably re-

---

23. Where $b_i$ is the Tobit coefficient for age group $i$, the ratio of giving between group $i$ and group $i-1$ is exp $(F(z)(b_i - b_{i-1}))$.

flecting the fact that the estate measure excludes lifetime gifts, some of which are included in the charitable deduction. The estimated price elasticity ($-2.79$), on the other hand, is much larger in absolute value than the corresponding elasticity in (A). The age and marital status variables are generally similar. In equation (C) the price elasticity is allowed to vary among estates according to three broad price categories, a variation that was suggested by the Boskin study noted above. Donors facing the lowest price (less than .60), those with the largest estates, had the smallest absolute price elasticity, $-1.77$. Those with prices between .60 and .80 had an elasticity of $-2.46$, and those in the highest price category had an implied elasticity of $-3.70$. This pattern of larger absolute elasticity values for smaller estates (higher prices) corresponds to Boskin's results for both the 1957–59 and the 1969 samples. However, the elasticities implied by the present analysis are consistently larger in absolute value. Moreover, the larger price elasticities found in the present analysis do not appear to be due to the functional forms that are used. A reestimation of Boskin's regression shown in equation (2) yielded much larger price elasticities and smaller estate elasticities than those implied by Boskin's estimates.[24]

One of the most important questions for tax policy is whether the price elasticity and the elasticity with respect to estate size vary significantly among estates of different sizes. This issue is addressed by Boskin and Feldstein and in tables 6.9 and 6.10 of the current chapter with different functional forms that allow some variation in elasticities. A more general functional form that allows interactions and nonlinear effects without specifying price or estate-size categories in the variable is a translog form. The estimated Tobit equation based on this form for the 1976 sample was:

$$(3) \quad \ln CB = -121.9 \ln P - 23.9 \ln NE + 22.2 \ln P \ln NE$$
$$+ 31.7 (\ln P)^2 + 2.95 (\ln ADE)^2 + 1.60 (\text{Age } 50\text{–}59)$$
$$+ 4.49 (\text{Age } 60\text{–}69) + 6.50 (\text{Age } 70\text{–}79) + 8.12 (\text{Age } 80+)$$
$$+ 4.81 \text{ Widow} + 10.62 \text{ Single} + 6.25 \text{ Divorced} + 17.0,$$
$$F(z) = 0.135, N = 6621.$$

24. The equation was:

$$CB = 0.0138 \, NE - 5564 \, P(P < 0.6) - 5158 \, P(0.8 > P \geq 0.6)$$

$$-4397 \, P(P \geq .80) - 284 \text{ Married} - 244 (\text{Age} < 65)$$

$$+ 2885, F(z) = 0.976.$$

The price elasticities calculated at the mean giving for the sample and mean price for each group are $-8.3$, $-10.8$, and $-12.4$ from lowest to highest price category. The estimated estate-size elasticity if 0.17, but is not significantly different from zero.

The price and estate elasticities may be caculated by differentiating the equation and substituting appropriate values of price and estate size. Because of the interaction and squared terms both elasticities depend on the value of the price and the estate size. To illustrate the pattern of implied price and estate effects, table 6.10 presents elasticities calculated for the mean values corresponding to four estate-size classes. For comparison, it also presents elasticities based on the translog form using adjusted disposable estate. Both equations support the earlier finding that the price elasticity tends to shrink as estate size increases. In the equation using net estate, the elasticity is −3.3 for the average net estate under $250,000 and goes in the positive direction until it is +1.36 for the largest estate class, a result that ranks with the implausible estimates obtained by Feldstein. These price elasticities appear to be balanced by an equally large variation in estate elasticities, from 0.17 for the smallest estates to 1.08 in the largest. The equation using adjusted disposable estate shows a similar pattern, but with less variation in both elasticities. For estates over $1 million it implies a price elasticity of −1.42 and income elasticity of 0.34. While the two equations yield similar elasticities for the lowest estate-size class, therefore, there is considerable difference at the top end.

Given the strong effects of age and marital status apparent in the equations above, it is useful to explore, finally, whether the price elasticity of bequest giving varies according to such personal characteristics. It is particularly interesting to determine whether the charitable bequests of single individuals show any greater price sensitivity than others, in light of the general lesser importance of family ties to single individuals, coupled with

Table 6.10    **Elasticities of Charitable Bequests Based on Translog Function**

| Elasticities by Estate Definition | | Estate Class (thousands) | | |
|---|---|---|---|---|
| | Under $250 | $250 under 500 | $500 under 1000 | $1000 or more |
| *Net estate* | | | | |
| Price | −3.30 | −1.81 | −0.46 | 1.36 |
| Estate size | 0.17 | 0.41 | 0.73 | 1.08 |
| *Adjusted disposable estate* | | | | |
| Price | −3.39 | −2.61 | −2.19 | −1.42 |
| Estate size | 0.21 | 0.23 | 0.29 | 0.34 |

*Note:* The sample sizes for the regressions were 6621 using net estate and 6451 using adjusted disposable estate.

their higher rate of bequest giving. To test for such differential price sensitivity, equation (A) in table 6.9 was reestimated by splitting the price term between single decedents and others. The implied price elasticities, shown in table 6.11, were − 2.30 for single individuals and − 1.64 for others, the latter being roughly the same overall price elasticity estimated in table 6.9, equation (A). Although these point estimates tend to support the hypothesis that single decedents are more responsive to tax-induced price effects in their charitable bequests, the difference is not statistically significant. If it exists, this difference may be in part due to the availability to married individuals of the marital deduction and its increasing attractiveness at higher marginal tax rates. A similar specification was employed to determine whether this marital status effect differs by age group as well. As shown in the second part of table 6.11, there is little difference in price responsiveness by age among single decedents. For others, the price elasticity for those 60 or over is approximately the same as for the entire sample. For those comparatively few decedents under 60 years of age, the price term is small and not significantly different from zero. Again, the differences among the coefficients are small relative to the estimated standard errors.

### 6.4.2 Estimates for Large Estates

Because of the very large share of total bequests given by the wealthiest decedents, it is especially important to focus on the price and estate-size elasticities for these decedents. The estimates presented above clearly do not yield definitive estimates for these larger estates. In order to provide better information on the responsiveness of these decedents to taxes, bequests by those with net estates over $1 million or more were analyzed separately. The average net estate size in this class was $2.2 million.

| Table 6.11 | Price Coefficients, Standard Errors, and Elasticities by Marital Status and Age Group | | |
|---|---|---|---|
| | | Single | Nonsingle |
| (A) | All | − 16.29 | − 11.65 |
| | | (5.02) | (2.74) |
| | | [− 2.30] | [− 1.64] |
| (B) | Under 60 | − 17.14** | − 7.72** |
| | | (9.18) | (5.88) |
| | | [− 2.42] | [− 1.09] |
| | 60 and over | − 16.32 | − 11.80 |
| | | (5.02) | (2.74) |
| | | [− 2.31] | [− 1.67] |

*Note:* All coefficients except those denoted by double asterisks were significantly different from zero at the 95 percent level.

For this group the estimated basic model is given in equation (4), which is estimated again using Tobit:

(4) $\ln CB = -6.22 \ln P + 3.04 \ln NE + 1.52$ (Age 50–59)
    (2.44)    (1.01)    (2.98)
    [−2.66]    [1.30]

+ 7.33 (Age 60–69) + 9.55 (Age 70–79) + 12.04 (Age 80+)
    (2.73)    (2.69)    (2.69)

+ 3.16 Widow + 7.40 Single + 3.06 Divorced − 39.6,
    (0.79)    (1.20)    (1.57)    (7.0)

$F(z) = 0.427, N = 2302.$

The coefficient of −6.22 for price implies an elasticity of the expected value of bequests of −2.66, and the corresponding estate-size elasticity is 1.30. Both of these estimates are clearly larger in absolute value than the values implied for large estates by the equations covering estates of all size. Their standard errors are also relatively larger, which is probably a reflection of the higher correlation between price and estate size for this more homogeneous group. The 95 percent confidence interval for the price elasticity is −0.61 to −4.70. While this range allows rejection of the hypothesis that the price elasticity is zero or positive, it nevertheless leaves considerable scope for uncertainty about the price response. For the estate elasticity the 95 percent confidence interval is 0.45 to 2.14, the lower value being close to the elasticity implied in the basic model (A) in table 6.9. To summarize, the point estimates in equation (4) imply that the estate tax exerts strong price and estate-size effects on bequests by very wealthy decedents, but these estimates are not extremely precise. The effects of age and marital status show similar patterns to those observed in equations for covering all estate classes, but the implied differences among groups are uniformly greater.

## 6.5 Summary and Implications

The deduction for charitable gifts in the estate tax complements the charitable deduction in the individual income tax by treating gifts at death in roughly the same way as lifetime giving. Although charitable bequests have averaged less than 10 percent of total giving, they are a significant portion of the total as well as a large percentage of gifts to certain types of organizations. The deduction has been a constant fixture of the tax over the years, but the changes in the effective tax schedule of the estate tax have altered tax liabilities and the relative price of charitable bequests.

There has been a limited amount of econometric analysis of bequest giving. Three basic conclusions emerge from it. First, bequests appear to be subject to a tax-induced price effect in much the same way as are contributions by living individuals. Second, the price elasticity of decedents with the largest estates appears to be not as large in absolute value as the elasticity of those with smaller estates. The third conclusion from the econometric work is a cautionary one, however. The estimates so far produced have not been as robust as those for individual giving. The estimates obtained by Boskin and those presented here appear most robust, but all together the econometric analysis of bequest giving suggests that point estimates should be applied only with caution.

With these reservations in mind, it is useful to consider the effect of recent and possible changes in the estate tax on charitable bequests. The effect of past tax policy can be understood only in the context of inflation; the consequence of policy and inflation was to raise marginal tax rates between 1943 and 1976 and increase bequest giving. Because the estate tax schedule was fixed in nominal terms over this period, an increasing proportion of estates became subject to the tax; thus the incentive effect of the deduction spread to more estates over time. In addition, as table 6.1 shows, the marginal tax rates applying to the largest estates rose over time, thus reducing the net price of bequest giving. For estates of $5 million in 1972 dollars, the increase in marginal tax rates resulted in a 45 percent decrease in price, from 0.55 to 0.30.

The changes since 1976 have reversed these trends. Tax legislation in 1976 and 1981 increased the minimum taxable estates through increases in the unified credit and lowered marginal tax rates for larger estates. The top marginal rate was reduced from 77 before 1976 to 70 percent between 1977 and 1981, and then, in steps, to 50 percent in 1985. As illustrated in table 6.1, this decline in tax rates implies for estates of $5 million in constant dollars an increase of almost 29 percent in the price of giving. Another change in the 1981 bill was the unlimited marital deduction. Although this provision certainly could have a significant impact on outright bequests by a married decedent, its long-run effect is likely to be considerably less since the marital exemption in the gift tax has long provided a limited means of delaying transfer taxation and since the estate is taxed at the time of the spouse's death.[25] The most important result of the 1981 tax

---

25. The 1981 law provided for special treatment of split-interest charitable remainder trusts. Under this treatment, a charitable deduction is allowed for the charitable portion at the time of death of the first spouse if the trust qualifies as a deductible charitable remainder unitrust or annuity trust and if the only noncharitable beneficiaries are the decedent or the spouse. This removes any incentive to make bequests to a spouse rather than leave a charitable bequest in a split-interest charitable remainder trust. See U.S. Congress, Staff of the Joint Committee on Taxation 1981, p. 238, or Arthur Andersen and Company 1982, pp. 48–51.

act on bequest giving appears to be, then, the restructuring of marginal tax rates, particularly the drop in tax rates for the very largest estates.

In order to give a rough idea of the effect of the post-1976 tax changes on bequests, table 6.12 presents two simulations of the change in bequest giving between 1976 and 1987. The number of estates by constant dollar class was assumed to be constant, and gross estate minus debt was assumed to increase with the price level. Taxes and tax rates were calculated using the respective tax schedules for 1976 and 1987. As can be seen in the third and fourth columns, the 1981 tax changes remove the tax liability for estates below \$500,000 in 1976 dollars. Except in the \$3 to \$5 million class, estates larger than \$500,000 will experience a decline in taxes. For the largest estate class the projected reduction in tax liability is 29 percent. Marginal tax rates for estates paying no tax in 1987 become zero, of course. Marginal rates for estates between \$500,000 and \$5 million are projected to rise while rates in the top two classes will fall.

Bequests in 1987 were estimated using the new values of net estate and price implied by these changes. For estates below \$1 million, elasticity values of $-1.6$ for price and 0.4 for net estate were used. For estates over \$1 million two sets of elasticities were used. The assumed price elasticity for this group was $-1.0$ in simulation I and $-2.4$ in simulation II. Estate elasticities for these top classes were 0.4 and 1.3 in simulations I and II, respectively. The first simulation generally reflects the results of equations based on estates of all sizes, while the second reflects the point estimates in equation (4). While these parameter values do not reflect the full variability of the parameter estimates, they are used to illustrate the implications of different values.

Both simulations imply that the 1981 estate tax changes will reduce bequest giving in real terms. Simulation I, using the comparatively smaller price elasticity for large estates, implies a fall in total bequests of 34 percent. The projected decline in the top class is over 50 percent. The second simulation, which gives greater weight to price changes as well as changes in net estate for wealthy decedents, implies even bigger declines. Total bequests fall by 52 percent, paced by a sharp decline in bequest giving in the top class. Obviously, the sheer size of bequests by the largest estates tends to dominate the overall change in bequests. Using methods such as those employed here, it is possible to project the likely effects of other changes in the estate tax, such as the elimination of the charitable deduction or its replacement with a credit. It is clear from the estimation and simulation results presented in this chapter, though, that the uncertainty surrounding the estimates of price and estate elasticities should serve as a caution flag in predicting the outcome of tax changes. As in discussing simulations of individual giving in chapter 3, two potential sources of error must be considered. First, the statistical uncertainty surrounding the coefficient estimates is important and much larger than that associated with models of

**Table 6.12    Estates, Charitable Bequests, and Taxes—1976 and 1987, Based on Taxable Estates in 1976 (dollar amounts in 1976 dollars)**

| Gross Estate Class (thousands) | Charitable Bequests (millions) | Average Estate Tax Less Credits | | Marginal Tax Rate | | Simulated Charitable Bequests, 1987 (millions)[a] | |
|---|---|---|---|---|---|---|---|
| | | 1976 | 1987 | 1976 | 1987 | I | II |
| 60–70 | 0.2 | 0.1 | 0 | .03 | 0 | 0.2 | 0.2 |
| 70–80 | 1.3 | 0.5 | 0 | .07 | 0 | 1.2 | 1.2 |
| 80–90 | 1.7 | 1.3 | 0 | .11 | 0 | 1.4 | 1.4 |
| 90–100 | 3.5 | 2.4 | 0 | .14 | 0 | 2.8 | 2.8 |
| 100–120 | 6.1 | 4.5 | 0 | .18 | 0 | 4.5 | 4.5 |
| 120–150 | 12.4 | 5.7 | 0 | .22 | 0 | 8.5 | 8.5 |
| 150–200 | 28.0 | 10.8 | 0 | .28 | 0 | 17.7 | 17.7 |
| 200–300 | 58.8 | 23.1 | 0 | .30 | 0 | 34.6 | 34.6 |
| 300–500 | 109.6 | 48.2 | 0 | .30 | 0 | 65.5 | 65.6 |
| 500–1000 | 142.0 | 105.2 | 45.4 | .32 | .39 | 176.1 | 175.1 |
| 1000–2000 | 158.7 | 240.9 | 210.6 | .37 | .35 | 181.7 | 234.4 |
| 2000–3000 | 98.8 | 486.2 | 404.8 | .45 | .50 | 110.7 | 134.2 |
| 3000–5000 | 121.2 | 809.8 | 826.9 | .49 | .50 | 123.3 | 126.5 |
| 5000–10,000 | 152.9 | 1583.2 | 1435.4 | .59 | .50 | 127.0 | 95.1 |
| 10,000 + | 1417.7 | 5268.1 | 3715.9 | .77 | .50 | 667.8 | 203.3 |
| TOTAL | 2312.8 | — | — | — | — | 1523.0 | 1105.1 |

*Source:* U.S. Internal Revenue Service, *Statistics of Income—1976, Estate Tax Returns* 1979, p. 8; pp. 15–19, table 1; and p. 27, table 5; *Internal Revenue Code* 1982, sec. 2001 and 2002, pp. 847, 849.

[a]Price elasticities used in simulations were: for estates less than $1 million: −1.6; for estates over $1 million: −1.0 in I and −2.4 in II. Estate elasticities were: 0.4 for all estates in I and estates less than $1 million in II; 1.3 for estates over $1 million in II.

individual giving. Second, fundamental shifts in giving patterns, due perhaps to an increased need by donees, could also modify the changes predicted by static econometric models. Having noted these caveats, one can summarize the findings of this section by stating that, other things equal, the 1981 tax act will probably cause a significant decline in real bequest giving and that the effect in the largest estates will predominate.

# 7    Foundations

It is impossible to make a full assessment of the effects of federal taxation on charitable giving without considering the unique role played by philanthropic foundations. Sometimes compared to banks or clearing houses,[1] foundations act primarily as intermediaries between contributors and the nonprofit organizations that provide charitable or other exempt services. As such, foundations do not originate charitable transfers; they merely complete them. In 1982 American foundations made grants amounting to $3.2 billion, or about one-fifteenth the size of donations by living individuals (*Giving U.S.A.* 1983, p. 36). Since these grants were made possible only by earlier contributions or bequests, it is improper to add foundation grants together with current contributions from all other sources. To do so would result in a double counting of gifts passing through foundations. Despite this intermediary role, foundations and their tax treatment loom large in the consideration of tax policy and the philanthropic sector. Tax provisions regarding foundations affect not only their institutional behavior but the nature and amount of gifts they receive.

The first section of this chapter provides a brief outline of the history, structure, and function of charitable foundations in the United States. The second section describes recent tax provisions affecting foundations, focusing particularly on the Tax Reform Act of 1969. The third section discusses the effects of tax laws—with emphasis on the 1969 act—on the behavior of foundations and potential donors. No econometric analysis is discussed because virtually none exists in this area comparable to the studies of tax effects in other areas of charitable behavior.

---

1. See, for example, Nielson 1979, p. vii, and Ture and Feulner in Butler 1980, p. ix.

## 7.1  Background

The modern charitable foundation traces its legal roots back into antiquity, but it was not until the twentieth century that its present form became solidified. Through a foundation, one or more individuals can establish a permanent mechanism to manage a sum of money and make charitable grants from it. The purposes to which the grants are to be applied may be stated in quite general terms. The tasks of managing the principal and distributing grants are left to directors or trustees who may well be related to the donor, but most of the largest foundations have come to be directed and operated by professionals and others largely unrelated to the donors.[2]

It is useful to distinguish several types of foundations, both for descriptive purposes and for the sake of understanding relevant tax legislation. The most visible are the large private institutions such as the Ford and Rockefeller foundations. There are many more smaller foundations of similar structure, most of which were established by the gifts of a single family or individual. Together these foundations are referred to as private nonoperating foundations. They are "nonoperating" because, for the most part, they make grants to other organizations rather than supplying services directly. In addition, their endowments come largely from one or several gifts from an individual or family rather than from the continuing support of a large number of contributors. It is the tax treatment of these private nonoperating foundations that has inspired the most intense policy debate in this area of nonprofit activity, and these foundations are the focus of the present chapter.

In order to point up the distinguishing features of private nonoperating foundations, it is useful to mention four other general categories of foundations. First, company foundations are those closely allied to firms, and their function is discussed in chapter 5. Second, community foundations (known also as community trusts) serve to centralize the administration for separate charitable funds in a community or region. Third, "operating foundations" such as endowed research or social-welfare organizations provide tax-exempt services directly. Although they are strictly a kind of private foundation, they act as ordinary charitable organizations rather than as grant-making entities. Finally, it is useful to distinguish a group of organizations that operate by attracting contributions from a wide spectrum of contributors and funneling that money to research or service organizations. Exemplified by organizations supporting health-related research, such "public charities" do not provide services directly, but are distinguished from private foundations by the breadth of their support.[3]

---

2. For historical descriptions of foundations, see Freemont-Smith 1965 or Karl and Katz 1981.
3. See Petska (1982a, p. 9) for examples of public charities or Freemont-Smith (1965, p. 12) for a similar categorization of foundations.

For the sake of clarity in evaluating data on foundations, it is important to note that the legal definition of *private foundation*—on which government statistics and tax treatment are based—covers more than just private nonoperating foundations. In particular, the definition of a private foundation as used by the IRS includes operating charities that fail to meet certain standards of public support (so-called failed public charities) or other conditions. Not only does this definition have important implications for the tax treatment of insitutions, it also means that government data on private foundations includes some number of organizations that do not conform to the usual definition of grant-making, nonoperating foundations. In fact, most private foundations are grant-making and nonoperating, thus conforming to the definition of private nonoperating foundations. Community foundations and most operating charities are not included in the IRS definition of private foundations. The distinction between private nonoperating foundations and the legal definition of private foundations is noted below in discussing the size and composition of the foundation sector.

Table 7.1 provides some idea of the magnitudes of the various foundation types, based on a sample of large foundations for 1979. Private nonoperating foundations constitute by far the most important category, accounting for 78 percent of these large foundations and 88 percent of their assets.[4] Company foundations accounted for 5 percent of assets, while community and operating foundations together made up the remaining 7 percent. As a percentage of assets, current contributions received by foundations were most important to company foundations, which is quite consistent with the idea that such foundations smooth out contributions rather than serve as repositories of endowments.[5] In contrast, current contributions received by private nonoperating foundations accounted for only 1.4 percent of assets, reflecting the general dominance of initial gifts relative to continuing outside support. Grants made by private nonoperating foundations amounted to 5.6 percent of assets, or four times as large as contributions received. In contrast, company foundations paid out slightly less than their receipts of contributions, though both amounts were large relative to total assets. The grants of community foundations were less than a third of their contributions received, and grants by operating foundations were of little importance.

## 7.1.1    Size and Function of Private Foundations

Because of the central role of private foundations in discussion of tax policy and recent tax legislation, it is useful to take a closer look at this segment of the foundation world. Based on mandatory tax and informa-

---

4. The Foundation Center uses the term *independent foundation* for private foundations (*Foundation Directory* 1981, p. ix).

5. For a further discussion of this point, see chapter 5.

**Table 7.1**    Assets, Contributions Received, and Grants Made for Large Foundations by Type, 1979 (dollar amounts in millions)

| | Private Nonoperating[a] | Company Sponsored | Community | Operating | All |
|---|---|---|---|---|---|
| Number[b] | 2,618 | 602 | 95 | 48 | 3,363 |
| Assets | $33,829 | $2,008 | $1,655 | $1,061 | $38,553 |
| Contributions received | $ 478 | $ 509 | $ 345 | $ 24 | $ 1,356 |
| As percentage of assets | 1.4 | 25.3 | 20.8 | 2.3 | 3.5 |
| Grants made | $ 1,910 | $ 438 | $ 102 | $ 33 | $ 2,483 |
| As percentage of assets | 5.6 | 21.8 | 6.2 | 3.1 | 6.4 |

*Source: Foundation Directory* 1981, p. vii.

[a]Identified as "independent" foundation by the Foundation Center.
[b]All foundations meeting specific size criteria were included in this tabulation.

tion returns, the IRS estimated that there were almost 28,000 private foundations in 1979. As large a number as this appears to be, returns for private foundations represented in 1975 only a quarter of the returns filed by all exempt organizations and only 7 percent of all expenditures for exempt purposes (Petska 1982a, p. 9). Of the 28,000 private foundations identified for 1979, IRS data indicate that some 27,000 were private nonoperating foundations (Petska 1982a, p. 23, table 9). In contrast, the Foundation Center estimated that there were only about 22,000 private nonoperating foundations in 1979 (*Foundation Directory* 1981, p. vii). Available data do not allow a precise determination of the reason for this discrepancy; thus it is impossible to determine how closely the IRS data on private foundations corresponds to the universe of private nonoperating foundations. Table 7.2 presents the size distribution of private nonoperating foundations, as defined by the IRS. Probably the most striking aspect of the table is the uneven distribution of assets among these foundations. Over half the foundations had less than $100,000 in assets; this group together accounted for only about 1 percent of total assets. At the other end, the largest 490 foundations (1.7 percent of the total) had 65 percent of total assets. A small minority of foundations thus accounted for the bulk of foundation assets.[6]

In order to suggest the areas of philanthropic activity in which foundations are involved, table 7.3 provides a breakdown of the number and assets of private foundations by major activity in 1974. Both operating and nonoperating private foundations are included in this tabulation. Of the

**Table 7.2**     **Number and Assets of Private Nonoperating Foundations, 1979**

| Asset Class[a] ($ thousands) | Number of Foundations | Percentage of Total | Total Assets[b] ($ millions) | Percentage of Total |
|---|---|---|---|---|
| Zero or not reported | 1,444 | 5.3 | 59 | 0.2 |
| Under $25 | 8,092 | 30.0 | 98 | 0.3 |
| $25 under 100 | 5,598 | 20.8 | 331 | 1.0 |
| $100 under 500 | 6,383 | 23.7 | 1,466 | 4.4 |
| $500 under 1000 | 1,961 | 7.3 | 1,276 | 3.9 |
| $1000 under 10,000 | 2,927 | 10.9 | 7,670 | 23.3 |
| $10,000 under 50,000 | 457 | 1.7 | 7,847 | 23.8 |
| $50,000 or more | 109 | 0.4 | 14,219 | 43.2 |
| TOTAL | 26,970 | 100.0 | 32,965 | 100.0 |

*Source:* Petska 1982a, p. 24, table 10.
[a]Market value.
[b]Book value.

6. The difference in asset sizes for the largest foundations identified by tables 7.1 and 7.2 appears to be due to the use of market value of assets in table 7.1 compared to book value in table 7.2.

**Table 7.3**    Private Foundations by Type of Activity, 1974

| Major Activity | Number of Foundations | Total Assets ($ millions) | Assets as Percentage of Total | Assets of Operating Foundations as Percentage of Class |
|---|---|---|---|---|
| Religious | 2,884 | 1,035 | 4.1 | 2 |
| Schools, colleges | 4,049 | 2,556 | 10.0 | 6 |
| Cultural and historical | 1,051 | 1,586 | 6.2 | 26 |
| Other instruction and training | 265 | 191 | 0.7 | 56 |
| Health services | 1,246 | 1,114 | 4.4 | 24 |
| Scientific research | 214 | 175 | 0.7 | 54 |
| Business and professional | 51 | 3 | 0.0 | —[a] |
| Employee or membership benefit | 87 | 20 | 0.0 | —[a] |
| Sports, athletic, recreational, or social | 191 | 116 | 0.5 | 7 |
| Youth | 457 | 217 | 0.9 | 9 |

| | | | | |
|---|---|---|---|---|
| Conservation, environmental or beautification | 160 | 300 | 1.2 | 55 |
| Housing | 112 | 129 | 0.5 | 63 |
| Inner city or community | 221 | 77 | 0.3 | —[a] |
| Civil rights, litigation | 57 | 38 | 0.1 | —[a] |
| Other activities directed to individuals | 746 | 2,380 | 9.3 | 5 |
| Activities directed to organizations not elsewhere classified | 12,148 | 14,715 | 57.7 | 1 |
| Other purposes | 174 | 95 | 0.4 | 29 |
| No activity reported | 2,748 | 760 | 3.0 | 5 |
| TOTAL[b] | 26,889 | 25,514 | 100.0 | 6 |

Source: U.S. Internal Revenue Service, Statistics of Income—1974–1978, Private Foundations 1981, pp. 25–26, table 1.

[a]Not reported separately.
[b]Total includes foundations engaged in farming activities, not shown separately.

specified activity areas, foundations accounting for 10 percent of total assets were devoted to the support of schools and colleges. Foundations with another 6 percent of assets were concerned with cultural and historical purposes, including museums and libraries. Foundations with 4 percent of assets had religious aims. By far the largest number of foundations, representing 58 percent of total private foundation assets, fell into the residual category, "activities directed to organizations not elsewhere classified." This reflects the generality of purpose with which most of the largest foundations were established—a generality that has allowed their trustees and directors considerable latitude to direct grants over time. Operating foundations constitute a significant part of several categories although they account for only a small portion of total private foundation assets. In the housing, other instruction and training, conservation and environmental, and scientific research classes, operating foundations accounted for over half of total assets.

### 7.2  Tax Treatment of Foundations

Few areas of tax policy have aroused more heated debate than the tax treatment of private foundations. As it developed in the early twentieth century, the legal form of the foundation received several distinct advantages: it could accumulate income without taxation, it could operate in perpetuity subject to the most general stated objective, and (after 1917) individuals making contributions to it could deduct those contributions in calculating their income taxes.[7] These advantages obviously gave foundations considerable autonomy and freedom from the hand of government. This autonomy has been defended as essential to the basic function of foundations in society. Stating that foundations offer a vital independent source of support for new ideas, proponents have argued that the taxation and regulation of foundations should be kept to a minimum.[8]

The special treatment of foundations has also received considerable criticism, and this opposition is apparent in the history of tax legislation regarding foundations. In 1915 the Walsh Commission attacked the concentration of wealth and influence in foundations and recommended limitations on their size, autonomy, and lifetimes (Freemont-Smith 1965, p. 51; Karl and Katz 1981, p. 249). Suspicion of foundations rose during the 1940s as foundations grew and abuses by foundations were made public. It was apparent that some donors derived economic benefit from establishing foundations. By making gifts of nonvoting stock or retaining control of the foundation, a donor could receive an immediate tax deduction

7. See Freemont-Smith (1965) for a discussion of the legal status of foundations, in particular the cy pres doctrine related to the foundation's objective.
8. See, for example, statements by Brewster quoted by Simon in U.S. Congress, Senate, Committee on Finance 1973 p. 179, or Ture and Feulner in Butler 1980.

without relinquishing control of a family business, for example. Or a donor could use his control to have the foundation make favorable grants or loans. In 1950 Congress passed a tax on the unrelated business income as well as restrictions on deferral of charitable gifts and transactions between donors and foundations. Congress showed further disfavor toward private foundations in 1964 by giving preferential tax treatment to "public charities"—organizations receiving "a substantial part" of their support from the public. The limit on charitable contributions to such public charities was raised from 20 to 30 percent of income, but the limit on gifts to private foundations remained at 20 percent. The justification given for this discrimination was the delay that commonly occurred between the establishment of a private foundation and actual grant-making activity (Nielson 1972, pp. 372–73; Freemont-Smith 1965, p. 160). A special Treasury study undertaken about this time confirmed that many private foundations did in fact pay out very small proportions of their assets. Table 7.4 presents a tabulation based on that study. It shows that over 9 percent of private foundations paid out 1 percent or less of their assets in 1962. To what extent these low rates of payout were due to a deliberate policy of capital accumulation or to the practice of some foundations to hold low-yield company stock is unclear.[9]

By 1969 there was strong sentiment in Congress to restrict private foundations further. Not only were the low payout rates a source of concern, there were also continuing problems with donors' attempts to control and manipulate foundations for personal gain (Nielson 1972, p. 373). According to foundation critic Congressman Wright Patman, foundations had by means of their tax exemption become "perverted into a vehicle for institutionalized, deliberate evasion of fiscal and moral responsibility to the nation" (Nielson 1972, p. 9).

As a result of concerns such as these, Congress enacted a set of fundamental changes in the tax treatment of private foundations as a part of the Tax Reform Act of 1969. The act provided for the first time a definition of private foundations. They were defined as nonprofit charitable institutions *other than* operating charitable organizations (such as churches, schools, hospitals, and the like), charitable organizations with broad-based public support, organizations supporting any of the above, or organizations that test for the public safety.[10] The act contained four sets of provisions related to private foundations. First, it established a minimum rate of payout or distribution of grants as a percentage of investment assets. After a phase-in period for existing foundations, the minimum

---

9. Worthy (1975, p. 244) states that foundations with major holdings in one corporation experienced lower rates of return.

10. *Internal Revenue Code* 1982, sec. 509(a). Broadly based organizations were those receiving over a third of their income from the general public in contributions, sales, or membership fees and less than a third from investment or unrelated business income.

**Table 7.4    Percentage Distribution of Private Foundations by Payout Rate and Asset Size, 1962**

| Ratio of Grants to Book Net Worth (percent) | Total | Asset Size | | | |
|---|---|---|---|---|---|
| | | Under $100,000 | $100,000 to 1,000,000 | $1,000,000 10,000,000 | Over $10,000,000 |
| 0 to 1 | 9.2 | 11.8 | 5.7 | 2.5 | 5.5 |
| 1 to 3 | 9.9 | 8.2 | 12.8 | 11.4 | 8.5 |
| 3 to 6 | 18.9 | 11.6 | 28.9 | 35.4 | 40.2 |
| 6 to 10 | 12.3 | 8.2 | 17.5 | 21.5 | 26.8 |
| Over 10 | 47.6 | 57.5 | 33.8 | 27.8 | 18.3 |
| Incomplete information | 2.1 | 2.7 | 1.2 | 1.5 | 0.6 |
| TOTAL | 100.0 | 100.0 | 100.0 | 100.0 | 100.0 |

*Source:* Testimony of H. Lawrence Fox in U.S. Congress, Senate, Committee on Finance 1974a, pp. 146–47. Based on Treasury Department Survey of Private Foundations (U.S. Congress, Senate 1965, p. 87).

payout rate was to be the greater of the foundation's actual investment income and a predetermined rate, originally set at 6 percent. This provision was a straightforward remedy for what were seen as insufficiently low rates of distribution by some foundations, as noted above. If funds were put into foundations but never expended for charitable purposes, many felt that it was difficult to justify the deduction for the original payment. The act's second provision was to impose an excise tax, originally at a rate of 4 percent, on the investment income of private foundations. The third provision that affected private foundations did so indirectly. This percentage-of-income ceiling on deductible contributions was raised from 30 to 50 percent for exempt organizations other than private nonoperating foundations; the percentage applying to private foundations remained at 20 percent. In addition, gifts exceeding the 20 percent limit were not eligible for carryover, and gifts of appreciated assets to private foundations were reduced by the capital gains exclusion rate as applied to the appreciation.[11]

Finally, the 1969 act imposed a set of regulatory measures intended to limit the potential for abuse by donors. Most important, that law prohibited "self-dealing" transactions between a foundation and its substantial donors and their families, including such transactions as loans, employment, purchases, or transfers of property. Previously such transactions were permitted if the donor and foundation acted independently and if the terms were no more favorable than could be obtained on the open market. This "arms-length" criterion had been difficult to enforce, however.[12] Next, the act limited a donor's power to maintain control over a foundation through the transfer of company stock. According to the act, a private foundation together with its major donors could hold no more than 20 percent of the voting stock of a corporation. Phase-in periods were allowed for foundations to divest themselves of any excess. Another provision required foundations to verify that grants to other foundations or to nonexempt organizations were actually used for their stated purposes. In addition to these provisions, private foundations were limited in their ability to make risky investments, participate in politics, make grants to individuals, or engage in nonexempt activities.[13] Taken together, these provisions of the Tax Reform Act of 1969 constituted a sweeping change in the tenor and substance of tax law regarding foundations. Even so, they

11. For a description of these provisions, see U.S. Internal Revenue Service, *Statistics of Income—1974–1978, Private Foundations* 1981, p. 5, or *Foundation Directory* 1981, p. xii.

12. *Internal Revenue Code* 1982, sec. 4946 specifies those disqualified from making such transactions. For a comparison of the rules on self-dealing before and after the 1969 act, see U.S. Internal Revenue Service, *Statistics of Income—1974–1978, Private Foundations* 1981, pp. 5–6.

13. See Labovitz 1974, pp. 64–71; U.S. Internal Revenue Service, *Statistics of Income—1974–1978, Private Foundations* 1981, pp. 5–7; or *1980 U.S. Master Tax Guide* (1979, pp. 192–94) for more detailed descriptions of these provisions.

are less stringent than some proposals, such as a provision rejected by the Senate to place a forty-year limit on the lives of private foundations (Council on Foundations 1977, p. 1559). The effects of these changes are the principal topic in section 7.3 below.

Since 1969 there has been some easing in the tax provisions related to private foundations. In 1976 the fixed portion of the minimum payout rate was lowered from 6 to 5 percent, and in 1981 the requirement that the payout rate meet or exceed the actual rate of return on investments was dropped, leaving a simple minimum payout rate of 5 percent. The excise tax on investment income also was reduced in 1978 to 2 percent.[14] Recently, proposals for more favorable treatment of private foundations have received increasing attention. Hearings in 1983 covered such possible changes as repeal of the 2 percent tax and easing of the divestiture rules.[15] Also under consideration was a proposal to end discrimination against private foundations in the deduction ceiling and rules concerning gifts of appreciated assets.[16]

As the law stood following the 1981 tax act, the rules governing private foundations could be quite important in the contribution decisions of some taxpayers. A donor's gift would generally fall under the private foundation provisions as long as he or his appointees retained control over the disposition of funds after the gift was credited. A donor could obtain a higher limit on gifts (30 percent) by giving up some control and establishing a support organization directed jointly by representatives of the donor and a charity.[17] In order to have the maximum deduction limits apply, a donor would have to relinquish control over the funds at the time of the gift; he would have to be content to influence the use of his contribution through a restricted endowment fund or recommendations to the charitable organization. For a class of large donors, however, the control available through the foundation form makes other forms of giving much less attractive. Important questions for tax policy concern the effect of these provisions on the creation of new private foundations, on the support of existing foundations, and on charitable giving in general. The following section addresses these questions.

### 7.3   The Impact of the 1969 Tax Reform Act on Foundations

Called "the most far-reaching legislation affecting private philanthropy in our two hundred–year history" (Worthy 1975, p. 232), the Tax Reform Act of 1969 has elicited widespread opposition among spokesmen for

14. See *Foundation Directory* 1981, pp. xii, 12, and Sugarman and Feinberg 1981, p. 5.
15. Hearings of the Subcommittee on Oversight of the Committee on Ways and Means covering rules for private foundations were held on 17–30 June 1983.
16. See, for example, "Tax Report," *Wall Street Journal,* 25 May 1983, p. 1.
17. See *Internal Revenue Code* (1982, sec. 509(a)(3)) or Sugarman and Feinberg (1981, pp. 8–11) for restrictions regarding support organizations.

foundations amid predictions of irreparable harm. Taggart stated ominously following the bill's passage: "The bell may well have faintly tolled for the private foundation; it is now to be found only in captivity and there are strong doubts about its ability to reproduce" (Taggart 1970, p. 63). Butler (1980, p. 14) agreed, saying the act will "jeopardize the existence of foundations."

In order to assess predictions such as these, it is useful to consider two sets of influences likely to have emanated from the 1969 act. First, the act's provisions are likely to affect the operation of private foundations, from its investment policy to its policies for making grants. Second, one would expect the act's provisions to affect the attractiveness of foundations as a vehicle for individual contributions or bequests. To the extent that the act's new restrictions lessen the attractiveness of the private foundation in relation to other means of giving—trusts or direct gifts to charities—it is reasonable to expect some substitution in favor of other forms. It is also possible that increases in other forms of giving will not compensate and that overall charitable giving will decline. Needless to say, effects on the operation of foundations and effects on contributions to foundations may also interact. Reductions in gifts may affect grant-making and investment decisions; restrictions on business dealings may affect the establishment of foundations. At the outset, it should be emphasized that as yet there exists little empirical investigation of these effects. What follows is a description of the available data relevant to the impact of tax law, and the 1969 law in particular, on foundations. The primary pieces of data relate to payout rates, other effects on foundation operations, donor support, and overall growth.

### 7.3.1 Payout Rate

A central pillar of the 1969 legislation was the requirement that private foundations distribute some minimum percentage of their assets annually. The provision arose out of concern that the immediate charitable deductions allowed at the establishment of a foundation might not be matched by actual grants to operating charitable organizations until much later. As Steuerle (1977, p. 1665) has pointed out, much of the discussion over this payout requirement has focused on the question of what rate would be appropriate, considering the investment opportunities open to foundations.

Probably the most useful question that can be posed in assessing the impact of the provision is whether the requirement actually increased payout rates. Since payout rates may be influenced by the rate at which contributions are received as well as by the performance of portofolios, however, it is impossible to isolate the requirement's independent effect. For example, Labovitz found that the median rate of return received by a sample of foundations fell between 1967 and 1970 for each asset group observed. As he suggests, these movements appear to be largely the effect of poor stock market performance (Labovitz 1974, pp. 89–92). In another analysis using a sample of 326 large foundations, Cushman (1979, pp. 155–56 table 6.3) found that the average payout rate rose from 4.2 to 6.6 percent between 1968 and 1973. Table 7.5 presents aggregate data on foundation distributions for various years, using two different series of data. The first data set covers all foundations. The second includes only a sample of the largest ones. The former shows a general rise in payout rates from the early or mid-1960s to 1979 while the second does not suggest any clear trend. Comparisons over time such as those in table 7.5 are hampered, however, because the calculated rates are based on different sample sizes, the smaller samples tending to be dominated by the largest foundations. In order to assess the implication of differing compositions of small and large foundations, it is useful to turn briefly to a consideration of the effect of asset size on rates of distribution.

The payout rates in the IRS sample covering all foundations are slightly higher than that based on the sample of large foundations. Most likely this difference reflects the generally higher payout rates for small founda-

**Table 7.5**    **Payout Rates for Foundations Based on Two Data Series (dollar amounts in millions)**

| | IRS Information Returns (990-PF): All Private Foundations | | | |
|---|---|---|---|---|
| Year | Number of Foundations[a] | Total Assets[b] | Contributions Paid | As Percentage of Assets |
| 1962 | 14,865 | $16,262 | $1,012 | 6.2 |
| 1974 | 26,889 | n.a | 1,953 | n.a. |
| 1977 | 27,691 | 34,817 | 2,289 | 6.6 |
| 1978 | 29,659 | 36,735 | 2,764 | 7.5 |
| 1979 | 27,980 | 44,648 | 2,801 | 6.3 |

| | Foundation Center Surveys of Large Foundations | | | |
|---|---|---|---|---|
| Year[c] | Number of Foundations[d] | Total Assets[b] | Grants | As Percentage of Assets |
| 1965 | 6,803 | $19,927 | $1,212 | 6.1 |
| 1969 | 5,454 | 25,181 | 1,513 | 6.0 |
| 1972 | 2,533 | 31,510 | 1,548 | 4.9 |
| 1975 | 2,818 | 28,635 | 1,808 | 6.3 |
| 1977 | 3,138 | 32,359 | 2,062 | 6.4 |
| 1979 | 3,363 | 38,553 | 2,365 | 6.1 |

*Sources:* Petska 1982b, p. 25; *Foundation Directory* 1967, p. 15; 1971, p. xi; 1975, p. xvi; 1977, p. xvii; 1979, p. xiv, 1981, p. vii.

[a]Includes non-grant-making foundations.

[b]Market value.

[c]Years covered by surveys are approximate.

[d]Includes all foundations meeting specific size criteria in each year.

tions, as indicated in table 7.6 for 1979. Expressed as a percentage of the book value of assets, payout rates ranged from 74 percent for foundations with less than $25,000 in assets to 6.5 percent for foundations with assets over $50 million. These payout rates correspond closely to the rates at which contributions were received. The implication of these differences, noted by Petska (1982a, p. 14), is that a percentage payout requirement such as that in the 1969 act poses a more serious constraint on large foundations than small ones, because of the latter's greater access to annual contributions as a source of funding. This suggestion finds support in table 7.7, which gives the required and actual distributions. While foundations in the lowest asset class distributed over three times what they were required to, the grants of the largest foundations exceeded the required amount by only 11 percent. To the extent that the payout requirement actually constrains the behavior of any foundations, therefore, its effect is most likely to be felt among the largest foundations, those least likely to receive a large portion of their incomes in the form of contributions.

Any increase in the payout rate, other things equal, will reduce the rate at which foundation assets grow. One frequently expressed concern among critics of the 1969 payout requirements is that they would force managers to "invade corpus" and distribute some portion of assets annually. Alternatively, foundations would be forced to switch away from growth stocks paying few dividends to assets offering higher interest rates but no growth opportunities. Indeed, one argument for payout requirements has been that foundations should not grow over time unless they

**Table 7.6**    **Gifts Received and Grants Made by Private Foundations, 1979**

| Asset Size[a] (thousands) | Gifts Received | | Gifts Paid Out | |
|---|---|---|---|---|
| | Total ($ millions) | As Percentage of Assets[b] | Total ($ millions) | As Percentage of Assets[b] |
| Zero or not reported | 8 | 13.4 | 16 | 26.6 |
| Under $25 | 78 | 77.6 | 75 | 74.2 |
| $25 under 100 | 70 | 20.4 | 59 | 17.3 |
| $100 under 500 | 227 | 13.6 | 193 | 11.5 |
| $500 under 1,000 | 145 | 10.9 | 145 | 10.9 |
| $1,000 under 10,000 | 682 | 8.3 | 716 | 8.7 |
| $10,000 under 50,000 | 562 | 6.7 | 652 | 7.8 |
| $50,000 or more | 510 | 3.5 | 946 | 6.5 |
| Total | 2,282 | 6.6 | 2,801 | 8.1 |

*Source:* Petska 1982a, p. 16, table 2.
[a]Market value.
[b]Book value.

Table 7.7    **Required and Actual Distributions for Exempt Purposes for Nonoperating Foundations, 1979**

| Asset Class | Number of Foundations | Required Distribution[a] ($ millions) | Actual Distribution ($ millions) | Required as Percentage of Actual |
|---|---|---|---|---|
| Under $100,000[b] | 15,833 | 83.4 | 279.5 | 29.8 |
| $100,000 under 1,000,000 | 7,862 | 196.9 | 375.1 | 52.4 |
| $1,000,000 under 10,000,000 | 2,761 | 559.3 | 786.5 | 71.1 |
| $10,000,000 or more | 514 | 1610.7 | 1791.6 | 89.9 |
| TOTAL | 26,970 | 2450.3 | 3233.3 | 75.8 |

*Source:* Petska 1982a, p. 26, table 12.
[a]"Distributable amount."
[b]Includes foundations with assets not reported.

continue to receive contributions. As Steuerle has noted, the real value of foundation assets will grow as long as the payout rate is not more than the sum of the real rate of return and the growth rate of assets due to new contributions (Steuerle 1977, pp. 1673–75.). In fact, the real value of private foundation assets has increased. Converting the asset values shown in table 7.5 to 1972 dollars shows an increase in real market value from $23.0 billion in 1962 to $27.4 billion in 1979 (Petska 1982b, p. 25). To summarize the evidence on payout rates, it seems likely that the law has been a binding constraint for some, mostly larger, foundations. The time-series evidence on payout rates is inconclusive, however, because the Foundation Center's sample was reduced between 1969 and 1972, raising the average size of the foundations included, and thus tending to lower observed payout rates. In any case, there is as yet no clear evidence to suggest that the payout requirement—in combination with asset yields and contributions received—has led to a decline in real asset values.

## 7.3.2 Formation of and Contributions to Foundations

Probably the most important measure of the impact of the 1969 legislation on private foundations is the law's effect on their creation and support by individual donors. The predictions of doom for foundations would indeed come about if the new restrictions on foundations caused potential donors to make other kinds of charitable gifts or forego making contributions altogether. In his testimony before the Finance Committee in 1973, John Simon argued that the 1969 lelgislation had reduced the birth rate of new foundations. He presented evidence that the number of new private foundations appearing annually had fallen by over half between 1969 and 1973 (U.S. Senate, Committee on Finance 1973, pp. 173–75).

In order to examine the possible effect of the 1969 act on the creation of new foundations, tables 7.8 and 7.9 present information on the number of foundations established over time. Table 7.8 displays the year of establishment for two samples of large foundations for 1969 and 1979. It shows that the number of births in the 1970s was only a third the level of the 1960s. However, it also shows that, in both samples, the 1950s was the most active period for the creation of large foundations: the number of foundations established in the 1960s was 40 percent less than the level for the 1950s. Table 7.9 shows, in the last two columns, the yearly average of the number of foundations receiving their tax exemption and their assets as of 1974 over several different periods from 1920 to 1974. In agreement with table 7.8, the period 1950–59 represented the most active (as measured by assets) period for the establishment of foundations. By this measure the decade of the 1960s was nearly as active, but the figures for that decade include institutions that had previously been established without securing official tax-exempt certification.[18] From 1970 to 1974, foundations with average assets of $421 million have been established annually,

Table 7.8    **Period of Establishment of Large Foundations**

| Period | 1969 Sample | | 1979 Sample | |
| --- | --- | --- | --- | --- |
| | Number | Percentage | Number | Percentage |
| Before 1900 | 18 | 0.3 | 25 | 0.8 |
| 1900–1909 | 16 | 0.3 | 17 | 0.5 |
| 1910–1919 | 75 | 1.4 | 58 | 1.7 |
| 1920–1929 | 157 | 2.9 | 136 | 4.1 |
| 1930–1939 | 259 | 4.8 | 176 | 5.3 |
| 1940–1949 | 1134 | 20.9 | 625 | 18.8 |
| 1950–1959 | 2546 | 46.8 | 1272 | 38.3 |
| 1960–1969 | 1231 | 22.6 | 759 | 22.8 |
| 1970–1979 | — | — | 255 | 7.7 |
| | 5436 | 100.0 | 3323 | 100.0 |

*Source: Foundation Directory*: 1969 Sample: 1971, p. x; 1979 Sample: 1981, p. xiv.

*Note:* Samples for tabulation consist of all foundations meeting specific size criteria in each year. For the 1969 sample, foundations with grants of $25,000 or more or with assets of $500,000 or more were included (*Foundation Directory* 1971, p. vii). For the 1979 sample, the comparable amounts were $100,000 in grants or $1 million in assets (1981, p. vii).

18. See U.S. Internal Revenue Service, *Statistics of Income—1974–78, Private Foundations* 1981, p. 24, for an explanation of the process by which institutions were granted tax-exempt status.

Table 7.9            **Number and Assets of Foundations by Year in Which Tax Exemption Was Obtained**

| Period | Total for Period | | Annual Average for Period | |
|--------|------------------|--|---------------------------|--|
|  | Number of Foundations | Assets ($ millions) | Number of Foundations | Assets ($ millions) |
| 1920–1939 | 401 | 3,784 | 20 | 189 |
| 1940–1949 | 2,071 | 4,283 | 207 | 428 |
| 1950–1959 | 6,061 | 7,792 | 606 | 779 |
| 1960–1969 | 12,094 | 7,181 | 1,209 | 718 |
| 1970 | 1,247 | 462 | 1,247 | 462 |
| 1971 | 1,092 | 367 | 1,092 | 367 |
| 1972 | 1,081 | 421 | 1,081 | 421 |
| 1973 | 809 | 475 | 809 | 475 |
| 1974 | 856 | 381 | 856 | 381 |

*Source:* Internal Revenue Service, *Statistics of Income—1974–1978, Private Foundations* 1981, p. 93, table 18.

much below the rate for the 1950s.[19] To summarize, the decline in the birth rate of new foundations began before the enactment of the Tax Reform Act of 1969 and appears to have accelerated slightly after it. Whether the act had an independent effect on this rate cannot be determined, however, on the basis of existing data. Not only might nontax influences have changed over the period, but some of the decline in the 1960s may have been due to actual or anticipated restrictions on foundations felt during the 1960s. The increase in the percentage limitation for gifts in 1964 was not extended to private foundations, as noted above. In addition, the hearings and reports on foundations may have had an adverse "announcement effect" on new foundations by signaling more stringent regulations to come.

Another deleterious effect seen as a possible result of the 1969 act was a drop in the rate at which individuals contributed to foundations. Labovitz's survey supported this fear, showing that the percentage of foundations receiving any contributions had fallen from 1967 to 1970 and that the average size of contributions had fallen in all but one asset class (Labovitz 1974, p. 99). In an attempt to provide a longer period for comparison, table 7.10 shows gifts received as a percentage of total assets of the large foundations covered in the Foundation Center's periodic surveys. These figures do in fact show a drop in contributions relative to assets between 1969 and 1972 as well as a lower rate of contributions after 1969.

19. Since some foundations created during the 1950s no longer exist, these figures understate the rate of births during that decade.

Table 7.10    **Gifts Received by Large Foundations, Selected Years**

| Year[a] | Number of Foundations | Gifts Received ($ millions) | As Percentage of Total Assets |
|---|---|---|---|
| 1965 | 6803 | 765 | 3.8 |
| 1969 | 5454 | 1,152 | 4.6 |
| 1972 | 2533 | 734 | 2.3 |
| 1975 | 2818 | 946 | 3.3 |
| 1977 | 3138 | 1,339 | 4.1 |
| 1979 | 3363 | 1,356 | 3.5 |

*Source: Foundation Directory*, various years. See table 7.5.
[a]Year is approximate.

However, this time series is subject to the same kind of bias affecting the comparison of payout rates over time. Because the sample size was reduced after 1969, leaving larger average foundations, one would expect observed contribution rates to be lower. Consequently, these data do not allow a satisfactory test of whether contributions have fallen off as a result of the 1969 tax act. The only comparable data on contributions received over time is Cushman's (1979, pp. 162–63, table 6.4) finding that gifts received by a sample of 326 large foundations fell between 1968 and 1973 from 15.1 to 8.3 percent of total income. The fall in stock prices over this period may have been a significant factor in this comparison, however.

### 7.3.3    Other Effects

There is some evidence that foundation behavior was influenced in other ways by the 1969 tax act. In general, however, these effects do not lend themselves readily to measurement. Labovitz's (1974) survey results suggest, for example, that many foundations modified their grant making as a result of the act's requirement to exercise "expenditure responsibility" over grants not made to exempt charities. As a result of the requirement, some foundations apparently shied away from making grants to controversial or unusual organizations (pp. 82–85). The survey results also indicate an increase in legal and administrative costs as a result of the act, though these could well have been short-term effects (pp. 78–82).[20] There was little evidence that the requirements to divest certain stock, imposed as they were over a long period, had had much effect by 1970 (pp. 94–98).

One other measure for the cumulative effect of these and other restrictions imposed by the 1969 act is the rate at which foundations terminate operations. Simon presented data to suggest that this death rate had risen

---

20. Cushman (1979, pp. 166–67, table 6.5) reports for his sample of 326 large foundations that the ratio of expenses to income rose from 7.0 to 12.2 percent between 1968 and 1973.

steeply since 1969 (U.S. Senate, Committee on Finance 1973, p. 174). While this is suggestive, it is difficult to draw any firm conclusions without a longer time series of observations on foundation deaths and births. More generally, it will be impossible to give a full assessment of the effect of the 1969 act without a more complete model of donors and foundations themselves.

## 7.4  Conclusion

The privileged position of foundations as autonomous, undying, and tax-exempt entities was challenged by a comprehensive set of provisions in the Tax Reform Act of 1969. The bill appears to have been motivated in large part by the perception that, in many cases, the private foundation was "little more than a tax shelter" (testimony by Patricia Senger, U.S. Senate, Committee on Finance 1974b, p. 50). Since 1969 the Congress has softened the restrictions somewhat, but most of the 1969 provisions remain in force. Because of the importance of the 1969 act, analysis of the effect of federal tax law on foundations must focus on the effects of these provisions. The chapter indicates quite clearly, however, that the analysis of these effects is severely hampered by the dearth of useful data for analyzing foundation behavior over time. Although foundation tax forms provide the groundwork for a useful data set, the data in this area remain far less developed than those used in studying other areas of philanthropy.

Based on the fragmentary data presented in this chapter, it appears that the 1969 act was successful in altering some forms of behavior by foundations and their donors without jeopardizing the continued use of the foundation form. Payout rates appear to have increased slightly due to the act. As for contributions to foundations, it is not clear whether they have risen or fallen overall as a result of the 1969 act. It is not clear that the act has reduced the rate at which foundations are established. Nor does the increase in the real value of foundation assets since 1962 suggest that the 1969 act has made foundations a dying breed. Given the available data, it appears indeed that the rumors of their demise may well have been exaggerated.

# 8    Charitable Giving Behavior and the Evaluation of Tax Policy

The preceding chapters have focused exclusively on positive questions related to the effect of federal taxes on charitable giving. The objective of this final chapter is to conclude the analysis by, first, summarizing the major findings and, second, providing a broader framework for the evaluation of tax policy toward charitable giving. The first section presents a brief summary of findings from empirical studies of tax effects on charitable giving, notes some of the important implications for tax policy, and lists several important unanswered questions. The second section discusses the normative evaluation of tax policy toward charitable giving, noting in particular the relevance of empirical work on charitable behavior.

## 8.1  Tax Effects on Charitable Giving: An Overview

From the evidence presented in the preceding chapters, it is possible to draw conclusions regarding the effect of tax policy on charitable behavior and to highlight some of the most important implications of this empirical work. It is useful to begin with a brief summary of the findings from econometric studies.

### 8.1.1  Summary of the Findings

Econometric analysis has focused on four major areas of charitable behavior: individual contributions, volunteering, corporate giving, and charitable bequests. There is also some empirical evidence on the effect of taxes on foundations, but no econometric studies have been done in that area. The bulk of econometric analysis and attention in economic studies has been directed toward individual giving, which seems appropriate given the large share of total gifts accounted for by individuals. Contribu-

273

tions by individuals vary widely by income level and age as well as among individuals within those classifications. The major tax policy instrument affecting individual giving is the charitable deduction allowed in the calculation of taxable income for taxpayers who itemize their deductions. As a result of this tax treatment, there are two major tax effects on individual giving: the tax liability affects the after-tax income from which taxpayers can make contributions and the deduction reduces the net price per dollar of contribution made. The econometric analysis of individual giving implies that the income tax has a strong effect on giving. This is not to say, however, that taxes are the only or the major influence on individual contributions, only that they are one significant factor.

Taken as a whole, the empirical work on tax effects and individual giving is notable for the number and variety of studies in the area and the consistency of the findings. In few other applied areas in public finance has there been such extensive replication of empirical findings using different data sets. Studies of charitable contributions have used aggregated and individual data, data from tax returns and survey data, and foreign as well as U.S. experience. The consensus of these studies is that the price elasticity for the population of taxpayers is probably greater than 1 in absolute value, although there are certainly estimates that are smaller and estimates that are considerably larger than this. The range of most likely values appears to be about $-0.9$ to $-1.4$. Taxes also influence giving through an income effect, with most estimates of the income elasticity falling between 0.6 and 0.9.

In order to appreciate the implications of these findings, it is necessary to consider the specific hypotheses, different uses of data, and qualifications that apply to the studies themselves. For example, one maintained hypothesis is that itemization status and marginal tax rate work together through the price effect to affect giving, and that there is no separate "itemization effect." Separate tests of such an effect, in fact, confirm this maintained hypothesis. Another important question is whether the price elasticity varies by income level. The extensive analysis on this question has failed to provide a definitive answer, but it appears that the elasticity rises in absolute value with income. It is reasonable to conclude, however, that the price elasticity is significantly less than zero even for low-income taxpayers. A question of particular importance for evaluating the impact of tax policy is whether taxpayers respond immediately to changes in price and income. Evidence on this question suggests that there are substantial lags in giving behavior, with the result that short-run responses are much less complete than those in the long run. One other question related to the impact of fiscal policy on contributions is whether increased government spending "crowds out" private giving. The econometric evidence on this question shows little if any effect of this sort in spite of the apparent relationship observed among nations in the size of government and the strength of private giving. Throughout this empirical literature certain econometric issues have had to be dealt with, in particular the high correlation between price and income. Based on attempts to correct for possible biases as well as the variety of data and models used in these studies, it appears that these econometric problems are not a major factor in explaining the pattern of estimates.

Along with individual contributions, volunteering is one of the two major sources of private support for the charitable sector. In contrast to individual giving, however, our knowledge about the tax effects on volunteering is quite limited. For one thing, data on volunteering are sparse, and data linking volunteering to tax variables are even more limited. In theory, income taxation can have two broad effects on volunteering: a direct effect through the influence of tax rates on the allocation of time, and an indirect effect, through the charitable deduction for donations. The former effect depends on whether volunteering is simply a competing use of time, such as leisure, work, and household production, or whether it is a form of investment in human capital. The latter depends on whether gifts of money and gifts of time are complements or substitutes. The evidence on these questions is both limited and mixed. An analysis of volunteering by women suggests that contributions and volunteering are complements, implying that the charitable deduction encourages volunteering as well as donations. Also, volunteering tends to be crowded out by market work. To the extent that work and volunteering are rival uses of time, tax policies that encourage labor force participation among women tend to reduce their volunteering.

There is a much larger econometric literature on the effect of taxes on corporate giving. The new evidence presented in this study is broadly consistent with earlier findings and suggests that the corporation tax has both a price and a net-income effect on corporate giving. Such behavior by firms would be consistent with a number of models other than pure profit maximization. The estimates of the income-effect elasticity using the cash flow measure of income are close to 1, suggesting that contributions are proportional to after-tax income. An important question remains, however, regarding the proper specification of this income measure. qualitatively similar results are obtained using after-tax net income. The estimated price elasticities appear to be smaller than those estimated for individual contributions, but the estimates presented here leave some doubt due to the difference in results using marginal and average tax rates, respectively. Taken together, these results suggest that the price elasticity is less than 1 in absolute value. Finally, there is evidence that corporations time their gifts in order to take more deductions during years in which tax rates are higher.

Tax effects are also apparent in bequest giving and foundation activity. The econometric evidence of bequest giving presented in this study, like previous work, produces estimates subject to substantial variation. Nevertheless, these estimates imply that the deduction in the estate tax has quite a strong effect by and large. Most estimates of the price elasticity are greater than 1 in absolute value. Bequests also rise with estate size, but the elasticity of estate size is substantially smaller than 1. On estimates obtained for the very important group of the wealthiest decedents, those with net estates over $1 million, the estimated price elasticity was greater than 2 in absolute value, and the income elasticity exceeded 1. In any assessment of the aggregate effect of estate tax changes on charitable bequests, the largest estates are of paramount importance because they account for most bequest giving. No comparable econometric evidence on foundation activity has as yet been produced. The limited information that is available suggests, though, that the provisions in the Tax Reform Act of 1969 related to private foundations had the effect of raising payout rates without threatening the existence of foundations.

### 8.1.2  Implications for Tax Policy and the Nonprofit Sector

The major conclusion arising from this empirical work is that federal taxes, especially tax provisions affecting charitable giving, have important effects on the size and distribution of giving. The deductions in the individual, corporate, and estate taxes are of course most important, in the sense that no other tax changes with comparable revenue effects would influence charitable giving as much as the elimination of these deductions. But other, more general tax provisions and changes also have profound effects on giving. Probably the most important of these effects arise from the combination of the standard deduction, nominal tax schedules, and inflation. The effect of inflation has been to erode the value of the standard deduction, causing an increase in the proportion of taxpayers who itemize their deductions. This in turn affects the price of giving. Another important set of tax changes not directly related to charitable giving has been revisions in the rate schedule itself. In particular, the decline in top marginal tax rates from 91 to 50 percent over the last three decades has had a sizable effect on the prices faced by taxpayers in the highest income classes. A tax change such as the 1981 tax act combines several changes likely to affect charitable giving. Simulations based on estimated models of individual giving suggest that the combined effect will be a slight increase in the rate of giving, resulting from a large increase in giving by nonitemizers due to the "above-the-line" deduction and a slight decline in giving among upper-income taxpayers due to the drop in tax rates.

Similarly, the econometric evidence presented here implies that federal taxes will affect other forms of giving as well. Policies that encourage labor force participation of women—for example, the deduction for secondary earners—may tend to discourage volunteering. The extension of the charitable deduction to nonitemizers, on the other hand, may encourage volunteering if gifts of time and money are complementary. The recent changes in the corporate tax resulting in an increase in the number of firms with no tax liability will tend to discourage corporate giving by raising its average net price. The implications of the empirical analysis of bequests are similar to those applying to individual contributions. The 1981 tax act, which reduces the number of taxable estates and lowers the marginal tax rate for many estates, is likely to discourage bequest giving by raising the net price of charitable bequests.

As the simulations of individual giving show, one of the most important implications of existing empirical work is that tax policy can affect the distribution as well as the level of contributions. Since donors at various income levels differ markedly in their propensities to make gifts to various kinds of charitable organizations, tax changes that affect the distribution of giving among income classes will tend to affect the distribution of support to various parts of the philanthropic sector. For example, the 1981 tax act had the effect of significantly reducing marginal tax rates for taxpayers in the top brackets in both the income and estate taxes. If the effect of such price changes outweighs the influence of changes in net income or net estate, which they in fact appear to do, these tax changes are likely to cut the relative share of giving undertaken by the wealthy. This would imply a decline in support for institutions such as colleges, universities, cultural institutions, and private foundations and toward religious organizations and certain health and welfare groups. It is important to emphasize, however, that implications such as these are based on price and income effects and do not account for any possible changes in behavior by donors or charitable organizations.

The econometric estimates also have implications for proposed or hypothetical tax provisions. Simulations in the text examine several proposals that involve changes in the charitable deduction or general tax rate revision. Probably the largest effect would be observed if the charitable deduction were eliminated altogether, perhaps as part of some comprehensive income tax. Such a change would have important effects on the distribution as well as the level of contributions, with gifts by wealthy taxpayers falling the most. Substituting a tax credit for the present deduction, depending on the rate used, would have the effect primarily of redistributing the pattern of gifts between low and high income groups. Smaller changes would come about as a result of less sweeping revisions, such as the constructive realization of appreciated assets given as gifts or the expansion of the deduction at low and middle income levels. Each of the proposals noted here would affect overall tax revenues, and it is important in simulating their effects to adjust for this. Similar effects could be calculated for bequest giving, with the elimination of the deduction in the estate tax having much the same kind of effect.

### 8.1.3  Unanswered Questions

Even though it encompasses many different studies, the econometric literature linking taxes to charitable giving still leaves a number of important questions unresolved. Some of these could in principle be answered within models such as those that have been estimated. In order to answer others, it would be necessary to employ more general models. Within the context of the models that have been estimated, questions remain in every major area of charitable giving. We still do not have a precise idea, for example, of the magnitude of the price elasticity for low-income households. This is an important policy question because of the introduction of the new deduction for nonitemizers and because of the distributional implications of general tax changes. A second unanswered question is how the response to taxes varies according to the type of donee organization being supported. Although it might be difficult to estimate separate price and income elasticities by detailed donee class, it might well be possible to determine whether religious giving is affected differently from other types of contributions. The estimation of tax effects on volunteering requires data on individuals' volunteering, wage rates, labor force participation, and taxes. Given the available studies, it is simply impossible to determine beyond any doubt whether the present deduction encourages or discourages volunteering. Although there is a fair amount of consistency among studies of corporate giving, there remains considerable uncertainty as to the precise price elasticity and the appropriate measure of corporate income. Within the context of the models estimated, however, there is one additional question on which more information is required. If the deduction for charitable contributions were limited or eliminated, corporations would have the incentive to substitute other deductible expenditures for corporate gifts. Because of this substitutability, the price elasticities based on the current regime of full deductibility would not be applicable. Concerning charitable bequests, the instability of elasticity estimates in several studies suggests that our knowledge about the tax effects is not as good as we would like.

Other questions left unanswered by existing empirical work would require broader models than have been used in previous work. The models underlying virtually all empirical work on charitable contributions are partial equilibrium in nature. They ignore interactions among various kinds of giving as well as interactions between donors and donee organizations. It seems reasonable to suppose that changes in the tax treatment of contributions in one tax could affect contributions made subject to another. For example, a restriction in the deductibility of charitable bequests might will increase lifetime giving. Except as between volunteering and lifetime gifts, there is no evidence on interactions of this kind. More generally, most of the empirical analysis of charitable giving subject to a given tax assumes that the tax base itself is given. A more general analysis would recognize the possibility of endogenous changes in the tax base. The models employed are also inadequate in their failure to reflect interactions among donors and interactions between contributors and charitable organizations. Contributions by peers may increase or decrease an individual's contributions, and this relationship has important consequences for tax policy effects. Charitable organizations, for their part, may respond to changes in tax policy by varying their solicitation efforts. As long as effects such as these are not reflected in econometric models, projected effects based on those models must be seen as conditional statements only.

## 8.2 Normative Criteria for Evaluating Tax Policy toward Charitable Giving

The fundamental normative questions in the evaluation of tax policy toward charitable giving are whether and to what extent such giving should be subsidized. If charitable giving were just another category of personal spending by consumers, there might be no reason to consider any form of subsidy whatsoever. A secondary question has to do with the proper form the subsidy should take, given that some subsidy is appropriate. In addressing questions such as these, it is useful to begin with the standard public finance criteria of efficiency and distributional equity. Other, more specific considerations may also be important. Before discussing these criteria, it is useful to note a fundamental distinction relevant to one specific form of subsidy—the deduction.

### 8.2.1 Two Views of the Charitable Deduction

Two quite different kinds of arguments have been offered to justify the present deductions for personal contributions and bequests. According to the first, the deductions are necessary adjustments in calculating the proper tax base. Andrews (1972) argues that contributions are properly excluded from the income tax base because they constitute neither accumulation nor consumption, the two components of income under the accretion concept.[1] Although contributions emanate from personal expenditures, he argues, they are not consumption in the usual sense because they effect a transfer of resources to others. Similarly, Wagner (1977) argues that a deduction is the correct mechanism for calculating the proper base for estate taxation, on the basis that funds set aside for charitable

---

1. See also Musgrave and Musgrave (1980, pp. 343–47) for a definition of the accretion concept of income.

purposes are funds that cannot be enjoyed by the heirs of an estate. By this reasoning, horizontal equity thus requires that contributions be deducted in calculating the tax base.[2]

An alternative justification for the current charitable deduction is to view the deduction as an incentive by which the tax law encourages desirable behavior. According to this view charitable giving is an item of discretionary spending that warrants an incentive. A deduction is only one of several forms such an incentive might take; a tax credit or some matching arrangements might be as good or better. Since contributions are seen as discretionary expenditures by this view,[3] there is no necessity to provide the incentive in the form of a deduction from income. In contrast, the first view plainly requires the use of a deduction.

The implications of these views for the normative analysis of the tax treatment of charitable giving should be clear. If the deduction is seen as an absolutely necessary adjustment to income, it becomes "a matter of principle" (Break 1977, p. 1530), and there remains little to discuss concerning the proper tax treatment of charitable giving. If it is an incentive, however, alternative subsidies are fair game for consideration. The tax policy debate over the last two decades suggests that the first view is by no means universally accepted. That debate has focused on the form as well as scope of incentives for charitable giving. And, due to the existence of the standard deduction, the charitable deduction iself (along with the other itemized deductions) has been effectively limited to a minority of taxpayers. Accordingly, the remainder of this chapter is predicated on the assumption that the form of tax subsidy is not determined a priori, but rather is a question subject to normative policy analysis.

## 8.2.2  Efficient Tax Incentives for Contributions

The concept of economic efficiency is important in any full assessment of tax provisions related to charitable contributions. Indeed, efficiency criteria are necessary for answering the primary question of whether charitable gifts should be subsidized at all. In order to give more concreteness to the application of economic efficiency to charitable contributions, it is useful to begin by presenting a stylized illustration of a tax policy decision involving incentives for charitable giving. Consider the choice be-

2. See also Posnett 1979 for a description of this view.

Similar reasoning underlay the justification for the deduction given in a 1938 Congressional Report: "The exemption from taxation on money or property devoted to charitable and other purposes is based upon the theory that the Government is compensated for the loss of revenue by its relief from financial burden which would otherwise have to be met by appropriations from public funds, and by the benefits resulting from the promotion of the general welfare" (U.S. Congress, House of Representatives 1938, p. 19). The statement makes no explicit reference to the proper income tax base.

3. Wagner (1977, p. 2342) notes, disapprovingly, that the "conceptualization of charity as an act of personal consumption is conformable to the proclivities of many economists."

tween an increase of $1 million in government expenditures and an increase of the same amount in tax subsidies for charitable giving, both being financed by an increase in tax rates. Further suppose the new incentive leads to an increase in charitable giving of $$X$ million. Obviously, government expenditures under the first option will be higher by $1 million. By the same token, charitable giving will be higher under the second; it will be $$X$ million higher if increased government expenditures do not crowd out private charity. Assuming no crowding out, the income available to households after taxes and charitable giving will be $$(X$-1)$ million less in the second case.

One definition of efficiency used in connection with tax policy for charitable giving focuses on the size of the incentive effect. As stressed in a number of empirical studies of tax effects on charitable giving, if the price elasticity of charitable giving is greater than 1 in absolute value, a tax incentive producing a marginal change in the rate of subsidy to contributions will increase giving by more than the associated revenue loss. Accordingly, some writers have defined the "efficiency" of the charitable deduction in terms of the ratio of increased contributions to foregone revenue.[4] By such a definition, the incentive described in the present example would be "efficient" if the elasticity is greater than 1 in absolute value because the rise in contributions ($$X$ million) would exceed the revenue cost ($1 million). Clearly this is quite a specialized definition of efficiency. This concept takes no account of the comparative social benefit derived from private contributions compared to public expenditures. Nor does it give any weight to the change in income after taxes and contributions.

In order to consider the implications of a more complete definition of efficiency, two kinds of theoretical models of incentives for contributions are discussed below. The first focuses on the presumed external benefits that result from contributions. The second includes more general optimal tax models that rest on an explicit maximization of welfare.

*External Benefits*

It appears to be widely agreed that in contrast to most other types of expenditures, charitable contributions often contain a substantial element of external benefit. While donors may reap some direct benefit from their contributions, much of that giving materially benefits others. It might also be argued that charitable organizations produce an external benefit for society to the extent that they offer alternatives to government services. One longstanding justification for public encouragement of charitable giving appeals to the value of diversity in a pluralistic society.[5] It is a

4. Feldstein testified: "a higher elasticity implies a greater efficiency; that is, more additional giving per dollar of lost tax revenues" (U.S. Congress, Senate 1980, p. 219). Also see Boskin (1976, p. 55) and Donee Group (1977, p. 73) for similar references.

5. See chapter 7 for a discussion of this point in relation to foundations.

basic theorem in applied welfare economics that goods producing external benefits tend to be underprovided in private markets and that economic efficiency can be served by subsidizing such goods. In equilibrium the price faced by each individual should ideally equal his personal marginal valuation of the good, with the subsidy making up the difference between marginal cost and marginal valuation. Where the "good" is dollars of charitable contributions, (with a marginal cost of $1), $v$ is marginal valuation per dollar, and $s$ is the subsidy per dollar, the relevant private optimality condition for individual $i$ is simply:

$$(1) \qquad\qquad v_i + s_i = 1.$$

Assuming the individual in equilibrium equates his marginal valuation with the price he faces $(1 - s_i)$, the social optimum will be achieved when $s_i$ is set at the marginal external benefit. The greater the external benefit, the larger the optimal subsidy.[6]

Hochman and Rodgers (1977) and Posnett (1979) analyze the tax treatment of charitable contributions using similar normative models in which contributions are assumed to be pure public goods. Hochman and Rodgers show that a set of tax subsidies based on a Lindahl solution achieves the optimal allocation.[7] They argue further that, for a wide class of cases, a constant subsidy rate such as a tax credit satisfies the optimality condition. Posnett demonstrates, however, that the general superiority of a constant rate of subsidy cannot be shown. About the most that can be gleaned from these theoretical studies is that tax subsidies of some kind for contributions can be justified on efficiency grounds.

Practically speaking, it is quite inconceivable that any subsidy scheme could be devised to meet the conditions of a Lindahl solution. Both the characteristics of gifts and the tastes of individuals differ too much. A more modest objective would be to set subsidy rates according to the average amount of external benefit from contributions of different kinds. Hochman and Rodgers (1977, pp. 13–15) recommend tax credits for contributions as a way of approximating the Lindahl solution and imply that subsidy rates might well differ by category of giving. They argue that religious giving may have a more important external component than gifts to organizations that have some government counterpart (p. 13). On the other hand, Schaefer (1968, p. 30) maintains that nonreligious giving involves much more redistribution than religious giving, the latter being used largely "to preserve houses of worship and to maintain the activities of congregations." Discrimination among donees on the basis of external benefits

6. For a general treatment, see Musgrave and Musgrave 1980, pp. 78–80.

7. A Lindahl solution to the public-good allocation problem is one in which each individual pays a price equal to his marginal evaluation and the sum of marginal valuations equals the marginal cost of the good. See Hochman and Rodgers 1977, p. 4.

would be difficult, both analytically and politically, but there are precedents. Contributions to private foundations are accorded less favorable treatment in the lower percentage limitation of gifts, lack of carryover, and limitations on the deductibility of gifts of appreciated assets. And contributions to schools practicing racial discrimination are not deductible at all.[8]

Although the present deduction does not provide for any discrimination in subsidy rates by type of charitable donee (except for the nondeductibility of some gifts), subsidy rates definitely do differ by income level. As illustrated for 1980 in table 2.7 the rate of subsidy tends to rise with income because the marginal tax rate rises with income. For example, the average taxpayer in the $10,000–15,000 class in 1980 faced a marginal tax rate of 0.16, compared to a rate of 0.49 for a taxpayer in the $50,000–100,000 class. Distributional issues aside, this variation in subsidy rates may be judged in the light of the welfare economics of subsidizing goods with external benefits. If the charitable activities supported by high-income taxpayers—such as higher education, cultural institutions, and private foundations—have a higher component of external benefits than activities supported by lower-income households   primarily religion and community-welfare agencies—this structure of subsidies may be justified. However, if these activities cannot be distinguished on the basis of their external benefits in this way, differing rates of subsidy would not be efficient.[9] In any case, it is important to identify the structure of subsidy rates as primarily a question of efficiency, although distributional equity is relevant to the resulting pattern of tax burdens and the distribution of the benefits of charitable activities.

*Optimal Tax Models*

A more general treatment of the efficiency of tax incentives for charitable giving can be obtained with an optimal taxation model, as developed by Atkinson (1976) and Feldstein (1980). Atkinson's model incorporates an additive social-welfare function in which individual utilities depend on their contributions. The well-being of a needy group in society can be affected either by contributions or government expenditures. The effectiveness of private giving in aiding this group can be more or less than that of government. Atkinson (p. 21) shows that the optimal tax-credit rate for contributions is higher, among other things, the more effective private giving is.

8. Private schools in North and South Carolina whose practices were found to be discriminatory were denied the right to receive deductible contributions in 1982. See *New York Times,* 16 October 1982, pp. 1, 7.

9. See Culyer, Wiseman, and Posnett (1976, pp. 44–46) for a proposal to replace the British deduction by a matching grant with rates determined according to the externality criterion. Posnett 1979 also endorses such a policy in general terms.

Atkinson also spells out the special assumptions under which the narrow "efficiency" concept noted above is an appropriate rule for determining whether the introduction of a charitable deduction improves social welfare. Two conditions are necessary: contribution dollars must be as effective as public expenditures in helping the needy group, and the social-welfare function must be Rawlsian, with all weight being given to the utility of recipients. In terms of the example given above, the first assumption allows dollars of giving to be compared directly to dollars of government revenue; the second makes it unnecessary to be concerned with donors' incomes after taxes and contributions. The deduction is a social improvement if the rise in contributions exceeds the revenue cost (if $X > 1$), that is, if the elasticity is greater than one in absolute value. In general, however, the desirability of a deduction depends not only on the effectiveness of contributions, but also on the weight given to the preferences of donors and the equity effects of a deduction compared to a credit.[10] An elasticity of $-1$ has no general efficiency connotations.

Feldstein's (1980) model compares the cost, measured by a representative individual's willingness to pay, of increasing the consumption of some preferred good through government expenditure versus private giving. The effectiveness of the two types of expenditure is allowed to differ. His model, like Atkinson's, implies that a subsidy for charitable contributions is desirable under certain conditions, particularly when the government is less efficient in provision, when labor supply is more sensitive to the marginal tax rate, and when there is no preexisting subsidy. Feldstein points out that these findings conflict with the view that all "tax expenditures" should be eliminated. Significantly, Feldstein's model implies that the optimal subsidy does not depend on the price elasticity of giving.

### Other Efficiency-Related Considerations

More generally, issues related to administrability or neutrality are proper considerations in the design of tax incentives for contributions. Administrability covers such issues as the compliance and administrative costs of tax provisions. As an illustration, proposals that would specify differing rates of subsidy for different types of charitable organizations might well entail higher enforcement costs. Alternatively, the extension of a tax subsidy for charitable gifts to low-income households might require significant increases in record keeping by taxpayers.

Neutrality arises as an issue particularly in the treatment of different types of charitable gifts. Long (1977) notes, for example, that the charitable deduction in the income tax provides neutral treatment as between gifts of time and money since the value of either kind of gift is excluded in the calculation of taxable income.[11] Thus any important change in the tax

---

10. See especially Atkinson 1976, p. 25.
11. Boskin (1976, p. 50) makes a similar point.

incentive for contributions in any major tax could distort taxpayers' choices among lifetime gifts, volunteering, bequests, and even gifts made through a corporation. Another way of putting this point is that such tax incentives may affect the various tax bases. The elimination of the charitable deduction in the estate tax might well increase the amount of wealth given away during life, thus reducing the size of estates.[12]

### 8.2.3 Distributional Aspects of Tax Incentives

The charitable deduction has come in for sustained and vigorous criticism for its alleged favoritism toward high-income taxpayers. Because the tax savings per dollar obtained from the deduction rises with one's marginal tax rate, high-income taxpayers enjoy a bigger proportional tax reduction in their giving than taxpayers at lower income levels. One critic (Nielson 1979, p. 16) states:

> the so-called "tax incentives" for charitable giving which are now embodied in the Internal Revenue Code are so extravagantly discriminatory as between poor and rich donors that for the social-action movements they are effectively meaningless as a help in soliciting individual gifts.
>
> The tax system as a whole is of no assistance in enabling them to be self-supporting through the contributions of their own members. Rather, it condemns them to dependence on baronial benefactors.

Others point out, however, that the differing rates of subsidy are merely an inevitable by-product of the progressive rate structure itself. If successive amounts are taxed at higher and higher rates, then a reduction of a dollar of taxable income must produce a bigger tax reduction at higher incomes.[13] Clearly this would not be the case with a tax credit, a fact that has led some critics of the deduction to favor a credit over the deduction on distributional grounds.[14]

It is important to ask whether this differential subsidy effect has any relevance for distributional equity. In doing so, it is useful to distinguish two kinds of effects resulting from the deduction: effects on the tax liabilities of taxpayers and effects of changes in giving patterns. On the "tax side" the deduction affects taxpayers in much the same way a price reduction does: there is both an income and a substitution effect. The income effect is associated with the improvement in utility for a taxpayer who makes donations, as illustrated in figure 2.3. The substitution effect is the change in the relative price of giving. This substitution effect has no importance for distributional equity per se; it is important primarily for its efficiency implications. Its only distributional importance is in its effect on the pattern of support for charitable organizations, discussed below.

12. See Boskin 1976 for a discussion of this point.
13. See, for example, Wagner 1977, p. 2344.
14. See, for example, Vickrey 1947, pp. 130–31, and Donee Group 1977, p. 72.

By contrast, there are clear distributional consequences in the deduction's income effect. These are reflected in the effect of the deduction on tax liabilities. If the charitable deduction were eliminated the distribution of taxable income would change, and along with it the measured progressivity of the income tax. As between any two taxpayers the elimination of the deduction would raise average rate progression[15] if

$$(2) \qquad m_2(G_2/Y_2) > m_1(G_1/Y_1),$$

where $Y$ is income, $m$ is marginal tax rate, $G$ is the level of contributions after elimination of the deduction, and the lower- and higher-income taxpayers are denoted by 1 and 2, respectively. In order to see the likely effects on progressivity, table 8.1 shows how tax liabilities would change, based on the simulation model presented in chapter 3. Revenues are held constant in each simulation by means of proportional changes in tax rates. The results show that it is quite likely that eliminating the deduction would in fact increase the progressivity of the income tax. Accounting for the anticipated fall in contributions, those simulations imply that tax liabilities for taxpayers with incomes under about $30,400 would decline due to the overall reduction in tax rates made possible by the expansion of the tax base. For taxpayers with incomes over $36,500, taxes would rise. Conversion to a tax credit would increase tax progressivity even more. It is clear, therefore, that the existence and form of the incentive accorded to charitable contributions has effects on tax progressivity. While it would certainly be possible to neutralize the impact of any change in the charita-

**Table 8.1**     **Ratio of Taxes under Two Proposals to Actual Taxes in 1983, by Income**

| Income (thousands)[a] | Elimination of Deduction | 20 Percent Tax Credit |
|---|---|---|
| $6.1 under 12.2 | 0.97 | 0.91 |
| $12.2 under 18.3 | 0.98 | 0.96 |
| $18.3 under 24.3 | 0.98 | 0.97 |
| $24.3 under 30.4 | 0.99 | 0.99 |
| $30.4 under 36.5 | 1.00 | 0.99 |
| $36.5 under 60.9 | 1.01 | 1.02 |
| $60.9 under 121.7 | 1.01 | 1.03 |
| $121.7 under 243.4 | 1.00 | 1.03 |
| $243.4 under 608.5 | 1.01 | 1.03 |
| $608.5 under 1217 | 1.03 | 1.05 |
| $1217 or more | 1.04 | 1.06 |
| All classes | 1.00 | 1.00 |

*Note:* Simulations use constant income and price elasticities. See chapter 3.
[a]Taxpayers under $6,100 have no tax liability under any of the simulated taxes.

15. Using the average rate progression measure, a tax is progressive if the average tax rate rises with income. See Musgrave and Musgrave 1980, p. 376.

ble deduction on tax progressivity by an appropriate restructuring in the tax schedule, it remains that the form of the incentive is a factor in determining the progressivity of the tax.

Tax incentives for giving may also have distributional consequences in their effect on giving patterns. Although the structure of net prices resulting from a tax incentive has no direct distributional effect on donors, the pattern of prices can affect the distribution of charitable support to various groups of charitable organizations. Because the present deduction results in net prices that fall with income, charities and charitable activities favored by the wealthy receive disproportionate encouragement. The result, in Vickrey's (1947, p. 131) words, is "a serious plutocratic bias to the activities of privately supported philanthropic, educational, and religious institutions."

To identify this bias is not to determine its ultimate distributional effect, however. A complete assessment of the distributional impact requires an examination of who ultimately benefits from the programs of charitable organizations. It is quite possible, as Schaefer (1968, p. 27) in fact suggests, that the charitable activities favored by the wealthy are more redistributive than organizations supported by lower-income taxpayers.[16] Unfortunately, little research into the distribution of benefits from charitable programs is available. Fragmentary evidence presented in chapter 2 on the distribution of church expenditures suggests that a significant portion of expenditures by religious groups is used in support of congregational needs rather than redistribution, but this may be a poor measure of the distribution of actual benefits. It is quite conceivable that charities favored by the wealthy have no larger redistributive component.

Finally, it is possible that the examination of the distributional impact of the charitable deduction should go beyond conventionally measured economic benefits to include the distribution of economic power. Some criticisms of the current deduction clearly imply that the present tax incentives for contributions have the effect of concentrating power at upper income levels.[17] This possibility is most evident in the private foundation. Simon writes (1978, p. 5):

> We have to acknowledge the fact that private economic power is being deployed, often dynastically, through the device of the charitable foundation and the power it gives the founder and the founder's family to select the objects of their charitable bounty and to manage the charitable assets.

He concludes that, while the legal form and tax treatment of private foundations make it easier to achieve power, the "spectre of privilege" applies

---

16. Boskin (1976, p. 50) also emphasizes the importance of identifying the beneficiaries of charitable programs, in the context of his discussion of the estate tax.

17. See, for example, Schaefer 1968, p. 25; Donee Group 1977; and Nielson 1979.

to some degree in all tax subsidies for giving available to wealthy taxpayers (Simon 1978, pp. 17, 27). Still, one would expect that the distributional impact of a tax credit would be different from that of a deduction.

## 8.3  Conclusion

Federal tax policy has a substantial impact on the level and distribution of charitable giving in the United States. The empirical analysis discussed in this study suggests that support for charitable organizations responds both to explicit tax incentives for charitable contributions and to general changes in effective tax schedules. Certainly responses of this sort are important for assessing the implications of actual or proposed tax provisions on the nonprofit sector.

In the normative evaluation of tax policy from the viewpoint of society as a whole, such behavioral response is only one of a number of considerations. Efficiency and distributional equity are the two principal criteria for judging the desirability of tax incentives for charitable giving. The present deductions in the income and estate taxes have effects on the overall progressivity of those taxes, and the degree of behavioral response to tax incentives is relevant in measuring this effect. The differential pricing of contributions arising from the deduction is not itself an equity issue, but this price structure has distributional implications due to the particular pattern of contributions that are encouraged and the benefits that are enjoyed as a result. Again, the degree of behavioral response determines the importance of this distributional effect. In judging the efficiency of tax incentives for contributions, the magnitude of the price elasticity of charitable contributions is only one of several important factors that need to be considered. Others include the external benefits derived from charitable giving, the value of diversity in the provision of services, the effectiveness of such giving compared to government expenditures, and the distributional impact on donors and recipients. Except under very special assumptions, it is impossible to state any simple relationship between the price elasticity and the efficiency of tax incentives for charitable giving.

The United States is distinctive among Western countries in its reliance on nonprofit institutions to perform major social functions. This reliance is rooted in American history and is fostered by federal tax provisions for charitable giving. This study had demonstrated that changes in tax policy—effected through legislation or inflation—can have a significant impact on the level and composition of giving. As long as the nonprofit sector retains its important role in the United States, understanding the effect of the tax structure on charitable giving will be an essential part of the study of public policy in education, health, and many areas of social welfare. Whether or not taxes are an explicit part of policy in any of these areas, taxes are certainly an important implicit component.

# Appendixes

## Appendix A
### Description of Pooled Data Set for Individual Contributions

The basic data source for the pooled sample covering contributions by individuals was the U.S. Internal Revenue Service's *Statistics of Income* tabulations by income class for selected years between 1948 and 1980. Data on itemized deductions were included in the reports for even years between 1948 and 1972 and for each year beginning in 1973. The number of income classes per year ranged from 12 to 49, giving a total number of class-year observations of 495. The observations in the pooled sample are averages pertaining to all itemizers within a given gross income class. For each class, average values of income, exemptions, and deductions are used to calculate a tax liability and a marginal tax rate. So as to apply to the first dollar of giving, both calculations are made assuming contributions were zero. The tax calculation routine uses tax schedules applying to each year for married taxpayers filing jointly. In years with tax surcharges, marginal tax rates were adjusted to reflect their effect.

An additional variable measuring per capita federal expenditures on welfare, education, and health was taken from the U.S. Bureau of the

Table A.1    Variable Definitions and Means for Pooled Data Set for Individual Contributions

|  | Full Sample | Net Income ≥ $4000 |
|---|---|---|
| Net income (Y) = adjusted gross income less tax liability if no contributions, in 1972 dollars | 74,686 | 91,318 |
| Logarithm of net income | 9.62 | 10.12 |
| Price (P) = 1 minus marginal tax rate if no contributions | 0.65 | 0.60 |
| Logarithm of price | −0.58 | −0.68 |
| Charitable giving (G) | 24,634 | 30,240 |
| Logarithm of giving | 6.50 | 7.30 |
| Per capita federal welfare expenditures = per capita direct and intergovernmental amounts for welfare, education, and health | 103.7 | 105.2 |

Census (1952–80) to measure federal spending in areas close to those in which many nonprofit organizations operate.

For estimation, all dollar figures were converted to 1972 dollars using the GNP price deflator. The means for the entire sample and a subsample based on classes with average incomes $4000 and above are given below. Classes with average incomes below $4000 were omitted because of the unusual circumstances that would typically be associated with very-low-income itemizers.

# Appendix B
## *Means, Estimated Coefficients, Variances, and Covariances for Individual Giving Equations, 1975*

| Variable | Mean |
|---|---|
| $\ln Y$ | 10.4384 |
| $\ln (G + 10)$ | 6.39861 |
| $\ln P$ | $-0.551671$ |
| $(\ln Y)(\ln P)$ | $-6.06453$ |
| $(\ln P)^2$ | 0.431233 |
| $(\ln Y)^2$ | 109.937 |

*Constant-elasticity form*

$$\ln G10 = \underset{\substack{(0.052) \\ (1)}}{-1.268 \ln P} + \underset{\substack{(0.018) \\ (2)}}{0.767 \ln Y} + \ldots$$

Relevant variances and covariances

|   | 1 | 2 |
|---|---|---|
| 1 | .00274055 | — |
| 2 | .000810734 | .000326516 |

*Variable-elasticity form*

$$\ln G10 = \underset{(0.266)}{0.706 \ln Y} + \underset{(0.629)}{4.306 \ln P} - \underset{(0.067)}{0.538 \ln Y \ln P}$$

$$- \underset{(0.124)}{0.247 (\ln P)^2} - \underset{(0.0132)}{0.0140 (\ln Y)^2} + \ldots$$

Relevant variances and covariances

|   | 1 | 2 | 3 | 4 | 5 |
|---|---|---|---|---|---|
| 1 | .0705098 | | | | |
| 2 | .132290 | .395040 | | | |
| 3 | − .0123079 | − .0408286 | .00448628 | | |
| 4 | − .00783861 | − .0462467 | .00633514 | .0152881 | |
| 5 | − .00346019 | − .00707766 | .000686385 | .000563653 | .000173322 |


# Appendix C
## *Volunteering and Giving in a Simple Model of Individual Behavior*

The theory of labor supply provides a useful framework for incorporating decisions concerning giving and volunteering in the presence of an income tax. It is convenient to begin with an individual who values hours of leisure $(H_1)$, hours spent volunteering $(H_v)$, his montary contributions $(D)$, and the consumption of other goods $(X)$:

(A1) $$U = U(X, D, H_v, H_1).$$

If this individual has a wage $w$, faces a tax rate $t$, and can itemize his deductions in calculating taxable income, his budget constraint is

(A2) $$X = [w(H^0 - H_1 - H_v) + I - D](1-t),$$

where $H^0$ is the total number of hours available and $I$ is exogenous non-wage income. Where $U_x$ is the marginal utility of $X$, $U_v$ is the marginal utility of $H_v$, and so forth, the familiar first-order conditions assuming interior solutions are:

(A3) $$U_x - \mu = 0,$$

(A4) $$U_D - \mu (1-t) = 0,$$

(A5) $$U_v - \mu (1-t)w = 0,$$

(A6) $$U_1 - \mu (1-t)w = 0.$$

The tax's incentive effect on donations is shown by the fact that in equilibrium the marginal rate of substitution between dollars spent on consumption and dollars donated is $U_D/U_X = (1-t)$ rather than one. The marginal rate of substitution between volunteering and donations is $U_v/U_D = w$, the same that it would be in the absence of taxation. For this reason, as Long (1977) points out, it is neutral to allow a deduction for gifts of money but not a deduction for gifts of time since there is already an implicit deduction in the nontaxation of imputed income from the activity.

Consider now a taxpayer who is not allowed to deduct monetary donations. In this case the budget constraint is

(A7)    $$X = [w(H^0 - H_1 - H_v) + I](1 - t) - D.$$

One first-order condition is changed:

(A8)    $$U_D - \mu = 0.$$

Since the marginal rate of substitution between donations and consumption in this case is unity, the tax has no price effect. The other important change is that the marginal rate of substitution between volunteering and donations becomes $U_v/U_D = (1 - t)w$.

In terms of this simple model, it is possible to specify what factors will affect an individual's volunteer effort. The first-order condition in (A5), which applies regardless of the deductibility of donations, can be rewritten as:

(A9)    $$B_v = (1 - t)w,$$

where $B_v = U_v/\mu$ is the individual's marginal valuation of an hour of volunteer work and the net wage $((1 - t)w)$ is the shadow price of time, or the marginal cost of volunteer effort. From this, it is possible to see that volunteer effort will *increase* if a) the marginal utility of income falls, b) the tax rate increases, c) the gross wage falls, or d) the marginal utility of volunteering increases.

Figure 4.2 illustrates the analysis for the special case of a separable utility function in which charity is a composite commodity $C(D, H_v)$. Utility is

(A10)    $$U(X, H_1, C(D, H_v)).$$

This special case of *(A10)* makes it possible to examine the individual's choice between donations and volunteering given an amount of "full income" (monetary income plus nonworking time) donated to charity. In the absence of a deduction for contributions, the budget set defined by this amount of full income is given by $D + (1 - t)w H_v = k^0$, where $D$ is again donations, $(1 - t)w$ is the net wage or shadow price of time, $H_v$ is hours of volunteering, and $k^0$ is a constant.

# Appendix D

## Description of National Study of Philanthropy and Related Transformations

The National Study of Philanthropy, conducted by the Survey Research Center at the University of Michigan, is described in detail in Morgan, Dye, and Hybels (1977). This appendix describes special computations used to calculate tax variables for the households in the file and presents mean values for variables used in equations in the text.

For the present study, it was necessary to calculate both the tax liabilities of households and their marginal tax rates. Because the survey did not include questions about all of the variables related to taxable income and tax liability, it was necessary to approximate some of them. Income in the survey is classified into fourteen intervals. (See Morgan, Dye, and Hybels 1977, p. 28). To convert these intervals to a continuous variable, households were assigned the mean adjusted gross income (AGI) for each income interval, as reported in the *Statistics of Income—1973, Individual Income Tax Returns* (U.S. Internal Revenue Service 1976, p. 7). These means are given in the third column of table A.2 for each income interval.

In order to calculate taxable income, it was necessary to estimate deductions for the itemizing taxpayers. The deduction for mortgage interest was calculated as a proportion of the household's mortgage as reported in the survey. A 5 percent interest-to-mortgage ratio was used, following experiments with several proportions and comparing the estimates to averages published in the *Statistics of Income*. Based on similar experiments, the

**Table A.2    Income Intervals for National Study of Philanthropy Sample**

| Income Class | Interval | Average AGI | Deductions Ratio |
|---|---|---|---|
| 1 | Under $1000 | 552 | 1.20 |
| 2 | $1000–1999 | 1,489 | 1.02 |
| 3 | $2000–3999 | 2,969 | .427 |
| 4 | $4000–7999 | 5,905 | .334 |
| 5 | $8000–9999 | 8,974 | .168 |
| 6 | $10,000–14,999 | 12,365 | .134 |
| 7 | $15,000–19,999 | 17,191 | .114 |
| 8 | $20,000–29,999 | 23,685 | .101 |
| 9 | $30,000–49,999 | 36,174 | .103 |
| 10 | $50,000–99,999 | 66,004 | .110 |
| 11 | $100,000–199,999 | 130,363 | .116 |
| 12 | $200,000–499,999 | 280,255 | .148 |
| 13 | $500,000–999,999 | 668,114 | .145 |
| 14 | $1,000,000 or more | 2,004,582 | .146 |

average property tax rate applied to reported house value was 1.3 percent (0.013). All other itemized deductions other than contributions were estimated as a proportion of AGI, where the proportion varied for each class. This set of proportions, calculated from figures for itemizers in the *Statistics of Income* (U.S. Internal Revenue Service 1976, p. 50) is given in the last column of table A.2. Exemptions were calculated from data on the number of adult taxpayers and dependents and on the age of husband and wife.

Taxable income (calculated without reference to contributions) was AGI minus exemptions and itemized deductions for those who itemized and AGI minus exemptions and the standard deduction for nonitemizers. Households were classified as single, joint, and head-of-household returns. By applying the appropriate 1973 tax table to taxable income, tax liability and marginal tax rate could be calculated. Price is normally one minus the marginal tax rate for itemizers and one for nonitemizers, but this was modified (as described in the text) for taxpayers for whom charitable contributions constituted the difference between itemizing and not itemizing.

Table A.3 lists the principal variables from the Michigan survey sample used in the present study.

| Table A.3 | Selected Unweighted Sample Means | |
|---|---|---|
| | All Households with Women | Households with Wives Not Employed |
| TOTAL | 2323 | 1122 |
| *Continuous variables* | | |
| Net income | 34,142 | 49,847 |
| Price | 0.755 | 0.681 |
| Age (women) | 37.7 | 48.3 |
| Hours of market work | 12.3 | 0.0 |
| Hours of volunteer work (women) | 71.3 | 103.4 |
| Number of children under 18 | 1.02 | 1.14 |
| *Dichotomous variables* | | |
| Any children under 5 | 0.158 | 0.175 |
| High school graduate only (women) | 0.437 | 0.602 |
| College graduate (women) | 0.390 | 0.235 |
| Head's parents contributed | 0.777 | 0.775 |
| New in neighborhood | 0.148 | 0.111 |

# Appendix E
## Calculation of Marginal Tax Rates on Corporate Income

The basic method of calculating marginal tax rates was to apply the tax schedules to mean values of income and other variables for each class in each year. While this approach is an improvement over simply using average tax rates or top-bracket rates, there are several limitations that remain. As noted in the text, it was impossible to account in detail for the numerous provisions of the tax law applying to insurance companies and other special classes of returns or to account for minor differences in the definitions of various tax bases within any given year. A second limitation to the use of average data for asset classes is that nonlinear functions of means will not in general be equal to means of those functions applied to disaggregated data. While the mean of taxable income falls in a certain bracket, for instance, it is possible that some individual companies fall outside that bracket. Where tax brackets have large discontinuities, calculation on the basis of mean values will be less reliable. In the present application, calculation on the basis of means gave much more accurate estimates of tax liability for the normal income tax than the excess-profits taxes. Thus when absolute amounts of the latter taxes were used in calculation of subsequent tax bases, means of actual taxes paid were used rather than calculated amounts.

Since some components of the corporate tax were often deductible in computing other parts, the marginal tax rate on income is not always the simple sum of each component's tax rate. The rules for deductibility are reflected in the equations below, where the component marginal tax rates are $RNT$ (normal tax), $RST$ (surtax), $RDEPT$ (declared-value excess-profits tax), $RWEPT$ (wartime excess-profits tax), and $RUNIT$ (undistributed net-profits tax).

1936–37
$$R = RDEPT + RNT + RUNIT (1 - RDEPT - RNT).$$

1938–39
$$R = RDEPT + RNT (1 - RDEPT).$$

1940
$$R = RDEPT + RWEPT (1 - RNT (1 - RDEPT)) + RNT (1 - RDEPT).$$

1941
$$R = RDEPT + RWEPT + RNT (1 - RDEPT - RWEPT) + RST (1 - RDEPT - RWEPT).$$

1942–45

(a) If subject to wartime excess-profits tax:

$$R = RDEPT\,(1 - RNT - RST) + RWEPT.$$

(b) If not subject to wartime excess profits tax:

$$R = RDEPT\,(1 - RNT - RST) + RNT + RST.$$

(c) If total tax is greater than 80 percent of net income,

$$R = .72\,(= (.8)\,(.9)).$$

1946–49

$$R = RNT + RST.$$

1950–53

$$R = RNT + RST + RWEPT.$$

1954–78

$$R = RNT + RST.$$

1979–80

$$R = RNT.$$

The wartime excess-profits tax during World War II is worthy of special mention. Companies could choose between two basic methods of calculating the excess-profits tax base. One method used a percentage of "invested capital" while the other was based on an average of previous years' income as well as the change in capital stock. Since most firms used the former method, it was applied in calculations for the present study.[1]

The credit allowed under this method is equal to "equity-invested capital" plus half of "debt-invested capital." For the purpose of tax calculation, equity-invested capital was approximated by capital stock and debt-invested capital was approximated by the liabilities other than capital stock. The credit was then calculated by applying tables for various years to the total invested-capital figure. Data published for 1940 on the amount of this credit by asset class showed that the average calculated credit was close to the average credit for firms paying the excess-profits tax. For example, the companies with assets between $500,000 and $1 million paying excess-profits taxes had an average excess-profits credit of about $35,900 (U.S. Internal Revenue Service, *Statistics of Income—1940, Corporation Income Tax Returns* (Part II), p. 251). The tax calculation algorithm estimated the average for that class to be $37,200. The average for the $10–50 million class was $1.16 million, compared to a calculated value of $1.08 million.

As noted above, the sum of the excess-profits tax, normal tax, and surtax was limited to 80 percent of net income; however, none of the class means in the present sample reached that constraint. Finally, a postwar refund of 10 percent of the excess-profits tax is reflected in the calculated

---

1. In 1945, for example, over two-thirds of companies paying excess-profits tax used the invested-capital method (U.S. Internal Revenue Service, *Statistics of Income—Corporation Income Tax Returns* 1950 (Part II), p. 358).

rates for 1942–45. For 1942 and 1943, this refund was immediately available to retire debt, and in 1944 and 1945 was an immediate tax credit. (U.S. Internal Revenue Service, *Statistics of Income—1945, Corporation Income Tax Returns* 1950 (Part II), p. 459).

To illustrate the calculations of marginal tax rates, table A.4 shows the calculation of marginal tax rates for two asset classes ($100,000–250,000 and $1,000,000–5,000,000) for the years 1939 and 1953. In each case,

**Table A.4**    **Calculation of Marginal Tax Rates for 1939 and 1953, Two Asset Classes**

|  | $100,000 –250,000 | $1,000,000 –5,000,000 |
|---|---|---|
| *1939* | | |
| Average net income + contributions | | |
| (*NI*) | $10,346 | $114,661 |
| Average capital stock (*CS*) | 65,200 | 671,235 |
| Declared-value excess-profits tax rate | | |
| (*RDEPT*) | .12 | .12 |
| 0 if *NI* < .10 *CS*, | | |
| .06 if .10 *CS* ≤ *NI* < .15 *CS*, | | |
| .12 if *NI* > .15 *CS*. | | |
| Income tax rate (*RNT*) | .14 | .19 |
| where Base *B* = *NI* − declared-value excess-profits tax | | |
| 0 if *B* < 0, | | |
| .125 if 0 < *B* ≤ $5000, | | |
| .140 if $5000 < *B* ≤ $20,000, | | |
| .160 if $20,000 < *B* ≤ $25,000, | | |
| .190 if *B* > $25,000. | | |
| Marginal tax rate | .243 | .287 |
| (*RDEPT* + *RNT*(1 − *RDEPT*)) | | |
| | | |
| *1953* | | |
| Average net income + contributions | | |
| (*NI*) | $13,085 | 154,937 |
| Income tax rate (*RNT*) | .30 | .30 |
| Surtax rate (*RST*) | 0 | .22 |
| 0 if *NI* < $25,000, | | |
| .22 if *NI* ≥ $25,000. | | |
| Excess-profits tax rate (*REPT*) | 0 | 0 |
| where *B* = *NI* − (83 percent of previous 4-year average of net income + 12 percent of increase in capital stuck over previous 3-year average), | | |
| 0 if *B* < $25,000, | | |
| .30 if *B* ≥ $25,000. | | |
| Marginal tax rate | .30 | .52 |

average net income is adjusted by adding average contribution back in. For the 1939 calculation, average capital stock was also necessary. In 1939 corporations in the $100,000–250,000 asset class had average net income of $10,346. Given their average capital stock, they were subject to a 12 percent marginal tax rate on net income from the declared-value excess-profits tax and a 14 percent rate on net income in the normal income tax. Using equation (11′) above, the overall rate was 0.243. Corporations in the $1–5 million asset class had average net income of $114,661, for an overall rate of 0.287.

The calculation of marginal tax rates is also illustrated for 1953, a year in which corporations faced a normal tax, a surtax, and an excess-profits tax based on increases in profits from a base period. The calculated marginal rates for the average firm in the two classes are 0.30 and 0.52. Although some firms in each class paid excess-profits tax, no excess-profits tax was due for the average net income of either of these classes, thus illustrating the disadvantage of calculating marginal rates using class averages when the rates are discontinuous and there is variation among firms.

**Appendix F     Top Marginal Tax Rates on Corporate Net Income, 1936–77**

| Years | Normal Tax | Surtax | Declared-Value Excess Profits | Excess Profits | Total, with Interations[a] |
|---|---|---|---|---|---|
| 1936–37 | .15 | .22[b] | .12 | — | .472 |
| 1938–39 | .19 | — | .12 | — | .287 |
| 1940 | .24 | — | .132 | .50 | .736 |
| 1941 | .24 | .07 | .132 | .60 | .815 |
| 1942–43 | .24 | .16 | .132 | .81[c] | .889[e] |
| 1944–45 | .24 | .16 | .132 | .855[c] | .932[e] |
| 1946–49 | .24 | .14 | — | — | .38 |
| 1950 | .30 | .19 | — | .15[d] | .64 |
| 1951 | .2875 | .22 | — | .30 | .808 |
| 1952–53 | .30 | .22 | — | .30 | .82 |
| 1954–63 | .30 | .22 | — | — | .52 |
| 1964 | .22 | .28 | — | — | .50 |
| 1965–74 | .22 | .26 | — | — | .48 |
| 1975–78 | .20 | .28 | — | — | .48 |
| 1979–80 | .46 | — | — | — | .46 |

[a]Calculated for return with top marginal tax rates for each component. Because of interactions, this may exceed the maximum total tax rate based on class calculations. See Appendix E.

[b]Undistributed net-income surtax.

[c]Includes 10 percent post-war tax credit.

[d]Prorated. Took effect 1 July 1950.

[e]Based on case (a). See Appendix E.

**Appendix G**　　**Comparison of Aggregate Tax-Rate Variables**

| Year | Marginal Tax[a] Rate | Average Tax[b] Rate | Nelson Estimate of Marginal Tax Rate |
|------|------|------|------|
| 1936 | .276 | .110 | .150 |
| 1937 | .307 | .114 | .150 |
| 1938 | .216 | .133 | .190 |
| 1939 | .246 | .140 | .190 |
| 1940 | .462 | .228 | .415 |
| 1941 | .626 | .397 | .678 |
| 1942 | .722 | .510 | .677 |
| 1943 | .717 | .555 | .717 |
| 1944 | .888 | .549 | .710 |
| 1945 | .894 | .488 | .664 |
| 1946 | .382 | .326 | .380 |
| 1947 | .367 | .329 | .380 |
| 1948 | .377 | .329 | .380 |
| 1949 | .376 | .321 | .380 |
| 1950 | .607 | .393 | .602 |
| 1951 | .755 | .488 | .673 |
| 1952 | .715 | .474 | .645 |
| 1953 | .726 | .475 | .640 |
| 1954 | .508 | .426 | .520 |
| 1955 | .508 | .432 | .520 |
| 1956 | .507 | .426 | .520 |
| 1957 | .507 | .423 | .520 |
| 1958 | .496 | .433 | .520 |
| 1959 | .504 | .441 | .520 |
| 1960 | .499 | .440 | .520 |
| 1961 | .495 | .424 | .520 |
| 1962 | .484 | .426 | .520 |
| 1963 | .496 | .429 | .520 |
| 1964 | .481 | .406 | .500 |
| 1965 | .464 | .392 | — |
| 1966 | .464 | .393 | — |
| 1967 | .463 | .385 | — |
| 1968 | .464 | .417 | — |
| 1969 | .463 | .422 | — |
| 1970 | .462 | .398 | — |
| 1971 | .464 | .388 | — |
| 1972 | .464 | .380 | — |
| 1973 | .466 | .379 | — |
| 1974 | .468 | .386 | — |
| 1975 | .457 | .390 | — |
| 1976 | .460 | .396 | — |
| 1977 | .459 | .394 | — |
| 1978 | .458 | .393 | — |
| 1979 | .435 | .373 | — |
| 1980 | .434 | .354 | — |

*Source:* Col. (3), Nelson 1970, Appendix A, p. 97.

[a]Where $R_i$ is the marginal tax rate for asset class $i$ and $NI_i$ is average net income for the class:

$$R = \frac{\sum_i R_i NI_i}{\sum_i NI_i}.$$

[b]Normal tax, surtax, and excess-profits taxes divided by net income.

# References

Aaron, Henry. 1972. Federal encouragement of private giving. In *Tax impacts on philanthropy.* Princeton: Tax Institute of America.

Abrams, Burton A., and Mark D. Schmitz. 1978. The "crowding-out" effect of government transfers on private charitable contributions. *Public Choice* 33:30–39.

———. 1983. The crowding-out effect of governmental transfers on private charitable contributions: Cross-section evidence. Typescript, University of Delaware.

Americans volunteer: A profile. 1982. *Public Opinion,* February/March, 21–31.

Andrews, F. Emerson. 1950. *Philanthropic giving.* New York: Russell Sage Foundation.

———. 1952. *Corporate giving.* New York: Russell Sage Foundation.

Andrews, William D. 1972. Personal deductions in an ideal income tax. *Harvard Law Review* 86:309–85.

Arthur Andersen and Company. 1977. Overview of governmental support and financial regulation of philanthropic organizations in selected nations. In *Research papers,* Commission on Private Philanthropy and Public Needs, 2:2975–93. Washington, D.C. Treasury Department.

———. 1982. *Tax economics of charitable giving.* Chicago: Arthur Andersen and Company.

Atkinson, Anthony B. 1976. The income tax treatment of charitable contributions. In *Public and urban economics: Essays in honor of William S. Vickrey,* ed. R. E. Grieson. New York: D. C. Heath.

Atkinson, Anthony B., and Joseph E. Stiglitz. 1980. *Lectures on public economics.* New York: McGraw-Hill.

Atwater, H. Brewster, Jr. 1982. The corporation as good citizen. In *Corporate philanthropy.* Washington, D.C.: Council on Foundations.

Auten, Gerald F., and Charles T. Clotfelter. 1982. Permanent versus transitory tax effects and the realization of capital gains. *Quarterly Journal of Economics* 98:613–32.

Baird, Peter D. 1972. Charitable deductions for *pro bona publico* professional services: An updated carrot and stick approach. *Texas Law Review* 50:441–47.

Barthold, Thomas, and Robert Plotnick. 1984. Estate taxation and other determinants of charitable bequests. *National Tax Journal* 37:225–37.

Becker, Gary S. 1974. A theory of social interactions. *Journal of Political Economy* 82:1063–93.

Bennett, Edmund C. 1977. Treatment of volunteer services and related expenses under the Internal Revenue Code. In *Research papers,* Commission on Private Philanthropy and Public Needs, 4:2287–96. Washington, D.C.: Treasury Department.

Bennett, James T., and Manuel H. Johnson. 1980. Corporate contributions: Some additional considerations. *Public Choice* 35:137–43.

Berger, Peter L., and Richard John Neuhaus. 1972. *To empower people: The role of mediating structures in public policy.* Washington, D.C.: American Enterprise Institute.

Bird, R. M., and M. W. Bucovetsky. 1976. *Canadian tax reform and private philanthropy.* Toronto: Canadian Tax Foundation.

Bolnick, Bruce R. 1975. Toward a behavioral theory of philanthropic activity. In *Altruism, morality, and economic theory,* ed. Edmund Phelps, 197–223. New York: Russell Sage Foundation.

———. 1978. Post-disaster cooperation: Utility interdependence, prices, and beyond. Typescript, Duke University.

Boskin, Michael J. 1976. Estate taxation and charitable bequests. *Journal of Public Economics* 5:27–56.

———. 1977. Estate taxation and charitable bequests. In *Research papers,* Commission on Private Philanthropy and Public Needs, 3:1453–84. Washington, D.C.: Treasury Department.

Boskin, Michael J., and Martin S. Feldstein. 1977. Effects of the charitable deduction on contributions by low-income and middle-income households: Evidence from the National Survey of Philanthropy. In *Research papers,* Commission on Private Philanthropy and Public Needs, 3:1441–52. Washington, D.C.: Treasury Department.

———. 1978. Effects of the charitable deduction on contributions by low income and middle income households: Evidence from the National Survey of Philanthropy. *Review of Economics and Statistics* 59:351–54.

Break, George F. 1957. Income taxes and incentives to work: An empirical study. *American Economic Review* 47:529–49.

———. 1977. Charitable contributions under the federal individual income tax: Alternative policy options. In *Research papers,* Commission on Private Philanthropy and Public Needs, 3:1521–39. Washington, D.C.: Treasury Department.

Brittain, John A. 1981. Comments. In *How taxes affect economic behavior*, ed. Henry J. Aaron and Joseph A. Pechman. Washington, D.C.: Brookings Institution.

Butler, Stuart M. 1980. *Philanthropy in America: The need for action*. Washington, D.C.: Heritage Foundation.

_____. 1981. Voluntarism and the Reagan economic program. *Backgrounder*, Nov.

Clotfelter, Charles T. 1980a. Explaining unselfish behavior: Crime and the helpful bystander. *Journal of Urban Economics* 8:196–212.

_____. 1980b. Tax incentives and charitable giving: Evidence from a panel of taxpayers. *Journal of Public Economics* 13:319–40.

_____. 1983a. Tax evasion and tax rates: An analysis of individual returns. *Review of Economics and Statistics* 65:363–73.

_____. 1983b. Tax-induced distortions and the business-pleasure borderline: The case of travel and entertainment. *American Economic Review* 73:1053–1065.

_____. 1984. Tax cut meets bracket creep: The rise and fall of marginal tax rates, 1964–1984. *Public Finance Quarterly* 12:131–52.

Clotfelter, Charles T., and Lester M. Salomon. 1982. The impact of the 1981 tax act on individual charitable giving. *National Tax Journal* 35:171–87.

Clotfelter, Charles T., and C. Eugene Steuerle. 1981. Charitable contributions. In *How taxes affect economic behavior*, ed. Henry J. Aaron and Joseph A. Pechman. Washington, D.C.: Brookings Institution.

Commission on Private Philanthropy and Public Needs. 1977. Commentary on commission recommendations. In *Research papers*, Commission on Private Philanthropy and Public Needs: 1:3–48. Washington, D.C.: Treasury Department.

*Congressional Record*. 1917 (7 Sept.); 1944 (3 and 19 May). Washington, D.C.

*Corporate support of higher education 1980*. 1981. New York: Council for Financial Aid to Education.

Corporation gifts to charities. 1935. *Social Service Review* 9:540–45.

Council on Foundations. 1977. Private foundations and the 1969 Tax Reform Act for Commission in Private Philanthropy and Public Needs. In *Research papers*, 3:1557–661. Washington, D.C.: Treasury Department.

Culyer, A. J., J. Wiseman, and J. W. Posnett. 1976. Charity and public policy in the UK: The law and the economics. *Social and Economic Administration* 10:32–50.

Cushman, John F., Jr. 1979. Charitable giving and philanthropic foundations: An economic analysis. Ph.D. dissertation, University of Virginia.

David, Martin, and Paul Menchik. 1981. Modelling household bequests. Paper presented at the Econometric Society meetings, December 28, Washington, D.C.

De Alessi, Louis. 1975. Toward a theory of postdisaster cooperation. *American Economic Review* 65:127–38.

Dennis, Barry, Gabriel Rudney, and Roy Wyscarver. 1982. Charitable contributions: The discretionary income hypothesis. Paper presented at meetings of the American Economic Association, December 28.

Dickinson, Frank G. 1970. *The changing position of philanthropy in the American economy.* New York: National Bureau of Economic Research.

Donee Group. 1977. Private philanthropy: Vital and innovative or passive and irrelevant. In *Research papers,* Commission on Private Philanthropy and Public Needs, 1:49–85. Washington, D.C.: Treasury Department.

Douty, Christopher M. 1972. Disasters and charity: Some aspects of cooperative economic behavior. *American Economic Review* 62:580–90.

Dye, Richard F. 1978. Personal charitable contributions: Tax effects and other motives. In *Proceedings of the Seventieth Annual Conference on Taxation,* pp. 311–21. Columbus: National Tax Association—Tax Institute of America.

————. 1980. Contributions of volunteer time: Some evidence on income tax effects. *National Tax Journal* 33:89–93.

Epstein, Marshall S. 1983–84. Preliminary income and tax statistics for 1982 individual income tax returns. *SOI Bulletin* 3, no 3: 11–22.

Falush, Peter. 1977. Trends in the finance of British charities. *National Westminister Bank Quarterly Review,* May:32–44.

Feenberg, Daniel. 1982. Identification in tax-price regression models: The case of charitable giving. National Bureau of Economic Research working paper.

Feldstein, Martin. 1975a. The income tax and charitable contributions: Part I—Aggregate and distributional effects. *National Tax Journal* 28:81–100.

————. 1975b. The income tax and charitable contributions: Part II—The impact on religious, educational, and other organizations. *National Tax Journal* 28:209–26.

————. 1977. Charitable bequests, estate taxation, and intergenerational wealth transfers. In *Research papers,* Commission on Private Philanthropy and Public Needs, 3:1485–1500. Washington, D.C.: Treasury Department.

————. 1980. A contribution to the "theory of tax expenditures": The case of charitable giving. In *The Economics of Taxation*, ed. Henry J. Aaron and Michael J. Boskin, 99–122. Washington, D.C.: Brookings Institution.

Feldstein, Martin, and Charles Clotfelter. 1976. Tax incentives and charitable contributions in the United States: A microeconometric analysis. *Journal of Public Economics* 5:1–26.

Feldstein, Martin, and Lawrence Lindsey. 1981. Simulating nonlinear tax rules and nonstandard behavior: An application to the tax treatment of charitable contributions. National Bureau of Economic Research Working Paper No. 682.

Feldstein, Martin, and Amy Taylor. 1976. The income tax and charitable contributions. *Econometrica* 44:1201–21.

Fiekowsky, Seymour. 1977. Pitfalls in the computation of "effective tax rates" paid by corporations. OTA Paper 23, Office of Tax Analysis, Treasury Department.

Fisher, Ronald. 1977. The combined state and federal income tax treatment of charitable contributions, 397–403. In *Proceedings of the National Tax Association*.

*Foundation directory.* 1967, 1971, 1975, 1977, 1979, 1981. New York: Russell Sage Foundation, 1967, 1971; New York: Foundation Center, 1975, 1977, 1979, 1981.

*Foundations today.* 1982. New York: Foundation Center.

Freemont-Smith, Marion R. 1965. *Foundations and government.* New York: Russell Sage Foundation.

⸻. 1972. *Philanthropy and the business corporation.* New York: Russell Sage Foundation.

Friedman, Milton. 1957. *A theory of the consumption function.* Princeton: Princeton University Press.

⸻. 1962. *Capitalism and freedom.* Chicago: University of Chicago Press.

Gallup Omnibus. 1979. *Survey of the public's recollection of 1978 charitable donations.* Princeton: Gallup Organization.

Gallup Organization. 1981. *Americans volunteer 1981.* Princeton, N. J.: Gallup Organization.

*Giving U.S.A.* 1981–83. New York: American Association of Fund-Raising Counsel, Inc.

Goldberg, Matthew S. 1979. Incentives and compensation of corporate managers: An application to charitable contributions. Typescript, University of Chicago.

Gonzalez, A. Miren, and Philip Tetlock. N.d. A literature review of altruism and helping behavior. Program in Non-profit Organizations Working Paper 16, New Haven, Institution for Social and Policy Studies.

Goode, Richard. 1976. *The individual income tax.* Washington, D.C.: Brookings Institution.

Griswold, Erwin J., and Michael J. Graetz. 1976. *Federal income taxation: Principles and policies.* Mineola, N.Y.: Foundation Press, Inc.

Gronau, Reuben. 1973. The intra family allocation of the housewives' time. *American Economic Review* 63:534–651.

Hammond, P. 1975. Charity: Altruism or cooperative egoism? In *Altruism, Morality, and Economic Theory,* ed. Edmund S. Phelps, 115–31. New York: Russell Sage Foundation.

Hansmann, Henry. 1981. Why are nonprofit organizations exempted from corporate income taxation? In *Nonprofit firms in a three sector economy,* ed. Michelle J. White, 115–34. Washington, D.C.: Urban Institute.

Harris, James F., and Anne Klepper. 1977. Corporate philanthropic public service activities. In *Research papers,* Commission in Private Philanthropy and Public Needs, 3:174–78. Washington, D.C.: Treasury Department. pp. 1741–88.

Hausman, Jerry A. 1981. Labor supply. In *How taxes affect economic behavior,* ed. Henry J. Aaron and Joseph A. Pechman, 27–72. Washington, D.C.: Brookings Institution.

Havrilesky, Thomas, Robert Schweitzer, and Scheffel Wright. 1973. The supply of and demand for voluntary labor in behalf of environmental quality. In *Proceedings of the Business and Economics Statistics Section of the American Statistical Association,* 170–79.

Heckman, James. 1979. Sample selection bias as a specification error. *Econometrica* 47:153–61.

Heckman, James J., and Thomas E. MaCurdy. 1980. New methods for estimating labor supply functions: A survey. Economics Research Center/NORC Discussion Paper.

Hirshleifer, Jack. 1978. Competition, cooperation, and conflict in economics and biology. *American Economic Review* 68:238–43.

Hochman, Harold M., and James D. Rodgers. 1969. Pareto optimal redistribution. *American Economic Review* 59:542–57.

———. 1973. Utility interdependence and income transfers through charity. In *Transfers in an urbanized economy: Theories and effects of the grants economy,* ed. Kenneth E. Boulding, Martin Pfaff, and Anita Pfaff, 63–77. Belmont, Calif.: Wadsworth Publishing Company.

———. 1977. The optimal treatment of charitable contributions. *National Tax Journal* 30:1–18.

Hodgkinson, Virginia Ann, and Murray S. Weitzman. 1984. *Dimensions of the independent sector.* Washington: Independent Sector.

Hood, R. D., S. A. Martin, and L. S. Osberg. 1977. Economic determinants of individual charitable donations in Canada. *Canadian Journal of Economics* 10:653–69.

Horvitz, Jerome S. 1974. Charity is good business. *Taxes* 52:249–54.

Hyman, Herbert H., and Charles R. Wright. 1971. Trends in voluntary association memberships of American adults: Replication based on secondary analysis of national sample surveys. *American Sociological Review* 36:191–206.

Interfaith Research Committee. 1977. A study of religious receipts and expenditures in the United States. In *Research papers,* Commission on Private Philanthropy and Public Needs, 1:365–450. Washington, D.C.: Treasury Department.

*Internal Revenue Acts, 1966–1970.* 1971. St. Paul, Minn.: West Publishing Company.

*Internal Revenue Code.* 1982. New York: Research Institute of America, Inc.

Ireland, T. T., and D. B. Johnson. 1970. *The economics of charity.* Blacksburg, Va.: Center for the Study of Public Choice.

Jantscher, Gerald R. 1967. *Trusts and estate taxation.* Washington, D.C.: Brookings Institution.

Johnson, J. A. 1982. The determinants of charitable giving with special emphasis on the income deduction under the income tax: A survey of the empirical literature. Working paper no. 82–29, McMaster University.

Johnson, Orace. 1966. Corporate philanthropy: An analysis of corporate contributions. *Journal of Business* 39:489–504.

Johnson, Orace, and Walter L. Johnson. 1970. The income elasticity of corporate philanthropy: Comment. *Journal of Finance* 25:149–52.

Kahn, C. Harry. 1960. *Personal deductions in the federal income tax.* Princeton: National Bureau of Economic Research.

Karl, Barry D., and Stanley N. Katz. 1981. The American private philanthropic foundation and the public sphere, 1890–1930. *Minerva* 19:236–70.

Keim, Gerald D., Roger E. Meiners, and Louis W. Frey. 1980. On the evaluation of corporate contributions. *Public Choice* 35:129–36.

Ketchum, David S. 1982. Fund raising in '82: Feast or famine? *Fund Raising Review,* February, 2–3.

Kmenta, Jan. 1971. *Elements of econometrics.* New York: Macmillan.

Kosters, Marvin. 1969. Effects of an income tax on labor suply. In *The taxation of income from capital* ed. Arnold C. Harberger and Martin J. Bailey. Washington, D.C.: Brookings Institution.

Kuh, E. 1959. The validity of cross sectionally estimated behavior in time series application. *Econometrica* 27:197–214.

Labovitz, John R. 1974. The impact of the private foundation provisions of the Tax Reform Act of 1969: Early empirical measurements. *Journal of Legal Studies* 3:63–105.

Lamale, Helen H., and Joseph A. Clorety, Jr. 1959. City families as givers. *Monthly labor review* 82:1303–11.

Landes, W. M., and R. A. Posner. 1978a. Salvors, finders, good samaritans and other rescuers: An economic study of law and altruism. *Journal of Legal Studies* 7:83–128.

———. 1978b. Altruism in law and economics. *American Economic Review* 68:417–21.

Levy, Ferdinand K., and Gloria M. Shatto. 1978. The evaluation of corporate contributions. *Public Choice* 33:19–28.

_____. 1980. The evaluation of corporate contributions: A reply. *Public Choice* 35:145–49.

Lewis, H. Gregg. 1969. Interes del empleador en las horas de trabajo del empleado (Employer interests in employee hours of work). *Cuadernos de economia* 6:38–54.

Liles, Kenneth, and Cynthia Blum. 1975. Development of the federal tax treatment of charities. *Law and contemporary problems* 39:6–56.

Lindsey, Lawrence B. 1981. Is the maximum tax on earned income effective? *National Tax Journal* 34:249–55.

Liston, Robert A. 1977. *The charity racket.* Nashville: Thomas Nelson, Inc.

Long, James E., and Frank A. Scott. 1982. The income tax and nonwage compensation. *Review of Economics and Statistics* 64:211–19.

Long, Stephen H. 1977. Income tax effects on donor choice of money and time contributions. *National Tax Journal* 30:207–11.

Long, Stephen H., and Russell F. Settle. 1979. Charitable contributions: The importance of relative income. Paper presented at the Econometric Society Meetings, December 1979.

Lynd, Robert S., and Helen Merrell Lynd. 1929. *Middletown.* New York: Harcourt, Brace.

Macauley, J., and L. Berkowitz. eds. 1970. *Altruism and helping behavior.* New York: Academic Press.

McDonald, John F., and Robert A. Moffitt. 1980. The uses of Tobit analysis. *Review of Economics and Statistics* 62:318–21.

McElroy, Katherine M., and John J. Siegfried. 1982a. The effect of firm size and mergers on corporate philanthropy. Working paper no. 82–W20, Department of Economics, Vanderbilt University.

_____. 1982b. The effect of firm size on corporate philanthropy. Working paper no. 82–W02, Department of Economics, Vanderbuilt University.

McFadden, Daniel. 1974. Conditional logit analysis of qualitative choice behavior. In *Frontiers in econometrics,* ed. Paul Zarembka, 105–42. New York: Academic Press.

McGuire, E. Patrick, and Nathan Weber. 1982. *Business voluntarism: Prospects for 1982.* New York: Conference Board, Inc.

McNees, Stephen K. 1973. Deductibility of charitable bequests. *National Tax Journal* 26:81–98.

Maddox, Katherine E. 1981. Corporate philanthropy. Ph.D. dissertation, Vanderbilt University.

Maddox, Katherine E., and John J. Siegfried. 1981. The effect of economic structure on corporate philanthropy. In *The economics of firm size, market structure, and social performance,* Bureau of Economics conference proceedings.

Menchik, Paul, and Burton A. Weisbrod. 1981. Volunteer labor supply in the provision of collective goods. In *Nonprofit firms in a three sector economy,* ed. Michelle J. White, 163–81. Washington, D.C.: Urban Institute.

———. 1982. Government crowding out and contributions of time—Or why do people work for free? Typescript, Michigan State University and University of Wisconsin.

Morgan, James N., Richard F. Dye, and Judith H. Hybels. 1977. Results from two national surveys on philanthropic activity. In *Research papers,* Commission on Private Philanthropy and Public Needs, 1:157–323. Washington, D.C.: Treasury Department.

Mueller, Marnie W. 1975. Economic determinants of volunteer work by women. *Signs* 1:325–38.

Musgrave, Richard A., and Peggy B. Musgrave. 1980. *Public finance in theory and practice.* New York: McGraw-Hill.

Myers, John H. 1977. Estate tax deduction for charitable benefits: Proposed limitations. In *Research papers,* Commission on Private Philanthropy and Public Needs, 4:2299–318. Washington, D.C.: Treasury Department.

National Study of Philanthropy. Unpublished survey data. See Morgan, Dye, and Hybels 1977.

Nelson, Ralph L. 1970. *Economic factors in the growth of corporation giving.* National Bureau of Economic Research Occasional Paper 111, New York, National Bureau of Economic Research and Russell Sage Foundation.

———. 1977a. A note on the estimation of personal giving. In *Research papers,* Commission on Private Philanthropy and Public Needs, 3:1501–13. Washington, D.C.: Treasury Department.

———. 1977b. Private giving in the American economy. In *Research papers,* Commission on Private Philanthropy and Public Needs, 1:115–155. Washington, D.C.: Treasury Department.

———. 1977c. Probable effect of extending the charitable contributions deduction to all tax return filers. Typescript, Queens College.

Nielson, Waldemer A. 1972. *The big foundations.* New York: Columbia University Press.

———. 1979. *The endangered sector.* New York: Columbia University Press.

———. *1980 U.S. master tax guide.* 1979. Chicago: Commerce Clearing House.

Obler, Jeffrey, 1981. Private giving in the welfare state. *British Journal of Political Science* 11:17–48.

Olson, Mancur. 1971. *The logic of collective action.* Cambridge: Harvard University Press.

O'Neill, June. 1981. Family issues in taxation. Paper presented for

American Enterprise Institute conference, Taxing the Family.

Owen, David. 1964. *English philanthropy, 1660–1960.* Cambridge: Harvard University Press.

Paqué, Karl-Heinz. 1982a. The efficiency of public support to private charity: An econometric analysis of the income tax treatment of charitable contributions in the Federal Republic of Germany. Working Paper No. 151, Institut für Weltwirtschaft an der Universität Kiel.

————. 1982b. Do public transfers "crowd out" private charitable giving? Some econometric evidence for the Federal Republic of Germany. Working Paper No. 152, Institut für Weltwirtschaft an der Universität Kiel.

Pechman, Joseph A. 1977. *Federal tax policy.* Washington, D.C.: Brookings Institution.

Penick, William C. 1960. Tax economics of charitable giving. *Taxes* 38:111–38.

Penner, Rudolph G. 1982. The price of giving: Charity begins with the tax laws. *Across the Board* 19:62–64.

Petska, Thomas B. 1982a. An examination of private foundations for 1979. *SOI Bulletin* 2, no. 2:9–29.

————. 1982b. The private foundation in a pluralistic society. Paper prepared for presentation at the August meeting of the American Statistical Association.

————. 1983. Charitable trusts: An IRS examination of non-exempt philanthropic organizations. Paper prepared for presentation at the August meeting of the American Statistical Association.

Posnett, John. 1979. The optimal fiscal treatment of charitable activity. Discussion Paper 552–79, Institute for Research on Poverty, University of Wisconsin, Madison.

Program on Non-profit Organizations. 1981. *Research Reports* 1: 3.

Reece, William S. 1979. Charitable contributions: New evidence on household behavior. *American Economic Review* 69:142–51.

Reece, William S., and Kimberly D. Zieschang. 1982. Consistent estimation of the impact of tax deductibility on the level of charitable contributions. Typescript.

Reiner, Thomas, and Julian Wolpert. 1981. The non-profit sector in the metropolitan economy. *Economic Geography* 57:23–33.

Revenue Canada. 1981. *1981 taxation statistics.* Ottawa: Canadian Government Publishing Centre.

Rose-Ackerman, Susan. 1981. Do government grants to charity reduce private donations? In *Nonprofit firms in a three sector economy,* ed. Michelle J. White, 95–114. Washington, D.C.: Urban Institute.

Rosen, Thomas. 1981. 1977 SOI, charitable deduction tabulations. Unpublished data and typescript, Office of Tax Analysis, Treasury Department.

Samuelson, Paul A. 1964. Tax deductibility of economic depreciation to insure investment valuations. *Journal of Political Economy* 72:604–06.

Schaefer, Jeffrey M. 1968. Philanthropic contributions: Their equity and efficiency. *Quarterly Review of Economics* 8:25–35.

Schwartz, Robert A. 1968. Corporate philanthropic contributions. *Journal of Finance* 23:479–97.

———. 1970a. Personal philanthropic contributions. *Journal of Political Economy* 78:1264–91.

———. 1970b. Reply. *Journal of Finance* 25:153–57.

Seidman, J. S. 1938. *Seidman's legislative history of federal income tax laws, 1938–1861.* New York: Prentice-Hall.

Sen, Amartya K. 1977. Rational fools: A critique of the behavioral foundations of economic theory. *Philosophy and Public Affairs* 6:317–44.

Shoup, Carl S. 1966. *Federal estate and gift taxes.* Washington, D.C.: Brookings Institution.

Siegfried, John J., and Katherine Maddox McElroy. 1981. Corporate philanthropy in the U.S., 1980. Working Paper No. 81–W26, Department of Economics, Vanderbilt University.

Sills, David L. 1957. *The volunteers.* Glencoe, Ill.: Free Press.

———. 1968. Voluntary associations: Sociological aspects. *International Encyclopedia of the Social Sciences* 16:362–79. New York: Macmillan.

Silverstone, Howard. 1964. Charitable giving: The need for a logically closed system. *Taxes* 42:429–54.

Simon, John G. 1978. Charity and dynasty under the federal tax system. *Probate Lawyer* 5:1–92.

Sorlien, Richard C., and Hans P. Olsen. 1970. Analyzing the new charitable contributions rules: Planning, pitfalls, problems. *Journal of Taxation* 32:218–25.

Sproull, Robert L. 1982. Cost-effective way to spur private giving. *Harvard Business Review* 60:62–65.

Statistics of Income. See U.S. Internal Revenue Service, *Statistics of Income.*

Steinberg, Richard. 1982. Problems in estimating the effect of federal tax policy on charitable donations. University of Pennsylvania. Typescript.

Steuerle, Eugene. 1977. Pay-out requirements for foundations. In *Research papers,* Commission on Private Philanthropy and Public Needs. 3:1663–78. Washington, D.C.: Treasury Department.

Sugarman, Norman A., and Paul H. Feinberg. 1981. *Charitable giving in light of the Economic Recovery Tax Act of 1981.* Paper prepared for the Council of Jewish Federations.

Sullivan, John, and Michael Coleman. 1981. Nonprofit organizations, 1975–1978. *SOI Bulletin* 1:6–38.

Sumariwalla, Russy D. 1983. Preliminary observations on scope, size, and classification of the sector. In *Working papers for spring research forum: Since the Filer Commission,* 181–228. Washington, D.C.: Independent Sector.

Sunley, Emil M., Jr. 1977. Dimensions of charitable giving reported on federal estate, gift, and fiduciary tax returns. In *Research papers,* Commission on Private Philanthropy and Public Needs, 4:2319–36. Washington, D.C.: Treasury Department.

Taggart, John Y. 1970. The charitable deduction. *Tax Law Review* 26:63–157.

Taussig, Michael K. 1967. Economic aspects of the personal income tax treatment of charitable contributions. *National Tax Journal* 20: 1–19.

Teitell, Conrad. 1977. Charitable deduction in grave jeopardy. *Philanthropy and Estate Planning* 116:486–87.

Theil, Henri. 1971. *Principles of econometrics.* New York: John Wiley and Sons.

Thomas, Ralph Lingo. 1966. *Policies underlying corporate giving.* Englewood Cliffs, N. J.: Prentice-Hall.

Throsby, C. D., and G. A. Withers. 1979. *The economics of the performing arts.* New York: St. Martin's Press.

Titmuss, Richard M. 1971. *The gift relationship: From human blood to social policy.* New York: Pantheon Books.

de Tocqueville, Alexis. 1835. *Democracy in America.* Trans. Henry Reeve. London: Saunders and Otley.

Tomes, Nigel. 1981. The family, inheritance, and the intergenerational transmission of inequality. *Journal of Political Economy* 89:928–58.

Troy, Kathryn. 1977, 1979, 1981, 1982, 1983, 1984. *Annual survey of corporate contributions.* 6 vols. New York: Conference Board.

U.S. Bureau of the Census. 1960. *Historical statistics of the United States, colonial times to 1957.* Washington, D.C.: Government Printing Office.

———. 1968–80. *Government finances.* 12 vols. Washington, D.C.: Government Printing Office.

———. 1982. *Current population reports.* Series P-25, no. 908, Estimates of the population of the United States to December 1, 1981. Washington, D.C.: Government Printing Office.

U.S. Bureau of Labor Statistics. 1979. *Marital and family characteristics of workers, 1970–1978.* Special Labor Force Report 219. Washington, D.C.: Government Printing Office.

U.S. Congress. 1982. *Tax Equity and Fiscal Responsibility Act of 1982.* 97th Cong., 2d sess. Public Law 97–248.

———. House of Representatives. 1917. *Revenue to defray war expenses.* 65th Cong., 1st sess. Conference Report No. 172.

————. 1938. Committee on Ways and Means. *The Revenue Bill of 1938.* 75th Cong., 2d sess. Report No. 1860.

————. Senate. Committee on Finance. 1965. *Treasury Department report on private foundations.* 84th Cong., 1st sess. Committee print.

————. 1973. *Private foundations: Hearing before the Subcommittee on Foundations.* 93rd Cong., 1st sess.

————. 1974a. *Impact of current economic crisis on foundations and recipients of foundation money: Hearing before the Subcommittee on Foundations.* 93rd Cong., 2d sess.

————. 1974b. *Private foundations: Hearing before the Subcommittee on Foundations.* 93rd Cong., 2d sess.

————. 1980. *Charitable contribution deductions: Hearing on S. 219.* 96th Cong., 2d sess.

————. Staff of the Joint Committee on Taxation. 1981. *General explanation of the Economic Recovery Tax Act of 1981.* Washington, D.C.: Government Printing Office.

————. 1982. *Summary of the revenue provisions of H.R. 4961 (The Tax Equity and Fiscal Responsibility Act of 1982).* Washington, D.C.: Government Printing Office.

U.S. Council of Economic Advisers. 1983. *Economic report of the President.* Washington, D.C.: Government Printing Office.

U.S. Department of Health and Human Services. 1982. *1978 vital statistics of the United States: Vol. 2—Mortality.* National Center for Health Statistics. Washington, D.C.: Government Printing Office.

U.S. Department of Labor. 1969. *Americans volunteer.* Manpower/Automation Research Monograph No. 10. Washington, D.C.: Government Printing Office.

U.S. Internal Revenue Service. Various years. Source book of statistics of income. Unpublished tax data.

————. 1939–83. *Statistics of income—1936–1980, Corporation income tax returns.* 44 vols. Washington, D.C.: Government Printing Office.

————. Various years. *Statistics of income, Estate Tax Returns,* 1943, 1947–50, 1953, 1954, 1958, 1960, 1962, 1965, 1969, 1972, 1976. Washington, D.C.: Government Printing Office.

————. 1977. *Statistics of income—1974, Fiduciary income tax returns.* Washington, D.C.: Government Printing Office.

————. Various years. *Statistics of income, Individual Income Tax Returns,* 1948–70, (even years only), 1972–81. 22 vols. Washington, D.C.: Government Printing Office.

————. 1981. *Statistics of income—1974–1978, Private foundations,* 4 vols. Washington, D.C.: Government Printing Office.

————. 1976 Estate Tax File. Unpublished tax data.

U.S. Office of Management and Budget. 1983. *Budget of the United States, Fiscal Year 1984.* Washington, D.C.: Government Printing Office.

U.S. Treasury Department. 1977. *Blueprints for basic tax reform.* Washington, D.C.: Government Printing Office.

Vickrey, William. 1947. *Agenda for progressive taxation.* New York: Ronald Press Co.

———. 1962. One economist's view of philanthropy. In *Philanthropy and public policy,* ed. Frank G. Dickinson. New York: National Bureau of Economic Research.

———. 1975. Private philanthropy and public finance. In *Altruism, morality, and economic theory,* ed. Edmund Phelps. New York: Russell Sage Foundation.

Wadsworth, Homer C. 1975. Private foundations and the Tax Reform Act of 1969. *Law and Contemporary Problems* 39:255–62.

Wagner, Richard E. 1977. Death, taxes, and charitable bequests: A survey of issues and options. In *Research papers,* Commission on Private Philanthropy and Public Needs, 4:2337–52. Washington, D.C.: Treasury Department.

Warner, W. Lloyd, and Paul S. Lunt. 1941. *The social life of a modern community.* New Haven: Yale University Press.

Weisbrod, Burton A. 1978a. Some collective-good aspects of non-government activities: Not-for-profit organizations. In *Proceedings of the 32nd Congress, International Institute of Public Finance,* ed. H.C. Rectenwald, 163–74.

———. 1978b. The forgotten economic sector: Private but non-profit. *Challenge,* Sept.–Oct., 32–36.

———. 1980. Growth of the non-profit sector: Implications for public employment and public finance. Institute for Research on Poverty Discussion Paper 623–80.

Weitzman, Murray S. 1983. Measuring the number, hours spent, and dollar value of volunteer activity of Americans. In *Working papers for spring research forum: Since the Filer Commission,* 261–89. Washington, D.C.: Independent Sector.

White, Michelle J. 1981. *Nonprofit firms in a three sector economy.* COUPE papers on Public Economics, vol. 6. Washington, D.C.: Urban Institute.

Williamson, Oliver E. 1964. *The economics of discretionary behavior: Managerial objectives in a theory of the firm.* Englewood Cliffs, N. J.: Prentice-Hall.

Worthy, K. Martin. 1975. The Tax Reform Act of 1969: Consequences for private foundations. *Law and Contemporary Problems* 39:232–54.

Zellner, Arnold. 1977. Evaluation of econometric research on the income tax and charitable giving. In *Research papers,* Commission on Private Philanthropy and Public Needs, 3:1515–19. Washington, D.C.: Treasury Department.

# Author Index

# Subject Index